Krosno by the Wislok River

Memorial Book of Jewish Community of Krosno, Poland

Compiled by

William Leibner

Edited by Jane W. Aronson and Toby Bird

Published by JewishGen

An Affiliate of the Museum of Jewish Heritage - A Living Memorial to the Holocaust
New York

Krosno by the Wislok River

Krosno by the Wislok River
Memorial Book of Jewish Community of Krosno, Poland

First Printing: February 2016, Adar 1 5776
Second Printing: March 2019, Adar II 5779

Compiled by William Leibner
Editors: Jane W. Aronson and Toby Bird
Layout: Alan Roth
Image Editor: Larry Gaum
Cover Design: Nina Schwartz
Indexing: Jonathan Wind

Published by JewishGen, Inc.
An Affiliate of the Museum of Jewish Heritage
A Living Memorial to the Holocaust
36 Battery Place, New York, NY 10280

Printed in the United States of America by Lightning Source, Inc.

Library of Congress Control Number (LCCN): 2015960980
ISBN: 978-1-939561-38-1 (hard cover: 536 pages, alk. paper)

Front Cover Image: "Krosner Jews in their traditional clothing," by the Polish artist Seweryn Bieszczad, 1923. Provided courtesy of Subcarpathian Museum of Krosno.

Back Cover Credit: Photograph of the synagogue dates to about 1924. Photographer unknown. Cemetery photograph were taken by Grzegorz Bozek in 2010.

JewishGen and the Yizkor-Books-in-Print Project

This book has been published by the **Yizkor-Books-in-Print Project,** as part of the **Yizkor Book Project** of **JewishGen, Inc**.

JewishGen, Inc. is a non-profit organization founded in 1987 as a resource for Jewish genealogy. Its website [www.jewishgen.org] serves as an international clearinghouse and resource center to assist individuals who are researching the history of their Jewish families and the places where they lived. JewishGen provides databases, facilitates discussion groups, and coordinates projects relating to Jewish genealogy and the history of the Jewish people. In 2003, JewishGen became an affiliate of the **Museum of Jewish Heritage - A Living Memorial to the Holocaust** in New York.

The **JewishGen Yizkor Book Project** was organized to make more widely known the existence of Yizkor (Memorial) Books written by survivors and former residents of various Jewish communities throughout the world. Later, volunteers connected to the different destroyed communities began cooperating to have these books translated from the original language—usually Hebrew or Yiddish—into English, thus enabling a wider audience to have access to the valuable information contained within them. As each chapter of these books was translated, it was posted on the JewishGen website and made available to the general public.

The **Yizkor-Books-in-Print Project** began in 2011 as an initiative to print and publish Yizkor Books that had been fully translated, so that hard copies would be available for purchase by the descendants of these communities and also by scholars, universities, synagogues, libraries, and museums.

These Yizkor books have been produced almost entirely through the volunteer effort of researchers from around the world, assisted by donations from private individuals. The books are printed and sold at near cost, so as to make them as affordable as possible. Our goal is to make this important genre of Jewish literature and history available in English in book form, so that people can have the personal histories of their ancestral towns on their bookshelves for themselves and for their children and grandchildren.

A list of all published translated Yizkor Books in the project with prices and ordering information can be found at:

http://www.jewishgen.org/Yizkor/ybip.html

Lance Ackerfeld, Yizkor Book Project Manager

Joel Alpert, Yizkor-Book-in-Print Project Coordinator

JewishGen
Yizkor Book Project

This book is presented by the
Yizkor Books in Print Project
Project Coordinator: Joel Alpert

Part of the
Yizkor Books Project of JewishGen, Inc.
Project Manager: Lance Ackerfeld

These books have been produced solely through volunteer effort
of individuals from around the world. The books are printed and
sold at near cost, so as to make them as affordable as possible.

Our goal is to make this history and important genre of Jewish
literature available in English in book form so that people can have
the near-personal histories of their ancestral towns on their bookshelves for themselves and for their children and grandchildren.

Any donations to the Yizkor Books Project are appreciated.

Please send donations to:
Yizkor Book Project
JewishGen
36 Battery Place
New York, NY 10280

JewishGen, Inc. is an affiliate of the
Museum of Jewish Heritage
A Living Memorial to the Holocaust

A Short History of Krosno

This is the Yizkor Book for the Jewish Community of Krosno, in Poland.

This edition of the Krosno Yizkor Book is nearly 500 pages long. It contains information on the town's institutions, organizations, buildings, and families as recounted by survivors and prewar emigrants in addition to first-hand reports of survivors of the killings and of Jews who vent into hiding, family histories of extended families of the town and all the photographs and illustrations are authentic of the city of Krosno.

Records of the earliest history show Jews living in Krosno as early as 1851. Local tradition had it that the Jews came because pursuing commercial opportunities. At the beginning of the twentieth century there were about 2,800 Jews or 18.5% of the population. A sizable number emigrated to the USA and Canada, settling primarily in New York City in teens, and 20s, by the late 1930s there were many Jews living in New York City, Newark and Toronto, Canada. The Jews were primarily in the commercial spheres.

When the Nazi forces occupied Krosno in 1939 the Jews were immediately expulsed and then permitted to return to the city. Most of the Jews of Krosno were sent to the Belzec death camp where they perished. Only a few survived the camps, hid, were hidden, or were in the Soviet Union. Their stories are presented in this volume as well as the dynamic story of Krosno when it was a living part of world Jewry prior to 1939 as recalled by prewar emigrants who contributed to the Yizkor project.

This Jewish community had existed for 90 years, during which time a vibrant Jewish community developed. In 1942 most of the Jews of Krosno were sent to the Belzec death camp where they perished. The remaining Jews of Krosno were then sent in December to the ghetto of Rzeszow. Krosno became "*Judenrein*" or clear of Jews.

Today there are a few descendents of Krosno living around the world, especially in the USA and in Israel. Read the details in the survivor's own words as they remember and bring to life the once vibrant Jewish community of Krosno. Today there are no Jews living in Krosno, Poland.

Geopolitical Information:

	Town	District	Province	Country
Before WWI (c. 1900):	Krosn	Krosn	Galicia	Austrian Empire
Between the wars (c. 1930):	Krosn	Krosn	Lwów	Poland
After WWII (c. 1950):	Krosno			Poland
Today (c. 2000):	Krosno			Poland

100 miles W of L'viv (Lvov), 42 miles ESE of Tarnów, 27 miles SSW of Rzeszów.

Alternate names: Krosno [Polish], Krossen [German], Kros(Yiddish)

Krosno, Poland is located at:
49°41' North Latitude and 21°47' East Longitude

180 mi South of Warszawa

Nearby Jewish Communities:

Jasienica Rosielna 6 miles ENE
Jedlicze 7 miles W
Domaradz 8 miles NE
Brzozów 9 miles E
Rymanów 9 miles SSE
Strzyżów 10 miles N
Niebylec 11 miles NNE
Dukla 12 miles SSW
Frysztak 12 miles NW
Zarszyn 13 miles SE
Nowy Żmigród 14 miles WSW
Jasło 16 miles W
Osiek Jasielski 16 miles WSW
Czudec 16 miles N
Błażowa 17 miles NE
Wielopole Skrzyńskie 18 miles NNW
Jaśliska 18 miles S
Kołaczyce 18 miles WNW
Bukowsko 20 miles SE
Tyczyn 20 miles NNE
Dynów 20 miles ENE
Sanok 20 miles ESE

Zgłobień 21 miles N
Brzostek 21 miles WNW
Wisłok Wielki 23 miles SSE
Nižný Komárnik, Slovakia 24 miles SSW
Jawornik Polski 24 miles ENE
Zabratówka 24 miles NE
Zagórz 24 miles SE
Rzeszów 24 miles NNE
Ropczyce 25 miles NNW
Sędziszów Małopolski 25 miles NNW
Jodłowa 25 miles WNW
Biecz 25 miles W
Čertižné, Slovakia 25 miles S
Szczawne 26 miles SSE
Dubiecko 26 miles ENE
Tyrawa Wołoska 26 miles ESE
Habura, Slovakia 27 miles S
Ladomirová, Slovakia 28 miles SSW
Pilzno 29 miles NW
Lesko 29 miles SE
Dębica 29 miles NW

BALTIC SEA   LITHUANIA

RUSSIA   Vilnius ●

POLAND   ● Stawiski

GERMANY   BELARUS

● Sierpc

● Poznan   Warsaw

● Lodz

● Prague   UKRAINE

Krakow
CZECH REPUBLIC   ●   ● KROSNO

SLOVAKIA

KROSNO

POLAND - Current Borders

├────────────────────┤ 250 miles
0

├──────────────────────────────┤
0   250 Km   500 Km

Map of Poland with Krosno indicated

Rear of the Krosner synagogue.

The synagogue was erected on a slope. The main entrance was the first floor where the main prayer hall was located, rabbi Samuel Fuhrer conducted here services. The second floor going downstairs was another prayer hall where the Hassidic rabbi Moshe Twersky conducted services. Further down were the *mikvehs* or ritual baths that received fresh water from the river Wislok, an apartment of the *shamash* or caretaker of the place and the slaughterhouse. Also the Krosno Jewish community had their offices in the building.

Front entrance of the Krosner synagogue

The entry to the synagogue was on the left side, next to it was small gate to go down to the facilities. On the extreme right was the small gate to go down to the lower level and farther down to the Mikva. In between the two gates and the entrance, were small storage places for the metal funeral casket, brooms and cleaning items.. One of the big 3 doors was the entrance for women.

Acknowledgements

I would like to thank the following people for their assistance in the preparation of this book:
  Avner Shalev, Chairman of the Yad Vashem Directorate;
  Rachel Barkai, Director of Commemoration and Public Relations, Yad Vashem;
  Dr. Robert Rozette, Director of Yad Vashem library;
  Rachel Cohen, Secretary of Yad Vashem library;
  David Sinai, chairman of manpower at Yad Vashem
  Mimi Ash at the Yad Vashem Media Center in Jerusalem;
  Yad Vashem staff at the various research stations in Jerusalem.
  National Library of Israel, Shachar Beer of the JDC (Joint Distribution Committee) archives in
    Jerusalem;
  Zvi Feine, former JDC official
  Misha Mistel of the New York JDC's media center.

We'd also like to thank Rochelle Rubinstein of the Central Zionist Archives; Itka at The Central
Archives for the History of the Jewish People, and as a JDC volunteer in DP camps in
Germany;Dora Weisman for her recollections of the British entry into the Bergen Belsen
concentration camp.

We would like to thank Dr. Alexander (Sender Bialywlos), for his his excellent information about
the Krosno Jewish community.

To Emil Leibner for his technical and computer assistance in getting the Yizkor book on paper.

To Claudette Leibner for endless patience and assistance while the project stretched on from
month to month.

Special thanks to Grzegorz Bozek for providing us with a rich collection of pictures of Jewish
Krsono.

I would like to thank Lance Ackerfield for editing the materials and Joel Alpert for publishing the
following books that I translate or compiled through the JewishGen.
        Translation of the Jaslo Yizkor Bok
        Translation of the Kroczyna Yizkor Book
        Compiler of the Nowy Zmigrod Yizkor Book
        Compiler of the Krosno by the Wislok River Yizkor Book

We thank all the people that contributed materials, pictures and information to enrich the Krosno
Yizkor book.

And apologizes to anyone unintentionally overlooked.

I would like to mention the fact that this is the fourth book that I translate or compiled.

                                                                William Leibner, Jerusalem, January 2016

Appreciation

Kudos to Mr. William Leibner for the years of time and effort compiling this Yizkor (Memorial) book in remembrance of the once living and vibrant Jewish community of Galician Kros or Krosno.

May their life so brutally murdered in the Holocaust be remembered for the present and future generations. "*Lo Tischkach*" (Don't Forget).

It should also serve to make the present inhabitants of the town aware of the past diversity of that area whenever they enter their homes previously inhabited by members of the Jewish community and their vital contribution to the progress and vitality of the town and area.

Dr. Alexander B White

Dr. Alexander B White

Alexander (Sender Bialywlos) White born June 1923 in Krosno, son of Mendel and Leah (Platner) Bialywlos who resided on Ordynacka street 8 Krosno. He survived the war working at the Krosno German military airport and later at the Krakow-Plaszow concentration camp from where he was sent to Schindler's camp in Brunnlitz (Brnenec), Czechoslovakia.He was liberatedby the Russian army May 9, 1945 Presently he lives with my family in retirement in the USA.

Notes to the Reader:

The on-line version can be seen at:

> http://www.jewishgen.org/yizkor/krosno/krosno.html

A list of this book and all books available in the Yizkor-Book-In-Print Project along with prices is available at:

> http://www.jewishgen.org/Yizkor/ybip.html

Table of Contents

IN MEMORIAM

Krosno by the Wislok River (Krosno, Poland)

49°41' / 21°47'

Acknowledgments
Compiled by
William Leibner

Edited by Jane W. Aronson and Toby Bird

Krosno by the Wislok River

William Leibner

In Memoriam

Yehuda Leibner

Dedicated to John (Yehuda) Leibner, son of
Jacob and Serl Leibner, a native of the city of
Krosno by the Wislok River. He died on the
slopes of Massada near the Dead Sea in Israel.
He loved the land of Zion.

May he rest in peace

Table of Contents

[Page 7]

Chapter I

Jews in Krosno

Introduction

The city of Krosno is an old historic city that developed slowly and reached its zenith in the "Middle Ages". The city was frequently refered to as "Little Krakow" due to the beautiful buildings that surround the "*rynek*" or market place. Krosno then started to stagnate and was dormant for a long period of time. One of the causes for the stagnation was the absolute stranglehold that the guilds imposed on the city. They prevented competition and did not admit Jews to the guilds. As a matter of fact, they even prevented Jews from living in the city. Jews were permitted to enter the city during the annual fairs. Krosno enforced the ban against Jews very effectively until the Austrian Empire changed the rules. Jews began to settle in Krosno. The Krosno population expands rapidly as does the Jewish population in the city. The railroad and the discovery of gas create an economic boom. Jews flock to the city from all the small villages. The Germans destroy this young Jewish community within a short period of time. The few survivors are scattered throughout the globe where they pass on in isolation from their birth place.

Dr. Herbert (Zvi) Breite formerly Breitowicz passed away on January 14, 2014 in New Jersey. He helped shape the Yizkor book.

Dr. Herbert Breite
May he rest in eternal peace

[Page 8]

The city of Krosno is a district city in Galicia, Poland
Administrative area of Krosno since 1945

The City of Krosno, by the Wislok River

Krosno is located in southeastern Poland, east of Krakow. The Wislok river flows next to the city. Since there are several places named Krosno, our Krosno is frequently referred to as Krosno on the Wislok. The city was founded in 1324 on lands belonging to the crown. Krosno's weaving industry played an important role in the development of the city and perhaps contributed to the name of the city, loom in Polish. The city was also an important trade center for Hungarian wines. In 1348 it was granted a municipal charter based on the Magdenburg laws. Somewhat later, Krosno was granted the right to hold an annual fair that became well known. This commercial boost and the protection of a city wall enabled it to flourish.

[Page 9]

The famous landmark of the city of Krosno, the commercial passages called "Pochenia" in Polish of Krosno

Known to the Jewish inhabitants as Kros, Krosno became an important industrial, trade and craft center in the 16th century and had about 250 artisans organized in 11 guilds, the total population exceeded 3000 people. The city attracted many artists and became known as "little Krakow". The various wars, invasions and partitions brought a halt to the growth of the city. It remained dormant until the second half of the 19th century.

According to Jerzy Potocki, historian of the area, Jews appear in Krosno in 1385 and 1427. The first actual residence is recorded by two brothers Nechemia and Lazar of Regensburg in Germany who received royal permission from Wladyslaw Jagiello in the 15th century to reside in the city for three years. But there was no continuity of Jewish life in the city. Here and there a Jew lived in the city but no trace of organized Jewish community life. Jews visited the city but did not reside in it. Jews lived in nearby Korczyna or Rymanow or Dukla. The city population vehemently opposed Jewish presence. The guild members led the fight to keep Jewish merchants out of the city. Krosno finally received from the crown in 1569 the so-called privilege "de non tolerandis Judaeis "barring Jews from residing and trading within the city walls. Jewish traders living in nearby townships of Korczyna, Rymanow or Dukla were frequently jailed and their wares confiscated for attempting to enter the city. Still, Jewish merchants from nearby towns maintained contact with the city and the property census of 1851 indicates that there were three

Jewish families in Krosno: Loje Grusnspan, Mojzesz Grunspan and Schije Dym.

[Page 10]

**Dr. Alexander B. White
(formerly Bialywlos)
a native of Krosno who
survived the Shoah**

The Austrian annexation of Galicia induced several major social changes that affected Jewish life in the area. The limitations on marriages were lifted, the limitations on the residence of poor Jews were eased, professions were opened to Jews, and Jews could purchase land. Finally, the new Constitution of 1867 granted all citizens equality before the law. All these changes encouraged and stimulated Jews to leave their villages and hamlets for the larger cities that offered larger opportunities. Krosno was no exception, by 1870 there were 26 Jewish families in the city The number grew to fifty families in the city by 1890. According to Dr. Alexander B. White (formerly Bialywlos) a native of Krosno, his maternal godfather Chaim Hersh Platner and his wife Mala were amongst the first Jewish to settle in Krosno. The family dealt extensively in coal, wood and coke. The Bialywloss family will develop the glass plate commerce in the city. Soon other 32 families arrived in the next ten years. To these official statistics we must add the unrecorded arrival of single people who lodged with families.

The population of Krosno

Year	Population	Catholic	Jews	Greek Orthodox
1870	2132	2100	26	6
1880	2461(2810)	2318	(127) 113	30
1890	2839 (3251)	2454	(567) 327	58
1900	3276 (3310)	2664	(961) 567	45
1910	4353 (5582)	3329	(1559) 961	63
1914	5521	3839	1558	70

[Page 11]

The numbers within the parenthesis are the numbers provided by Yad Vashem in Jerusalem, Israel.

Column 1 is Year, total population, Roman Catholics, Jews, and Greek Catholics Column 2 represents the total population of Krosno that grew by 96.5% between the years 1870-1910. Column 3 represents the Catholic population that grew by 60.5% between the same years. Column 4 represents the Jewish population that grew between the same years by 376%. If we go by the numbers within the brackets provided by Yad Vashem, the Jewish population even grew by a much larger percentage. Column 5 represents the Greek Catholic church that grew between the same years by 17.2%

The above figures show the rapid growth of the Jewish population which outpaced the overall growth of the city as oil was discovered in the area and money flowed in to develop the industry. The railway, linking Krosno with Jaslo and Europe, followed in 1884. Industries began to develop especially the weaving and glass producing sectors. Krosno was in the midst of an economic boom. Jews kept streaming to the city and even beyond it to the distant lands of the Austrian Empire, Germany and the USA.

The Jewish population of Krosno grew in numbers and influence. The leaders collected money and build a big modern synagogue, a religious school and a mikvah or ritual bath. The leaders also petitioned the provincial governor to grant the Jewish community of Krosno the right to form a Jewish community council or kahal that would administer to the needs of the Krosno Jews. At present, all decisions were made in the Korczyner Jewish community council. On January 1st, 1900, the governor of Galicia granted the Jews of Krosno the right to organize their community and select the leaders of the community. The kahal or community leadership then proceeded to search for a rabbi to represent the community. They chose Shmuel Fuhrer to be their rabbi and head of the religious council that adjudicates khalakhic matters. The rabbi was born in 1863 in the historic village of Sekowa near Gorlice,

Galicia. He was a bright Talmudic student and gifted in in mathematics. In 1883 he was ordained rabbi and chosen by the Milowka, near Krakow, Jewish community to be their rabbi. He remained there until 1904 when he moved to Krosno. Rabbi Fuhrer urged the community to establish a cemetery which it did. Up to this point, Krosno Jews buried their deaths in Korczyna. With the consecration of the cemetery, the community created the "Hevrah Kadisha" or voluntary burial society to handle burials. The association worked in close conjunction with the rabbi. Rabbi Fuhrer was the only rabbi that Krosno had. He served the community for 35 years.

He would be shot during one of the "actions" that liquidated the Krosner ghetto. A memorial stone would be erected for him following the war.

[Page 12]

The Krosno synagogue survived the war but disappeared with time. The building is no longer in existence

Rabbi Samuel Fuhrer, rabbi of Krosno

[Page 13]

German permission for Rabbi Samuel Fuhrer
to return to Krosno

[Page 14]

He was familiar with financial matters and frequently arbitrated monetary disputes between merchants. He authored the scholarly Khalic book entitled "Har Shafar" that was published in Bardajow, present day Slovakia. In his later years, he was assisted by his son Shlomo Fuhrer. With the outbreak of the war, rabbi Fuhrer moved to Eastern Galicia where he remained until the Germans occupied the area. The rabbi received permission from the Germans to return to Krosno. The permit was issued in Brzezany district in Eastern Galicia on November 11, 1941. On the back of the permit are listed 5 people that were permitted to return with the rabbi, namely; Shlomo Fuhrer, son of the rabbi, born 1902, Roth Taube born 1924, Hemerling Ruchel born1927, Pinter Meyer born 1900, and Horowitz Schija born 1925.

At last the rabbi was at home where he had a large family and many followers. The Germans killed the rabbi in one of their actions of rounding up Jews during WW II in Krosno in 1942.

The Hassidic rabbi of Krosno, Rabbi Moshe Twerski

Krosno also had an elderly Chassidic rabbi named Aaron Twerski or better known as "Arale". He was a descendant of the famous Twerski Hassidic rabbinical family. On his death, late 1920, a typhoid fever epidemic raged in Krosno. Aaron's son, rabbi Moshe Twerski assumed his father's position. The rabbi and his wife Frida, sister of the famous Radomsker chasidik rabbi lived with my maternal grandfather Chaim Lang and his wife Feige Reisel Findling-Lang.

[Page 15]

The rabbi's family lived upstairs where the rabbi conducted services. The rabbi was very popular and had many Hassidic followers. He conducted services in his apartment and occasionally attended services at the main Krosno synagogue. At the beginning of World War II, he left Krosno with many other Jews and headed to Eastern Poland which was then occupied by the Soviet Army.

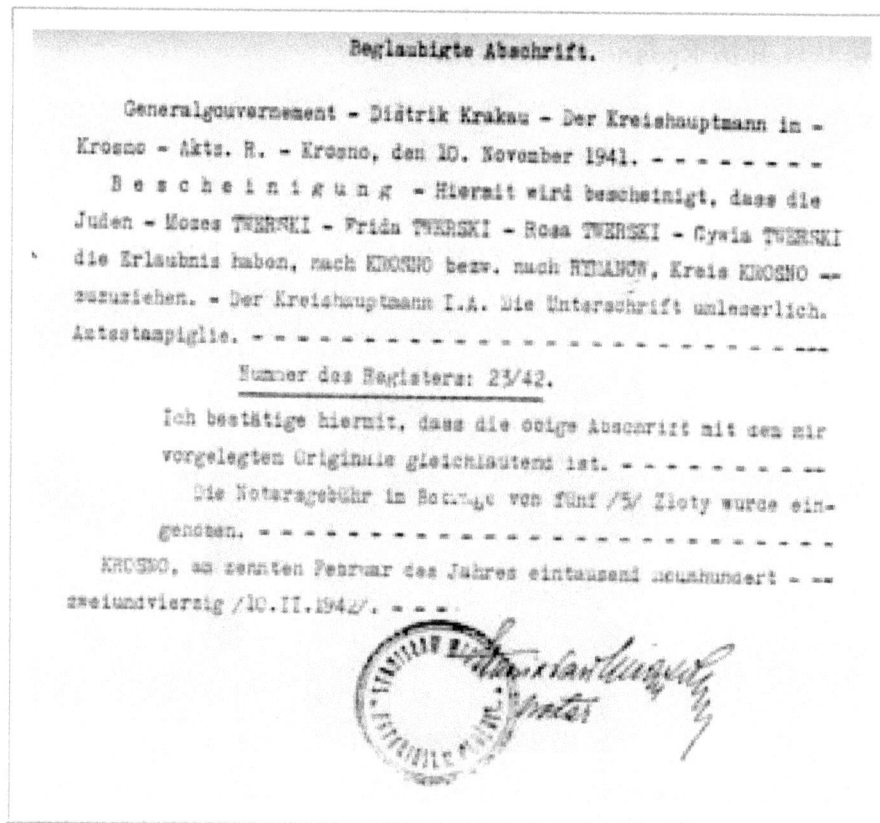

**Official German military document enabling rabbi Moses Twerski, his mother Rosa, his wife Frida, and his daughter Civia to return to Krosno.
Document dated February 10, 1942**

[Page 16]

**Yaacov Breitowicz at
the end of the war**

According to Yaacov Breitowicz, a native of Krosno and a Shoah survivor, he met the Rabbi's starving family and brought them some food. He spread the words among Krosner Jews in the area and they helped the rabbi's family. Furthermore, he states in his book "Through Hell to Life" that he urged his acquaintances to help get the rabbi back to to Krosno. Indeed, the rabbi family consisting of rabbi Moshe Twerski, his wife Frieda, his daughter Tzivia and his mother Rosa received permission from the German authorities to return to Krosno. The permission dated November 10, 1941. The style is typical Nazi German style of writing, the permission talks of Jews, no reference to the rabbi as a person. He even had to pay for the permit. At least the family received permission to return to Krosno. We do not know how many strings or money had to be given to the Gestapo to obtain the permits for the two rabbis to return to Krosno. Other Krosno Jews that were stranded in the formerly Russian areas were also permitted to return to Krosno. The Gestapo was not the friendliest organ in dealing with Jews in general, especially with very religious Jews. The road back to Krosno was long and tedious but the rabbi finally made it.

[Page 17]

Chaim Lang

The rabbi shared the house with my maternal grandfather Chaim Lang. He and his wife Feige Reisel Findling-Lang and children lived downstairs in the back while their clothing store faced to the market or rynek. The Langs were natives of Nowy Zmigrod hamlet and moved to the city prior to World War I. Chaim Lang opened a clothing store that operated until the Germans entered Krosno. In World War I he served in the Austrian army where he acquired the German language. Both Chaim Lang and his wife Feige Reisel Lang managed to to smuggle their way from German occupied Krosno across the new German-Soviet border in Poland. They reached the hamlet of Lesko or Linsk in Yiddish where they had distant relatives. They remained in Lesko for a while and then were asked to apply for Soviet citizenship. They refused to become Russians. During the summer of 1940, they were arrested by the Soviet secret police known as the NKVD at night. They were told to pack a few things and were escorted to the train station.

[Page 18]

Feige Reisel Findling-Lang

A special cargo train awaited them. The Langs were helped to board the train. The loading proceeded very rapidly since everything was prepared in great detail. Hundreds of Polish Jews who had fled their homes in German occupied Polish areas were rounded up like the Langs and pushed aboard the train. Many similar trains left the area with Polish refugees mainly Jewish. Some Krosno Jews like the Mintzes, or the Platners, and many more were aboard these trains. It is estimated that about 200,000 Polish refugees were transported during the summer of 1940 to the depths of Russia. The Lang train reached Siberia where they would remain until the Polish-Russian agreementwould be signed July 30, 1941 that would restore their Polish citizenship. The agreement is also known as the Sikorski-Mayski accord was extended on August 11, 1941 and gave the Polish refugees permission to leave the miserable Siberian camp for warmer areas in the Soviet Union.

The Langs and the other Polish refugees soon left the desolate camp and made their way to a nearby train station that took them to the big city of Dzhmbul in Kazakhstan. They were helped by the Polish Red Cross and Russian aid offices to settle in the city. Hunger and disease were rampantand many refugees died of sheer exhaustion. Everything was in short supply since the Russian armies at the front needed everything. The black market was thriving and food prices were prohibitive. Most of the refugees managed to find work and barely sustained themselves with basics like bread. Many Polish refugees died of hunger, starvation, diseases and loneliness. My maternal grandparents; Chaim and Feige Reisel Lang died in Dzhambul one after the other. Both were buried in this city.

[Page 19]

Chaim Lang the son of Yehuda and Dworah Lang died on July 5th 1943 in Djambul, Kazakhstan	**Feige Reisel Findling –Lang , wife of Chaim Lang died in Dzhambul**

The growing Jewish population in Krosno created the need to open special Jewish stores such as butcher shops, fish stores and bakeries. In 1906 there were already two established baking families in the city, one belonged to Selig Findling, and the other one to Chaim Oling. Krosno had three Jewish slaughterhouses belonging to Fulka Breitowitz, Moses Breitowicz, and Wolf Mahler. Sender Fessel, Jacob Grunspan, and Tobiah Nagiel, owned kosher butcher shops. Dawid Mehl led the metal industry that included Chaim Korba, Jakub Pinkas and Jonasz Steifel.The spirit industry was headed by Schije Dym and Isaac Hertzig. Tax collections were in the hands of Hersh Wasserstrum and the Dym family. Jewish tailors, barbers, glaziers, shoemakers opened stores or workshops. Ritual slaughters and Hebrew teachers found employment in the city. The Jews dominated and expanded the commercial base of the city. They also developed small industries. Jewish artisans and craftsmen opened and expanded workshops.

List of Jewish merchants in the city of Krosno 1912-1915

The translation of the Polish document

Grocery; Hersz Roth, Eliasz Horowitz, Szymon Pastor, Ozjas Weinstein
Slaughterhouses: Salomon Storch, Samuel Trenczer
Charcoal; Chaim Platner, Jakob Schoenberg, Eliasz Matzner, Feldes Wolf
Construction materials; Simche Eisenberg, Abraham Pel, Israel Winter, Dawid Trencher, Jakob Margules
Agricultural machines; Seld Szamroth
Furniture; Regina Fishbein, Mojzesz Hirschfeld
Utensils; Mayer Dunkel, Mayer Ellowicz, Dawid Ozjas Pasternak
Oil; Hersz Just, Naftali Just
Ready made clothing; Hersz Beer, Chaim Lang,Chaim Zwiebel, Hersz Wasserstrum
Fruits and foods; Menashe Bodnar, Izaak Eisenberg, Hersz Heller
Agricultural implements; Jacob MayerKleiner, Hersz Roth, Leizer Rozner
Leather goods; Eliasz Blazer,Chaim Feitelbaum,Israel Heferling,Izaak Chaim Hares, Saul Weinberger. Eliasz Zeller
Draperies;Sara April,Jozef Grunspan, Chaim Muller,Regina Schneider,Chaim Eisenberg, Abraham Meilech
Haberdashery; Jozef Horowitz, Adolf Biednar,Abraham Gleicher,Rachela Truncher, Samuel Klein
Household goods; Chana Gartner,Ozjass Gerlich, Israel Helfering, Leja Herbstman, Naftali Margules, Chaim Orgler, Mojzesz Pasternak, Samuel Safran, Mendel Stroh,Edi Vogel.
Coal and Coke; Chaim Platner,Meilech Denn
Metal and metal products; Tomasz Stiefel,Samuel Vogel,Izaak Kinderman, Mendel Margules, Hersz Kinderman

[Page 21]

Przedmiot handlu	Imię i nazwisko kupca
Artykuły spożywcze	Hersz Roth, Eliasz Horowitz, Szymon Pauler, Ozjas Weinstein
Bydło rzeźne	Salomon Storch, Samuel Trenczer
Drzewo opałowe	Chaim Platner, Jakób Schonberg, Eliasz Matzner, Feldes Wolf
Materiały budowlane	Simcha Einsenberg, Abracham Pel, Israel Winter, Dawid Trenczer, Jakób Margules
Maszyny rolnicze	Szamroth Seid
Meble	Regina Fischbein, Mojzesz Hirschfeld
Naczynia	Majer Dunkel, Majer Ellowicz, Dawid Ozjas Pasternak
Nafta	Hersch Just, Naftali Just
Odzież gotowa	Hersz Beer, Chaim Long, Chaim Zwiebel, Hersz Wasserstrum
Owoce i warzywa	Menasze Bodnar, Izaak Eisenberg, Hersz Heller
Płody rolne	Jakób Majer Kleiner, Berusz Roth, Rozner Leibmar
Skóry i futra	Eliasz Blaser, Chaim Feinelbaum, Israel Heferling, Izzak Chaim Hares, Saul Weinberger, Eliasz Zeller
Towary bławatne	Sara April, Józef Grunspan, Chaim Muller, Regina Schneider, Chaim Eisenberg, Abraham Meilech
Towary galanteryjne	Józef Horowitz, Adolf Biednar, Abraham Gleicher, Rachela Trenczer, Samuel Klein
Towary mieszane	Chane Gartner, Ozjas Gerlich, Israel Heferling, Laja Herbstman, Naftali Margules, Chaim Orgler, Mojzesz Pasternak, Samuel Safran, Mendel Stroh, Edi Vogel
Węgiel i koks	Chaim Platner, Denne Meilech
Żelazo i wyroby żelazne	Jonasz Stiefel, Samuel Vogel, Izaak Kinderman, Mebel Margules, Hersz Kinderman

List of Jewish merchants in Krosno 1912-1915

During the Austrian period, some Jews served in government offices. These officials were later retired with Polish independence. There were only two Jews that worked for the civil service in Krosno namely Dr. Samet who gave Jewish religious instruction in the city school system and Spiegelman who worked in the post office. Jews were by and large absent from the ranks of the police forces, officer corps, judicial branch or local or governmental civil service. They concentrated in the fields of commerce, commercial services, professions and small industry. Jews were not hired as industrial workers in the Krosno plants, notably the glass plant, the linen factory, the Tepege tool and dye plant and the the "Wudeta" rubber plant that produced footwear and bicycle tires. Two Jews built the factory namely Wurzel and Daar from Tarnow. Some Jews worked in the offices of the plants but not on the production line.

With the advent of World War I, many Jews left the city and headed to the interior of the Empire namely Vienna or Budapest. The city was occupied for a while by the Russian army. The Russian soldiers looted and robbed Jewish stores and apartments. The Jewish population was instantly pauperized. Food shortages and the lack of medical facilities caused serious harm to the Jewish population in Krosno. With the end of the war, the city's economic life was in shambles. Many of the Jews that left the city did not bother to return. Those that returned found their places ransacked or destroyed. Commercial links shrunk since the Austro-Hungarian Empire disintegrated and many national countries appeared instead, each with its rules and regulations. The new Polish administration did not look with favor on Jewish commercial interests. The Jewish community of Krosno was seriously affected by these changes.

The Jewish community of Krosno was in dire financial straights following World War I. There were many orphans and widows and the able bodied men had no work.

[Page 23]

The Jewish population received assistance from the American Joint Organization and from former Krosno Jews in America. The slow process of economic recovery also improved the conditions of the Jewish community. In 1921, there were 49 workshops that employed 112 people. 38.4% of the workers were the actual owners of the places, 16% were members of the family and 45.5 were salaried workers. 82.4% of the latter were Jews. 49% of the workshops dealt with clothing, 21.8% dealt with food, 14.6% were connected with the building line and 10.9% dealt with metal.

The Jewish community of Krosno appealed for financial help and the American Joint Organization and the Krosner landsmanshaft in the USA (former Jews of Krosno) helped financially the revitalization of the Jewish community. Slowly the city resumed life and with it the Jewish economic sector. Suddenly in 1921, a serious Typhoid Fever epidemic swept the city, mainly the Jewish section of the city that was concentrated around the market square. The kahal or community leadership appealed for help to the Polish government and various health organizations, the American Joint Distribution Committee (AJDC and to the Krosner landsmanschaft in New York.

The former Krosno residents in conjuction with the former Jedliczer residents established, a shtetl near Krosno, established in New York City the "The First Krosno Jedliczer Young Men's Benevolent Society".

The entrance gate of the Krosner-Jedliczer cemetery in New York The above picture was graciously presented by Elissa Sampson

[Page 24]

The officers of the Krosner-Yedliczer landsmanschaften were; Isidor Moskowitz, President, I. Kalb, V. Moskowitz, M. Spindler, A. Calitzky and P. Moskowitz

The cemetery was just outside New York City. The gate entrance to the cemetery is dated May 30, 1928 and listed the officers of the society. The Landesmanschaften also provided financial assistance to the communities of Krosno and Jedlicze in Poland. organization was to aid new immigrants in the new country, assist the new arrivals to take the first steps in the new country, provide some assistance to needy families and provided burial plots for the deceased members of the society. The cemetery of the society was located in the Beth David cemetery

The Krosno community also appealed to the AJDC for medical help and it responded by sending a medical investigator who made the following report found amongst the AJDC records relating to the epidemic in Krosno of 1921.

[Page 25]

"Information reached my office (AJDC representative in Poland) on May 15th, that an epidemic of typhoid Fever broke out at Krosno, a small town in

West Galicia, with a total population of 8,000 of which 2,000 are Jews. There are no hospitals in the city and the patients are being cared for at their homes. The general sanitary conditions of ths city are primitive and poor. No water system nor sewers are there. Neither can be found a bath house. It was discovered that nearly all persons affected have been using the water from the local river (Wislok) for drinking purposes. The Epidemic was found concentrated among the Jews who dwell around the market place and who were compelled to use river water for their homes because of the fact, that the well pump situated on the market place was out of order and their non-Jewish neighbors did not allow the Jews to draw water from their wells.

Upon the recommendation of the city physician, orders were issued by the local authorities prohibiting the use of the river water for consumption and that all private wells should be free for public use. We furnished the Jewish community, under the supervision, of the local Jewish physician, a supply of lime, carbolic acid and corrosive sublimate for disinfectiom; also a supply of 5O suits of underwear, 50 sheets and 50 pillow cases and soap for the use of the patients and their families, also 15,000 Mk. in cash.

We furnished 300 doses of antityphoid vaccine to the Jewish physician Dr. Siegel for the purpose of Inocculating all the contacts, thereby immunizing them against the disease. Upon my request the Health Commissioner of Krakau furnished Krosno two trained nurses Misses Dobrsanska and Szulgenia who together with our sanitarian Mr, A. Mlrowski, visited the affected families giving than instruction to the care of the sick and how prevent the healthy persons of becoming contaminated and infected

We also requested the local Jewish Community to prohibit, for the present, the use of the Mickvah by all persons convalescent from Typhoid fever. The Community was also requested to prepare a plan and budget for the construction of a bathhouse in Krosno, thereby promising them support in the undertaking.   signed, *Dr Irvin Michlin*

The report is an excellent historical document describing the Jewish community at the time. Notice the discrepancy between the figure of Jews given by the Joint and those of the official Polish census. The Polish historian Elzabeta Raczy that did extensive research on Jews in Krosno and published her findings in a historical series on Jews in Krosno calls our attention to the discrepancy of figures. The census only registered legal residents while the Joint figure represents the actual total Jewish population as in the community. Furthermore, the document describes the poor health conditions of the Jewish population in the city, and also the financial poverty of the community that needed underwear for the sick and poor Jews. The AJDC not only helped Krosno to overcome the epidemic but also helped build a bathhouse to improve the health situation of the Jewish community.

[Page 26]

The AJDC organization also provided financial help to the following Jewish families in Krosno.

Bobka, Breitowitz, Burd,
Englehardt, Findling, Fleischer, Freff, Fries,
Hornik, Kempler, Krill, Kurschner, Kurz,
Lindenberg, Michlin, Muschel, Oling,
Ranozy, Reizer, Rettig, Rezmovits, Rubenfeld,
Sauer, Schildkraut, Spira, Steifel, Steiner, Szklint, Stolina,
Tag, Trenczer (multiple),
Weissman, Zeman

The above stated document revealed the extent of Polish resentment toward the Jew, his neighbor. Of course not all Poles were bitter anti-Semites but there was a sizable percentage that made Jewish life very unpleasant to say the least. Unfortunately, the latter group grew in strength as time passed. They organized the boycotts aimed at Jewish stores or commercial enterprises. Polish students frequently broke show case windows of Jewish stores. Jewish students were frequently mistreated or verbally abused by the Polish students. Some of the Polish adults did not behave better, Dr.White writes in his book entitled "Be a Mentch" that he and his uncle were transporting glass for repairs and suddenly the coach driver pulled sharply to the right and then to the left, he repeated the sharp movements several times while driving until the passengers and their glass fell to the floor. The glass splintered all over the place and the passengers were cut in many places. The driver claimed that the horse panicked. Here is another simple event as told by the late Shimshon Lang, the son of Chaim Lang of Krosno. One Saturday, Chaim Lang dressed in his Hassidic garb with a shtreimel or fur hat \was walking home from the synagogue followed by his sons. A pair of Polish military air force cadets from the Krosno air base passed them and demonstratively knocked off the fur hat from Chaim Lang's head. Shimon and Shimshon Lang, sons of Chaim Lang lounged at the attacker and his friend and beat them mercilessly. They ripped of their shoulder epaulettes and left them on the floor. In the ensuing commotion both brothers made their escape and hid at the apartment of their sister Seril Lang-Leibner. They would remain for a few days in hiding. Both brothers were well built and had an appetite to go with the size. They could finish between themselves all the rolls that were backed for the Sabbath for the entire family. They also tore the insignias of the shoulders of the Polish fliers, something unheard of in Poland. During the confusion, both brothers disappeared prior to the police arrival The police intervened and looked for the attackers who were hidden in a closed at their sister's apartment, Seril Lang-Leibner.

[Page 27]

The matter was subsequently hushed up when money was placed in the right pocket. These type of incidents continued until the outbreak of World War II.

**Shimshon Lang,
son of Chaim and Feige
Reisel in the Polish Army**   **His brother, Shimon Lang**

[Page 28]

Chapter II
Between the Wars

Social life

Jews were by and large excluded from the social life of the city. They met the general population throughout the day for purposes of business or professional consultations. Monday was market day in Krosno where almost everybody appeared. Merchandise was sold and bought. The farmers brought their produce to the market for sale. The Jewish stalls and stores provided all goods and services. There was no socialization after work hours between the Jewish and the Christian population. The Jews organized their own societies to provide for their social, religious and cultural needs.

Krosno had a burial society or "Hevrah Kadisha" that tended to the needs of the deceased and their families. Chaim Fruhman and Jacob Palant headed the society. The family usually had to pay for the burial plot and funeral expenses unless they could not afford it, then the community assumed the financial burden. The "Bikur Kholim" society tended to the sick of the city while the "Tomchei Aniim "society headed by Kalmen Bogen supported the needy Jewish population. The "Linas Kholim" society provided beds for the sick people while the "Khanassat Orchim" society provided lodging for people that were stuck in the city and had no place to sleep. He also headed the society for helping poor indigenous Jews that were not residents of the city. This hospice provided sleeping accommodation for one or two nights without charge and was located near Teitelbaum's inn. There was also a society to help unwed Jewish girls to marry. There was also the Ludowy bank headed by Minc. Yossef Platner was a member of the board of directors. The bank granted loans to merchants at low interest. Krosno also head several private banks that granted small short term loans. There was the "Gmilas Khessed" society that helped people in need. The group launched appeals and collected money for various projects in the community. Below is a letter of appeal that was sent to the Krosner landsman in the USA. The Yiddish letter is dated January 16, 1939. The lengthy letter explains the difficult situation of the Krosno Jews. Especially the small merchants or peddlers. The letter urges the American brethren to help the Krosno "Gmilass Chessed" provide loans for the needy.

The Jews of Krosno did not forget needy Jews in Palestine and made small contributions to the "Meir Baal Haness" charity organization that helped Jews in Palestine. Here is a partial list of the Krosno contributors:

[Page 29]

AFTENGUT	Shlomo	HADNER	Sara
AKSLER	Yossi	HALBERSHTAM	Dawid
ALTER	Yaakow	HASHNIK	Kalman
AMSTERDAM	Chaim	HERMAN	Israel Ber
BAUMEN	Kalman W	HERTZFELD	Hersh
BIALYWLOSS	Mendel	HERTZFELD	Tzwi
BLUMBERG	Shmuel	HERTZIG	Itshe
BOBKER	Yehezkel	HERTZIGER	Yossef
BOIGEN	Nahum	HERTZLICH	Kalman W
BRANDER	Yossef	HERTZOG	Yehuda
BREITOWICZ	Israel	HOFFERLING	Israel
BREITOWICZ	Moshe	HOLOSHITZ	Shmuel
BRONFELD	Yaakow	HOLTZER	Yossef
BRUDESHEWKI	Noach	HOROWITZ	Menachem
BUCH	Lewi	IMMERLING	Akiva
DAWID	Mechel	JUST	Tzwi
DERSHEWITZ	Hawa	KALB	Asher
DIAMAND	Klaman	KALB	Betzalel
DIM	Lea	KALMENSOHN	Lipa
DIM	Chana	KANNER	Moshe Ye
DOMINITZ	Klaman	KATZ	Zishe
DUNKEL	Meir	KERNKRAUT	Yehoshua
DYM	Riwka	KITZELSTEIN	wolf
EDELHEIT	Tzwi	KLATCH	Chaim
EISENBERG	Itzhak	KLEINBERGER	Yakow
FAST	Israel	KLOTZ	Itzhak
FESSEL	Hide	KLOTZ	Sara
FEUERLICHT	Yakow	KOENIG	Chaim
FEURLICH	Elimelech	KRIELER	Baruch
FISHBEIN	Dawid	KRILL	Hersh
FISHLER	Tzwi	KRILL	Reisel
FISHLICH	Yaakow	LAM	Yehiel
FITTER	Awrahm	LANDAU	Shmuel
FLAM	Fima	LANG	Chaim
FRENKEL	Itzhak	LANGBLUM	Moshe
FREUND	Shmuel	LEHRER	Tali
FRUMAN	Chaim	LIEBER	Anshel
FRUSHTAG	Yossel	LIEBER	Berish
FUSS	Sender	LIEBER	Tzwi
GERLICH	Menachem	LITTMAN	Israel Mos
GRINSHPAN	Moshe	LONDON	Zindel
GRINSHPAN	Aaron	LONDON	Feibish
HABER	Yossef	LUDENBERG	Mendel

[Page 30]

MAHLER	Wolf	SHOENBERG	Yaakow
MAHLER	Eliezer	SHOSS	Sender
MARGOLIS	Moshe	SHPINDLER	Chana
MARIN	Aaron	SHTIMMER	Miriam Ze
MEBEL	Moshe	SHUB	Yaakow
MECHLECH	Menachem	SHWATSCH	Nute
MEHLICH	Yehoshua	SHWEIBEL	
MELAMED	Awraham	SOBOL	Shia
MELLER		STROWBURGER	Awraham
MELLER	Shprintze	TAUBENFELD	Moshe
MINTZ	Awraham	TEITELBAUM	Haya
MORGENSTERN	Benyamin	TEITELBAUM	Mechel
MOSES	Awraham	THALER	Mordechai
NORD	Hersh	TRANCHER	Manas
NUSSBAUM	Wolf	TRAUBER	Getzel
OLING	Amshel	TRAUBER	Mania
OLINK	Awraham	TRENCHER	Manes
PASTERNAK	Moshe	TZELLER	Eliayhu
PERETZ	Reuven	TZWIBEL	Yaakow
PINKUS	Lemel	TZWIK	Awraham
PLATNER	Awraham	WALKER	Itzhak
PORUSH	Ozer	WALTER	Tzwi
POSTACH	Shimon	WARFEL	Zelig
POSTER	Shimon	WEINFELD	Shmuel
PRESSER	Baruch	WEINMAN	Moshe
REICHMAN	Leibish		Itzhak
RIEDER	Seril	WEISNER	Daw
RINGEL	Shaul	WESTREICH	Feivel
RINGLER	Awraham	WIENER	Itahak
ROZNER	Eliyahu	WILNER	Leibish
RUBIN	Hersh	WILNER	Itzhak
SAMIT	Yenta	WILNER	Leibish
SHAMROT	Zelde	WILNER	Nuta
SHAMROT	Moshe	WINTER	Israel Ber
SHEINBERG	Yaakow	WOLFF	Leibish
SHEINER	Naphtali	ZELTZER	Zeew
SHENKER	Moshe	ZIMET	Leibish
SHILDKRAUT	Zelig	ZWASS	Yakow
SHLANGER	Miriam Ze		

[Page 31]

Religion

The great preponderance of the Jewish population of Krosno was religious. The religious range extended from the Hassidic or very pious to the moderate or traditional religious Jews. Of course, there were some non-believers, agnostics and assimilated Jews but their numbers were limited. Jewish life revolved around the synagogue and synagogue related activities. The community built a beautiful synagogue that had three floors. The upper floor was the main synagogue of the community where Rabbi Fuhrer conducted services. The cantor of the main synagogue was Reuben Peretz Kaufman, a brother in law of the famous world-renowned cantor Yossele Rosenblat. The lower floor served as a synagogue where the Hassidic Rabbi Arale (Aaron) Twerski, and later Moshe Twerski, conducted services. The lower synagogue attracted the more religious and Hassidic elements in the city. The small yeshiva of Krosno also used the synagogue for studies.

The second floor also had another synagogue called the "Yad Harutzim" headed by Awraham (Adolph) Muenz where merchants and artisans prayed. The third floor contained the "mikvah" or ritual bath, there was a cold and a heated ritual bath connected to an underground spring that provided constantly fresh water. There was also a steam room with a row of benches anchored to the floor. The highest bench was extremely hot and humid.People used to take with them a bucket of cold water to splash their faces in order to cool down. The sauna was open Saturday morning and still steaming. The sexton of the synagogue and his family lived on this floor. The city also had a few small "shtibelech" or one room service halls notably the Gerer shtibel next to **Wilner's** residence where followers of the Rabbi of Gur prayed. The community also maintained a religious judge or "dayan" **Akiva Hammerling,** son in law of Rabbi Fuhrer. He was in charge of the rabbinical court. The community maintained "heders" or religious schools where youngsters were thought the prayers. The community assumed the costs for those that could not afford to pay. Of course, there were private heders and advanced cheders for students that continued their studies with the Talmud. There were also a few religious slaughterers that charged the customers for their services. The community also baked matzot for Passover at the bakery of Krill and provided the needy with the staple for the holiday. The budget of the community was based on taxes raised by the kehilla of all Jewish residents in the city.

Political life

The major Polish political parties did not encourage Jews to join their ranks. Very few Jews held positions in the major political parties. The Jews flocked to their own parties or representatives to protect their interests. Since the Jews were a minority in Poland, their representation in Parliament was small.

[Page 32]

This representation was further reduced through various gerrymandering tactics regularly employed in Polish elections of the period. The Jewish parliamentary representation was usually isolated and had few allies in the governing bodies of Polish politics. While the Jewish representation in the Sejm- or parliament was small by contrast, Jewish representation at the local level was more representative.

Jews participated heavily in municipal elections and supported usually moderate city councilmen or they voted for Jewish lists that combined several political parties. There were always Jewish city councilmen in Krosno to defend the Jewish interests in the city. Some of these councilors were frequently re-elected, namely, Eber Englander, Leopold Dym and the Stiefel brothers. The mayor of Krosno was always Christian. Jewish voters supported their candidates particularly following the great depression of 1928 and 1930 hat seriously affected the Jewish community. The campaign of the Polish cooperatives to boycott Jewish firms further deteriorated the Jewish economic situation. To strengthen their economic base, the Jewish workshop owners formed a close supportive economic association (in the mid-twenties) called "Yad Harutzim" and the Jewish merchants association headed by Jozef Stiefel also formed an association of self-assistance. The associations established a financial institution, namely, the "Gmiles Chessed," cooperative bank suported by the AJDC. The bank provided financial loans to merchants in need at very low interest. The capital of the bank was subscribed by the members of the association and the Joint. The members selected a board of officers. Below is a list of the officers of the bank and the subscribing members.

[Page 33]

The Management

Stowarzyszenie Dobroczynne
„Gemiłus Chesed"
Kasa Bezprocentowych Pożyczek
w KROŚNIE.

Krosno, dnia .... 193_

1. Goldstein, Samuel , president
2. Platner, Jozef, vice president
3. Fink, Israel, Mgr. secretary
4. Ader, Jakub, member of the board
5. Apfel, Maneshe, member of the board
6. Breitowicz, Israel, member of the board
7. Freund, Samuel, member of the board
8. Feurlicht, Meilech, member of the board
9. Elowicz, Saul, member of the board
10. Trenczer, Leiser, member of the board
11. Weinstein, Szyzion, member of the board
12. Weisman, Markus, member of the board
13. Willner, Herman, member of the board
14. Moses, Abraham, member of the board
15. Shmutz, Natan, member of the board

[Page 34]

„Gemiłus Chesed"
Kasa Bezprocentowych Pożyczek
w KROŚNIE.

Krosno, dnia _____ 193__

L. _____

Halpern Feuerlicht	Knobel Kalman
Kiselstein Moses	Amsterdam Chaim
Goldberg Izrael	Rössler Peretz
Podner Chaskel	Tronczer Czarna
Platner Markus	Trenczer Samuel
Zwas Jakub	Klagsbald Eber
Grünspan Moses	Platner Abraham
Halpern Jakub	Goldberg Izrael
Beer Mendel	Weissman Cyla
Peim Benzion	Waks Debora
Wenig Naftali	Gross Henoch
Schachne L. D.	Winter Sala
Ramras Eidel	Rubenfeld Chajka
Stern Dawid	Herbstman Lea
Margulies Machcia	Zimet Leib
Winter Izral Beer	Platner Dora
Weissman Mendel	Puretz Samuel
Epstein Berisch	Manler Abraham
Frühman Sara	Schönker Moses Hersch
Grünspan Jakub	Schreier Aron
Zwik Flima	Flik Moses
Ehrenreich Jakub	Margulies Nachel
Breitowicz Lina	Samuel Hajer
Beer Nechemia	Charis Subina
Menner Aron	Breitowicz Cila
Winter Jakub	Horen Lea
Cling Aron	

[Page 35]

Granted loans

Halpern, Feurlicht	Eiselstein Moses	Goldberg, Israel
Podner, Chaskel	Platner, Markus	Zwas, Jakub
Grunspan, Moses	Halpern, Jakub	Beer, Mendel
Beim, Benzion	Wenig, Naftali	Schachner, L.D.
Ramras, Eidel	Stern, Dawid	Margules, Machcia
Winter, Izrael Ber	Weisman, Mendel	Epstein, Berisch
Fruhman, Sara	Grunspan Jakub	Zwik, Flima
Ehrenreich, Jakub	Breitowicz, Lina	Beer, Nehemia
Menner, Aron	Winter, Jakub	Sling, Aron
Knobel, Kalmen	Amsterdam, Chaim	Rossler, Peretz
Trenczer, Czarna	Trenczer, Samuel	Klagsbald, Eber
Platner, Awraham	Goldberg, Izrael	Weisman, Cyla
Waks, Debora	Gross, Henoch	Winter, Sala
Rubenfeld, Chajka	Herbstman, Lea	Zimet, Leib
Platner, Dora	Puretz, Shmuel	Manlar, Abraham
Schenker, Moses Hersh	Schreier, Aron	Flik, Moses
Margolies, Mechel	Neuman, Mayer	Caras, Sabina
Breitowicz, Cilia		

[Page 36]

**Stowarzyszenie Dobroczynne
„Gemiłus Chesed"
Kasa Bezprocentowych Pożyczek
w KROŚNIE.**

Krosno, dnia

L.

[illegible] Pi??l	Bauman Markus
[illegible] Leopold	Botker Moses
Karner Moses Juda	Stern Szymon
Dawid Mi??s	Kleinman Hela
Kleinman Salomon	Katz Rafael
Weinstein Maria	Weiser Wolf
Zimet Hersch	Breitowicz Izak
Trancer Fajga	Maroka Chana
Trancer Fischel	Lam Chaim
Freund Salomon	Poth Salomon
Sprecher Naftali	Schiff Leib
Steinmetz Mirjam	Schenker Dawid
Rubenfeld Osias	Fink Klara
Nord Salomon	Ellowicz Majer
Galander Mendel	Beer Izrael
Herzfeld Hersch	Margulies Moses
Montag S??g	Taubenfeld Zischu
Wedbel Berl	Frank Jozef P
Weinfeld Markus	Frühman Sara
Spitz Gizela	Jamel Mendel
Richter Hitla	Stern Moses
Bal? Izrael	Peiles Mina
[illegible] Izrael	Schildkraut Selig
Stiefel Joachim	Mahor Jozef
Lambik Hersch	Knopf Izak
Trafner Roza	Teplicki J??t

[Page 37]

Fendar, Feivel	Blum, Leopold	Kanner, Moses L
Dawid , Pinkas	Kleinman, Salomon	Weinstein, Mania
Zimet, Hersh	Trenczer, Fajga	Trenczer, Fishel
Freund, Salomon	Sprecher, Naftali	Stainman, Mirjam
Rubenfeld, Osias	Nord, Salomon	Gelander, Mendel
Hershfeld, Hersh	Montag, Szyja	Wrobel, Berl
Weinfeld, Markus	Spitz, Gizela	Beim, Izrael
Haferling, Izrael	Stiefel, Joachim	Lambik, Hersh
Trattner, Roza	Bauman, Markus	Botker, Moses
Stern, Szymon	Kleinman, Hela	Katz, Rafael
Neiser, Wolf	Breitowicz, Isak	Maroka, Chana
Lem, Chaim	Roth, Salomon	Schiff, Leib
Schenker, Dawid	Fink, Klara	Ellowicz, Mayer
Beer, Israel	Margolies, Moses	Taubenfeld, Zisha
Grank, Jozef	Fruhman, Sara	Jamal, Mendel
Stern, Moses	Peiles, Nina	Schildkraut, Selig
Haber, Jozef	Knopf, Izak	Taplicki, Saul

[Page 38]

Stowarzyszenie Dobroczynne
„Gemiłus Chesed"
Kasa Bezprocentowych Pożyczek
w KROŚNIE.

Krosno, dnia

Kimmel Izak Wolf	Beer Jozef
Sroka Mindel	Stern Majer
Ehrlich Alter	Kaufman Ruben
Geller Feiwel	Lam Perl
Den Wolf	Schleien Alter
Horowitz Sara	Dawid Mechel
Gotlieb Benjamin	Tanz Salomon
Ramras Lazar	Margulies Kalmen
Oling Gena	Schönbach Mechel
Kanner Leib	Weisman Lazar
Scheiner Abraham	Strassfeld Nuchem
Mandel Jakub	Dorf Mendel
Fried Eliezer	Steiner Zudik
Leichtberg Juda	Ratz Chaim
Türk Izrael	Gerlich Osias
Schiff Moses	Spigelman Dawid
Feitelbaum Moses	Krans Jozef
Alter Jakub	Pinsel Chaja
Grün Chawa	Münz Ruben
Breitowicz Leib	Beim Süssman
Engelhard Mendel	Pogen Kalmen
Meisels Lazar	Wisslstein Ch. W.
Weiner Aron	Gunik Moses
Beer Mendel	Kornreich Alter
Friedman Mendel	Engelhard Ojzer
Riemer Jakub	Landau Leo
Edelheit Tubin	Berger Benjamin
Rieder Jozef	

[Page 39]

Kimel, Izak Wol.	Sroka, Mindel	Ehrlich, Alter
Geller, Feivel	Den, Wolf	Horowitz, Sara
Gottlieb, Benyamin	Ramras, Lazar	Oling, Genia
Kanner, Leib	Schainer, Abraham	Mandel, Jakub
Fried, Eliezer	Leitberg, Juda	Turk, Izrael
Schiff, Moses	Teitelbaum, Moses	Alter, Jakub
Grun, Chzwa	Breitowicz, Leib	Engelhardt, Mendel
Meisels, Lazar	Weiner, Aron	Beer, Mendel
Friedman, Mendel	Riemer, Jakub	Edelheit, Rubin
Rieder, Jozef	Beer, Jozef	Stern, Mayer
Kaufman, Rubin	Lam, Perl	Schleien, Alter
Dawid, Mechel	Tanz, Saloman	Margulies, Kalmen
Scheinbach, Mechel	Weisman, Lazar	Strasfeld, Nuchim
Dorf, Mendel	Steiner, Zudik	Ratz, Chaim
Gerlich, Osias	Spigelman, Dawid	Kranz, Jozef
Pinsel, Chaja	Munz, Reuben	Beim, Sussman
Pogon, Kalmen	Kieselstein, Ch.	Guzik, Moses
Kernreich, Alter	Engelhardt, Ojzer	Landau, Leia
Berger, Benjamin		

[Page 40]

Stowarzyszenie Dobroczynne
„Gemiłus Chesed"
Kasa Bezprocentowych Pożyczek
w KROŚNIE.

Krosno, dnia

ךרבעה ןרק ןולסרק

Melamed Rachela	Friedman Manes
Akselrad Izak	Fischler Wolf
Montag Moses	Gotlieb Benjamin
schenker Wolf	Pelm Salmon
Wittman Moses	Zimet Samuel
Schuldenfeld Leib	Rössler Aron
Flapan Lazar	Metzger Rachela
Hornik Kalman	Fütter Abraham
Weinstein Szymon	Silberberg Osias
Bobker Markus	Weinfeld Ascher
Moses Wolf	Bodner Chaim
Gelb Chaim	Goldfinger Drezel
Bogen Muchem	Ettinger Moses
Salomon Lea	Wilner Leib
Weinberger Saul	Weiser Wolf
Pinkas Lemel	Fenig Chawa
Berger Jakub	Dunkel Majer
Freund Moses	Schreier Aron
Salz Mendel	Diamand K. M.
Kanner Chaskel	Engelhard Schulim
Trenczer Helena	
Engelhard Izak	
Fürst Izrael Jakub	
Possner Rosa	
Weber Jozef	
Tatz Josef Leib	
Akselrad Lipe	

[Page 41]

Melamed Rachela	Akselrod, Izak	Montag, Moses
Schenker, Wolf	Pittman, Mozes	Schuldenfeld, Leib
Flapan, Lazar	Hernik, Kalmen	Weinstein, Szymon
Bobker, Markus	Moses, Wold	Gelb, Chaim
Bogen, Nuchem	Salomon, Lea	Weinberger, Saul
Pinkas, Lemel	Berger, Jakub	Freund, Moses
Salz, Mendel	Kanner, Chaskel	Trenczer, Helena
Engelhardt, Izak	Furst, Izrael Jak.	Possner, Rosa
Weber, Jozef	Ratz, Jozef Leib	Akselrad, Lipa
Friedman, Manes	Fishler, Wolf	Gottlieb, Benjamin
Beim, Salmen	Zimet, Samuel	Rossler, Aron
Futter, Abraham	Silbeberg, Osias	Weinfeld, Asher
Bodner, Chaim	Goldfinger, Drezel	Ettinger, Moses
Wilner, Leib	Weiser, Wolf	Fenig, Chawa
Dunkel, Mayer	Schreier, Aron	Diamand, K.W
Engelhard, Schulem		

[Page 42]

Some of the names seem to repeat themselves since the list extends over a long period of time. The fund was very helpful to the small business people. There was also the "Ludowy Bank" or People's bank that was a Jewish banking institution in Krosno.

The Yiddish letter below was sent to the USA to appeal for contributions.

[Page 43]

גמילות־חסד־קאסע   דעם 16 יאנואר 1939

אין קראסנע

צו

אונדזערע השובע ברידער אין אמעריקע.

די פאראאלסונג פון דער גמילות־חסד אין קראסנע, ווענדעט זיך
צו אײך מיט א הײסן אפעל אין דער ה"גסיקער שווערע לאגע פון דער־דישער
באפעלקערונג אין פוילן, וועלכע אײך דארף אײך נישם שילדערן, און קען ז"
לידער אײך נישם שילדערן. די גויטסענדיק"ם מים אײך זיך צו שטעלן אין
פארבינדונג, כדי איר זאלם מימען, וואָס ב" אונדז אין קראסנע מערם געמון או
גע"ססעם פאר דער דישער באפעלקערונג מים דער מיסהילף פון דעם
"רזשא"נס".

עס איז געשאפן געמאָרן ב" אונדז צ" קאַאָפעראסי"ע־בעגק, וועלכע
פארס"לן יערלעך חלואות אויף צינזן אויף דער סומע פון א האלבן מיליאָן
זלאָסעס, נאמירלעך, אז דאָס איז פאר מיטל־סוחרים. דאקעגן האבן מיר גאָך
דר"סיק ביז פינף און דר"סיק פראצענט באפעלקערונג, וועלכע גענוסן נישם
פון די קאָאָפעראסי"ע־בעגק, ה"ל ז" זענען נישם אין דער לאגע פון ז"ערע
מאָרטשאָסן אָדער קל"נע געשעפטעלך צו צאָלן צינזן, צוליב דעם האָבן מיר
געשאָסן ב" אונדז אין קראסנע א גמילות־חסדים קאסע, וועלכע האָם די אויפ־
נאַגע צו סיסצן די ר"גע 35 % באפעלקערונג, וועלכע קען נישם גענוסן פון
די בעגק צוליב די צינזן. די נ"ח־קאסע האָם אן א"גן קאפיקאל צוזאמען־
געסעלם פון דעם אָנ"ל פון דער דישער באפעלקערונג אין די ה" הוי"ך פון
3500 גילדן. דער "רזשא"נס" האָם אונדז געצוערנס אלגעגעבם 8000 זלאס.
דא ה"סם צוזאמען האבעם די קאסע מים א קאפיקאל פון א 12000 זלאסעס.
נאסירלעך געניואָ נישם צו באשפ"זן די 35 % פון דער ווי'סבאדערפסיקע
דישער באפעלקערונג און ז" באנארן מים חלואות, מיר ל"גן ב" אן אויס־
צוג, אימל מיר האבן פארסיילם אין די לעצסע מאָנאם און אויך די נעמען
פון די לוים זי אויך די נעמען פון די פאראאלסונגס־מיסגלידער.

מיר זענען איבערצ"גם, אז ב"ם דורכל"ענעם דעם גר"ה, זי אויך ג"ם

[Page 44]

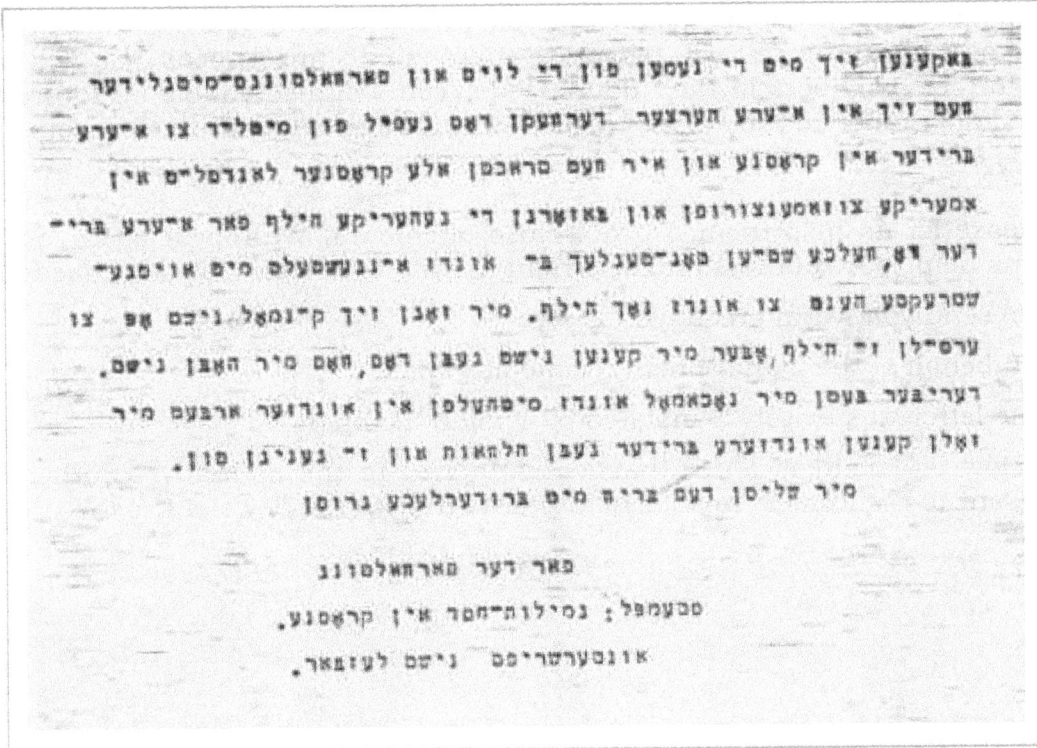

The Yiddish letter dated Januaey 16, 1939 is addressed to the Krosner landsman in the USA

The Yiddish letter dated January 16, 1939 is addressed to the Krosner landsman in the USA.

The letter states that the management of the "Gmiless Chessed" in Krosno desperately appeals for help during this difficult period for the Jews in Poland. I do not need to explain the situation nor am I capable of describing it. The needs are urgent therefore we decided to inform you of the activities we undertook on behalf of the Jewish population in Krosno with the cooperation of the "Joint".

We established two cooperative banks that provide annual loans amounting to a half a million zlotys. The benefactors of these interest bearing loans are of course the stronger situated merchants. The bank operations leave out between 30-35% of the smaller merchants or artisans that can not afford to pay interests. We therefore created a special fund that would provide non-interest loans to these people. The fund has managed to obtain from various sources the sum of 3500 zlotys. The Joint provided another 8000 zloty. The fund started to operate with 12000 zlotys at its disposal. Of course, the sum could not feed all the small merchants but the fund could assist many merchants with needed financial assistance. Below are the names of the management committee and the list of loan receivers.

The list of names is published with the intent to show you the extent of the needs and hopefully you will respond generously to this appeal. You will help your former neighbors in their daily needs. You will also enable us to provide needed assistance to the Jews of Krosno who struggle daily with their lot.

[Page 45]

Please let us help them. Do not close our doors. We repeat again, please help us help your brothers and sisters in Krosno with loans for their needs.

We send you warm greetings.

On behalf of the management. Name illegible.

The letter was loosely translated by William Leibner.

Below is a Yiddish letter that was attached to the lists abve. Both items were sent to the former Krosner inhabitants to help the Jews of Krosno.

[Page 46]

Another leetter of appeal was sent by the Gmilass Chessed
society of Krosno to the USA begging for help

[Page 47]

AMERICAN JOINT DI   UTION COMMITTEE, WARSAW

IG/947/1251   Warsaw, March 17th, 1939

Landsmannschaft Department

American Joint Distribution Committee
P a r i s .

RE: G. Ch. Kassa in Krosno /Voiv. Lwów/
/ Letter of appeal /

Dear Sirs,

We append a letter of appeal to the Landsmannschaft of the G. Ch. Kassa in Krosno.

This is a middle-size town in the Lwów voiv. with 13.500 inhabitants including about 2.000 Jews.

Krosno is a industrial centre, with many factories, a glass-blowing shop, and oil-refining plants. In the mills Christian workers are almost exclusively employed save for some Jewish clerks.

Until recently trade was wholly in Jewish hands. Of late however several non-Jewish co-operative societies have been established which compete keenly with the Jewish traders. Still, in view of the industrial nature of the town there is still enough elbow-room for the Jewish trade.

The local G. Ch. Kassa is of great importance for the local petty traders who largely benefit from its free credit. Its activity is satisfactory. An enrollment action has been carried out, which brought the number of members to 300. As much as a third of the Jewish population enjoys the services of the Kassa to which they are chiefly indebted for the competing ability of their shops.

Following are the chief items of the balance sheet of the Kassa on October 1st, 1938 .

Working capital	Zł. 14.655,10
Own capital	" 5.154,50
Credits from the J. D. C.	" 7.303.-
Deposits	" 3.647,50
Loans granted from 1.IV.38 till 30.IX.38	" 9.590.-
Loans repaid " " " "	" 9.088,15
Local income " " " "	" 495,50
Administr. expenses " " " "	" 333.-

Number of loans granted within the period under review was 81.

The need for more capital is very pressing to enable the G. Ch. Kassa to enhance its beneficial activity.

Yours very truly,
American Joint Distribution Committee

I. GITERMAN

Encl.
IG/mk

Joint report from Krosno to the Joint headquaters in Paris regarding the small revolving fund in Krosno that provides small interest free loans to small Jewish merchants and artisans. The figures represent 1938

[Page 48]

Community Politics

Jewish political life revolved around the community. Who will control the community? Factions and sub factions based on personalities, wealth, political views, religious feelings and social issues fought for control of the The elected candidates selected the officers of the community. Usually the community or kehilla. The elections were proportional and very democratic. The council consisted of 8 members. Only male residents could vote in the elections that were hef every four years. Officers represented coalition forces within the community. **The more prominent community leaders were; Bendet Akselrod, Mojszes Wieisenfeld, Meshulem Weinberg, Wolf Hirshfeld, Samuel Stiefel, Leopold Dym and Ozjasz Heller**. Bendet Akselrod was born in Korczyna to the well-known industrial family of Meshulam Akselrod Father and son were distinguished community leaders. Bendet Akselrod was born on April 14th 1886 and killed on July 15th 1943 at the Szebnie concentration camp in Poland. He was the head of the Jewish community in Krosno for many years until the Germans occupied the city. He was active on behalf of Jewish interests during in the early stages of the German occupation of the Krosno and then went into hiding in Krosno. (See Akselrad chapter).

Bendet Akselrad

[Page 49]

The Krosno Jewish community had many political parties partie; some local and others Zionist parties. **Hirshprung and Fessel** headed the Aguda or very religious party. **Dr. Leopold Dym** headed the Mizrahi or moderate Zionist religious party. **Josef Horowitz, Samuel Rosshandler, Samuel Stiefel, and Aron Wallach** led the General Zionist party. **Hersh Altman and Itzik Salomon** led the Revisionist or right wing Zionist party. There was also a Hitachdut group that represented several left wing groups that supported the working movement in Palestine. The Bund was also represented in Krosno. Of course, there were also independent or unaffiliated Jews. All these political parties had youth branches that were very active in Krosno, for the youth saw no outlet for their hopes since most avenues of general life were closed to them in Poland.

The Betar youth movement on the right was headed by **Moshe Montag**, the Noar Dati was the youth wing of the moderate religious party, Noar Iwri represented the center group. Gordonia and Shomer Hatzair represented the left groups. There was also the **Hehalutz movement** that organized and trained youngsters to settle in Palestine. As a matter of fact, most of the Zionist youth groups stressed the study of the Hebrew language and stressed the importance of Palestine as a home of the Jews. Many young did in fact leave for Palestine, legally or illegally. One of these immigrants was Shimshon Lang. Following his discharge from the Polish army, he saw no future in Poland and decided to leave for Palestine. His illegal ship was intercepted by the British navy and he was offered a choice: join the British army or face prison. He joined the army and fought World War Two with the British 8th army.

[Page 50]

Shimshon Lang in the Polish army   **Some years later, Shimshon Lang in the British army**

The Jewish youth societies had their own clubs that provided a social meeting ground for the Jewish youngsters. Krosno had two Jewish sport clubs; Maccabi and Gideon that provided athletic outlets for Jewish youngsters.

[Page 51]

The Krosner Beis Yaacov or girls school

Education

Most Jewish children, especially boys, started "cheder" or school at the age of three. The cheder usually consisted of one room with 10-15 students. The parents selected the cheder and paid the teacher. The community also provided some help with tuition for orphans. Krosno had several cheders, notably the one of **Moshe Feivel by the river, Chaim Just, Chaim Lam and Kuflick**. Students studied for some years with the teacher where they learned how to read the prayers and the weekly portions of the bible. Most of them then went on to a higher cheder where the religious instruction was more intensive. Here they studied various commentaries on the bible and started to study the Talmud or religious judicial law. Some students continued their studies with private tutors but this was expensive.

Rabbi Twerski organized a small Yeshiva named "Keter Hatorah" for those students that wanted to continue to study in an organized framework. The head of the Yeshiva was **Mr. Seligman**. A "Beis Yaacov" or school for girls was also established in Krosno under the leadership of Mr. Hirschfeld. A school where Hebrew was the official language of instruction was also established in Krosno. The school was small but grew in numbers with the years; it was affiliated with the "Tarbut" movement or cultural movement that had a network of schools in Poland. Most Jewish children went to the Polish public elementary schools where their experiences were far from happy.

[Page 52]

Very few students continued their studies, since secondary school was very expensive. Some Jewish students opted for trade or commercial classes, but the number of students was very limited due to the expense and the built in system of limitations for Jewish students. Very few students continued higher education that required extensive financial backing. Furthermore, Polish universities limited the number of Jewish students. Some of the students went abroad to study. Still the number of Jewish professionals was impressive. Krosno boasted several Jewish medical doctors, lawyers and engineers.

Jewish doctors in Krosno. Siegel, Buchholz, Yacov Baumring, Awraham Rosenberg, and Leopold Dym. Esther Moskowitz was a dentist.

Lawyers: Leib Rosenbaum, Weinberger.

Engineers; Oscar Gross Otto Lieberman

Youth

Postcard from an outing of the Betar youth movement. Notice the stamp with the inscription of Brit Trumpeldor (official name of the youth division), Krosno. Polish greetings from some participants, dated 29 November 1933

Most Jewish youngsters finished their education with the elementary school. They then assisted their fathers in the business or the mothers at home. The very religious youngsters continued their heder study. Some became apprentices. Most of the youth, however, saw few opportunities. The civil service, the government industries, the municipal services were closed to them. They could only hope to work in Jewish places and these were few in numbers.

[Page 53]

Thus, the attraction to the Zionist youth movements in Poland, especially in smaller cities like Krosno. These movements offered hope and provided an outlet for intellectual, social and physical activities. The youth clubs staged plays, musicals, literary evenings and various outings that involved both sexes. The stress of the political youth clubs was Hebrew, Jewish History, Zionism, Palestine geography, songs and group dances. and They also provided the great support for the two sport clubs in Krosno, namely the Gideon club with goalkeeper **Gobel** and the Maccabi club headed by **Mendel Fish**. The more prominent players of Maccabi were Jossel and Mendel Friss. Soccer was the most popular game amongst the spectators. Some Jewish youth also supported the "Bund" or Jewish socialist group, the Polish socialist movement and even the Polish communist party that was officially outlawed in Poland. The party was very active and one of its leaders was Wladyslaw Gomulka, a native of Krosno. Following World War II he became leader of the Polish Communist party and then Prime-Minister of Poland.

From left; Wolf Mozes, Zalek Weinfeld, Yossek Weissman, Srulek Spitz, Malka Fruhman, Mundek Bieder, Mayer Goldstein, David Fruhman, and Tulek Katz

[Page 54]

Krosno youth players

[Page 55]

Play staged by Krosno's Jewish youth

Krosno Jews Youth
From left; Yossef Margolis, Moniek Fruhman, Chune Altman,
Yossef Lang, Olek Steigbigel and BarUch Minc

[Page 56]

The motor age arrives to Krosno. Moniek Fruhman with
small Salek Beim on his motorcycle

Jewish Residences

Krosno did not have a specific Jewish neighborhood or quarter. Jews lived throughout the city but certain areas or streets had a large Jewish concentration notably around the market. The Jews of Krosno were predominantly religious. According to White, you did not need a calendar to know that Shabbat or a Holiday was approaching. "The aroma of the gefilte fish and parsley in the soup penetrated even in the street air. At home after the Friday evening service , we sat down at the table , sang the prayer greeting the Sabbath and sanctified the wine, homemade grape juice. Everybody received a sip of wine. The challah was blessed and distributed to every person. Then the gefilte fish was followed by chicken soup with farfel or noodles. Chicken and compote followed. Between courses, religious songs were sung at the table". "Saturday morning, the streets were empty, the stores in the city mostly Jewish owned were closed. Jews went to the synagogues to pray that would last until noon." The men returned home and a big elaborate meal would be served interspersed with religious songs praising God and Sabbath.

Jewish Refugees

The Jews of Krosno as well as those of Poland were accustomed to seeing Jews leave Poland. Mainly they headed to Germany, Austria and the USA. This trend continued for many years until the USA established a quota system following World War I that in effect barred Polish Jews from entering the USA.

[Page 57]

This act was soon followed by other nations that faced massive unemployment caused by the severe financial world depression. Each country tried to stop the flow of immigrants. Hitler assumed power in Germany and not only stopped Jewish from entering Germany but proceeded to expel them by any and all means, especially non-German citizens. Jews who lived in Germany for many years suddenly faced expulsion. Most of them were deprived or stripped of everything and sent to Poland. The expulsions were rigidly enforced and sometimes split families that consisted of German and foreign citizenships. The Jewish expulsions were vividly described in the German press that launched vitriolic attacks against Jews. Of course, the Germans saw to it that the anti-Jewish campaign also appeared in the neighboring countries under various disguises. The Polish press or rather a good part of it fell prey to this anti-Jewish campaign and further incited the Polish public against the Jewish population.

The Polish government was not crazy about accepting the German Jewish residents of Polish descent but it had no choice. The refugees returned usually to their native places. Krosno received a number of them; Yehuda Engel and Moshe Kleiner who will play tragic roles later in Krosno. These Jews left Krosno in the hope of finding a better life in Germany which they did. But wwith Hitler's rise to power, they were persecuted and finally chased out of Germany under one or another pretext. Close to 200 Jews from Germany arrived in Krosno, most of them penniless. One exception was the **Leiner family** that brought a mechanical ice-cream machine and began to sell the product. Up to this time, ice cream was made by hand and rather expensive. The community launched an appeal to help these refugees. The refugees described in great detail the situation in Germany, particularly the Jewish situation. Many Jews found it hard to believe that the Germans who behaved decently to the Polish Jews during World War I sunk to such bestial behaviour. Slowly the facts were digested but the Jews could do very little about the situation. The world was closed to the Jews and they had no place to go. Even Palestine slowly closed the doors to Jewish immigrants. The Krosno Jew like all Jews in Poland and Eastern Europe became trapped with no exit.

The Polish government encouraged Jews to leave the country for it wanted to reduce the Jewish population in Poland. Following the official and honest census of 1921, the government never published demographic information regarding the number of Jews in Poland. The estimates are that the Jewish population reached about 10% of the population of the country or about 3.5 million people. Various Polish governments tried to reduce this estimated number by various intentional misrepresentations that the public and the Polish Jewish community did not accept. The fact remained that the estimated figure of 3.5 million Polish Jews was the accepted figure.

My father Jakob Leibner a native of Zmigrod left the place to marry my mother Seril Lang of Krosno. He had to register the move with both localities.

[Page 58]

- - - - - - - - - -

Top registration note states that Jakob Leibner left his Zmigrod residence and moved to Krosno to the Lang residence in the market place.
Bottom note states that he left Zmigrod and moved to Krosno

The Polish government maintained a close watch over the movement of people depression spread and the entrance gates to most countries closed. The Zionist movement in Poland began to ship illegally young Jews to Palestine. The demand for passage steadily increased. A number of Krosno Jews left Poland for Palestine. While Poland encouraged Jews to leave Poland, it kept a close watch over the Jews in Poland. As a matter of fact, the Polish authorities encouraged Jews to leave Poland. Internally, however, the government kept close watch over Jewish movements as can be seen by the document above.

[Page 59]

ikob Leibner as he appeared on his Polish identity card

**Seril Lang-Leibner, daughter of Chaim and Feige Lang,
married to Jakob Leibner**

In 1935, Pilsudski died. General Smigly-Ridz took over the reins of Poland. A wave of anti-Semitic propaganda descended on Poland. Anti-Semitic Polish parties and groups began openly to agitate against Jews, notably the National Democratic party known by the letters ND. The members were familiarly called the "Endekes". They refused to recognize the Polish Jews as Polish citizens. They staged a violent campaign against the Jewish manner of slaughtering animals claiming that it was cruel to animals. Apparently hunting animals was humanitarian.

[Page 60]

The "anti-Schitah" laws or ritual slaughter laws were passed in a modified manner that immediately increased the price of "Kosher meat". Illegal slaughtering appeared on the Polish scene. The entire meat business industry received a serious shock and affected the Krosno Jewish butchers and customers. Other laws aimed at Jewish economic and financial interests were passed. The Polish street was incited against Jews. In Krosno, graffiti slogans such as "Jews to Palestine", "Out with Jews" , "Kill Jews" appeared on the city walls. Polish students returning from schools for their summer holidays organized boycotts of Jewish stores and prevented buyers from entering the stores. The students also attacked the Maccabi sport club and caused a great deal of damage. Part of the Polish press encouraged these activities and created the illusion that the Polish Jew was the enemy of Poland. While the real enemy of Poland, Germany incited the Polish masses. Of course, the German press and radio did their best to incite the Poles against the Jews. Hitler wanted to detract attention from his military activities in Germany.

Germany was very pleased with this anti-Jewish campaign in Poland. It also supported and egged on Poland to insist on territorial changes along the Polish-Czechoslovak border in favor of Poland. The Czechs refused to negotiate. The Poles were furious and waged an aggressive publicity campaign against Czechoslovakia in the Polish press. Germany was of course interested in keeping these two Slavic nations apart for Czechoslovakia was an industrialized country with a large military industry at its disposal that could provide military hardware to its allies in time of need. And the Polish army needed modern weapons. The Germans were determined to keep the feud between the two Slavic countries going to prevent any Polish –Czech logical alliance. Hitler succeeded beyond his wildest dream. Poland joined militarily Germany in dismembering Czechoslovakia. Czech prisoners of war soon appeared in the city of Krosno for the city was close to the border between the countries. Now Poland faced Germany alone in the east.

[Page 61]

Chapter III
Germany attacks Poland

Before long, Germany was beginning to demand Polish territorial concessions. Poland refused to grant concessions and signed hasty alliances with France and England. As German pressure mounted, Poland was facing powerful Germany armies reinforced with Czech weapons. The Polish army was no match for the highly mechanized German army that surrounded Poland from several sides. Poland began to mobilize the military reserves and prepared for war. The Polish radio constantly repeated code names for military units to present themselves at their designated places. Soldiers began to appear on the streets heading to their military bases. The process was slow, cumbersome and never completed.

Here is eyewitness account of the beginning of the war in Krosno.

"September 1 1939 Hitler's armies invaded Poland. In my hometown of Krosno Southern Poland where I was born and raised I had just turned 16. Hours before Hitler officially declared war on Poland, German Stukas (dive-bombers) raided and bombed our military airport in Krosno. I was awakened by the sirens and bombing. It was around 4 AM. As an appointed warden for the street and trained to use a gas mask at school, I ran outside to urge people to get down into the cellars that had been designated as make-shift bomb shelters. Instead, we were just standing in the street watching the end of the precision bombing of our airport. Little damage was sustained by the neighboring homes. At the same time in the proximity of Krosno, the oil refinery in Jedlicze and the electricity plant in Mecinka were bombed. The Stukas returned later in the day but didn't bomb the Airbase again. A wing of a shot-down plane with it's cross and swastika was later seen being hauled on the main road".

Although certain preparations for the war commenced earlier as the winds of war swept through Poland, the sudden "Blitz" (lightning) attack came as a shock. In the days following, chaos reigned. While Hitler's highly mechanized armies were rapidly overrunning Poland, the Polish army unprepared for war was still being mobilized. Polish Jews were among the enlisted men and officers.

The German armies raced across Poland as though they were on maneuvers. The Polish government soon left Warsaw and headed southeast near the Polish- Rumanian border. The Polish government urged all military units to head East and form a battle line along the Vistula or Wisla river. The Polish roads became clogged with military units and civilians heading East. The Stuka dive bombers had a field day machine-gunning these long human columns of civilians and soldiers. Meanwhile the German armies continued their rapid advance through Poland.

Krosno was occupied on September 8, 1939 by German troops under the command of General Wilhelm List that came from occupied Czechoslovakia. Many Jews of Krosno had left the city prior to the German arrival and were now stranded along the roads leading from Krosno to the Soviet border. But the city received many Jews who were heading East but were cut off by the German army and could not continue their trip. Finally, Russian forces entered Poland and occupied Eastern Poland in accordance with the secret agreement signed between Russia and Germany. The Polish government crossed the Rumanian border and headed to the West. Hitler appointed Hans Frank governor general of Poland with his seat in Krakow.

The German panzer columns swept across Poland. The poorly equipped Polish army was no match for the Germans. The market square of Krosno became a huge parking lot for German tanks, armored vehicles and trucks. Military kitchens were set up to provide the soldiers with hot food. Telephone wires were stretched across balconies and poles that lead to the military headquarters. The Jews immediately felt the iron hand of the occupiers. Jews were rounded up for work details to clean the streets and debris of the bombing. Jewish store owners were forced to open the stores. German soldiers bought everything in sight, paid in zlotys, marks or worthless paper coupons. The purchases were immediately packaged and sent back home to Germany via military post. Jakob Leibner was forced to open his clothing store and sell or give away the merchandise to German soldiers. Most of the merchandise was removed from the store prior to the German arrival and buried in his father-in law's, Chaim Lang's cellar. He closed the store when there was nothing left on the shelves and headed home. He was lucky for in some stores the soldiers worked over the owners.

Some SS officers also came to my maternal grandfather, Chaim Lang's store. They entered the store with their long black leather coats, their spit polished boots, their suspended daggers, indeed messengers of Satan. They inquired about the lack of merchandise in the store. Chaim Lang informed them in German that he acquired during World War I (he served with Austrian Imperial forces during World War I) that the Poles took everything. The Germans asked him where he studied German and he told them whereupon they asked him with what regiment he served. He named the regiment and the commanding officers in a typical Austrian Imperial military manner that impressed the visitors. The SS men were Austrian and warned my grandfather to disappear. They left the store and we all began breathing again. The SS men went next door and practically destroyed the store and beat the Jewish owner. We had luck that they met an ex-comrade in arms, although Jewish, still an old soldier and decided not to make an issue. Indeed, the entire stock of merchandise of Chaim Lang's store and that of Jakob Leibner were buried in the cellar. The family also buried the silver candelabra and other expensive items. The place was sealed and invisible to the naked eye.

The German army ruled the city for a while then the German civil administration took over. Krosno was part of the "General Government" headed by governor general Hans Frank. Michael Zuzik was appointed administrator of Krosno, he was later replaced by Dr. Heimisch. The Gestapo appointed Hauptsturmfuehrer Gustav Schmatzler to head the Krosno Gestapo. He was born January 17, 1895 in the village of Neindorf. He finished public school. His assistant was Oberstumrfuhrer Ludvik Von Davier. Other Gestapo men in Krosno were sturman Oskar Backer who was born in Grodek Jagelonski. He was a descendant of German colonists in Poland and resided in Katowice where he was a butcher. Gehard Sachar, Untersturmbanfuhrer Stengler, Karl Hauch, and Paul Stenzel were also members of the Krosno Gestapo. The city itself was in the district of Jaslo whose Gestapo chief was Hauptsturmfuhrer Wilhelm Raschwitz. He was chief of the Gestapo office in Jaslo from 1941 to 1943. He was killed later in battles with the partisans. The Gestapo harassed Jews notably religious Jews.

Then the order was given that all Jews must leave Krosno. The city was near the new border between Germany and Russia, The Germans wanted to push the Jews of Krosno to the Russian side of the border To the Jews it was a terrible blow to leave everything behind and begin to wander not knowing what the tomorrow will bring. Some Jews prepared to leave Krosno, others decided to hide in the country side or in nearby villages until things calmed down. Age-old strategy used by Jews throughout their history, hide when in doubt until things calm a bit and things settle down. Soon Jews began to return to Krosno from their nearby hiding places or cellars. All Jewish organizations, associations and group activities were disbanded. Jews decided not to attend the synagogue for fear of being grabbed by the Germans. They prayed at home or in small groups in private homes. Many religious Jews abandoned their traditional caftans for jackets and tried to avoid the streets. Most of the Jewish stores or workshops were handed over to German agents. Intimidation was the order of the day. Public executions or hangings were quite common. The Gestapo arrested the Polish mayor of Krosno, Mr. Bergman his brother, some influential Polish leaders and nobody saw them again. The Gestapo ruled Krosno with an iron hand. The Gestapo encouraged Jews to move to the Soviet occupied zone of Poland. Sometimes the Russians let them stay and sometimes they send them back to the German side.

The Germans made it extremely difficult for Polish Jews to return to heir former homes in Poland from Russian occupied areas of Poland. The Germans accepted quite readily ethnic Germans and Poles from the Soviet occupied zone. Some Krosno Jews braved all dangers and smuggled their way back home while other Krosno Jews headed the other way. The Soviet authorities then opened a registration office where all Polish refugees could indicate whether they wanted to become Russian citizens. The overwhelming majority of Polish refugees refused to accept Russian citizenship. The regular inhabitants of the Soviet zone were automatically made Soviet citizens. The Soviets decided to deport all Polish refugees who refused to become Russian citizens to Siberia. Thousands of refugees were deported to Siberia throughout

1940, amongst them many Krosner Jews, notably Chaim Lang and family, Awham Munz with family, Joseph Platner with family etc.

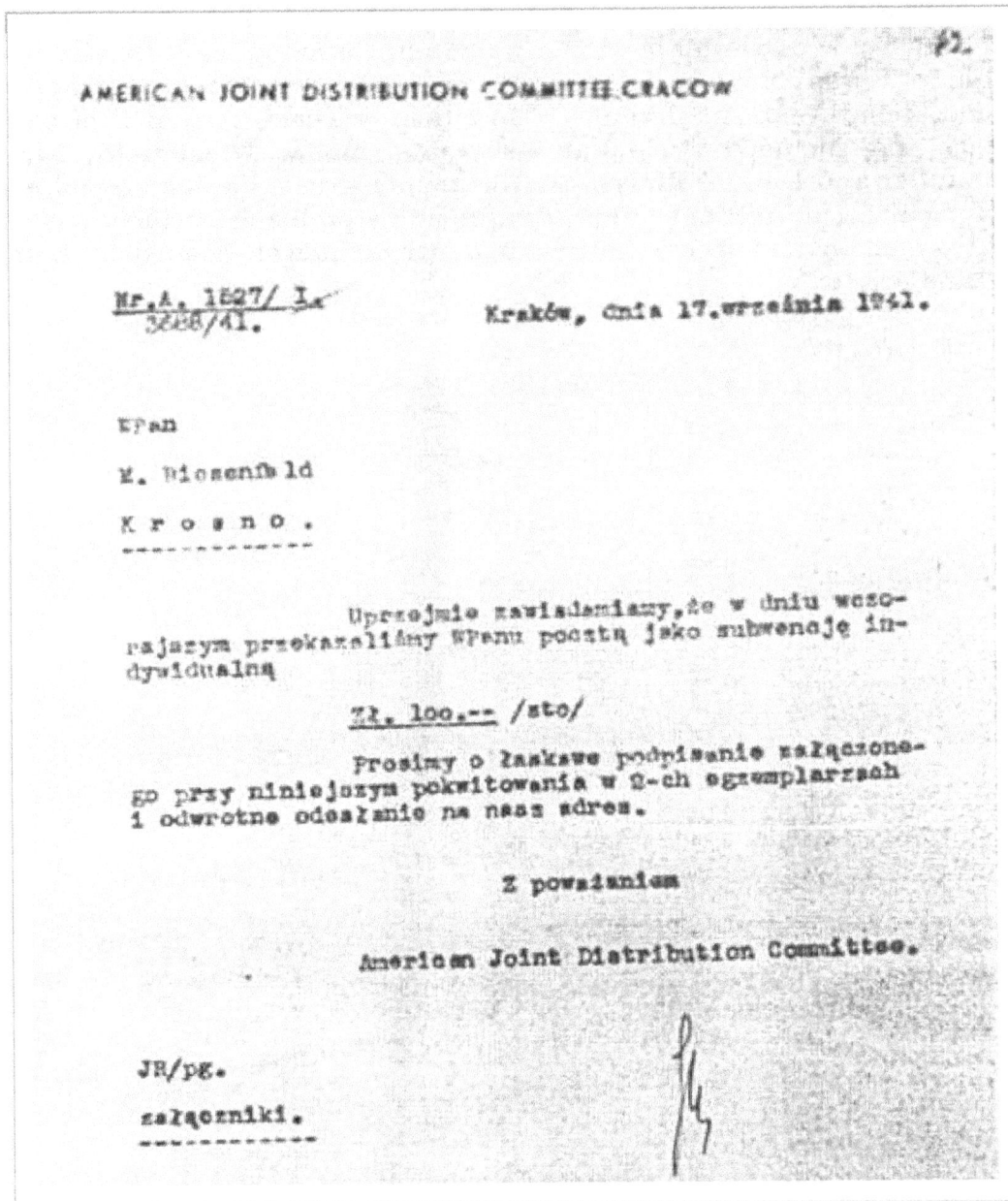

Letter from the American Joint office in Krakow to Mr. M. Wiesefeld, member of the Krosno Judenrat that he was issued a subsidy of 100 zlotys. Acknowledgement is requested. Letter dated September 17. 1941

In Krosno, all Jews were ordered to wear a white armband with a blue star. They were forbidden to enter parks or public institutions but most remained in their apartments. The Gestapo confiscated many nice apartments for their own use but Krosno had lots of empty places since many Krosno Jews had left the city. The Germans appointed **Yehuda Engel** head of the "Judenrat". He was a native of Krosno that lived many years in Germany and was kicked out by Hitler. He was fluent in German. His assistant **was Moshe Kleiner** who also lived many years in Germany. They then selected a council of several members that included **Dr. Jakob Baumring, Mosze Wiesenfeld, Samuel Rosshandler and Mendel Bialywlos.** The council created a Jewish police and some special social tments to cope with the many problems, notably, housing, heath, sanitation and food. The health department was headed by **Samuel Rosshandler**.

The Krosno Judenrat income and expense sheet for the month of April 1941

Translation of the income and expense sheet of April 1941

The Jewish Community Admistration of Krosno - May 7, 1941
April 1941 - Financial Statement in zlotys

	Income	Expense
Cash on hand April 1 1941	2341.39	
Passover 1941 contributions	2757	
January taxes	385	
"Centos" – orphans organisation	315	
People's kitchen	408.90	
Various incomes	3185.67	
Sender account	377.5	
Guard expenses	599	
Legal expenses	49.5	
"Joint"	1250	
Netstandsabgabe		28
Needy		4788
Medicines		54
Public kitchen		1459.06
Sonder account		597.50
Various expenses		1010.99
Loan taxes and medical expenses		346.11
Salaries		1845
"Centos"		28.20

Notice the large Joint contribution to the community and the Passover contribution by the J.S.S. in Krakow. We also notice the small contribution made by the "Centos" organization that was created to help Jewish orphans. We even see that some people had to pay a minimal charge for the meals that the community kitchen provided. On the expense side notice the large expense for the needy, the public kitchen and the salaries of the Judenrat officials. Needless to say the expenses exceeded the income with the contributions. Frequently, the community kitchen had to reduce the number of free meals for lack of money.

The Germans constantly demanded of the Judenrat workers. The workers were hardly paid by the Germans and worked very hard. The Judenrat supplemented their measly pay. Some Jews were sent far away from the city to construct roads and bridges. Others were sent to the air force base.   The Judenrat collected taxes from the Krosno Jews to pay for the various programs notably schooling for the children, medical help for the needy, food for the poor. A special problem posed the Jewish from Lodz, later from Krakow and other areas in Poland. These Jewish refugees were practically dumped at the Krosno railway station. Most of these refugees arrived penniless and without luggage. The Judenrat had to provide them with lodging and the bare necessities. Engel launched an appeal requesting Krosno Jews to help the refugees. Some were lodged at the synagogue of Krosno. Others were lodged in abandoned Jewish apartments. All these activities cost money and the Krosno Jewish tax base kept declining.

As mentioned earlier, most Jewish welfare associations were disbanded with the German occupation. The Judenrat intensified its appeals to former Krosner Jews in America, the Krosner Jewish Association the American JDC and the JDC in Poland. The Joint organization continued to work in occupied Poland since the USA remained neutral in the war in Europe. Joint officials in Poland such as Isaac Borenstein born in 1899 in Kovel, Volyhn region, joined the Joint organization in Poland in 1930. In early 1940, he managed to contact German officials in Krakow and received from them permission for the Joint to operate in the "General government" territory. Krosno was of course part of this territory and entitled to get help from the Joint. The Joint was also instrumental in establishing a Jewish welfare organization called "Judische Soziale Selbsthilfe" or J.S.S. for short. The head of the J.S.S. was Dr. Michael Weivhert who had his office in Krakow The office urged all Jewish communities to establish branches of the J.S.S. in their localities to help the needy Jews.

The Krosno Judenrat received substantial help from both organizations as the above documents indicate. The Krosno Judenrat established a J.S.S. committee in Krosno headed by Samuel Rosshandler. The members of the committee were Bendet Akselrod, Mendel Bialywloss. Moshe Wiesenfeld, and dr. Jakub Baumring. The committee established a free kitchen that provided meals to the needy Jews of Krosno. The kitchen also charged a minimal fee of those that were able to pay. There were frequent clashes between the Engel and Rosshandler over money allocations for the kitchen. The needs of the kitchen increased as the Jewish population was getting poorer by the day. More and more Jewish artisans and shopkeepers were unemployed. Their ranks were constantly increased by the additional Jewish arrivals from the vicinity of Krosno. The Krosno Jewish population steadily increased but the economic situation worsened.

Engel executed everything that Schmatzler asked for. Still Engel tried to lighten the burden of the Jews in Krosno. To a certain extent he managed to do so since the Gestapo behavior in Krosno was brutal but nothing compared to the one of Krakow or other places in Poland. Helena Stiefel, a native of Krosno and a shoah survivor, states that the Jewish situation in Krosno was much better than in the eastern part of Poland where she resided for some time. Engel did work with Schmatzler and manged to help many Jewish refugees in the city. He arranged for the safe return of Krosno Jews to their native city notably both rabbis. In many localities, returning Jews were executed on arrival to their former home. The Krosno Jews killed in Dynow were buried at the local Jewish cemetery by the Krosner "Hevrah Kadisha". Schmatzler allowed the Judenrat and the J.S.S. to distribute to the Krosno Jews money, "matzos" or unleavened bread oil, flour and eggs prior to the Passover holiday of 1941. The Judenrat kept a record of the distribution as shown in the following pages.

Partial list of Krosno Jews that received money, matzos, oil, flour and eggs for Passover 1941. The cash amounts were in zlotys, the matzos in kilos, the oil in decagrams, the flour in kilograms and the eggs in numbers. We have not been able to find all distribution sheets.

Blatt 2

Krosno, den 19...

Vor- und Zuname:	Geld:	Matzen
Uebertrag:	Zł 545.--	kg 10
Basche Litwok	Zł 15.--	kg 3
Jakob Ehrenpreis	" 5.--	" 1
Ruchen Strassfeld	" 30.--	" 6
Salomon Gelb	--	" 2
Isaak Sitzer	" 25.--	" 3
Regina Rawski	" 5.--	" 1
Dina Gabrilewicz	--	" 1
Jakob Wohlrauch	--	" 2
Mendel Marchewka	--	" 7
Moses Langbaum	" 25.--	" 3
Franla Reisenbach	--	" 1
Elias Haferling	" 28.--	" 2
Josef Spritzer	" 10.--	" 2
Berta Holloschuetz	" 25.--	" 4
Tobias Axelrad	" 10.--	" 2
Sala Buchsbaum	" 25.--	" 2
Pinkas Mendel	" 28.--	" 1
Jakob Alter	" 25.--	" 1
Elias Infeld	--	" 4
Benjamin Gottlieb	" 21.--	" 1
Markus Seemann	" 20.--	" 1
Lea Salomon	" 5.--	" 1
Salig Schildkraut	" 10.--	" 1
Taube Glowinski	--	" 1
	" 15.--	" 1

Blatt 3

Krosno, den 29. Apr.

Vor- und Zuname:	Geld:	Matzen	Oel
Uebertrag:	Zł 955.--	kg 199	280
Jasek Knopf	Zł 36.--	--	--
Aron Maenner	" 25.--	kg 5	--
Jakob Zwass	" 35.--	" 3	--
Leiser Koninski	" 20.--	" 4	--
Jhuda Fessel	" 15.--	" 3	--
Regine Pelzmann	--	" 2	15
Reisel Pelzmann	--	" 4	30
Liepe Biedermann	--	" 6	45
Hirsch Burstanowicz	--	" 7	55
Chiel Goldfarb	--	" 5	40
Mottel Einreder	--	" 2	15
Mendel Silberberg	--	" 4	30
Berek Nissenbaum	--	" 4	30
Sische Enzweig	" 10.--	" 2	--
Bendet Steinberg	--	" 4	30
Liepe Fessel	" 40.--	" 6	--
Markus Pelczer	--	" 6	45
Alta Poznanska	--	" 1	25
Frimet Rosenblatt	--	" 2	--
Elias Zajdow	--	" 2	15
Eidel Bogen	--	" 4	30
Gitel Rieder	" 25.--	" 5	--
Josef Vogel	--	" 8	65
Rachel Lamberg	--	" 2	15
Feiwel Geller	" 20.--	" 4	--

Blatt 4

Krosno, d...

Vor- und Zuname:	Geld:	Matzen:
Uebertrag:	Zł 1207.--	kg 3...
Alta Rybak	Zł --	kg 1...
Simon Ehrlich	" --	" ...
Elias Lustig	" --	" ...
Chane Ehrenreich	" 20.--	" ...
Renia Huttner	" 10.--	" ...
Moses Schlanger	--	" ...
Berel Welkes	" 40.--	" ...
Pinkas Bealan	--	" ...
Ryfka Landau	--	" ...
Simon Teitelbaum	" 10.--	" ...
Mordche Weingold	--	" ...
Isaak Vogelfluegel	--	" ...
Chaim Wiazwowski	--	" ...
Sara Dina Gora	--	" ...
Josef Verstaendig	" 25.--	" ...
Benzion Beil	" 25.--	" ...
Ite Friedrich	" 5.--	" ...
Chane Breitowicz	" 10.--	" ...
Hirsch Magel	" 5.--	" ...
Golde Oknowski	"	" ...
Meilech Stuhl	" 35.--	" ...
Sali Weiss	--	" ...
David Aronowicz	--	" ...
Hirsch Bleichfeld	--	" ...

Krosno, den 29. April 1941

Blatt 5

Vor- und Zuname:	Geld:	Matzen:	Oel:	
Uebertrag:	Zł 1392.--	kg 409	1200	d...
Sand Jermias	Zł 25	kg 5	--	
Moses Gruenspan	" 27	" --	--	
Joel " "	" 27	--	--	
Mordche Hirsch Schenker	" 3	--	--	
Chane Asner	" 5	" 1	10	dkg
Perla Baruch	--	" 1	10	"
Hirsch Baer Berkowicz	--	" 2	15	"
Fischel Kopfzucker	--	" 3	25	"
Isaak Schenker	" 20	" 4	--	
Akiba Hemmerling	" 250	" 2	--	
Samuel Hirsch Ranras	" 130	" 5	--	
Gitel Fuehrer	" 50	--	--	
Frieda Pinther	" 80	" 12	--	
Aron Leib Fuehrer	" 100	" 15	--	
Marjem Selde Schlanger	" 10	" 1 1/2	--	
Hirsch Niawadomski	--	" 2	15	"
Nuchem Piwonja	" --	" 3	25	"
Leie Schapiro	--	" 1	10	"
Salomon Jakubowicz	--	" 4	30	"
Sara Kieselstein	" 15	" 3	--	
Samuel Lambik	" 5	" 1	--	
...	" 27	--	--	

Kresno, den 2?.

Blatt 6

Vor- und Zuname:	Geld:	Massen:
Uebertrag:	Zl 2240.--	kg 476
Jakob Lieber	Zl 21	kg ?
Rlime Rubenfeld	" 15	" ?
Adolf Scheibe	--	" ?
Beile Turek	--	" 7
Hirsch Horowitz	" 20	" ?
Scheindel Salz	" 10	" ?
Ester Smorodina	--	" ?
Frieda Kanner	" 10	" ?
Abraham Korb	" 45	--
Rosalie Westreich	--	" ?
Moses Goldfinger	" 25	" ?
David Leibel	" 20	" ?
Golda Karsch	--	" ?
Regine Retter	" 10	" ?
Malke Berger	" 5	" ?
Majer Reinhold	" 5	" ?
Ryfka Schenker	" 5	" ?
Chane Axelrad	" 25	" ?
Liepe Axelrad	" 25	" ?
Ester Tuerk	" 15	" ?
Chaje Rudnicki	--	" ?
Meilech Kanner	" 20	" ?
Moses Rosenberg	--	" ?
Jakob Judenherz	--	" ?
Getzel Trenczer	" 20	" ?

Kresno, den 29. April

Blatt 7

Vor- und Zuname:	Geld:	Massen:	Cal:
Uebertrag:	Zl 2508.--	kg 580	1570
Bronia Thaler	Zl 10	kg 8	--
Moses Goldmann	--	" 4	30
Anna Keil	" 25	" 5	--
Oskar Sternlicht	--	" 2	--
Ferdinand Lippner	--	" 4	--
Mialkus Brilloski	--	" 1/4	--
David Engel	--	" 1	10
Meilech Jhude Kanner	" 30	" 2	--
Eber Klagsbald	" 12	--	--
Wolf Hausmer	" 30		--
David Oitler	" 5	" 1/2	--
Nathan Beil	" 25	--	--
Friederiske Trataner	--	" 1	--
Chaim Schlanger	--	" 4	--
Oalas Silberberg	" 50	" 10	--
Kalf Weiser	" 50	" 6	--
Chaje Stern	" 15	" 5	--
Samuel Raibscheldt	" 5	" 1	--
Beile Fuehrer	--	" 10	--
Moses Wissenfeld	--	" 10	--
Apotheke Korczyna	--	" 14	--
Jhude Leichtberg	--	" 8	--
Ite Schreier	--	" 8 1/2	--

The Krosner Jews were busy with the Passover preparations while the Germans were busy transporting nightly troops and war materials to the border areas with the Soviet Union. Suddenly large military units appeared in the vicinity of Krosno. According to Batia Eisentein (formerly Akselrod) who lived in hiding near the airbase, the Krosno base became a beehive center of activity. Planes constantly landed and took off. Then on June 22, 1941, German armies attacked Russia. The surprise was total according to the pilots of the German air force. According to White who worked at the airbase, the German pilots openly described the bombing raids within Russia. The German armies raced across the Soviet Union as they did in Poland and France. Nobody seemed capable of stopping the German might. The first Soviet war prisoners reached Krosno and were sent to the death camp of Szebnie where 5,000 of them will be shot. The Jewish situation in Krosno worsened by the day as the poverty increased and the Judenrat collected less and less money yet the number of needy Jews increased for the Gestapo was expulsing Jews from the villages near Krosno.

The Gestapo ordered the Judenrat in Krosno to conduct a census of the Jewish population of Krosno. All Jews were ordered to stay at home while the census was conducted on June 22, 1941. All Jews who resided in Krosno on this date were recorded in the census. Krosno Jews that were out of Krosno were not recoded. Jews that preferred to hide were also not recorded Below is a list of Jews as compiled by the Krosno Judenrat on June 22, 1941 and released February 10,1942. The list has 2072 names. We don't know the reason for the list nor do we know the exactness of the list. Most Jews of Krosno appear on the list and most of them would be sent to the death camp of Belzec where there would be no survivors.

Here is the list as it appeared at the Judenrat office and presumably at Gestapo headquarters in Krosno.

[Page 85]

Chapter IV
The Census

The list was extensive and recorded almost all the Jews who were present that day in Krosno but we do not know how many of these Jews were residents of the city. For many Jews were deported to the city of Krosno. Of course, some Jews were hiding while others managed to avoid being registered. The list contained 2072 names of which 1172 were women, 885 men, 172 old people, 395 children and 84 babies.

The census was in German and the occupations are listed in German. Then the question whether they are fit to work; "ja" means yes and "nein" means not fit. The censor defined the fitness. We translated freely the trades to English. The trade given was not always correct.

Administration of the Jewish Community in Krosno

Administration of the Jewish Community in Krosno.

Krosno, February 10th, 1942

1st Part
Alphabetical local Jews – Recording list
[Made] here before the 22nd of June, 1941

Four copies made in accordance with the order / reference code of the *Kreishauptmann* [district chief] dated 7th and 8th and of the *Stadtkommissar* [town inspector] dated 9th of the previous month.

Family name	First name	Birth date	Trade (German)	Able to work	Trade (English)
ABRAHAM	Rosa	1914	Stickerin		embroider [female]
ABRAHAM	Sara	1891			
ABRAHAM	Moses	1921	Arbeiter		worker
ABRAHAMSON	Berisch	1888	Beamter		clerk
ABRAHAMSON	Feige Leie	1886			
ABRAHAMSON	Chaim	1923	Glaser		glazier
ABRAHAMSON	Salomon	1908	Fellsortierer		furs sorter
ABRAHAMSON	Chane	1909			
ABRAHAMSON	Wella	1935			
ABRAHAMSON	Dora	1939			
ADER	Benjamin	1906	Friseur		barber
ADER	Hene	1917			
ADER	Sara	1939			
ADER	Jakob	1877			
ADER	Ester	1880			
ADER	Pene	1910			
ADER	Lola	1915			
ADER	Sara	1917			
AFTERGUT	Salomon	1893	Kaufmann		merchant

AFTERGUT	Sala	1892		
AFTERGUT	David	1923	Elektrotechniker	electrician
ALTBACH	Sender	1873		
ALTBACH	Helene	1877		
ALTBACH	Helene	1877		
ALTBACH	Ester	1914		
ALTER	Jakob	1881	Arbeiter	worker
ALTER	Sime	1920		
ALTER	Osias	1923	Arbeiter	worker
ALTHOLZ	Moses	1899	Uhrmacher	watchmaker
ALTHOLZ	Debora	1902		
ALTHOLZ	David	1928	Arbeiter	worker
ALTHOLZ	Zila	1931		
ALTMANN	Leib	1878	Klempner	plumber
ALTMANN	Sara	1888		
ALTMANN	Moses	1907	Bäcker	baker
ALTMANN	Osias	1908	Klempner	plumber
ALTMANN	Hirsch	1909		
ALTMANN	Marie	1914		
ALTMANN	Chune	1917	Monteur	mechanic
ALTMANN	Poje	1919		
ALTMAN	Sala	1900	Lehrerin	teacher [female]
AMSTERDAM	Chaim	1889	Kaufmann	
AMSTERDAM	Regina	1889		
AMSTERDAM	Gerson	1911	Arbeiter	worker
AMSTERDAM	Ester	1913		
AMSTERDAM	Naftali	1923	Schäftemacher	upper shoe maker
APFEL	Guetl	1896		
APFELBAUM-BEER	Mendel	1898	Friseur	barber
APFELBAUM-	Freida	1908		

BEER				
APFELBAUM-BEER	Rosa	1929		
APFELBAUM-BEER	Rosa	1929		
APFELBAUM-BEER	Leib	1930		
APFELBAUM-BEER	Samson	1934		
APFELBAUM-BEER	Shmaja	1939		
APELSTEIN	Sala	1911	Hausmädchen	housemaid
APRIL	Sarah	1864		
ARON	Ite	1865		
ARONOWICZ	David	1908	Arbeiter	worker
AUSSENBERG	Menashe	1911	Arbeiter	worker
AUSSENBERG	Regina	1913		
ATLAS	Salomon	1864		
AXELRAD	Zile	1890		
AXELRAD	Shulim	1913	Beamter	clerk
AXELRAD	Leib	1930		
AXELRAD	Beile	1932		
AXELRAD	Helene	1900		
AXELRAD	Moses	1928		
AXELRAD	Zile	1933		
AXELRAD	Chaim	1927	Arbeiter	worker
AXELRAD	Luser-Lipe	1907	Arbeiter	worker
AXELRAD	David	1934		
AXELRAD	Chaim	1935		
AXELRAD	Jochwet	1937		
AXELRAD	Chawa	1884		
AXELRAD	Leie	1919		
AXELRAD	Ester	1923		
AXELRAD	Fradel	1926		

AXELRAD	Jsaak	1930		
AXELRAD	Tobias	1890	Kaufmann	merchant
AXELRAD	Hadassa	1905		
BEILES	Henoch	1889	Arbeiter	worker
BEILES	Minna	1886	Schneiderin	seamstress
BARTH	Josef	1860		
BARUCH	Perl	1883		
BAUMANN	Berta	1910	Köchin	cook
BAUMRING	Jakob	1895	Arzt	doctor of medicine
BAUMRING	Anna	1904		
BAUMRING	Theodor	1934		
BAUMRING	Gina	1939		
BEER	Moses	1902	Kutscher	coachman
BEER	Sara	1906		
BEER	Henoch	1933		
BEER	Hinde	1936		
BEER	Marjem	1939		
BEIGEL	Chaje	1884		
BEIGEL	Moses	1923	Arbeiter	worker
BEIGEL	Naftali	1924	Arbeiter	worker
BEIGEL	Ester	1927	Arbeiter	worker
BEIGEL	Solomon	1893		
BEIL	Benzion	1892		
BEIL	Abisch	1930		
BEIL	Mendel	1925	Arbeiter	worker
BEIL	Rachel	1923		
BEIM	Moses Jakob	1920		
BEIM	Josef	1893	Arbeiter	worker
BEIM	Perl	1893		
BEIM	Rachel	1920		
BEIM	Hinde	1923		

BEIM	Mendel	1925	Arbeiter	worker
BEIM	Golde	1927		
BEIM	Solomon	1898	Klempner	plumber
BEIM	Berta	1895		
BEIM	Ester	1922		
BEIM	Feiga	1925		
BEIM	Salke	1923	Schäftemacher	upper shoe maker
BEIM	Niche	1928		
BEIM	Suessman	1928	Elektrotechniker	electrician
BEIM	Suessman	1893	Kutscher	coachman
BEIM	Toni	1894		
BEIM	Salomon	1927	Arbeiter	worker
BEIM	Josef	1920	Arbeiter	worker
BEIM	Chana	1924		
BEIM	Jakob	1921		
BEIM	David	1920	Kutscher	coachman
BEIM	Jsrael	1870		
BEIM	Regina	1905		
BEIM	Nathan	1890	Klempner	plumber
BEIM	Sala	1908		
BEIM	Samuel	1925	Arbeiter	worker
BEIM	Siegmund	1926	Arbeiter	worker
BEIM	Rachel			
BELZYCKI	Pinkas	1890	Uhrmacher	watchmaker
BELZYCKI	Feige Leie	1890		
BELZYCKI	Jsaak	1912	Elektriker	electrician
BENKENDORF	Rosa	1907	Köchin	cook
BERGER	Malke	1921		
BERGER	Jakob	1872	Schneider	tailor
BERGER	Reisel	1893		
BERGER	Moses	1912	Schneider	tailor
BERGER	Osias	1915		

BERGER	Solomon	1919			
BERGER	Mechel	1921			
BERLINSKI	Sara	1916	Arbeiter		worker
BERLINSKI	Dine	1906			
BERMAN	Lisa	1917			
BIALYWLOS	Mendel	1891	Glaser		glazier
BIALYWLOS	Leie	1896			
BIALYWLOS	Marjem	1922	Angestellte		employee [female]
BIALYWLOS	Alexander	1923	Glaser		glazier
BIALYWLOS	Salomon	1923			
BIALYWLOS	Henoch	1931			
BIDERMAN	Liepe	1886	Arbeiter		worker
BIDERMAN	Malke	1886			
BIDERMAN	Zile	1914	Verkäuferin		saleswoman
BIDERMAN	Poje	1915			
BIEDERMAN	Sara	1920			
BIDERMAN	Hirsch	1925	Arbeiter		worker
BIGAJER	Chaim	1915	Schneider		tailor
BIGAJER	Reisel	1916			
BIGAJER	Aron	1941			
BLADY	Samuel	1913	Monteur		mechanic
BLAU	Moses	1904	Schirmmacher		umbrella maker
BLAU	Rosa	1897			
BLAU	Adele	1938			
BLEICHFELD	Herman	1879	Bauer		farmer
BLUMENFELD	Berisch	1894	Kaufmann		merchant
BLUMENFELD	Berta	1898			
BLUMENFELD	Salomon	1920	Arbeiter		worker
BLUMENFELD	Abraham	1922	Angestellter		employee [male]
BLUMENFELD	Naftali	1927	Arbeiter		worker

BIRNKRAUT	Sabine	1903			
BIRNKRAUT	Efraim	1912	Bäcker		baker
BIRNKRAUT	Ester	1939			
BIRNKRAUT	Rachel	1907	Verkäuferin		saleswoman
BOBKER	Markus	1901	Kaufmann		merchant
BOBKER	Ester	1903			
BOBKER	Mendel	1928			
BOCIAN	Pinkus	1903	Schneider		tailor
BOCIAN	Chaje	1907			
BOCIAN	Jente	1932			
BOCIAN	Hirsch	1935			
BODNER	Chaskel	1877			
BODNER	Abraham	1878			
BODNER	Blime	1877			
BODNER	Suesal	1915			
BODNER	Chaje	1940			
BODNER	Blueme	1917	Friseuse		coiffeuse
BODNER-LECH	Benjamin	1912	Schneider		tailor
BODNER-LECH	Scheindel	1912			
BODNER-LECH	Marjem	1937			
BODNER	Regina	1914			
BOGEN	Kalmen	1885	Buchbinder		bookbinder
BOGEN	Nuchim	1909	Buchbinder		bookbinder
BOGEN	Ascher	1915	Arbeiter		worker
BOGEN	Chaje Eidel	1880			
BOGEN	Eidel	1880			
BOGEN	Chaim	1907	Schuster		shoemaker
BOGEN	Hirsch	1910	Musiker		musician
BOGEN	Schlama	1923	Arbeiter		worker
BORGERNICHT	Simon	1922	Schuster		shoemaker
BORKOWSKI	Jsaak	1894	Schuster		shoemaker
BORKOWSKI	Feige	1900			

BORKOWSKI	Chane	1920		
BORKOWSKI	Dine	1923		
BORKOWSKI	Abraham	1927	Schuster	shoemaker
BRAND	Ester	1888		
BRAND	Modche	1931		
BRAUSS	Sonia	1912		
BRAUSS	Stephan	1937		
BREITOWI	Czaron	1914	Fleischer	butcher
BREITOWICZ	Moses	1906	Bäcker	baker
BREITOWICZ	Pepi	1910		
BREITOWICZ	Ete	1912		
BREITOWICZ	Hene	1918		
BREITOWICZ	Luise	1889		
BREITOWICZ	Fradel	1920	Buchhalterin	bookkeeper [female]
BREITOWICZ	Kreindel	1921	Schneiderin	seamstress
BREITOWICZ	Gutel	1926		
BREITOWICZ	Chana	1927		
BREITOWICZ	Chana	1867		
BREITOWICZ	Leib	1900	Fleischer	butcher
BREITOWICZ	Rachel	1905		
BREITOWICZ	Naftali	1936		
BREITOWICZ	Rosa	1938		
BREITOWICZ	Jsaak	1902		
BREITOWICZ	Ester	1903		
BREITOWICZ	Schifra	1931		
BREITOWICZ	Rosa	1934		
BREITOWICZ	Abraham	1938		
BREITOWICZ	Abraham	1904	Fleischer	butcher
BREITOWICZ	Chaje	1906		
BREITOWICZ	Hirsch	1933		
BREITOWICZ	Ester	1935		

BREITOWICZ	Janke	1936		
BRINGS	Lola	1886		
BRIESS	David	1909	Arbeiter	worker
BRZEZINSKI	Sische	1892	Arbeiter	worker
BRZEZINSKI	Ryfke	1889		
BRZEZINSKI	Josef	1923		
BRZEZINSKI	Abraham	1924		
BRZEZINSKI	Aron	1930		
BUCH	Levy David	1902	Schneider	tailor
BUCH	Ester	1903		
BURSTANOWICZ	Hirsch	1898	Arbeiter	worker
BURSTANOWICZ	Rachel	1902		
BURSTANOWICZ	Rosa	1924	Schneiderin	seamstress
BURSTANOWICZ	Jakob	1926	Arbeiter	worker
BURSTANOWICZ	Jonas	1928		
BURSTANOWICZ	Sische	1931		
BURSTANOWICZ	Moses	1934		
BUCHSBAUM	Sara	1903		
BUCHSBAUM	Freide	1927		
BUCHSBAUM	Ete	1929		
BUCHSBAUM	Aron	1930		
BUCHSBAUM	Feiwel	1931		
CHAJES	Mendel	1909	Schäftemacher	upper shoe maker
CHAJES	Berta	1909		
CHAJES	Schlama	1941		
DAVID	Mechel	1863	Klempner	plumber
DAVID	Sabina	1861		
DAVID	Hinde	1865		
DAVID	Luser	1932		
DAVID	Leie	1922	Arbeiter	worker
DAVID	Sala	1913		
DAVID	Pinkas	1897	Klempner	plumber

DAVID	Sara	1896		
DAVID	Jochewet	1925		
DAVID	Neche	1927		
DAVID	Chana	1930		
DAVID	Ester	1936		
DAVID	Sprinze	1880		
DAVID	Rachel	1909	Schneiderin	seamstress
DAVID	Freide	1915	Lehrerin	teacher [female]
DAVID	Markus	1920	Tischler	carpenter
DAVID	Berel	1901	Klempner	plumber
DAVID	Rosa	1903		
DAVID	Suessl	1930		
DAVID	Anita	1935		
DAVIDOWICZ	Mendel	1898	Glaser	glazier
DAVIDOWICZ	Marjem	1911		
DAVIDOWICZ	Brandel	1935		
DAVIDOWICZ	Chane	1941		
DENN	Abraham	1906	Kaufmann	merchant
DENN	Selde	1905		
DENN	Leib	1935		
DENN	Pinka	1936		
DENN	Wolf	1893	Arbeiter	worker
DENN	Leie	1891		
DENN	Jsaak	1925	Arbeiter	worker
DENN	Sprinze	1869		
DENN	Berel	1901		
DICK	Beile	1879		
DICK	Marie	1909		
DIAMANT	Kalmen	1887	Kaufmann	merchant
DIAMANT	Pessel	1886		
DIAMANT	Chaje	1916		

DIAMANT	Sime	1922		
DIAMANT	Rachel	1924		
DIAMANT	Mindel	1926		
DIAMANT	Sara	1929		
DIAMANT	Leib	1931		
DILLER	Yossef	1907	Bademeister	bath attendant
DILLER	Chaja	1900		
DILLER	Feige	1924		
DILLER	Jsaak	1926	Arbeiter	worker
DILLER	Uri	1929		
DILLER	Pessel	1935		
DILLER	Saul	1909	Angestellter	employee [male]
DORSCHOWITZ	Chaje	1890		
DORSCHOWITZ	Naftali	1920	Sattler	saddler
DUNKEL	Mayer	1865		
DUNKEL	Luser	1911	Arbeiter	worker
DUNKEL	Eisig	1916	Arbeiter	worker
EHRLICH	Chaskel	1934		
EISEN	Jhuda	1922	Bäcker	baker
EDELHEIT	Blueme	1916		
EDELHEIT	Moses	1937		
EDELHEIT	Hirsch	1887	Bürstenmacher	brush maker
EDELHEIT	Golde	1894		
EDELHEIT	Beile	1925		
EDELHEIT	Berel	1930		
EHRENREICH	Ester	1912		
EHRLICH	Alter	1888	Eierpacker	egg sorter
EHRLICH	Scheindel	1886		
EHRLICH	Sara	1916		
EHRLICH	Rachel	1920		
EHRLICH	Chane	1923		

EHRLICH	Leib	1924	Darmputzer		cleaner
EHRLICH	Leie	1929			
EHRENBERG	Hadass	1902			
EHRENBERG	Majer	1935			
EHRENPREIS	Jakob	1898			
EICHORN	Regin	1922	Arbeiter		worker
EICHORN	Netti	1920			
EICHORN	Feiwel	1907	Arbeiter		worker
EICHORN	Ester	1909			
EICHORN	Hinde	1939			
EINHORN	Rubin	1904			
EICHORN	Ester	1902			
EICHORN	Rische	1931			
EICHORN	Hudes	1932			
EINHORN	Hirsch	1935			
EINLEGER	Jhuda	1887	Arbeiter		worker
EINLEGER	Leie	1898			
EINLEGER	Rita	1932			
EINREDER	Mottel	1880	Arbeiter		worker
EINREDER	Leie	1888			
EISENBERG	Saul	1887	Perückenmacher		wigmaker
EISENBERG	Liebe	1890			
EISENBERG	Menachem	1928			
ELLOWITSCH	Mayer	1872			
ELLOWITSCH	Simche	1871			
ELLOWICZ	Saul	1879			
ELLOWICZ	Luser	1907	Arbeiter		worker
ELENBERG	Rosa	1925			
ENGEL	Jhuda	1896	Judenrat		Judenrat
ENGEL	Mirjam	1899			
ENGEL	Jhudith	1926			
ENGEL	Helene	1901			

ENGELHARDT	Moses	1916	Taschenmacher	bag maker
ENGELHARDT	Sabine	1863		
ENGELHARD	Jsaak	1909		
ENGELHARDT	Chaje	1912		
ENGELHARDT	Chane	1936		
ENGELHARDT	Chawe	1937		
ENGELHARDT	Mendel	1879	Lehrer	teacher
ENGELHARDT	Marjem	1878		
ENGELHARDT	Benzion	1901	Kaufmann	merchant
ENGELHARDT	Chaje	1901		
ENGELHARDT	Rachel	1922		
ENGELHARDT	Ester	1924		
ENGELHARDT	Leib	1930		
ENGELHARDT	Ryfke	1888		
ENGLAENDER	Hirsch	1895	Kellermeister	cellarer
ENGLAENDER	Malke	1890		
ENTNER	Abrahan	1907	Bäcker	baker
ENTNER	Regina	1898		
ENTNER	Malke	1932		
ENTNER	Hene	1934		
ENTNER	Simon	1937		
ENTNER	Leie	1902		
ENTNER	Hene	1930		
ENTNER	Berisch	1931		
ENZWEIG	Zische	1903	Arbeiter	worker
ENZWEIG	Haim Aron	1933		
EPSTEIN	Berisch	1891	Arbeiter	worker
EPSTEIN	Rachel	1888		
EPSTEIN	Chume	1916		
EPSTEIN	Guetl	1918		
EPSTEIN	Israel	1921	Arbeiter	worker
EPSTEIN	Ida	1923		

EPSTEIN	Zile	1925			
EPSTEIN	Nissim	1927	Arbeiter		worker
EPSTEIN	Benjamin	1920			
ERREICH	Jsaak	1928	Schneider		tailor
ERTEL	Abisch	1907	Arbeiter		worker
ERTEL	Hene	1903			
ERTEL	Rosa	1907			
ERLBAUM	Josef	1883	Arbeiter		worker
ERLBAUM	Suessl	1884			
ERLBAUM	Tonka	1913	Näherin		seamstress
ETTINGER	Moshe	1893	Kaufmann		merchant
ETTINGER	Malke	1896			
ETTINGER	Scheindel	1924			
ETTINGER	Debora	1928			
FALLMAN	Hirsch	1876			
FELCZER	Mordche	1888	Kantor		cantor
FELCZER	Czarne	1884			
FELCZER	Ita	1931			
FELCZER	Chane	1923			
FELCZER	Mindel	1924			
FELCZER	Chiel	1925	Arbeiter		worker
FELDER	Machle	1886			
FEILHARDT	Anna	1894			
FEILHARDT	Rosa	1922			
FEILHARDT	Lola	1923			
FEILHARDT	Ete	1927			
FEIN	Jakob	1899	Sockenstricker	ja	sock needle worker
FEIN	Liebe	1898			
FEIN	Chawa	1925			
FEIN	Wolf	1929			
FEIN	Ester	1934			

FEIT	Leib	1921	Schneider	ja	tailor
FENIK	Salomon	1906	Schneider	ja	tailor
FENIK	Feige	1928			
FENIK	Simon	1930			
FENIK	Chaim	1932			
FENIK	Wele	1934			
FENSTER	Salomon	1906	Schneider		tailor
FENSTER	Debora	1907			
FENSTER	Moses	1936			
FESSEL	Zile	1915	Schneider		tailor
FESSEL	Chane	1920			
FESSEL	Jhuda	1907	Arbeiter		worker
FESSEL	Rosa	1907			
FESSEL	Wolf	1933	Arbeiter		worker
FESSEL	Hinde	1876			
FESSEL	Rachel	1915	Verkäuferin		saleswoman
FESSEL	Feige	1906			
FESSEL	Wolf	1927	Arbeiter		worker
FESSEL	Sara	1932			
FEUERLICHT	Anna	1898			
FEUERLICHT	Feige	1921	Verkäuferin		saleswoman
FEUERLICHT	Marjem	1925			
FEUERLICHT	Hinde	1926			
FEUERLICHT	Jakob	1875			
FEUERLICHT	Sprinze	1878			
FEURLICHT	Zipora	1914			
FINDLING	Jdes	1905	Hausmädchen		housemaid
FINK	Kiara	1879			
FINK	Helene	1915			
FISHBEIN	Jetti	1895			
FISHLER	Leie	1905			
FISHLER	Josef	1930			

FLAPPAN	Luser	1867	Musiker		musician
FLAPPAN	Rachel	1884			
FLAPPAN	Frania	1910			
FLAPPAN	Hella	1912			
FLAPPAN	Feige	1914			
FOGEL	Josef	1878			
FOGEL	Chaja	1883			
FOGEL	Freide	1923	Näherin		seamstress
FREIFELD	Chaskel	1899	Arbeiter	ja	worker
FREIFELD	Marjem	1932			
FREIFELD	Rosa	1903			
FREIREICH	Chaim	1883	Arbeiter	ja	worker
FREIREICH	Feige	1892			
FRAENKEL	Rachel	1872			
FRAUWIRTH	Jsaak	1917	Kaufmann	ja	merchant
FRAUWIRTH	Rifke	1916			
FRAUWIRTH	Ite	1912			
FRAUWIRTH	Beile	1911			
FREUND	Zalel	1859			
FREUND	Chane	1920			
FREUND	Majer	1877			
FREUND	Deborah	1873			
FREUND	Salomon	1911	Arbeiter	ja	worker
FREUND	Adele	1914			
FREUND	Berel	1897	Arbeiter	ja	worker
FREUND	Beile	1906			
FRIED	Jakob	1870			
FRIED	Ziwie	1884			
FRIEDMANN	Mannes	1890	Uhrmacher	ja	watchmaker
FRIEDMANN	Leie	1895			
FRIEDMANN	Pinkas	1923	Arbeiter	ja	worker
FRIEDMANN	Abraham	1924	Arbeiter	ja	worker

FRIEDMANN	Chiel	1926	Arbeiter	ja	worker
FRIEDMANN	Naftali	1929	Arbeiter	ja	worker
FRIEDMANN	Chaskel	1931			
FRIEDMANN	Hinde	1933			
FRIEDMANN	Luser	1905	Arbeiterin		worker [female]
FRIEDMANN	Mendel	1906	Arbeiter		worker
FRIEDMANN	Brandel	1901	Arbeiter	ja	worker
FRIEDMANN	Samuel	1903	Schuster	ja	shoemaker
FRIEDMANN	Eva	1899			
FRIEDMANN	Freide	1930			
FRIESS	Tille	1892			
FRIESS	Ester	1917	Näherin		seamstress
FRIESS	Rosa	1920			
FRIESS	Jsrael	1923	Schuster	ja	shoemaker
FRIESS	Adele	1936			
FRIESS	Dora	1934			
FIRESS	Ojzer	1887	Arbeiter		worker
FRIESS	Malka	1887			
FIRESS	Josef	1915	Zuschneider		cutter
FIRESS	Ester	1917			
FIRESS	David	1914	Schäftemacher	ja	upper shoe maker
FRIESS	Regina	1914			
FRISCH	Feige	1899			
FRISCH	Rachel	1920	Näherin		seamstress
FRISCH	Chaje	1921			
FRISCH	Dine	1925			
FRUEHMANN	Sara	1884			
FRUEHMANN	Chaim	1880	Kaufmann	ja	merchant
FUCHS	Israel	1920	Friseur	ja	barber
FUEHRER	Leib	1902	Arbeiter	ja	worker
FUEHRER	Beile	1901			

FUEHRER	Abraham	1928			
FUEHRER	Jsaak	1931			
FUEHRER	Mirel	1934			
FUERST	Osias	1919	Arbeiter		worker
FUERST	Samuel	1896	Kaufmann	ja	merchant
FUERST	Chaje	1890			
FUERST	Abraham	1920	Arbeiter	ja	worker
FUERST	Meilech	1921	Arbeiter	ja	worker
FUERST	Osias	1923	Arbeiter	ja	worker
FUERST	Rosa	1925			
FUERST	Sara	1926			
FUERST	Nissen	1928			
FUERST	Henoch	1930			
FUSS	Malke	1912			
FUSS	Leie	1937			
FUSS	Berisch	1878			
FUSS	Feige	1878			
FUSS	Pessel	1913			
FUSS	Brandel	1914			
GABLINGER	Marjem	1906			
GABRYLEWICZ	Dine	1924			
GALON	Frimet	1907	Näherin		seamstress
GALON	Liebe	1933			
GALON	Ite	1934			
GELB	Osias	1894	Arbeiter	ja	worker
GELB	Pessel	1896			
GELB	Dora	1922			
GELB	Aron	1924	Arbeiter	ja	worker
GELB	Salomon	1876			
GELB	Debora	1894			
GEBEL	Moses	1874	Schneider		tailor
GEBEL	Beile	1871			

GEBEL	Fishel	1915	Schneider	ja	tailor
GELBART	Sara	1912			
GERLICH	Pinkas	1884	Kaufmann	ja	merchant
GERLICH	Brandel	1882			
GERLICH	Sara	1911			
GERLICH	Osias	1881	Kaufmann	ja	merchant
GERLICH	Hinde	1881			
GERLICH	Mathias	1910	Arbeiter	ja	worker
GERLICH	Chaje	1911	Buchhalterin		bookkeeper [female]
GERLICH	Brandel	1913			
GERLICH	Pinkas	1918	Arbeiter	ja	worker
GOETZLER	Leib		Fischer		fisher
GOETZLER	Feige				
GOETZLER	Jsrael				
GAERTNER	Leie	1900	Näherin		seamstress
GAERTNER	Feige	1902	Näherin		seamstress
GAERTNER	Sara	1906	Näherin		seamstress
GOETZ	Samuel	1910	Arbeiter	ja	worker
GOETZ	Sara	1903			
GLEICHER	Abraham	1886	Kaufmann		merchant
GLEICHER	Beile	1885			
GLEICHER	Ete	1914	Arbeiter	ja	worker
GLEICHER	Jehuda				
GLUECK	Max	1903	Beamter	ja	clerk
GLUECK	Regina	1910			
GLUECK	Baruch	1934			
GLUECK	Markus	1907	Arbeiter	ja	worker
GLUECK	Guetl	1907			
GLUECK	Regina	1935			
GLOWINSKI	Taube	1899			
GLOWINSKI	Chaje	1919	Näherin		seamstress
GOLDBERG	Peisech			nein	

GOLDFARB	Chiel	1903	Arbeiter	ja	worker
GOLDFARB	Reisel	1904			
GOLDFARB	Moses	1929			
GOLDFARB	Ester	1938			
GOLDFARB	Abraham	1940			
GOLDFINGER	Moses	1873			
GOLDFINGER	Rosa	1880			
GOLDFINGER	Chaje	1920			
GOLDFINGER	Simon	1915	Goldschmied		goldsmith
GOLDFINGER	Jetti	1910			
GOLDFINGER	Zile	1936			
GOLDFINGER	Genia	1914			
GOLDMAN	Moses	1898	Chauffeur	ja	driver
GOLDMAN	Selde	1902			
GOLDMAN	Leie	1921			
GOLDMAN	Zlate	1929			
GOLDMAN	Sara	1884			
GOLDSTEIN	Ester	1887			
GOLDSTEIN	Reisel	1914	Arbeiter		worker
GOLDSTEIN	Debora	1917	Arbeiter		worker
GOLDSTEIN	Matel	1923	Arbeiter		worker
GOLDSTEIN	Anna	1904	Näherin		seamstress
GOLDSTEIN	Mechel	1905	Kaufmann	ja	merchant
GOLDSTEIN	Leie	1904			
GOLDSTEIN	Naftali	1930			
GOLDSTEIN	Abraham	1933			
GORA	Sara	1874			
GOTTLIEB	Benjamin	1892	Arbeiter	ja	worker
GOTTLIEB	Eva	1895			
GOTTLIEB	Schiffre	1924	Näherin		seamstress
GRAJOWER	Salomon	1892	Arbeiter	ja	worker
GRAJOWER	Feige	1898			

GRAJOWER	Sara	1922			
GRAJOWER	Jakob	1928			
GRAJOWER	Mechel	1932			
GRAJOWER	Chane	1939			
GRAEBER	David	1895		nein	
GRAEBER	Feige	1895			
GRAEBER	Zierl	1926			
GRAEBER	Moses	1935			
GRUESS	Mendel		Arbeiter		worker
GRUESS	Suessl		Arbeiter	ja	worker
GRUESS	Chune				
GROSS	Wilhelm				
GROSS	Ryfke	1939			
GROSS	Henoch	1889	Bäcker	ja	baker
GROSS	Ite	1898			
GROSS	Sala	1919			
GROSS	Pepe	1921			
GROSS	Chaim	1923	Arbeiter	ja	worker
GROSS	Leib	1927	Arbeiter	ja	worker
GROSS	Malke	1929			
GROSS	Jsaak	1931			
GROSS	Neche	1934			
GROSS	Feige	1936			
GROSS	Ryfke	1939			
GROSS	Sime	1917	Näherin		seamstress
GROSS	Josef	1920	Schneider		tailor
GRUEN	Aron	1872			
GRUEN	Guetl	1868			
GRUEN	Wolf	1903	Arbeiter	ja	worker
GRUEN	Sala	1903			
GRUEN	Freide	1932			
GRUEN	Marjem	1938			

GRUENSPAN	Moses	1888			
GRUENSPAN	Ryfke	1878			
GRUENSPAN	Feivel	1916	Schneider	ja	tailor
GRUENSPAN	Jacob	1864	Fleischer		butcher
GRUENSPAN	Guetl	1868			
GRUENSPAN	Getzel	1910	Arbeiter	ja	worker
GUENSPAN	Moses	1878			
GRUENSPAN	Ryfke	1878			
GRUENSPAN	Feiwel	1916	Schneider		tailor
GRUENSPAN	Joel	1902	Arbeiter	ja	worker
GRUENSPAN	Jente	1912			
GRUENSPAN	Meilech	1937			
GRUENSPAN	Gene	1922			
GURKE	Regina	1903			
GURKE	Henoch	1929			
GUETER	Flora	1898			
GUETER	Chaje	1925			
GUETER	Sara	1923			
GUZIK	Moses	1876			
GUZIK	Debora	1879			
GUZIK	Jakob	1910	Arbeiter	ja	worker
GUZIK	Feige	1912			
GUZIK	Markus	1901	Arbeiter	ja	worker
GUZIK	Regina	1897			
GUZIK	Poje	1927			
GUZIK	Simon	1924	Arbeiter	ja	worker
GUZIK	Rachel	1924			
GUZIK	Jakob	1933			
HABER	Josef	1886	Arbeiter	ja	worker
HABER	Rachela	1886			
HABER	Malke	1920	Arbeiter		worker
HAFERLING	Israel	1877			

HAFERLING	Leib	1908	Arbeiter	ja	worker
HAFERLING	Rosa	1882			
HAFERLING	Sime	1922			
HAFERLING	Baruch	1920	Arbeiter		worker
HAFERLING	Sara	1933			
HAFERLING	Moses	1902	Schuster	ja	shoemaker
HAFERLING	Blueme	1902			
HAFERLING	Hinde	1932			
HAFTEL	Jsrael	1883	Drucker	ja	printer
HACKWOLF	Beer	1870			
HACK	Adele	1888			
HACK	Moses	1911	Arbeiter	ja	worker
HACK	David	1924	Arbeiter	ja	worker
HACK	Ester	1924			
HALBERSTAMM	David	1895	Kaufmann	ja	merchant
HALBERSTAMM	Rachel	1899			
HALBERSTAMM	Beile	1929			
HALBERSTAMM	Osias	1936			
HALBERSTAMM	Naftali	1938			
HALPERN	Jakob	1868			
HALPERN	Dora	1898			
HALPERN	Gene	1923			
HAMMER	Chane	1906			
HAMMER	Ruth	1931			
HAMMERMANN	Luise	1908			
HASENFELD	Liebe	1912			
HASENFELD	Rosa	1915			
HAUSNER	Sara	1873			
HAUSNER	Jakob	1903			
HAUSNER	Moses	1912	Arbeiter	ja	worker
HAUSNER	Beile	1906	Verkäuferin		saleswoman
HAUSNER	Chane	1925	Schneiderin		seamstress

HAUSNER	Zile	1877			
HAUSNER	Rosa	1903			
HAUSNER	Moses	1939			
HAUSNER	Wolf	1882			
HAUSNER	Meilech	1915	Arbeiter	ja	worker
HAUSNER	Chaim	1920	Arbeiter	ja	worker
HEINBERG-KARP	Reisel	1879			
HEINBERG-KARP	Moritz	1904	Arbeiter	ja	worker
HEINBERG-KARP	Martin	1921	Arbeiter	ja	worker
HELLER	Moses	1905	Glaser	ja	glazier
HELLER	Rachel	1914			
HELLER	Guetl	1940			
HELLER	Ryfke	1940			
HEMMERLING	Akiba	1895	Beamter	ja	clerk
HEMMERLING	Ryfke	1894			
HEMMERLING	Hirsch	1922	Arbeiter	ja	worker
HEMMERLING	Leie	1927			
HEMMERLING	Taube	1930			
HEMMERLING	Pessel	1933			
HAENDLER	Sara Taube	1909			
HAENDLER	Eduard	1940			
HERBSTMAN	Lea	1878			
HERBSTMANN	Feige	1904	Produktenkäufer		merchant
HERBSTMANN	Rachel	1929			
HERBSTMANN	Dora	1924			
HERBSTMANN	Abraham	1937			
HERBSTMANN	Malke	1907	Produktenkäufer		merchant
HERBSTMANN	Feige	1936			
HERSON	Jakob	1892	Arbeiter	ja	worker
HERSON	Dora	1898			
HERSON	Abraham	1924	Schneider	ja	tailor

HERSON	Sara	1925	Mützenmacher		capper
HERSON	Chaje	1927			
HERZFELD	Henoch	1864			
HERZIG	Osias	1871	Mützenmacher		capper
HERZIG	Rachel	1877			
HERZIG	Sender	1901	Arbeiter	ja	worker
HERZIG	Chane	1906			
HERZIG	Neche	1936			
HERZIG	Chaskel	1907	Mützenmacher	ja	capper
HERZIG	Rosa	1919			
HERZIG	Hella	1939			
HERZIG	Sabine	1883			
HERZIG	Dora	1913			
HIRSCH	Malke	1899			
HIRSCHFIELD	Leib	1905	Bäcker	nein	baker
HODYS	Jakob	1875	Fleischer		butcher
HOFFMAN	Jda	1881			
HOFSTAEDER	Mendel	1932			
HOLLANDER	Chane	1915			
HOLLOSCHUETZ	Debora	1931			
HOLLOSCHUETZ	Chaskel	1937			
HOLLOSCHUETZ	Berta	1888			
HOLLOSCHUETZ	Ester	1933			
HOLLOSCHUETZ	Jsaak	1889			
HOLLOSCHUETZ	Sara	1875			
HONIGSTOCK	Mira	1907			
HONIGSTOCK	Alice	1929			
HORNIK	Kalman	1887	Fleischer	ja	butcher
HORNIK	Feige	1893			
HORNIK	Beile	1922	Photograph		photographer
HORNIK	Abraham	1924	Arbeiter	ja	worker
HORNIK	Mirel	1929			

HOROWITZ	Sara	1892			
HOROWITZ	Benno	1890	Arbeiter	ja	worker
HOROWITZ	Moses	1924	Arbeiter	ja	worker
HOROWITZ	Benno	1878	Arbeiter	ja	worker
HOROWITZ	Chaje	1900			
HOROWITZ	Rafael	1916	Arbeiter	ja	worker
HOROWITZ	Norbert	1922	Konditor	ja	confectioner
HOROWITZ	Eva	1912	Schneiderin		seamstress
HOROWITZ	Golde	1907	Schneiderin		seamstress
HOROWITZ	Hirsch				
HOROWITZ	Guste				
HOROWITZ	Netti	1912	Schneiderin		seamstress
HOROWITZ	Moses	1915	Tapezierer	ja	upholsterer
HUDES	Chaim	1891	Mützenmacher	ja	capper
HUDES	Ester	1890			
HUDES	Abraham	1919	Arbeiter	ja	worker
HUDES	Aron	1921	Mützenmacher	ja	capper
HUDES	Berisch	1926	Arbeiter	ja	worker
HUTTNER	Reisel	1912			
HUTTNER	Leib	1936			
GROSSSIME		1917	Schneiderin		seamstress
GROSS	Josef	1920	Schneider	ja	tailor
INFELD	Elias	1886	Fleischer	ja	butcher
INFELD	Hinde	1887			
INFELD	Pinkas	1921	Metzger	ja	butcher
INFELD	Josef	1923	Schneider	ja	tailor
JAKUBOWICZ	Brandel	1907			
JAKUBOWICZ	Salomon	1901	Arbeiter		worker
JAKUBOWICZ	Sala	1924			
JAKUBOWICZ	Beile	1925			
JAKUBOWICZ	Rafael	1904	Klempner	ja	plumber
JAKUBOWICZ	Beile	1902			

JAKUBOWICZ	Sala	1930			
JAKUBOWICZ	Marjem	1937			
JAKUBOWICZ	Zila	1917			
JAMEL	Mendel	1895	Arbeiter	ja	worker
JAMEL	Chane	1897			
JAMEL	Ryfke	1920	Verkäuferin		saleswoman
JAMEL	Leie	1923	Schneiderin		seamstress
JAMEL	Leib	1925	Monteur	ja	mechanic
JAMEL	Markus	1928			
JAMEL	Chaim	1931			
JAMEL	Rosa	1933			
JERUCHIM	Feiwel	1895	Lehrer	ja	teacher
JERUCHIM	Leie	1894			
JERUCHIM	Simon	1921	Arbeiter	ja	worker
JERUCHIM	Aron	1923	Arbeiter	ja	worker
JERUCHIM	Chawa	1928			
JERUCHIM	Malke	1929			
JOSEFOWICZ	Osias	1906	Bauer	ja	farmer
JOSEFOWICZ	Toni	1916			
JOSEFOWICZ	Leib	1938			
JUDENHERZ	Hene	1910			
JUDENHERZ	Jocheweth	1915			
JUST	David	1896	Arbeiter	ja	worker
JUST	Guetl	1897			
JUST	Sabine	1922	Strickerin		needle worker [female]
JUST	Amalie	1925			
JUST	Naftali	1928			
JUST	Perl	1899			
JUST	Naftali	1930			
JUST	Dobe	1934			
JUST	Chaje Ete	1929			

JUST	Jacob	1898	Arbeiter	ja	worker
JUST	Sala	1904			
JUST	Debora	1929			
JUST	Naftali	1932			
JUST	Hirsch	1881	Kaufmann	nein	merchant
JUST	Feige	1885			
JUST	Tille	1916			
JUST	Abraham	1913	Arbeiter	ja	worker
JUST	Don	1894	Kaufmann	ja	merchant
JUST	Ryfke	1895			
JUST	Chaje	1921	Verkäuferin		saleswoman
JUST	Rische	1925			
JUST	Rachela	1876			
JUST	Baruch	1911	Arbeiter	ja	worker
JUST	Leib	1910	Arbeiter	ja	worker
JUST	Osias	1882	Kaufmann	nein	merchant
JUST	Kreindel	1893			
JUST	Malke	1916			
KACHAN	Moses	190?	Schuster	ja	shoemaker
KACHAN	Ester	192?			
KACHAN	Rosa	1923			
KACHAN	Jakob	1925	Arbeiter	ja	worker
KACHAN	Sara Ryfke	1928			
KACHAN	Frimet	1930			
KACHAN	Jsaak	1939			
KALB	Moses	1874			
KALB	Leie	1870			
KALB	Ascher	1878			
KALB	Chaje	1881			
KALB	Rachel	1904			
KALB	Schulim	1905	Arbeiter	ja	worker
KAMPEL	Samuel	1910	Schuster	ja	shoemaker

KAMPEL	Freide	1912			
KANAREK	Aron	1904	Bäcker	ja	baker
KANAREK	Chaje	1907			
KANAREK	Victor	1928			
KANAREK	Ester	1931			
KANNER	Sara	1864			
KANNER	Chawa	1908			
KANNER	Meilech	1895	Arbeiter	ja	worker
KANNER	Leie	1890			
KANNER	Sali	1926	Arbeiter	ja	worker
KANNER	Chaje	1929			
KANNER	Leib	1900	Arbeiter	ja	worker
KANNER	Rosa	1908			
KANNER	Fischel	1933			
KANNER	Fradel	1870			
KARSCH	Golda	1895			
KATZ	Chaim Wolf	1885	Arbeiter	ja	worker
KATZ	Zile	1893			
KATZ	Chane	1910			
KATZ	Sala	1907			
KATZ	Ester	1936			
KATZ	Hene	1914			
KATZ	Suesmann	1876			
KATZ	Chaje	1882			
KATZ	Klara	1892			
KATZ	Mathias	1912	Arbeiter	ja	worker
KATZ	Osias	1910	Arbeiter	ja	worker
KATZ	Sara	1908			
KATZ	Zwi	1936			
KATZ	Sime	1940			
KATZ	Ettel	1865			
KATZ	Leie	1894	Arbeiter		worker

KATZ	Neche	1900			
KATZ	Feige	1925			
KATZ	Guetl	1929			
KATZ-HERMAN	Ryfke	1881			
KATZ-HERMAN	Hirsch Leib	1917	Uhrmacher	ja	watchmaker
KEIL	Anna	1901			
KEIL	Feige	1931			
KEIL	Neche	1929			
KEIL	Leie	1926			
KEIL	Abraham	1924	Friseur	ja	barber
KERN	Leie	1871			
KERN	Baruch	1912	Arbeiter	ja	worker
KERN	Mala	1909	Verkäuferin		saleswoman
KERN	Taube	1926			
KERN	Anne	1892			
KERNKRAUT	Machla	1888			
KERNKRAUT	Fischel	1925	Arbeiter	ja	worker
KIJOWSKI	Taube	1937			
KIESELSTEIN	Sala	1891			
KIESELSTEIN	Chaje	1923			
KIESELSTEIN	Chiel	1922	Arbeiter		worker
KIESELSTEIN	Dora	1890			
KIESELSTEIN	Moses	1892	Expedient		dispatch clerk
KIESELSTEIN	Samuel	1916	Arbeiter		worker
KIESELSTEIN	Chane	1923	Näherin		seamstress
KIESELSTEIN	Mendel	1925	Arbeiter	ja	worker
KIESELSTEIN	Zile	1926			
KINDERMAN	Jakob	1894	Kaufmann	ja	merchant
KINDERMAN	Ida	1892			
KINDERMAN	Recha	1922			
KINDERMANN	Zierl	1865			

KINDERMAN	Perl	1909	Arbeiter		worker
KIRSCHNER	Ida	1900			
KIRSCHNER	Georg	1925	Verkäuferin	ja	saleswoman
KIRSCHNER	Mirel	1929			
KLAGSBALD	Eber	1902	Arbeiter	ja	worker
KLAGSBALD	Amalia	1902			
KLAGSBALD	Freide	1925			
KLAGSBALD	Debora	1927			
KLAGSBALD	Rachel	192			
KLAGSBALD	Guetl	1933			
KLEINBERGER	Jakob	1878			
KLEINBERGER	Berta	1878			
KLEIN	Samuel				
KLEINERMAJER					
KLEINER	Mandel	1885	Arbeiter	ja	worker
KLEINER	Malke	1897			
KLEINER	Leia	1926			
KLEINER	Pauline	1930			
KLEINERMOSHE	Judenrat			ja	
KLEINER	Yaacov				
KLEINER	Moses	1893	Arbeiter		worker
KLEINER	Ella	1898			
KLEINER	Samuel	1923	Uhrmacher	ja	watchmaker
KLEINER	Feige	1926			
KLEINER	Jakob	1863			
KLEINER	Jhuda	1901	Kaufmann		merchant
KLEINMANN	Salomon	1908			
KLEINMANN	Adele	1908			
KLEINMANN	Leie	1913	Näherin		seamstress
KLEINMANN	Sara	1918			
KLEINMANN	Blueme	1937			
KLEINMANN	Chane	1938			

KLEINMANN	Pepi	1911	Arbeiter		worker
KLEINMANN	Ester	1901			
KLEINMANN	Mendel	1935			
KLOTZ	Sara	1880			
KLUCZKOWSKI	Rachel	1854			
KLUCZKOWSKI	Abraham	1886			
KLUCZKOWSKI	Chaje	1886			
KLUCZKOWSKI	Brandel	1926	Näherin		seamstress
KNOBLECH	Chaim David	1913	Arbeiter		worker
KNOBLECH	Reisel	1909			
KNOPF	Jsaak	1899			
KNOPF	Chaje	1904			
KNOPF	Naftali	1932			
KNOPF	Debora	1934			
KOLBER	Berel	1893	Arbeiter	ja	worker
KOLBER	Basche	1898			
KOLBER	Baruch	1933			
KOLBER	Ester	1936			
KONINSKI	Samuel	1892	Arbeiter	ja	worker
KONINSKI	Helene	1897			
KONINSKI	Siegmund	1920	Drucker	ja	printer
KONINSKI	Ignaz	1923	Arbeiter	ja	worker
KOENIG	Leie	1880			
KOENIG	Jsaak	1904	Konditor	ja	confectioner
KOENIG	Hella	1906			
KOENIG	Moses	1908			
KOENIG	Chaje	1910			
KOENIG	Ruth	1937			
KOPITO	Sala	1910			
KORB	Hirsch	1898	Klempner	ja	plumber
KORB	Leie	1889			

KORB	Brandel	1921			
KORB	Stella	1940			
KORB	Abraham	1897	Klempner	ja	plumber
KORB	Reisel	1905			
KORB	Berta	1932			
KORB	Malke	1864			
KORB	Brandel	1905	Verkäuferin		saleswoman
KORB	Tamara	1937			
KORNITZER	Guetl	1878			
KORNREICH	Regina	1893			
KORNREICH	Anna	1914			
KORNREICH	Sabine	1895	Schneider		tailor
KORNREICH	Seinwel	1923	Verkäuferin	ja	saleswoman
KORNREICH	Feige	1925			
KORNREICH	Sara	1926			
KRANZ	Feige	1873			
KRANZ	Berel	1897	Schuster	ja	shoemaker
KRANZ	Eva	1896			
KRANZ	Hinde	1928			
KRANZ	Jsaak	1932			
KRANZ	Basche	1936			
KRANZ	M.		Gastwirt		innkeeper
KREISBERG	Hene	1910			
KRESCH	Naftali	1900	Lehrer	ja	teacher
KRESCH	Ete	1910			
KRESCH	Ziwie	1939			
KRESCH	Fiwel	1941			
KRIEGER	Baruch	1881	Bäcker	ja	baker
KRIEGER	Sara	1890			
KRIEGER	Jakob	1936			
KRIEGER	Brandel	1907			
KRIEGER	Jsaak	1936			

KRIEGER	Charles	1905	Bäcker	ja	baker
KRIEGER	Marjem	1913			
KRIEGER	Rosa	1929			
KRIEGER	Hirsch	1929			
KRIEGER	Suessl	1931			
KRIEGER	Markus	1934			
KRIEGER	Anne	1938			
KRIEGER	Meilech	1918	Arbeiter	ja	worker
KRIEGER	Josef	1903	Arbeiter	ja	worker
KRIEGER	Rosa	1904			
KRIEGER	Jsrael	1939			
KUDLER	Simche	1921	Arbeiter	ja	worker
KUDLER	Markus	1921	Arbeiter	ja	worker
KUDLER	Irene	1920	Verkäuferin		saleswoman
KUDLER	Feige	1929			
KUDLER	Frieda	1896			
KUDLER	Guetl	1921			
KUFLIK	Leib	1883	Kaufmann	ja	· merchant
KUFLIK	Ester	1880			
KUFLIK	Leie	1919			
KUENSTLINGER	Jakob	1907	Schneider	ja	tailor
KUENSTLINGER	Leie	1905			
KURZER	Henryke	1864			
KUPPERMANN	Ryfke	1898	·		·
KUPPERMANN	Etsche	1927			
KURZMANN	Siegmund	1904	Uhrmacher	ja	watchmaker
KURZMANN	Rosa	1912			
	Moses	1899	Friseur	ja	barber
KIRES	Ester	1904			
KRESCH	Feiwel	1941			
LACHNER	Ester	1919			
LAMBERG	Feige	1882	Arbeiter		worker

LAMBERG	Ides	1917			
LAMBIK	Herzke	1886	Arbeiter	ja	worker
LAMBIK	Ryfke	1886			
LAMBIK	Samuel	1923	Arbeiter	ja	worker
LAMBIK	Mordche	1921	Arbeiter	ja	worker
LAMBIK	Rosa	1904			
LAMBIK	Brandel	1923			
LAMBIK	Simon	1925	Klempner	ja	plumber
LAMBIK	Israel	1932			
LAMBIK	Samuel	1897	Arbeiter	ja	worker
LAMM	Samuel	1901	Fleischer	ja	butcher
LAMM	Fannie	1906			
LAMM	Osias	1933			
LAMM	Rafael	1937			
LAMM	Gerson	1939			
LAMM	Barel	1872			
LAMM	Malka	1874			
LAMM	Josef	1904	Arbeiter	ja	worker
LANDAU	Tile	1883			
LANDAU	Dine	1878			
LANDAU	Sindel	1882	Kaufmann	ja	merchant
LANDAU	Schifre	1909			
LANDAU	Osias	1913	Verkäuferin	ja	saleswoman
LANDAU	Chane	1917	Arbeiter		worker
LANDAU	Mechel	1920	Arbeiter	ja	worker
LANDAU	Samuel	1907	Arbeiter	ja	worker
LANDAU	Feige	1907			
LANDAU	Sara	1935			
LANDAU	Moses	1938			
LANDAU	Chaim	1940			
LANDAU	Ryfke	1911	Lehrer		teacher
LANDGARTEN	Feige	1906	Schneiderin		seamstress

LANG	Sima	1912			
LANG	Yosef	1916	Angestellter	ja	employee [male]
LANGBAUM	Moses	1870			
LANGBAUM	Chane	1871			
LAUTMAN	Berta	1889			
LEHRMAN	Majer	1913	Arbeiter	ja	worker
LEHRMAN	Ziwie	1939			
LEHRER	Leiser	1900	Tischler	ja	carpenter
LEHRER	Leie	1905			
LEHRER	Feige	1934			
LEHRER	Helene	1936			
LEHRER	Chaim	1937			
LEHRER	Aron	1941			
LEIBEL	David	1892	Schneider	ja	tailor
LEIBEL	Rosa	1900			
LEIBEL	Levy	1932			
LEIBEL	Ete	1937			
LEICHTBERG	Wolf	1880			
LEICHTBERG	Jhuda	1882			
LEICHTBERG	Ete	1886			
LEICHTBERG	Chaim	1912			
LEINER	Regina	1876			
LEINER	Arthur	1912	Kürschner	ja	furrier
LEINER	Rosa	1916			
LEINER	Chaim	1901	Kaufmann		merchant
LEINER	Luise	1902			
LEISER	Aron	1898	Kaufmann	ja	merchant
LEISER	Sala	1896			
LEISER	Ides	1927			
LEISER	Chaim	1930			
LEMBERG	Rachel	1891	Arbeiter		worker

LEMBERG	Marjem	1896	Arbeiter		worker
LERNER	Wolf Beer	1885	Lehrer	ja	teacher
LERNER	Reisel	1890			
LERNER	Golde	1913	Friseur		barber
LERNER	Hirsch	1914	Taschenmacher	ja	bag maker
LERNER	Moses	1916	Arbeiter	ja	worker
LERNER	Schaje	1917	Arbeiter	ja	worker
LERNER	Chaje	1923			
LERNER	Jakob	1925	Arbeiter	ja	worker
LERNER	Meilech	1927	Arbeiter	ja	worker
LERNER	Simon	1930			
LICHELET	Chaje	1924			
LIEBER	Ryfke	1896			
LIEBER	Moses	1925	Arbeiter	ja	worker
LIEBER	Feige	1929			
LIEBER	Samuel	1922	Arbeiter		worker
LIEBER	Himde	1886			
LIEBER	Chaje	1925	Schneiderin		seamstress
LIEBER	Jakob	1888	Lehrer	ja	teacher
LIEBERMANN	Hirsch	1906			
LIEBERMANN	Ilona	1906	Arbeiter	ja	worker
LIEBERMANN	Jsrael	1929			
LIEBERMANN	Ascher	1933			
LIPPINER	Feige	1875			
LIPPINER	Pepi	1918			
LIPPINER	Rosa	1914			
LIPPINER	Siegmund	1913	Arbeiter	ja	worker
LIPINER	Ester	1918	Köchin		cook [female]
LIPPNER	Josephine	1896			
LIPPINER	Ferdinand	1885	Beamter	ja	clerk
LIPPINER	Olga				
LITWOK	Basche	1903			

LITWOK	Chaim	1895	Arbeiter	ja	worker
LITWOK	Samuel	1932			
LIZEWSKI	Feiwel	1902	Sockenstricker	ja	sock needle worker
LIZEWSKI	Leie	1903			
LIZEWSKI	Chaim	1928			
LIZEWSKI	Chane	1931			
LOEBEL	Ite	1915			
LOEBEL	Sabine	1919			stylist
LOEBEL	Chaim Leib	1940			
LOEBEL	Rachel	1922			stylist
LOEBEL	Chane	1929			
LOEBEL	Eva	1892			
LOEBEL	Abraham	1914	Schneider	ja	tailor
LUSTIG	Elias	1894	Klempner	ja	plumber
LUSTIG	Sara	1898			
LUSTIG	Rachel	1925			
LUSTIG	Matel	1930			
LUSTIG	Osias	1933			
LESSIG	Nathan	1921	Elektriker	ja	electrician
MAHLER	Leiser	1890	Bäcker	ja	baker
MAHLER	Regina	1900			
MAHLER	Hirsch	1923	Bäcker	ja	baker
MAHLER	Genia	1896			
MAHLER	Hirsch	1923	Bäcker	ja	baker
MAHLER	Rafael	1902	Fleischer	ja	butcher
MAHLER	Marjem	1916			
MAHLER	Nissen	1940			
MALZ	Mindel	1885			
MALZ	Leie	1917			
MALZ	Jocheweth	1922	Schneiderin		seamstress
MANDEL	Pinkas	1906	Schneider	ja	tailor

MANDEL	Dora	1910			
MANDEL	Chaim	1935			
MANDEL	Sprinze	1938			
MANDEL	Jakob	1877	Schuster		shoemaker
MANDEL	Ryfke	1877			
MANDEL	Debora	1910			
MANDEL	Pessel	1915	Schneiderin		seamstress
MAENNER	Aron	1894	Arbeiter	ja	worker
MAENNER	Chaje	1905			
MAENNER	Markus	1931			
MAENNER	Jsrael	1933			
MAENNER	Jsaak	1941			
MARCHEWKA	Mnadel	1886	Lehrer		teacher
MARCHEWKA	Chume	1894			
MARCHEWKA	Basche	1924	Schneiderin		seamstress
MARCHEWKA	Schulim	1927	Arbeiter	ja	worker
MARCHEWKA	Scheindel	1930			
MARCHEWKA	Jsaak	1932			
MARCHEWKA	Leie	1936			
MARFELD	Selig	1898	Expedient	ja	dispatcher
MARFELD	Hadassah	1897			
MARFELD	Samuel	1928			
MARFELD	Chaje	1930			
MARFELD	Selde	1936			
MARGULIES	Moses	1900	Beamter	ja	clerk
MARGULIES	Eva	1905			
MARGULIES	Moses	1885	Expedient		dispatcher
MARGULIES	Ester	1888			
MARGULIES	Matel	1912			
MARGULIES	Pessel	1927			
MARGULIES	Machla	1886			
MARGULIES	Reisel	1875			

MARGULIES	Hirsch	1875			
MARGULIES	Malke	1908			
MARGULIES	Chai	1877			
MARGULIES	Sara	1878			
MARGULIES	Amalia	1911			
MARGULIES	Jocheweth	1912			
MARGULIES	Anna	1910			
MARGULIES	Markus	1903	Arbeiter	ja	worker
MARGULIES	Salomon	1901	Konditor		confectioner
MARGULIES	Minna	1902	Konditorin	ja	confectioner [female]
MARGULIES	Josef	1939			
MARGOLIES	Hinde	1890			
MAJEROWITZ	Schaje	1895	Kaufmann	ja	merchant
MAJEROWITZ	Leie	1898			
MAJEROWITZ	Eva	1924			
MAJEROWITZ	Marjem	1926			
MAJEROWITZ	Sala	1932			
MELAMET	Leie	1912			
MELAMET	Beile	1921			
MELAMET	David	1923	Arbeiter	ja	worker
MELAMET	Suessl	1925			
MELLER	Sprin	1870			
MAISELES	Mala	1904			
MAISELES	Sala	1926			
MAISELES	Chaje	1906			
MAISELES	Feige	1914			
MEISLICH	Jsrael	1898	Beamter	ja	clerk
MEISLICH	Frimet	1908			
MEISLICH	Guetl	1929			
MEISLICH	Ryfke	1931			
MEISLICH	Jhuda	1934			

MOHR	Chaje	1903	Maniküre		manicurist [female]
MOLLER	Alte Chane	1898			
MOLLER	Chiel	1933			
MONHEIT	Malke	1884			
MONHEIT	Feige	1914			
MONHEIT	Samuel	1919	Verkäufer	ja	salesman
MONHEIT	Naftali	1922	Verkäufer	ja	salesman
MONHEIT	Mechel	1924			
MONTAG	Josef	1911	Kaufmann	ja	merchant
MONTAG	Mindel	1917			
MONTAG	Ete	1940			
MORGENSTERN	Benjamin	1904	Kaufmann	ja	merchant
MORGENSTERN	Minna	1904			
MORGENSTERN	Schifre	1930			
MORGENSTERN	Sara	1936			
MORGENSTERN	Blanka	1910	Beamter		clerk
MOSES	Ascher	1849			
MOSES	Rachel	1849			
MOSES	Wolf	1875			
MOSES	Chane	1880			
MOSES	Abraham	1885	Beamter	ja	clerk
MOSES	Sala	1888			
MOSES	Suessl	1927			
MOSKOWICZ	Chaje	1898			
MOSKOWICZ	Hinde	1909			
MOSKOWICZ	Ester	1910	Arzt		doctor of medicine
MOSKOWICZ	Nischl	1913			
MOSKOWICZ	Moses	1914	Schuster	ja	shoemaker
MOSKOWICZ	Ite	1918	Beamter		clerk
MOSKOWICZ	Ilona	1933			
MOSKOWICZ	Moses	1932			

MOSKOWICZ	Pinkas	1930			
MOSKOWICZ	Josef	1925			
MUEHLRAD	Benzion	1897	Arbeiter	ja	worker
MUEHLRAD	Chane	1899			
MUEHLRAD	Saul	1927	Arbeiter	ja	worker
MUEHLRAD	Kalman	1928			
MUEHLRAD	Chaim	1929			
MUEHLRAD	Reisel	1931			
MUEHLRAD	Guetl	1933			
MUEHLRAD	Moses	1935			
MUEHLRAD	Sime	1936			
MUEHLRAD	Jsaak	1938			
MUEHLRAD	Chawe	1939			
MUEHLRAD	Jsrael	1941			
MUENZ	Jakob	1918	Schlosser	ja	locksmith
MUENZ	Schaje	1911	Schneider	ja	tailor
MUENZ	Sara	1907	Schneiderin		seamstress
MUENZ	Deborah	1937			
MUENZ	Ruben	1892	Klempner	ja	plumber
MUENZ	Rosa	1910			
MUENZ	Majer	1922	Klempner	ja	plumber
MUENZ	Eisig	1924	Klempner	ja	plumber
MUENZ	Abraham	1936			
MUENZ	Salomon	1940			
MUENZ	Simon	1941			
NAGEL	Tobiasz	1884	Fleischer	ja	butcher
NAGEL	Samuel	1914	Fleischer	ja	butcher
NAGEL	Guetl	1917			
NAGEL	Jakob	1920	Arbeiter	ja	worker
NAGEL	Markus	1924	Arbeiter	ja	worker
NAGEL	Sara	1856			
NAGEL	Nathan	1932			

NAGEL	Markus	1925	Arbeiter	ja	worker
NAGEL	Rachela	1900			
NAGEL	Markus	1922			
NAGEL	Halinka	1932			
NEISS-AKSELRAD	Zipora	1896			
NEISS-AKSELRAD	Sara	1929			
NEUMANN	Majer	1896	Arbeiter	ja	worker
NEUMANN	Sime	1908			
NEUMANN	Schaje	1930			
NEUMANN	Abraham	1932			
NIEWIADOMSKI	Hirsch	1888	Korbmacher	ja	basketmaker
NISSENBAUM	Berek	1908	Arbeiter	ja	worker
NISSENBAUM	Jente	1910			
NISSENBAUM	Rosa	1933			
NISSENBAUM	Sala	1937			
NORD	Hirsch	1875	Schneider		tailor
NORD	Rosa	1911			
NORD	Jocheweth	1917			
NORD	Zipora	1919			
NORD	Jsaak	1924	Schneider	ja	tailor
NORD	Rachel	1860			
NORD	Salomon	1881	Kaufmann	ja	merchant
NORD	Dine	1883			
NORD	Zeche	1917			
NOVEMBER	Ryfke	1874			
NOVEMBER	Samuel	1912	Weißbinder	ja	[house] painter
NUSSBAUM	Wolf	1876			
NUSSBAUM	Henoch	1909	Kaufmann	ja	merchant
NUSSBAUM	Ida	1909			
NUSSBAUM	Abisch	1935			
NUSSBAUM	Debora	1914			
OKNOWSKI	Golde	1884			

OKNOWSKI	Josef	1908	Tapezierer	ja	upholsterer
OLING	Aron	1886	Beamter	ja	clerk
OLING	Leie	1890			
OLING	Melke	1912	Friseur		barber
OLING	Chane	1915			
OLING	Mindel	1922	Schneiderin		seamstress
OLING	Jakob	1928			
PARNESS	Mirel	1913	Schneiderin		seamstress
PARNESS	Scheindel	1909			
PASTERNAK	Taube	1900			
PASTERNAK	Toni	1937			
PASTERNAK	Leib	1894	Kaufmann	ja	merchant
PASTERNAK	Leie	1896			
PASTERNAK	Gerson	1924	Verkäufer	ja	salesman
PASTOR	Simon	1895			
PASTOR	Regina	1905			
PASTOR	Ester	1914			
PELZMAN	Regina	1908			
PELZMAN	Samuel	1933			
PELZMAN	Reisel	1878			
PELZMAN	Feige	1920			
PELZMAN	Rachel	1921			
PELZMAN	Chaje	1928			
PELZMAN	Meilech	1872			
PELZMAN	Chaje	1903			
PELZMAN	Sara Ryfke	1939			
PINKAS	Jakob	1864	Klempner		plumber
PINKAS	Adele	1908	Schneiderin		seamstress
PINKAS	Lemel	1901	Kaufmann	ja	merchant
PINKAS	Freide	1899			
PINKAS	Samuel	1931			
PINKAS	Abraham	1933			

PINKAS	Neche	1935			
PINKAS	Reisel	1937			
PINKAS	Sabine	1941			
PINTER	Abraham	1934			
PINTER	Abraham	1934			
PINTER	Frieda	1906			
PINTER	Jsaak	1936			
PINTE	Guetl	1935			
PINSEL	Mendel	1886	Arbeiter	ja	worker
PINSEL	Chaje	1886			
PINSEL	Fischel	1913	Arbeiter	ja	worker
PINSEL	Brandel	1918	Scheiderin		seamstress
PINSEL	Leib	1922	Arbeiter	ja	worker
PINSEL	Liepe	1924	Arbeiter	ja	worker
PINSEL	Naftali	1929			
PIRBIAK	Mose	1918	Buchhalter		bookkeeper
PIRBIAK	Hirsh	1919	Buchhalter		bookkeeper
PIRBIAK	Rahela	1921	Korsettmacher		corsetmaker
PIRBIAK	Moses	1940			
PIRBIAK	Jakob	1904	Arbeiter	ja	worker
PIRBIAK	Leie	1907			
PIOTRKOWSKI	Sara	1878			
PIOTRKOWSKI	David	191	Arbeiter	ja	worker
PIWONJA	Chaje	1892			
PIWONJA	Nachim	1918	Arbeiter	ja	worker
PIWONJA	Leie	1919			
PLATNER	Markus	1879			
PLATNER	Chane	1878			
PLATNER	Debora	1913			
PLATNER	Abraham	1887	Glaser	ja	glazier
PLATNER	Helene	1887			
PLATNER	Sara	1919			

PLATNER	Rachel	1922			
PLATNER	Aron	1925	Glaser	ja	glazier
POZNANSKI	Alte Neche	1889			
PRESSER	Golde	1911			
PRESSER	Rachel	1879			
PROBKER	Anna	1912			
PROBKER	Sala	1938			
PROBKER	Ryfke	1940			
PRUEFER	Moses	1903	Schneider	ja	tailor
PRUEFER	Leie	1903			
PRUEFER	Naftali	1930			
PRUEFER	Chaim	1906	Arbeiter	ja	worker
RABI	Feiwel	1909	Schuster	ja	shoemaker
RABI	Chaje	1916			
RABI	Tile	1872			
RABI	Berl	1938			
RABI	Siegmund	1938			
RABINOWICZ	Perl	1905			
RABINOWICZ	Rosa	1934			
RABINOWICZ	Abraham	1938			
RAKOSZYNSKI	Feie	1888			
RAKOSZYNSKI	Mordche	1914	Arbeiter	ja	worker
RAMRAS	Samuel	1875			
RAMRAS	Ryfke	1876			
RAMRAS	Eidel	1901			
RAMRAS	Rachel	1939			
RATZ	Rachel	1870			
RECK	Moses	1903	Schneider	ja	tailor
RECK	Rachel	1900			
RECK	Rosa	1928			
RECK	Benjamin	1929			

REIBSCHEID	Samuel	1895	Arbeiter	ja	worker
REICH	Adam	1896	Ingenieur	ja	engineer
REICH	Malke	1912			
REICH	Schulim	1891	Glaser	ja	glazier
REICH	Rosa	1901			
REICH	Salomon	1930			
REICH	Regina	1935			
REINHOLD	Majer	1923	Vulkaniseur		vulcanizer
REISS	Salomon	1906	Arbeiter	ja	worker
REISS	Niche	1890			
REISS	Alter	1940			
RUBENFELD	Osias	1898	Verkäufer	ja	salesman
RUBENFELD	Chaje	1909	Schneiderin		seamstress
RIEDER	Berel	1897			
RIEDER	Jsrael	1903	Mützenmacher	nein	capper
RIEDER	Guetl	1889			
RIEDER	Mendel	1925	Arbeiter	ja	worker
RIEDER	Leib	1928	Arbeiter	ja	worker
RIEDER	Beile	1930			
RIEDER	Sprinze	1920			
RIEMER	Leie	1904			
RIEDER	Guetl	1930			
RIEDER	Moses	1935			
RINGLER	Amalie	1869			
RINGLER	Simon	1898	Kaufmann	ja	merchant
RINGLER	Pauline	1907			
RINGLER	Abraham	1931			
RINGLER	Malke	1927			
RINGLER	Pepi	1900			
RINGLER	Abraham	1907			
ROGALIK	Feige	1884			
ROGALIK	Marjem	1928			

ROSENBERG	Abraham	1904	Arzt	ja	doctor of medicine
ROSENBERG	Serl	1920			
ROSENBERG	Moses	1879			
ROSENBERG	Chaje	1877			
ROSENBERG	Berl	1917	Arbeiter	ja	worker
ROSENBERG	Ryfke	1918			
ROSENBLATT	Frimet	1909			
ROSENBLATT	Chaskel	1936			
ROSENBLUM	Chawe	1909			
ROSENBLUM	Leib	1887	Advokat	ja	lawyer
ROSENBLUM	Fanziska	1891			
ROSENBLUM	Ester				
ROSENBLUETH	Franziska	1885			
ROSENTHAL	Moses	1885	Holzarbeiter	ja	woodworker
ROSENTHAL	Liebe	1885			
ROSENTHAL	Neche	1911			
ROSSENHENDLER		1890	Kaufmann	ja	merchant
ROSSENHENDLER	Rosa	1898			
ROSSENHENDLER	Elias	1927	Monteur	ja	mechanic
ROSSENHENDLER	Irene	1932			
ROSSLER	Aron	1890	Weißbinder	ja	[house] painter
ROSSLER	Ester	1895			
ROSSLER	Isaak	1922	Weißbinder	ja	[house] painter
ROSSLER	Moses	1923	Weißbinder	ja	[house] painter
ROSSLER	Beile	1925	Schneiderin	ja	seamstress
ROSNER	Rosa	1895			
ROSNER	Blueme	1938			
ROSNER	Leiser	1870			
ROSNER	Feiwel	1895	Schneider	ja	tailor

ROSNER	Chana	1896			
ROSNER	David	1927	Arbeiter	ja	worker
ROSNER	Chaskel	1928			
ROTH	Jhuda	1896	Kaufmann	ja	merchant
ROTH	Zierl	1898			
ROTH	Moses	1928			
ROTH	Guetl	1936			
ROTH	Chaskel	1900	Glaser	ja	glazier
ROTH	Lonke	1910			
ROTH	Dora	1902			
ROTH	Sprinze	1881			
ROTH	Osias	1898	Weißbinder	ja	[house] painter
ROTH	Samuel	1933			
ROTH	Eisig	1931			
ROTH	Mechel	1940			
ROTH	Salomon	1905	Schneider	ja	tailor
ROTH	Malke	1905			
ROTH	Aron	1932			
ROTH	Eisig	1936			
ROTH	Hersh				
ROTHENBERG	Sara	1911			
ROTHENBERG	Josef	1936			
ROTHENBERG	Guetl	1937			
ROTTER	Regina	1871			
ROTTER	Goerg	1901	Arbeiter	ja	worker
ROTTER	Leib	1882	Schneider	ja	tailor
ROTTER	Feige	1884			
ROTTER	Saul	1919	Photograph	ja	photographer
ROTTER	Isaak	1923	Weißbinder	ja	[house] painter
ROTTERSMAN	Zile	1894			
ROTTERSMAN	Guetl	1916	Verkäuferin		saleswoman

ROTTERSMAN	Anna	1922			
ROTTERSMAN	Ester	1925			
ROTTERSMAN	Suess	1935			
RUBIN	Oskar	1905	Verkäufer	ja	salesman
RUBIN	Golde	1941			
RUBIN	endel	1904	Kaufmann	ja	merchant
RUBIN	Friede	1908			
RUBIN	Mechel	1930			
RUBIN	Naftali	1933			
RUBIN	Suessl	1936			
RUBIN	Chane	1939			
RUBIN	Jsaak	1915	Arbeiter	ja	worker
RUBINFELD	Blueme	1895			
RUBINFELD	Wolf	1929			
RUBINFELD	Abraham	1936			
RUBINFELD	Basche	1880			
RYBACH	Alte	1892			
SAFERN	Chawa				
SAFERN	Osias	1906	Arbeiter	ja	worker
SAFERN	Pinkas	1915	Arbeiter	ja	worker
SAFERN	Guetl	1904			
SAFERN	Sprinze	1927			
SAFERN	Feige	1931			
SAFERN	Malke	1932			
SAFERN	Josef	1935			
SAFERN	Jsaak	1937			
SAFERN	Chaje	1939			
SALOMON	Leie	1880			
SALZ	Selde	1905			
SALZ	Jocheweth	1917			
SAMUEL	Jetti	1886			
SAMUEL	Leie	1910	Korsettmacherin		corsetmaker

					[female]
SAND	Jeremias	1898			
SAND	Sala	1908			
SAND	Samuel	1931			
SAND	David	1933			
SAND	Chaim	1937			
SANDOWSKI	Frimet	1920	Maniküre		manicurist [female]
SEEMAN	Markus	1876			
SEEMAN	Guetl	1875			
SEIFMAN	Alter David				
SEIDENFELD	Abraham	1882	Arbeiter	ja	worker
SEIDENFELD	Rachel	1878		ja	
SILBERBERG	Osias	1894	Bauer	ja	farmer
SILBERBERG	Ester	1897			
SILBERBERG	Chane	1923	Schneiderin	ja	seamstress
SILBERBERG	Jocheweth	1925	Arbeiter		worker
SILBERBERG	Anna	1927		ja	
SILBERBERG	Chaim Jak	1928			
SILBERBERG	Dora	1930			
SILBERBERG	Feige	1932			
SILBERBERG	Moses	1934			
SILBERBERG	Perl	1937			
SILBERBERG	Chane	1888			
SILBERBERG	Chaim	1920	Arbeiter	ja	worker
SILBERBERG	Chaje	1925			
SILBERMANN	Regina	1901			
SILBERMANN	Abraham	1935			
SILBERMANN	Berl	1938			
SINGER	Fradel	1880			
SORODINA	Ester	1890			
SMORODINA	Chaje	1924			
SMORODINA	Abraham	1929			

SOBEL	Osias	1885	Arbeiter	ja	worker
SOBEL	Feige	1887			
SOBEL	Ester	1920			
SOBEL	Fradel	1927			
SONNENSCHEIN	Siegmund	1899	Kürschner	ja	furrier
SPANNDORF	Simche	1885	Arbeiter	ja	worker
SPANNDORF	Suessl	1887			
SPERBER	Dora	1915			
SPIEGEL	Josef	1900	Angestellter	ja	employee [male]
SPIEGEL	Sara	1899			
SPIEGELMANN	Leie	1917			
SPITZ	Guetl	1878			
SPITZ	Schaje	1916	Arbeiter	ja	worker
SPRECHER	Naftali	1897	Arbeiter	ja	worker
SPRECHER	Chaje	1900			
SPRECHER	Regina	1934			
SPRECHER	Sala	1912			
SPRECHER	Gerson	1910	Tapezierer	ja	upholsterer
SPRINGER	Jsaak	1893	Mechaniker	ja	mechanic
SPRINGER	Rudolfine	1897			
SPRINGER	Majer	1920	Arbeiter	ja	worker
SPRINGER	Heinrich	1922	Autoschlosser	ja	car locksmith
SPRINGER	Eugenie	1924			
SPRINGER	Erwin	1927	Arbeiter	ja	worker
SPRINGER	Regine	1872			
SPRINGER	Ester	1914	Verkäuferin		saleswoman
SPRINGER	Eugenia	1913			
SPRINGER	Moses				
SROKA	Mindel	1884			
SROKA	Aron	1906	Schneider	ja	tailor
SROKA	Anna				

SROKA	Jonas	1919	Friseur	ja	barber
SROKA	arjem	923	Schneiderin		seamstress
SROKA	Beile	1926			
SROKA	Moses	1892	Arbeiter	ja	worker
SZYJOWICZ	Samuel	1912	Fleischer	ja	butcher
SZYJOWICZ	Scheindel	1913			
SZYJOWICZ	Blueme	1940			
SUESSHOLZ	Ester	1914			
SUESSHOLZ	Rosa	1918			
STADTFELD	Chaim	1898	Schneider	ja	tailor
STADTFELD	Chume	1891	Schneider	ja	tailor
STADTFELD	Taube	1893			
STADTFELD	Dine	1891			
STADTFELD	Hirsch	1925	Schneider	ja	tailor
STADTFELD	Chaje	1924			
STADTFELD	Abraham	1930			
STADTFELD	Berl	1933			
STEINBERG	Freide	1894			
STEINBERG	Salek	1923	Arbeiter	ja	worker
STEINBERG	David	1924	Arbeiter	ja	worker
STEINHORN	Pinkas	1904	Arbeiter	ja	worker
STEINHORN	Ryfke	1912			
STEINHORN	Moses	1936			
STEINHORN	Baruch	1874			
STEINHORN	Ryfke	1917			
STEINHORN	Sara	1923			
STEIGBUEGEL	Chaim	1885	Arbeiter	ja	worker
STEIGBUEGEL	Leie	1889			
STEIGBUEGEL	Lugen ?	1925	Arbeiter		worker
STEIN	Chaskel	1899	Kaufmann		merchant
STEIN	sara	1901			
STEIN	Meilech	1925	Arbeiter		worker

STEIN	Feige	1929			
STEIN	Beile	1931			
STEIN	Marjem	1934			
STEIN	Simon	1936			
STEINER	Zudik	1911			
STEINER	Ziwie	1915			
STEINMETZ	Hirsch	1882			
STEINMET	Minna	1888			
STEINMET	Malke	1920			
STEINMET	Markus	1928			
STERN	Chaje	1909			
STERN	Chaim	1936			
STERN	Simon	1877			
STERN	Chane	1912	Schneiderin		seamstress
STERN	Eva	1881			
STERN	Majer	1934			
STIEBER	Gusta	1877			
STIEFEL	Joachim	1894	Arbeiter	ja	worker
STIEFEL	Charlotte	1894			
STIEFEL	Marcin	1923	Schlosser	ja	locksmith
STIEFEL	Moses	1925	Arbeiter	ja	worker
STIEFEL	Josef	1928			
STRASSFELD	Nuchim	1889	Schneider	ja	tailor
STRASSFELD	Scheindel	1922			
STRASSFELD	Regine	1923			
STRASSFELD	Jente	1926			
STRASSFELD	Berisch	1928			
STROH	Anna	1876			
STROBING	Beile	1876			
STUHL	Meilech	190	Arbeiter	ja	worker
STUHL	Salomon	1941	Kaufmann	ja	merchant
STRYCK	Wolf	1898	Kaufmann	ja	merchant

SABINE		1903			
STRYCK	Leie	1933			
STRYCK	Guetl	1935			
STRYCK	Majer	1911	Arbeiter	ja	worker
STRYCK	Jente	1910			
STRYCK	Ester	1937			
STRYCK	Moses	1885	Kaufmann	ja	merchant
STRYCK	Anna	1888			
STRYCK	Chaim	1911	Arbeiter	ja	worker
STRYCK	Jsrael	1912	Arbeiter	ja	worker
STRYCK	Basche	1927			
SCHACHNER	David	1886	Arbeiter	ja	worker
SCHACHNE	Guetl	1880			
SCHACHNER	Helene	1918			
SCHACHNER	Moses	1936			
SCHACHNER	Salek	1910	Elektromonteur	ja	electrician
SCHALL	Abraham	1877			
SCHAL	Leie	1885			
SCHAL	Ziwie	1920			
SCHAMROTH	Moses	1904	Elektromonteur	ja	electrician
SCHAMROTH	Chaje	1910			
SCHAMROTH	Jsaak	1934	Arbeiter	ja	worker
SCHAMROTH	Rachel	1936			
SCHAMROTH	Selde	1886			
SCHAMROTH	Regine	1914			
SCHAMROTH	Lola	1906			
SCHAMROTH	Rubin	1910	Arbeiter	ja	worker
SCHAMROTH	Wolf				
SCHAMROTH	Suessl				
SCHAMROTH	Marjem				
SCHAPIRO	Leie	1886			
SCHARF	Feiwel				

SCHATTEN	Rosa	1920			
SCHATTEN	Ester	1922			
SCHENKER	Ryfke	1875			
SCHENKER	Jsaak	1905			
SCHENK	Ester Sara	1905			
SCHENK	Moses	1937			
SCHENK	Rachel	1940			
SCHEINBACH	Mendel	1857			
SCHEINBACH	Osias	1896	Arbeiter	ja	worker
SCHEINBACH	Regina	1897			
SCHEINBACH	Serl	1923			
SCHEINBACH	Chaim	1930	Kassiererin		cashier [female]
SCHEINBACH	Elias	1898	Arbeiter	ja	worker
SCHEINBACH	Chane	1901			
SCHEINBACH	Josef	1931			
SCHEINBACH	Serl	1937			
SCHOENBACH	Mechel	1900	Arbeiter	ja	worker
SCHEINBACH	Dora	1898			
SCHEINBACH	Leib	1931			
SCHEINBACH	Sime	1937			
SCHEINER	Abraham	1910	Kutscher	ja	coachman
SCHEINER	Rachel	1912			
SHEINER	Naftali	1858			
SCHENKER	Rosa	1854			
SCHERER	Sabine	1918			
SCHIFF	Leib	1870			
SCHIFF	Ester	1872			
SCHIFF	Moses	1904	Arbeiter	ja	worker
SCHIFF	Debora	1862			
SCHLAF	Israel	1885	Arbeiter	ja	worker
SCHLAF	Anna	1890			

SCHLAF	Rosa	1920			
SCHLAF	Hella	1922			
SCHLAF	Leie	1928			
SCHLANGER	Mose	1896	Kürschner	ja	furrier
SCHLANGER	Ryfka	1906			
SCHLANGER	Feige	1929			
SCHLANGER	Selde	1862			
SCHLEIN	Feige	1908			
SCHLEIN	Ryfke	1876			
SCHLEIN	Marjem	1912	Näherin		seamstress
SCHMALBERG	Wolf	1902	Kaufmann	ja	merchant
SCHREIER	Ite	1893			
SCHREIER	Abraham	1919	Arbeiter	ja	worker
SCHOULDENFREI	Leib	1903			
SCHOULDENFREI	Taube	1902			
SCHOULDENFREI	Dora	1932			
SCHOULDENFREI	Hirsch	1933			
SCHWEBEL	Alter	1887	Kaufmann	ja	merchant
SCHWEBEL	Anna	1889			
SCHWEBEL	Regin	1922			
SCHWEBEL	Mendel	1923	Arbeiter	ja	worker
SCHWEBEL	Brandel	1926			
SCHWEBEL	Chaje	1929			
TABACZNIK	Isaak	1889	Arbeiter	ja	worker
TABACZNIK	Ryfke	1888			
TABACZNIK	Ides	1922			
TABACZNIK	Sara	1923			
TANZ	Salomon	1872			
TANZ	Scheindel	1878			
TANZ	Brandel	1906			
TANZ	Golde	1908			
TANZ	Ester	1914	Näherin		seamstress

TANZ	Debora	1916			
TANZ	Ryfke	1920			
TAUBENFELD	Moses	1882	Kaufmann	ja	merchant
TAUBENFELD	Mania	1921			
TAUBENFELD	Wolf	1908	Arbeiter	ja	worker
TAUBENFELD	Josef	1917	Arbeiter	ja	worker
TAUBENFELD	David	1919	Arbeiter	ja	worker
TEITELBAUM	Chaje	1876			
TEITELBAUM	Mechel	1904	Hausmeister	ja	janitor
TEITELBAUM	Ete	1927			
TEITELBAUM	Mirjam	1927			
TEITELBAUM	Basche	1930			
TEITELBAUM	Chane	1931			
TEITELBAUM	Benjamin	1933			
TEITELBAUM	Osias	1917	Arbeiter	ja	worker
TEITELBAUM	Debora	1914			
TEITELBAUM	Ester	1937			
TEITELBAUM	Moses	1901	Beamter	ja	clerk
TEITELBAUM	Liebe	1902			
TEITELBAUM	Hirsch	1931			
TEITELBAUM	Sara	1933			
TEITELBAUM	Samuel	1910	Arbeiter	ja	worker
TEITELBAUM	Abraham	1891	Arbeiter	ja	worker
TEITELBAUM	Berta	1901			
TEITELBAUM	Minna	1926			
TEITELBAUM	Moses	1932			
TEITELBAUM	Josef	1936			
TEITELBAUM	Josua	1895	Arbeiter	ja	worker
TEITELBAUM	Feige	1906			
TEITELBAUM	Freide	1934			
TEITELBAUM	Mechel	1938			
TEITELBAUM	Jsaak	1932	Beamter	ja	clerk

TEPLICKI	Jakob	1882			
TEPLICKI	Liebe	1883			
TEPLICKI	Anna	1913			
TEPLICKI	Helene	1923			
TEPPER	Mathilde	1900			
TEPPER	Feige	1924			
TEPPER	Eidel	1889			
TEPPER	Hinde	1916	Näherin		seamstress
TEPPER	Scheindel	1921			
TEICHER	Mirja	1902			
TESTYLIER	Feige	1889			
TESTYLIER	Emma	1920	Näherin		seamstress
THALER	\Sala	1929			
THALER	Bruche	1905			
THALER	Markus	1887	Beamter	ja	clerk
THALER	Hene	1880			
THALER	Scheindel	1920			
THALER	Pinkas	1921	Arbeiter	ja	worker
THALER	David	1909	Bäcker	ja	baker
THALER	Golde	1911			
THALER	Emanuel	1939			
TISCHLER	Jakob	1904	Kutscher	ja	coachman
TISCHLER	Reisel	1905			
TISCHLER	Rachel	1932			
TISCHLER	Anna	1933			
TISCHLER	Sala	1934			
TISCHLER	Chiel	1935			
TISCHLER	Josef	1872			
TISCHLER	Chaje	1875			
TISCHLER	Berel	1905	Stricker	ja	needle worker
TISCHLER	Zipora	1910			
TISCHLER	David	1936			

TRATTNER	Markus	1894	Kaufmann	ja	merchant
TRATTNER	Rosa	1891			
TRATTNER	Abraham	1924	Arbeiter	ja	worker
TRATTNER	Moses	1925	Arbeiter	ja	worker
TRATTNER	Ester	1932			
TRATTNER	Efraim	1855			
TRATTNER	Freide	1905			
TRENCZER	Shmuel	1859	Fleischer		butcher
TRENCZER	Anna	1872			
TRENCZER	Gene	1905			
TRENCZERLEIZER		1887	Arbeiter	ja	worker
TRENCZER	Chaya	1890			
TRENCZER	Osias	1913	Beamter	ja	clerk
TRENCZER	Bianka	1914			
TRENCZER	Yosef	1917			
TRENCZER	Chawe	1883			
TRENCZER	Schifre	1914			
TRENCZER	Getzel	1886	Fleischer	ja	butcher
TRENCZER	Feige	1858			
TRENCZER	Mathilde	1887			
TRENCZER	Anna	1911			
TRENCZER	Etel	1914	Näherin		seamstress
TRENCZER	Erna	1923	Verkäuferin		saleswoman
TRENCZER	Ignaz	1926	Arbeiter	ja	worker
TRENCZER	Chawe	1882			
TRENCZER	Rosa	1916	Näherin		seamstress
TRENCZER	Matel	1909	Arbeiter	ja	worker
TRENCZER	Fischel	1901	Arbeiter	ja	worker
TRENCZER	Ete	1911			
TRENCZER	Salomon	1935			
TRENCZER	Jsrael	1906	Fleischer	ja	butcher
TRENCZER	Freide	1912			

TUREK	Beile	1888			
TUREK	Zipora	1917	Näherin		seamstress
TUREK	Joel	1918	Arbeiter	ja	worker
TUREK	Frimet	1919	Näherin		seamstress
TUREK	Sueskind	1921	Schneider	ja	tailor
TUREK	Malke	1923	Näherin		seamstress
TUREK	Moses	1925	Arbeiter	ja	worker
TUREK	Ester	1880			
TUREK	Markus	1923	Arbeiter		worker
TUREK	Leie	1925			
UNGER	Neche	1913	Näherin		seamstress
UNGER	Moses	1939			
UNGER	Chyawe	1900			
UNIKOWSKI	Schije	1895	Konditor	ja	confectioner
VERSTAENDIG	Josef	1893	Arbeiter	ja	worker
VERSTAENDIG	Beile	1907			
VERSTAENDIG	Mechel	1932			
VERSTAENDIG	David	1929			
VERSTAENDIG	Malke	1935			
VOGEL	Frime	1924	Näherin		seamstress
VOGEL	Feige	1924	Modistin		dressmaker [female]
VOGEL	Josef	1927	Schneider	ja	tailor
VOGEL	Mechel	1928			
VOGELFLUEGEL	Jsaak	1882	Arbeiter	ja	worker
VOGELHUT	Regina	1905			
VOGELHUT	Adolf	1929			
WAGSCHAL	Sara	1887			
WAGSCHAL	Chane	1914			
WAGSCHAL	Samuel	1918	Verkäuferin		saleswoman
WAGSCHAL	Ete	1921			
WAGSCHAL	Guetl	1925			
WAGSCHAL	Gene	1923			

WALDNER	Sali	1925			
WALDNER	Therese	1916			
WALDNER	Feige	1890			
WALKER	Berl	1941			
WALKER	Chaim	1900	Arbeiter	ja	worker
WALKER	Chaje	1910			
WALKER	Hirsch	1939			
WANDER	Moses	1880			
WANDER	Anna	1922			
WDOWINSKI	Rosa	1920			
WEHRMANN	Jda	1893			
WEHRMANN	Berl	1913	Arbeiter	ja	worker
WEHRMANN	Richard	1921	Arbeiter	ja	worker
WEHRMANN	Zile	1921			
WEHRMANN	Moses	1938			
WEINBERGER	Saul	1885	Arbeiter	ja	worker
WEINBERGER	Sara	1882			
WEINBERGER	Nathan	1917	Monteur	ja	mechanic
WEINBERGER	Sime	1921			
WEINBERGER	Schmerl	1908	Monteur	ja	mechanic
WEINBERGER	Taube	1900			
WEINBERGER	Chane	1934			
WEINBERGER	Samuel	1936			
WEINBERGER	Chaje				
WEINBERGER	Meshulim	1877	Beamter	ja	clerk
WEINBERGER	Ninna	1888			
WEINBERGER	Chaskel	1898	Arbeiter	ja	worker
WEINBERGER	Mendel	1904	Arbeiter	ja	worker
WEINBERGER	Chane	1900			
WEINBERGER	Chaje	1934			
WEINBERGER	Jsaak	1879			
WEINBERGER	Sime	1920			

WEISSBERGER	Ilona	1900			
WEISSBERGER	Eva	1922	Sekretärin		secretary
WEISSBERGER	Berta	1925	Näherin		seamstress
WEINFELD	Suessl	1889			
WEINFELD	David	1923			
WEINFELD	Jsrael	1914	Tapezierer	ja	upholsterer
WEINFELD	Naftal	1924	Tapezierer	ja	upholsterer
WEINFELD	Chane	1926			
WEINFELD	Jsaak	1888			
WEINFELD	Rachel	1894			
WEINFELD	Jsrael	1914	Weber	ja	weaver
WEINFELD	Hadassa	1916	Modistin		dressmaker [female]
WEINFELD	Salek	1918	Monteur	ja	mechanic
WEINFELD	Ascher	1897	Kaufmann	ja	merchant
WEINFELD	Rachela	1897			
WEINFELD	Hirsch	1917	Arbeiter	ja	worker
WEINFELD	Naftal	1930			
WEINFELD	Reisel	1931			
WEINSTEIN	Wolf	1896	Kaufmann	ja	merchant
WEINSTEIN	Margule	1894			
WEINSTEIN	Suessl	1926			
WEINSTEIN	Gene	1928			
WEINSTEIN	Jonas	1931			
WEINSTEIN	Jsrael	1902	Kutscher	ja	coachman
WEINSTEIN	Malke	1908			
WEINSTEIN	Scharne	1938			
WEINSTEIN	Chane	1940			
WEINSTEIN	Pinkas	1908	Arbeiter	ja	worker
WEINSTEIN	Leib	1907	Arbeiter	ja	worker
WEINSTEIN	Hene	1873			
WEINSTEIN	Zile	1907			
WEINSTEIN	Salomon	1906	Arbeiter	ja	worker

WEINSTEIN	Rosa	1892			
WEINSTEIN	Samu	1924	Arbeiter	ja	worker
WEINSTEIN	Hirsch	1924	Arbeiter	ja	worker
WEINSTEIN	Jsaak	1928			
WEINSTEIN	Josef	1929			
WEINSTEIN	Pinkas	1931			
WEINSTEIN	Chemje	1900	Kutscher	ja	coachman
WEINSTEIN	Beile	1902			
WEINSTEIN	Chaim	1935			
WEISS	Elias	1907	Beamter		clerk
WEISS	Jutta	1909			
WEISS	Rudi	1935			
WEISER	Wolf	1895	Beamter	ja	clerk
WEISER	Brandel	1900			
WEISER	Jsrael	1930			
WEISER	Chume	1923			
WEISER	Suessl	1924			
WEISER	Mendel	1927	Arbeiter	ja	worker
WEISS	Sali		Arbeiter	ja	worker
WEISS	Beile	1891			
WEISS	Leiser	1890	Arbeiter	ja	worker
WEISS	Feige	1921	Näherin		seamstress
WEISS	Poje	1914			
WEISS	Jakob	1928			
WEISSBERGER	Ilona	1900			
WEISSBERGER	Eva	1922	Sekretärin		secretary
WEISSBERGER	Berta	1925	Näherin		seamstress
WEISSMANN	Rosa	1914			
WEISSMANN	Beile	1939			
WEISSMANN	Markus	1886	Expedient	ja	dispatch clerk
WEISSMANN	Zile	1890			

WEISSMANN	Hirsch	1925			
WEISNER	Rosa	1899			
WELKES	Berl	1868			
WELKES	Baruch	1924	Arbeiter	ja	worker
WELKES	Chaim	1911	Arbeiter	ja	worker
WELKES	Malke	1913			
WELKES	Guetl	1912			
WELKES	Chane	1922			
WELKES	Sala	1921			
WELKES	Beile	1868			
WENIG	Jsaak	1889	Arbeiter	ja	worker
WENIG	Rosa	1889			
WENIG	Freide	1914			
WENIG	Guetl	1918			
WENIG	Solomon	1919	Arbeiter	ja	worker
WERTHEIMER	Hinde	1923			
WESTREICH	Blueme	1864			
WESTREICH	Rosa	1899			
WIAZOWSKI	Chaim	1907	Arbeiter	ja	worker
WIAZOWSKI	Guetl	1913			
WIAZOWSKI	Mordche	1939			
WIENER	Chane	1909			
WIENER	Rosa	1935			
WILLNER	Nathan	1898	Bäcker	ja	baker
WILLNER	Sala	1896			
WILLNER	Freide	1925	Verkäuferin	ja	saleswoman
WILLNER	Salomon	1930			
WILLNER	Naftal	1931			
WILLNER	Leib	1896	Arbeiter	ja	worker
WILLNER	Chaje	1884			
WILLNER	Berisch	1922			
WILLNER	Leie	1924	Näherin		seamstress

WILLNER	Freide	1931			
WILLNER	Moses	1929			
WILLNER	Jsrael	1935			
WILLNER	Helene	1889			
WILLNER	Sulamith	1925			
WILLNER	Leie	1927			
WILLNER	Eidel	1932			
WICHNER	Chane	1904			
WINTER	Jakob	1886	Arbeiter	ja	worker
WINTER	Sara	1900			
WINTER	Leie	1870			
WISTREICH	Mille	1918	Näherin		seamstress
WITTKIND	Beile	1900	Lehrer		teacher
WROBEL	Leie	1917			
WROBEL	Berel	1876			
WROBEL	Debor	1886			
WROBEL	Guetl	1920			
WROBEL	Freide	1924			
WROBEL	David	1921	Schneider	ja	tailor
ZAJDOW	Ele	1915	Arbeiter	ja	worker
ZAJDOW	Jocheweth	1880			
ZAJDOW	Jocheweth	1880			
ZIMET	Chaje	1884			
WISTREICH	Mille	1918	Näherin		seamstress
ZWASS	Jakob	1889	Schneider	ja	tailor
ZWASS	Marjem	1886			
ZWASS	Hillel	1923			
ZWASS	Markus	1926			
ZWASS	Aron	1927	Arbeiter	ja	worker
ZWICK	Blueme	1870			
ZWIEBEL	Jakob	1889	Bäcker	ja	baker
ZWIEBEL	Feige	1891			

ZWIRN	Salomon	1902	Friseur	ja	barber
ZWIRN	Feige	1905			
ZYCHOHOLZ	Hirsch	1904	Schneider	ja	tailor
ZYCHOHOLZ	Leie	1925			
ZYCHOHOLZ	Chaim	1928			
ZYCHOHOLZ	Sara	1929			
ZYZAK	Genendel	1884			
ZYZAK	Ester	1921			

[Page 162]

Chapter V
Germany Attacks Russia

KROSNO, Rynek – Podcienia

The main market square or rynek of Krosno is renamed Adolf Hitler Platz

The Germans lived very well in Krosno; they had special stores, clothing shops, and other facilities. But there was a tension in the air. There was a constant movement of troops and armor at night towards the Russian border. The formations were spread out in the country side but many officers made their appearance in the city. The Judenrat was constantly asked for more workers who were involved in building barracks, roads, tracks, and all kind of military emplacements.

Then the war started. The German armies attacked the Soviet Union across the entire frontier. The German panzers were cutting the Russian armies into pieces. Thousands of prisoners of war soon appeared on the roads leading west. Krosno also received several thousand starving Russian soldiers who were eventually sent to Szbnie where they were murdered. The German armies continued their advance. Nothing seemed to stop the German war machine. According to White, the Krosno air base was very active in supporting the German military drive. The German pilots described the bombings and strafing of Russian cities. Soon the rains started and converted the poor

Russian roads into quagmires of mud. Then the winter arrived and froze everything.

The German armies soon faced the bitter Russian winter and the battle-hardened Soviet soldiers. Germany did not provide the German soldiers with warm clothing to protect them from the cold Russian weather. The Gestapo was ordered to collect furs and woolen materials from all over Poland. The Krosno Judenrat was called to the Gestapo office and ordered to collect all furs, fur pieces, woolen items of clothing from the Jews of Krosno. The order was given that anyone disobeying the order would be shot. Becker shot a Jew for allegedly disobeying the order. He also killed Mrs. Furst in her kiosk for allegedly hiding a pair of gloves. Several Krosno Jews were shot by Gestapo men for supposedly withholding woolen goods. A wave of terror began with the collection of furs and woolens. Breitowicz stated in his book that the Gestapo men shot Tolba Pineles, daughter of the religious scribe Pineles, in front of him for wearing a coat with a fur collar.

Worse news was yet to arrive. On December 11, 1941, Germany declared war against the USA. The American Joint operations in Poland came to an official end. The Joint continued to support indirectly the J.S.S. organization in Poland through various illegal connections. But officially, the Joint had to stop all activities in Poland. The J.S.S. funds declined rapidly as did the funds of the Krosno Judenrat.

German photographers force Jews to pull the beard of the other Jew. The couple on the right side is that of Rabbi Shmuel Fuhrer on the left and Nussbaum on the right. We could not identify the couple on the left side. All Jews involved display their arm bands. The event took place in the center of town.

**A Krosner Jew with his
white armband in the
street of the city**

The area of the ghetto in Krosno

In May of 1942, the Gestapo ordered the creation of a ghetto in Krosno. The ghetto consisted of 4 to 5 houses and it had to absorb about 4,000 Jews. The ghetto extended from the Franciscane Street next to the Franciscan church to the Dym house. The Judenrat had to settle the Jews in the ghetto. The ghetto was terribly overcrowded and several families had to share a room. To leave the ghetto you needed special permission. Hunger, despair and hopelessness affected the Jews of Krosno. Some began to contact non–Jewish friends to seek shelter. Hiding Jews was very dangerous for both the Jew and the non–Jew. Some people saw an opportunity to make money and offered assistance only to denounce the family after they received the money. Still others built hiding places while some Jewish women tried to get so–called "Aryan' papers to be able to volunteer for work in Germany.

At the end of July, or possibly early August 1942 according to others, the Gestapo announced a plan of "resettlement" of the Jews of Krosno to the East. They initially requested a "kotribucja," a contribution of a large sum of money, and/or an equivalent amount of precious valuables in order to postpone the edict. The Judenrat scrambled to collect the money as best as possible in order to obtain a reprieve. After delivering the contribution, the resettlement was supposedly called off for the time being. This was a Gestapo scheme to extract money from the Jews.

The decision to resettle had nothing to do with the local Gestapo. The Reinhardt Operation that called for the elimination of the Jews proceeded in accordance with a master plan in great detail and did not allow for local commanders to play with time schedules. About a week later a final order from the Gestapo was received for every Jew to appear at 9 A.M. on Monday August 10, 1942, at the Targowica (a large plaza used as the cattle market) Square located near the railroad station on Koleiowa Street. Every person was limited to a 10 kilo suitcase. Everybody, regardless of age, gender or state of health, was to show up at the square. Anyone found hiding or disobeying the order would be shot on the spot.

White's description of the so–called resettlement operation: "Monday morning, the few thousand Jews made their way to the Targowica. A mass of wretched humanity with babies in their arms, in wheelchairs; some on stretchers were making their way as ordered. It was a very sad and depressing sight." Hivis (SS volunteers), mostly Ukrainian, were already there and cordoned off the Targowica Square with their machine guns aimed at us. Local Poles kept arriving at the periphery to observe this sad and horrible spectacle. Among them I recognized Mr. Bazentkiewicz, in whose building we had our "kitownia" (putty–making shop).

Was he there to see us being taken away and so he could take over the shop? Were the others there for a similar purpose — glad to see the Nazis take care of their "Jewish problem" and they take over their properties? Didn't the pre–war Polish foreign minister Josef Beck declare to the Polish parliament that Poland's problem was too many Jews? Didn't he try to get the French who ruled Madagascar to get Jews from Poland transferred there? Such thoughts entered my mind at that time. I preferred to give the onlookers the benefit of the doubt that they were there out of curiosity and maybe of concern as to what would happen to us and concern that they might be next.

There was also the Gestapo from Krosno, some from Jaslo, and some that I had never seen before. The Gestapo from the outside seemed mainly in charge. We were ordered to line up in rows of five. One SS–man who was unknown to me had a whip in his hand and ordered some of the assembled Jews to move out of the line to the far corner of the plaza.

They appeared to be the elderly, the handicapped, those in wheelchairs and stretchers. There was crying and wailing as some family members tried to join their loved ones in the corner but were beaten, whipped, and ordered to get back in line. One scene I remember was where a very pretty young girl from Lodz was stubbornly sticking to her mother in spite of being whipped mercilessly to turn back, but to no avail. There were a few trucks waiting on which they and the stubborn girl were forcibly loaded. The trucks were covered and SS men with machine guns got on top.

Soon two Jeeps with mounted machine guns and SS men in them stopped by the plaza and were dispatched by the SS–man with the whip pointing them to leave in a certain direction. A truck, with SA or sturm abtailung men, German Nazi para military organization, sitting on benches and holding shovels as if presenting arms, came by and was ordered to drive off in the same direction. Subsequently the trucks with the victims were ordered to leave in the same direction. The dispatched Jews appeared to me doomed. The SA men in the truck with their shovels were probably sent to bury the victims after the shooting by the machine gunners in the Jeeps.

German civilians and military officials, including an officer from the Krosno air base with some airmen, arrived with lists of their Jewish employees. The Jews working for them were released and allowed to march off to their jobs and thereafter to the ghetto or to barracks built for them at their workstations. Others working in the oil refinery and those working for other German outfits were released for work to their supervisors.

Then Gestapo man Stengler called out names. They were given blue identification cards and ordered to march back to the ghetto. The bulk of the people on the Targowica were marched later to the nearby railroad station. They were loaded into cattle cars. Each wagon contained 100 people. Even the Jewish prisoners at the Krosno jail were escorted to the train station. The train stood for hours at the station and finally left Krosno under SS guard. The head of the Judenrat of Krosno, Yehuda Engel and his family, was aboard the train.

The Jews transported by trucks were taken to the woods near Brzozow where they were shot. The train transport waited for hours without food or water before it left Krosno. It stopped again in Iwonicz–Zdroi where Dr. Baumring complained to the SS escort through the barbed wired small window of the wagon, begging to allow some water but instead was ordered out of the wagon and shot. There were no survivors from the transport. Considering the death of the "resettled" in Belzec via carbon monoxide (CO) gas from a Soviet diesel tank (cyanide had not been used yet), Dr. Baumring's death by shooting was a blessing. About 80–90 percent of the Krosno Jews perished during this first "resettlement" action.

All day of the action, the Germans searched the city for hidden Jews and shot them on the spot. Their bodies were scattered through the ghetto areas. Some eye witnesses stated that Rabbi Shmuel Fuhrer was amongst the killed Jews. Identification was difficult since many Jews were shot in the head. The same evening, a small ghetto that already existed for several weeks was sealed off from the rest of the city. Moshe Kleiner, who also resided in Germany, was appointed head of the new Judenrat.

The ghetto had between 300–600 Jews. Many Jews were hiding and the Gestapo knew it. Posters appeared stating that blue cards would be distributed to everyone who would appear at the office of the Judenrat. Some Jews came out of hiding and received the blue cards that would permit them to work. A short while later, similar posters appeared and hidden Jews appeared. The Gestapo rounded them up and then proceeded to arrest all the Jews who were just recently issued blue cards. Most of the men were sent to Szebnie camp and the rest to the ghetto of Rzeszow. It was now obvious that the Krosno ghetto was heading toward dissolution. On Friday, December 4th, 1942, the week of Chanukah, all Jews were ordered to appear at the milk and butter market of Krosno. The entire ghetto was surrounded by SS, Gestapo, and Ukrainian Hiwis – soldiers. Those who had working places were sent to the side where the military and civilian German officials took possession of their workers. The rest would be marched to the railway station where they would board a train for the ghetto of Rzeszow. Amongst them would be Rabbi Moshe Twerski with his family. While the selection took place, policemen searched the entire ghetto for hidden Jews. Most of them were shot on discovery. The search for Jews would continue in Krosno until mid–March 1943.

The remnants of the Krosno Jews were led to the railway station by brutal guards who did not hesitate to shoot stragglers. The column reached the train station and the Jews were pushed into cattle cars, with no standing or sitting room and no knowledge about the real destination of the train. Finally the train arrived at Rzeszow and the Jews were forced to march several kilometers to the ghetto.

The Krosner Jews in the ghetto of Rzeszow would slowly die of starvation or sickness, amongst them Rabbi Moshe Twerski. Most of the Krosner Jews would be sent to the Belzec death camp or Szebnie labor camp where they would be worked to near death and then sent to Auschwitz–Birkenau.

Some young Krosner Jews like Yaacov Breitowicz managed to survive all the labor and death camps and slowly resume life following liberation.

```
B R E I T O W I C Z    Jakob      306  708

    12.12.05        Krosno                        -

1.42 - 6.44        Gh.Krosno, Reichshof, Huta-
                   Komorska, Misloce
6.44 - 4.45        KZ Plaszow-Flossbg.

1.1.47      Cham/Opf.


URO Mü.
G/USA
```

He started in the ghetto of Krosno where he lived before the war. He was then sent to the ghetto of Rzeszow and then to Huta Komorska labor camp, a sub branch of the Plaszow labor camp. Later he was sent to Misloce labor camp. In June 1944 he arrived at the Plaszow concentration camp near Krakow. With the approach of the Russian army, he was sent to the Flossenberg concentration camp in Germany. He was liberated by the American army. January 1, 1947 we find him at the Cham D.P. in Germany.

Another survivor was Josef Lang, son of Chaim and Feige Reisel Lang, a native of Krosno. He was arrested by the Gestapo in June of 1940 and sent to a forced labor camp in Frysztak near Krosno where he remained until December 1940. He was then sent to Dukla where he worked until December 1942. He was then sent to Plaszow where he remained until January 1944. He was then sent to Skarzysko forced labor camp where he remained until November 1944. He was then sent to the concentration camp of Buchenwald where he remained three weeks and was transferred to Schlisban forced labor camp that was soon evacuated to the Theresienstadt concentration camp where he was liberated on May 5 1945 by the Russian army.

Josef Lang

```
                                          281 914

        L A N G        Josef
    28.11.17         Krosno/ Polen              —

    Am 1.1.47 ?
    6.40 - 12.40   ZAL. Prystak
    12.40 - 12.42    "  Dukla
    12.42 - 1.44   KZ. Plassow b/Krakau
    1.44 - 11.44   ZAL. Skarzysko Werk "C"
    11.44 3 Wochen KZ. Buchenwald Zig. Lg.
                          Gef. No. 67816

    12.44- Ende 4.45   ZAL. Schlieben
    4.45 - 5.5.45      KZ. Theresienstadt
```

Josef Lang's German war record card

Below is Dr. White's (formerly Bialywlos) index card during the war.

Alexander Bialywlos residing at 84 Ordinacka Street, Krosno. The index card is barely legible so we decided to print the context. The original text is in English since it was typed at the D.P. camp following the war

The Bialywlos family was in the glazing business. When the Germans entered Krosno, they used the facilities of the family to repair the broken car and truck windows. The store was soon "aryanized" or confiscated and given to a German who let the Bialywlos family work in the store. Business declined due to all the anti–Jewish regulations and Alexander and his father, Mendel Bialywlos, were soon forced to look for work.

Official index card relating to Alexander Bialywlos and his status

Alexander Bialywlos was a resident of the Landzberg D.P.
refugee camp. He applied for emigration to the USA

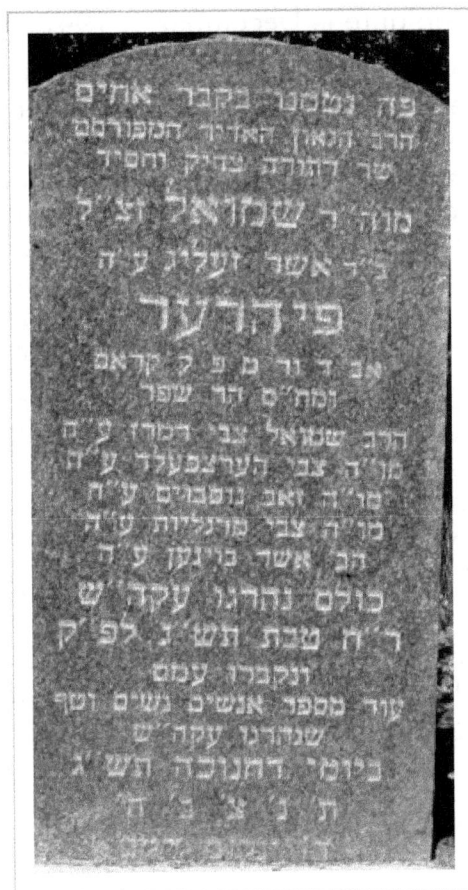

After the war a tombstone was erected in the memory of Rabbi Shmuel Fuhrer (above), other rabbis, and unnamed Jewish people. Here is buried in a brotherly grave the great scholar and saint Rabbi Shmuel Fuhrer, son of Rabbi Asher Zeelig Fuhrer, may he rest in peace. Rabbi Shmuel Fuhrer was the head of the Jewish religious court in Krosno and authored the scholarly book "Har Shefer."

Buried are also Rabbi Zwi Demrez, Rabbi Zwi Herzfeld, Rabbi Ze'ev Nussenbaum, and the son of Asher Bogen. All were killed as Jewish martyrs. May they all rest in peace.

Dated the first day of the Jewish month of Tevet, the year Tashag–or 5703. The exact conversion date is December 19, 1942. (The date is confusing since there were no longer Jews in Krosno at this date. According to some people, Rabbi Fuhrer was shot by Oscar Baecker during the round–up of Jews that took place on August 10, 1942. There seems to be another problem, namely Krosno had three rabbis: Rabbi Shmuel Fuhrer, Rabbi Moshe Twerski, and the so–called Reishpoler rabbi. The stone seems to refer to other rabbis of Krosno that we have not been able to substantiate. Buried with them were men, women, and children whose names are unknown. They were killed on the 4th day of the month, the first day of Hannukah in the year Tashag – or 5703. The exact conversion date is December 4, 1942.

They worked at various places until the the big selection in Krosno when most of the Jews were sent to the death camp of Belzec. They were assigned to work at the Krosno military air field. They worked at the base until January 1944. Alexander was then sent to the Szebnie labor camp. In March 12, 1944 he was transferred to the Plaszow concentration camp and attached to the Schndler compound. With the advance of the Soviet army, Plaszow was being dismantled and Alexander was sent to the Gross Rozen concentration camp on October 15, 1944. He was then sent to the Schindler camp at Brunlitz, Czechoslovakia where he was liberated by the Soviet army.

The German officials took their assigned workers and led them to their new quarters. The air force led their assigned workers to the base. Many saw the city for the last time. The city was not officially "Juden rein," or free of Jews. Of course, there were some hidden Jews namely Stefan Stiefel, Helena Stiefel, Pinkas Thaler and family, Stiebel and family, Lieber Wolf, Jozef Guzik, and a few Jewish children like Batia Akselrad, the daughter of Bendet Akselrad, and Benjamin Nussbaum.

The Jewish community of Krosno ceased to exist on December 4, 1942, during Chanukah, the festival of light and resistance. The relatively young Polish Jewish community was thus totally erased.

[Page 180]

Chapter VI
The Krosno Airfield

me-1963

The Jewish workers, amongst them Dr. White and his father Mendel Bialywloss, were escorted to the base. Some hidden Jews of Krosno attached themselves to the column and walked to the base without being hindered by the air force guards. The base was already surrounded by SS and Gestapo men who checked papers. They had a list of the authorized civilian workers at the base, especially the Jewish workers. The latter were ordered to appear at an assembly point. The SS then searched the entire base for hidden Jews and found them. All Jews were lined up and a selection took place. All sick people, children, women, and old people were shunted to one side. Now, the remainder of Jewish workers were checked against the official list. Only those that were on the list were permitted to stay at the base. The column of Jews that just arrived from the ghetto of Krosno was also selected. According to Dr. White, only about two dozen people who had the blue identification cards were permitted to stay and join the other 100 Jewish workers at the base. The rest of the Jews were forced to march to the railway station of Krosno, amongst them Yaacov Breitowicz and his six–year–old son Henek (Zvi) Breitowicz. The SS wanted Breitowicz to stay at the base without his son. The father refused. Both were ordered to join the column marching to the Krosno railway station where the train heading for the ghetto of Rzeszow was waiting for them.

The late Dr. Herbert (Zvi) Breite (formerly Breitowicz) a native of Krosno and a Shoah survivor. His father refused to part with him and both were sent to the ghetto of Rzeszow where most of the Jews of Krosno would perish

Dr. White was familiar with the base since he and his father glazed some of the buildings there. Batia Eisensenstein nee Akselradwas also familiar with the place seeing daily Jewish workers marching to and from the air base in the initial stage of the war, since there were no sleeping accommodations at the air base for civilians. She of course assumed that her brother was one of the laborers but she was not sure since she was afraid to get too close and have a look. Besides, there were always police guards walking alongside the column and it was very dangerous for her to expose herself and she knew the consequences of being caught as a Jew. So she observed the Jewish workers from a hidden distance. We decided to research the matter and below is the result of our work.

The Polish government decided to build a military airfield in 1932 on the outskirts of the city of Krosno, Galicia, Poland. The airfield construction took a number of years and gave an economic boost to the local economy. Local artisans and technicians, amongst them the Bialywloses who were glaziers, helped built the airfield under the overall supervision of the engineer Zalekowski. The airport was officially opened in 1938 with the arrival of the Polish air force cadets. They were previously stationed in Bydgoszcz in

Northern Poland. The cadets represented the cream of the Polish military youth and were highly nationalistic and tended to be anti–Semitic. Many of them were of German descent and some of them would later openly identify with Nazi Germany. As a matter of fact, one cadet named Peck would later open in Krosno the "Deutsches Geshaeft" store that would only sell goods to Germans during the occupation of Poland.

No Jews worked at the airport and the cadets had little if any contact with the Jewish population. The higher–ranking officers including the Jewish medical base officer lived in Krosno. The junior officers, the non-commissioned officers, and cadets lived at the base. On weekends some of them received liberty and came to the center of the city to let off some steam. They were often involved in brawls or fights with religious Jews who were going to or coming from the synagogues dressed in their Sabbath clothes, as happened to my maternal grandfather, Chaim Lang. We already described the incident in an earlier chapter

The tense international situation, especially in Eastern Europe, forced Poland to expand and enlarge the military defenses at the airfield of Krosno. These expansions were in full swing when the German air force bombed the Krosno airport in the early hours of September 1, 1939. The Luftwaffe also bombed the railway station, the refinery, the electric power station, and Stuka dive–bombers terrorized the industrial section of the city. The Polish anti-aircraft managed to down one German plane. The German air force returned the following days to continue to bomb and strafe everything that moved. The German armies soon rolled over Poland and reached the city and the airfield of Krosno on September 8, 1939. The German soldiers immediately began to loot stores, especially Jewish stores. Stores were forced to open and the German soldiers began to buy everything. They even asked the owners to wrap the packages and took them to the military post to be mailed home. Some paid with zlotys that they had in their pockets; the amount never reached the sum demanded. The storekeeper could protest but to no avail when facing armed soldiers. Other German soldiers paid in all kind of valueless promissory notes. The SS were of course the worst of the lot since they took items without even bothering to inform you that they took merchandise.

The German soldiers soon began to round up Jews for work details. Some of these details consisted of cleaning the streets while others consisted of clearing extensive bombing debris. Many Jews were immediately rounded up and marched to the airport to begin cleaning the place. The Germans did a very good job of bombing the airfield, so there was a great deal of work and there was a need for many hands. The work was extremely difficult and the pay hardly remunerative. The next day few Jews showed up for this work detail, which forced the Germans to seize people in the city and send them to the airport. They also rounded up Jews for clearing the debris at the bombed railway station, to clear the roads and fix damages, and to clear the bombed industrial sites.

Soon the SS and Gestapo took matters in hand. They ordered the Judenrat headed by Idel (Yehuda) Engel of Krosno to provide Jewish laborers for the airfield. Engel lived for many years in Germany and was expulsed from Germany following the order to send all Polish citizens back to Poland regardless of the number of years they lived in Germany. He spoke German fluently and was terrified of the new masters.

The number of workers increased daily since the Jews needed bread. Most of the Jewish stores were closed since they could not get supplies so they closed shop and started to look for work, preferably with German outfits that also provided security from street arrests. Jews worked at the refinery, at the railway, along the poorly maintained roads of Poland, and at the airfield. The German air force began to rebuild the entire airbase according to Yaakov Breitowicz, a survivor of the Shoah who worked at the base. According to him, the total number of Jewish workers at the airfield of Krosno reached its peak in December of 1942 when there were between 300–500 forced Jewish workers. Most of them were from Krosno or the surrounding vicinity. Some of them, like shia Wolf Zafern of Krosno, even smuggled their wives and children into the area of the airfield.

At first the Jews resisted the work details at the base because of the hard work and low pay but as time went by, the base became a desirable place for it offered the opportunity to buy food from the Polish or even German co-workers at the base and bring it home to starving family members. Most workers went home at the end of the workday. The base was relatively safe from the harassment that was a daily event in the city of Krosno. Air force personnel were by and large indifferent to the Jewish workers. The official designation of the base was "Fliegerhorstkommandantur Krosno, Fliegertechnischeschule 4, Luftgaukommando 8, Breslau."

The head of the base was Oberst, or Colonel, Hugo Giegold, who was appointed to this base on August 10, 1942. He was born September 6, 1893 in Schwartzenbach, Germany. He was a pilot and participated in World War One on the western front. Following the defeat of Germany, the air force was disbanded. With rise of Hitler, the Luftwaffe was restored and he rejoined the air force. Promotions came rapidly and by June 1, 1939 he reached the rank of Oberst. Oberst Hugo Giegold is appointed cammander of the Krosno air base the same day that the big "action" removes most of the Jews of Krosno.

Giegold's assistants are Major Hildebrand, Captain Hoelzl was the sport officer and very friendly to Jewish people. We must also mention Oberzahlmeister or assistant payroll officer Frankfurter who led the Jewish workers from the Targowice market place to the base. His immediate superior, Captain Pflauman dealt extensively with the head of the Jewish workers Langsam. These officers and enlisted men set the tone of the base and did not concern themselves with the Jewish or Polish workers as long as they did the work.

Of course the Polish workers were paid higher salaries than the Jewish workers who did the same work. All Jewish workers at the base were the property of the SS and the German air force paid each Jewish laborer a daily fee. The Gestapo and the SS on occasion visited the air base to check the people and the place. After these visits, the airfield returned to normal work routine.

There were Germans who sympathized with the plight of the Jews and even tried to help on occasion. According to Dr. White, a survivor of the air base, the "Zahlmeister" or paymaster Frankfurter was a real "mentsh" or human being when it came to Jews. During the first big selection of the Krosno Jews during the summer of 1942, he assembled all the Jewish workers of the base in Krosno and escorted them out of the city to the base. The SS and the Gestapo were not too happy with the base commander's attitude to his Jewish workers but he apparently had the backing of the air force to continue with his work. Indeed the Krosno airfield became an important air base where all types of planes took off and landed at all times according to Batia Eisenstein, nee Akselrad who lived in proximity of the airfield. She was certain that her brother Awraham worked at the airbase but had no proof.

The airfield played an important role in the attack on Russia on June 21st 1941, since it was very close to the Russian border. The fighting role diminished as the Wehrmacht advanced into Russia and the distances became longer by the day. The airfield operated around the clock during the initial weeks of the war against Russia according to Batia. Planes constantly flew over their house to and from the airport. The Jewish workers went back and forth daily to their homes in Krosno. They worked alongside Polish salaried workers and German air force technicians. These daily contacts enabled the exchange of goods among the workers. The Jewish workers traded everything for food that was scarce in the city. The SS and Gestapo were starving the Jewish population. So the food that was smuggled into the city was a blessing for the Jewish population. The air force police at the base was rather lax and permitted the trade. Occasionally the Gestapo and the SS searched the workers and found food that resulted in severe punishments, but the necessity of food overrode all regulations and dangers.

The situation changed radically when posters were plastered throughout Krosno that ordered all Jews to report on August 10th 1942, to the Targowa square (old cattle market) with small suitcases. Most of the Jews including those that were just expulsed from nearby villages, appeared at the indicated place. Here the selection began. All people who worked for German firms and had permits were pushed to the side. The old, feeble, and sick were taken to a nearby forest and shot. Some young and strong people were also pushed to the side. The rest of the crowd was pushed into an awaiting train that will head to the death camp of Belzec. The transport will include the head of the Judenrat, Yehuda Engel. According to Dr.White, about 80% of the Jewish population of Krosno was on that train. There would be no survivors of this transport. Throughout the day, the Germans searched for hidden Jews and on discovery shot them. The survivors of the selection were then escorted to a small–enclosed ghetto. Then Frankfurter came and escorted the Jewish workers to the air base.

The base commander kept his usual quota of Jewish workers despite the fact that the activities of the air base steadily declined, for the front lines were far away in Russia. The SS was anxious to get rid of all the Jews at the base, but the air force prevailed and kept all the Jewish workers and some of the women and children. Occasionally the SS raided the base but the pickings were small. Then the ghetto of Krosno was ordered closed on December 4th 1942. All the Jews in the ghetto of Krosno were marched to the railway station where a train consisting of cattle cars awaited them to ship them to the ghetto of Rzeszow ("Reishe" in Yiddish) except for essential skilled workers who were issued special passes and escorted to their places of work. They would no longer return to the ghetto that was officially closed.

The Gestapo and SS men began to search for hidden Jews and shot them on discovery. 24 Jews were assigned to the air base among them Alexander Bialywlos. Mendel Bialywlos, Zalman Beim, and his son Zishe Beim. They were immediately taken to their place of work at the air base According to Zishe Beim, the airfield was extensively enlarged and handled many planes. Simultaneously with the final action in the city of Krosno, another selection was taken place at the airfield. The entire air base was thoroughly searched by the SS and they permitted only 100 Jewish workers to remain at the base. The rest of the Jewish workers were all marched to the railway station in Krosno where the transport for the ghetto of Rzeszow awaited them. The horrible trip is still vividly remembered by Dr. Herbert Breite (formerly Henek Breitowicz) who was then six–and–a–half years old. The train was crowded, standing room only, some people were dying or dead, and everybody feared the destination. According toDr.White, 124 Jewish workers remained at the base; some of them were Krosner Jews, the last remnants of the Jews of Krosno. The city was now " Judenrein" except for a few hidden Jews like the Akselrads, or Pinhas Thaler.

The 100 Jewish workers at the base were reinforced by the contingent of 24 Jewish workers from the Krosno ghetto. The entire Jewish force of 124 workers was headed by Langsam, a Jew from Gorlice, Galicia. The force continued to work and live at the base. They were fed and treated fairly well in view of the general Jewish situation in German occupied areas. One Jewish worker named Frauwirth from Krosno died at the base after a prolonged disease and was buried at the Jewish cemetery of Krosno by his brother.

Two Jewish workers named Zishe Beim and his cousin Dolek Beim broke out of the enclosed camp and headed to the area of the ghetto of Krosno. The father of Zishe Beim, Zalman Beim was a religious person and very involved in community affairs. He was a member of the Krosner "Hevrah Kadisha" or burial society. He knew that that the "shochet" or ritual slaughterer and "dayan" or religious judge Klagsbald and his family was hidden in a bunker. Zalman Beim did not see them during the second and final round–up of Jews in Krosno. He therefore assumed that they were still in the hidden and now deserted place. Thus the request to his son to help the Klagsbald family.

The two boys left the camp, cut the barbed wires that circled the base, and headed to the ghetto area in Krosno. They reached the area and started to search for the bunker, and at last they found it. They tapped on the door and it opened. They decided to take Klagsbald, his wife, and three children to the air base for the ghetto was now deserted. They started to walk and re–entered the base where they had cut the wires. The family was hidden and the cousins of course presented themselves at their work posts on time. The Gestapo later discovered the family, since they did not appear on the list of authorized workers and removed them from the base. All these activities were hushed up for there were no reprisals.

The Jewish laborers hoped to survive the war since they knew the military situation by reading the German newspapers and listening to the base radio. The Soviet armies defended Stalingrad with determination, the Allies were in North Africa and the hopes of the Jewish workers became a bit brighter.

According to Dr. White, the Jewish workers at the base were treated correctly and were provided with ample food. The tone of the base was one of tolerance when all around madness seemed to prevail. The Oberst was even brought before a military tribunal for his accepting an invitation to participate at a party given by a Polish countess Lesikowska on October 10, 1943. The Oberst was penalized for accepting the invitation and for participating at the party. He did not consider his action detrimental to Germany. On the contrary, he showed a deep respect for people and treated them as people.

The airport activities began to increase as the German armies began to retreat. Dr. White saw Messerschmitt fighter planes, the famous Me–109, Dormier bombers, and Heinkel planes on the strips of the airport. The Germans also expanded the anti–aircraft defense forces at the base.

As the year progressed, the front moved closer to Krosno. Of course the German press constantly talked of retrenchments, but in reality the German army retreated and the Krosno airbase was busier than ever. Then in December 1943 or January 1944, the commander of the base, Colonel Giegold and his entire staff as well as his entire air formation were transferred. Another air force unit and 400 Russian Uzbeck prisoners of war arrived to provide labor. The SS jumped at this opportunity and rounded up all Jewish workers and sent them to the Szebnie concentration camp. The camp was officially closed but there were still a few Jews left who were dismantling the camp. The work lasted several weeks and the Jewish workers of the air base of Krosno were sent to the Plaszow concentration camp near Krakow, Poland.

The Krosno airfield following the war. We see Doctor Herbert Breite, formerly Herbert Breitowicz, a survivor of the airport visiting the place. Dr. Breite spent many a day roaming around the base where his father was forced to work. Then the family was rounded up and shipped to the Rzeszow Ghetto in December of 1942, with many other Jewish workers

Jews of Krosno who worked at the Krosno air base:

Abrahamson, Szymek n the son of Berish Abrahamson
Amsterdam
Beim Zalman
Beim Zishe still alive in Haifa, son of Zalman
Beim, Joseph in NJ.
Beims Yankele (Jack) living in CA
Beim, Dolek
Bialywlos, Mendel
Bialywloss Alexander (son of Mendel, presently Dr. White)
Breitowicz Abraham with family
Breitowicz, Yaakov,
Breitowicz, Henek (son of Yaakov, presently Dr. Herbert Breite)
Frauwirth, died at the base
Frauwirth brother of above
Grayower, Sonia
Gross Oscar
Klaksbald and family

Langsam from Gorlice was in charge of Jewish workers at the base
Mahler, Moses
Mahler, Raphael
Polaner, Moshe (Heller)
Polaner, Rachel wife of Moshe Polaner
Spitz brothers,
Taubenfeld with his son,
Trenczer Shiek,
Trenczer Yosek
Weinfelds from Gorlice.
Zafern, Shia Wolf with his wife and children

Many of the Jewish workers at the base survived the war due to the relative decent living condition that the base headed by Oberst Giegold provided to all the workers.

[Page 193]

Chapter VII
The End of the War

On September 11, 1944 the Russian army liberated the city of Krosno. The city was seriously affected by the war, notably the industry and the airfield. Slowly the few hidden Jews in Krosno began to emerge. Slowly and fearfully they began to appear in the streets. They were soon joined by Jews that survived in the countryside of Krosno. Their numbers were abysmally small in comparison to the pre–war Jewish population of Krosno. Of the estimated 3.3 million Jews who lived in Poland when the Nazis invaded on September 1, 1939, only 42,662 Jews remained by May 1945. Soon starving survivors from the labor camps and concentrations camps returned home and increased the number of Jews to 80,000. By January 1946 the numbers increased to 106,492 with the discharge of Jewish soldiers from the Polish and Russian armies. By all accounts the number of surviving Jews in Poland was minute and Krosno was no exception. Many Jewish camp survivors did not return to Poland, not even for a visit. They said goodbye to their native country from a distance.

Some Krosner Jews came back, visited the city and then left. The city was strange to them and the faces were unfamiliar. It seemed to the returnees that this was not their Krosno. Their families were gone, their homes occupied by Poles, and their businesses destroyed. The returnees would have to start from scratch, and many decided against it. They packed their few belongings and decided to leave Krosno for the big cities or to leave Poland altogether. Other Jews decided to stay in Krosno and even established a Jewish community committee to help the returnees settle in the city.

Members of the Jewish community in Krosno following World War II

The lists are difficult to read so we decided to rewrite them. We have two pages of names that follow the original name sheets. The second page has the official stamp of the Jewish committee of Krosno.

Last name	First name	Birth year	Place	Last name	First name	Birth year	Place
Koenig	Helena	1910	Krosno	Landsberger	Isydor	1885	Krosno
Koenig	Ruta	1937	Krosno	Fries	Zofia	1921	Krosno
Sternbach	Zofia	1910	Krosno	Lipiner	Israel	1890	Zrecin
Pferferbaum	Jan	1937	Krosno	Lipiner	Helena	1900	Zrecin
Pferferbaum	Manes	1903	Krosno	Lipiner	Estera	1923	Zrecin
Pferferbaum	Fani	1917	Krosno	Lipiner	Sonia	1935	Zrecin
Maisels	Hela	1906	Krosno	Morgenstern	Chaskel	1901	Zrecin
Maisels	Fela	1914	Krosno	Brozinska	Irena	1918	Zrecin
Trynopolski	Jozef	1909	Krosno	Bergman	Awraham	1927	Zrecin
Schwebel	Alter–Aron	1887	Krosno	Schenker	Regina	1908	Zrecin
Schwebel	Anna	188	Krosno	Grunspan	Herman	1899	Zrecin
Schwebel	Mendel	1922	Krosno	Fessel	Pinkas	1907	Zegwice
Schwebel	Brononia	1924	Krosno	Bigayer	Awraham	1892	Zegwice
Schwebel	Chaja	1924	Krosno	Bigayer	Regina	1888	Jedlice
Taller	Pinkas	1928	Krosno	Emer	Genia	1908	Jedlice
Engel	Jozef	1921	Krosno	Emer	Alfred	1930	Jedlice
Grunspan	Donia	1920	Krosno	Neuman	Menashe	1908	Jedlice
Rabi	Klara	1922	Krosno	Schenker	Rosa	1920	Jedlice
Gelb	Dora	1922	Krosno	Riess	Jozef	1898	Jedlice
Grunspan	Awraham	1921	Krosno	Riess	Mala	1930	Jedlice
Kalb	Mania	1906	Krosno	Riess	Regina	1915	Jedlice
Kalb	Osina	1936	Krosno	Feld	Osias	1926	Jedlice
Bergman	Dawid	1907	Krosno	Feld	Menasche	1927	Jedlice
Bergman	Saul	1910	Krosno	Feld	Sonia	1938	Jedlice
Bergman	Osias	1908	Krosno	Denholtz	Dawid	1908	Jedlice
Bergman	Rubin	1919	Krosno	Denholtz	Poldek	1926	Jedlice
Bergman	Markus	1916	Krosno	Denholtz	Lola	1922	Jedlice
Bergman	Lazar	1907	Krosno	Lerman	Eljas	1896	Jedlice

Schachner	Stanislaw	1908	Krosno	Lerman	Leona	1902	Jedlice
Schachner	Hela	1918	Krosno	Lerman	Bronia	1922	Jedlice
Schachner	Moniek	1936	Krosno	Lerman	Salomon	1928	Jedlice
Elowitz	Samuel	1878	Krosno	Ber	Estera	1893	Jedlice
Stiefel	Samuel	1878	Krosno	Ber	Jakub	1905	Jedlice
Stiefel	Hela	1912	Krosno	Denholtz	Gehardt	1906	Jedlice
Katz	Hela	1917	Krosno	Turk	Herman	1918	Jedlice
Lieber	Wolf	1900	Krosno	Turk	Dawid	1906	Jedlice
Engelhard	Iza	1901	Krosno	Kimel	Dawid	1896	Jedlice
Schiff	Pinkas	1901	Krosno	Kimel	Esla	1920	Jedlice
Schiff	Necha	1888	Krosno	Unger	Lea	1912	Jedlice
Schiff	Josef	1928	Krosno	Unger	Samuel	1929	Jedlice
Schiff	Rozia	1925	Krosno	Unger	Inis	1928	Jedlice
Kuflick	Rpsa	1916	Krosno	Roth	Alter	1902	Jedlice
Keller	Markus	1912	Krosno	Lacher	Lea	1899	Jedlice
Keller	Chune	1919	Krosno	Lacher	Leon	1929	Jedlice
Spira	Ida	1913	Krosno	Fels	Sara	1891	Jedlice
Spira	Mania	1938	Krosno	Fels	Chana	1925	Jedlice
Spira	Meilech Her	1919	Krosno	Hiller	Samuel	1942	Jedlice
Guzik	Szyja	1903	Krosno	Schenbach	Ricchard	1909	Krosno
Guzik	Jozef	1909	Krosno	Stern	Cesia	1915	Krosno
Linsker	Sara	1908	Krosno				
Rosenthal	Nuchim	1910	Krosno				
Trum	Jakub	1925	Krosno				
Tenzer	Leib	1910	Krosno				
Ehrenreich	Wolf	1914	Dukla				

We copied the names as they were written with their mistakes. We notice that the list contained many Jews who were not native of Krosno but settled in the city following World War II to increase their personal security. The hamlets were near Krosno.

On May 15, 1945, the Jewish committee of Krosno also submitted a list of officers who were elected to represent the community. Their names and titles are as follows:

President Schachner,

1.   Stanislaw Guzik, Vice–president, University graduate

2.   Josef Helena Stein Secretary, University graduate

3.   Stein, Helena Secretary, University graduate

4.   Helena Katz Treasurer

5.   Wolf Lieber, Member of the board

All members are residents of the city of Krosno. Notice the community stamp and the official notations of the city of Krosno.

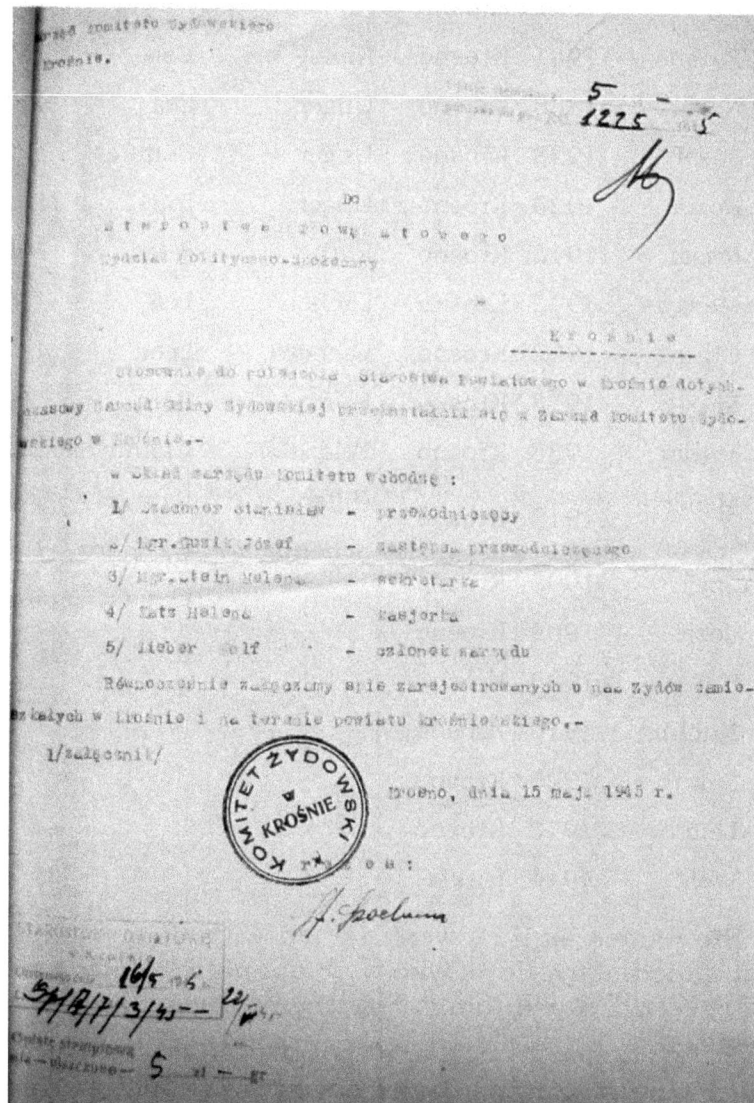

Official letter to the mayor of Krosno.

The Soviet–established Polish government steadily strengthened the Polish Communist party in its quest for total power. These moves were strongly opposed by the Polish nationalist forces that were well organized. Soon armed clashes took place between these two forces. The nationalist forces considered the Polish Jews outsiders and barely tolerated them. Their hatred of the Jews increased with the appointments of Jewish ministers like **Jakub Berman** and **Hilary Minc** to important cabinet posts.

A rare event in Poland between the wars was the appointment of a Jewish official to a high position in the government. This policy changed after the war. There were some Jewish ministers and high officials in the administration. Attacks against Jews began to take place in the countryside that was controlled by the nationalist forces. In September of 1945, a pogrom against Jews took place in Krakow, Galicia. Anti–Jewish incidents multiplied across Poland, their intensity increasing as Polish citizens began to return from the Soviet Union.

The first transports were primarily Polish farmers and skilled workers where the number of Jews was relatively small. As the transports kept coming, the percentage of Jews increased substantially. By July 1946, with the massive arrival of repatriated Polish Jews from the Soviet Union, the number of Jews in Poland swelled to 240,489. Most of the recent arrivals were sent to the new Polish areas where there were plenty of apartments and jobs. The German residents of these areas were forced to leave Poland. Large Jewish communities began to appear, namely Wroclaw (Breslau) and Walbrzych (Waldenburg), among others.

The Polish government and the American Joint helped the returnees settle, but the Polish countryside continued the fight against the Government and the Polish Jews. The height of the campaign reached the city of Kielce where 41 Jews and four Poles were killed on July 4, 1946[1].

The news of the pogrom made headlines across the world and forced the Polish government to take action. The Polish government was sympathetic and understood the plight of the Jews, but it was powerless to restore order and also did not want to be too closely allied with the Jews. The Polish government decided to let the Jews leave Poland, regardless of internal or external consequences. The Polish government was primarily concerned with its own existence. The Assistant Minister of Defense of Poland, **Marshal Marian Spychalski**, was ordered to conduct secret negotiations with Itzhak or **Antek Tzuckerman**, one of the leaders of the Jewish ghetto uprising in Warsaw in 1943 and presently a member of the Central Committee of Polish Jews in Poland. They worked out a secret agreement whereby only Jews would leave Poland. No gold or foreign currency was permitted to leave the country, and all transportation arrangements were the responsibility of the Polish Brichah. All medical and special problems were to be handled by the Polish Brichah. The Polish government and the Polish official institutions were not officially involved in the Jewish exodus. Last but not least, no individual papers would be needed to leave Poland. The agreement was to commence on July 27, 1946, and end about February 1947. The agreement was secret and applied to the Polish–Czech borders.

The mass grave at Kielce, Poland following the pogrom. Under the pretext that a Christian child was kidnapped by Jews for ritual purposes, the Poles attacked the surviving Jews of Kielce. The fact that Polish security and police forces joined the mob sent alarm warnings to all Jews of Poland. Jews began to worry about their safety.

In 1945, about 5,000 Polish Jews left Poland and crossed illegally to Czechoslovakia. The stream became stronger and in May of 1946, 3,052 Polish Jews entered Czechoslovakia. The number jumped to 8,000 in June. After the pogrom in Kielce, the tide turned to an avalanche. 19,000 Jews left Poland in July; 35,346 in August; and 12,379 in September of 1946. During 5 months, 77,700 Polish Jews left Poland and crossed the border at Nachod in Czechoslovakia. This was a major crossing point, but Jews crossed the border at several border points. According to American Joint records, it is estimated that 90,000 Jews left Poland in 1946. Fear struck the Jews and they decided to pack and seek safety. The Polish countryside was losing the Jews who headed to the various crossing points along the long Polish–Czech border. The main crossing points were at Kladzko, Walbrzych, Wroclaw, Krosno and Sanok.

Crossing points of the Brichah at Krosno and Sanok, Poland to Slovakia, Subcarpathis and Romania.

The old Brichah road that went from Rowno through Czernowitz, Soviet Union, was closed with the arrest of the Brichah leaders.. The Brichah leader, Abba Kovner, ordered 3 of his assistants to explore a new route that led to Romania[1]. He selected Velvele Rabinowitz from Wilno as head of the group and send them to Krosno, across the Carpathian Mountains to Humene, Slovakia, Chust in Subcarpathia and Sato Mare in Romania[2].The group reached Bucharest and met Moshe Auerbach, chief of the Brichah in Romania. Rabinowicz returned to Krakow, Poland and reported to the Brichah that the route was now open for Polish Jews to head to Romania and eventually to Palestine. Mordechai Rosman head of the Polish Brichah decided to open permanent bases for Jews, crossing the border at Rzszow and at Tarnow in Galicia. From there small groups would proceed to Krosno or Sanok where they would rest and then proceed cross the border to Slovakia where the Slovakian Brichah would take over.

---

[1] Bauer, Flight, p.28

לופם אפרים ושימה

לב פיטה

A group of Polish Brichah agents, amongst them Moshe Meiri or better known as Ben. He is at the right corner at the bottom of the picture.

The Krosno Brichah station was headed by Ben or Moshe Meiri[3].

Ben proceeded to Krosno and organized a base where the Brichah brought small groups of Jews that were about to cross the Carpathian Mountaines. They had to rest, stock up on food and prepare for as long trip over the mountains. The Krosno station grew in importance as the number of Jewish refugees increased. The Krosno Brichah station would soon decline in importance as the crossing points shifted West.
The road changed in a Westerly direction since the Romanian authorities closed the Constanta port facilitirs to the Brichah.So there was no point in sending Jewish refugees to Romania. Instead, the refugees were sent to Czechoslovakia and then to Germany and Austria where they entered the D.P. camps mainly in the American zones.Still, individual Jews who ventured into the Polish countryside took their lives in their hands as the tombstone above shows. Jews continued to live in the big cities like Krakow, Warsaw, Lodz, and Wroclaw.

[2] Bauer, Flight, p.28

Brichah agents in Krosno; from right to left; Sarah Pressman, Lena Hemel, Stefan Grajek, Vi Feishter and a police official. The city of Krosno was located near the Polish-Czechoslovakian (presently Slovakian) border. The Brichah would bring groups of Jews that wanted to go to Palestine. In Krosno they received their final directions and instructions before they set out.

Yechiel Proper, the son of Arieh Proper of Sanok. This important and kind man was murdered by blood–thirsty killers on the 8th day of the Jewish month of Elul in the year Tashav or 5706. [August 17, 1945]

With the liberation of the city of Krosno, some Jewish survivors began to appear, amongst them **Salek Berger**, a native of Krosno, who survived the war in Eastern Ukraine and with the liberation of the area was drafted into the Polish Army. He fought the Germans and was discharged at the end of the war. He returned to Krosno but decided not to stay in the city. Berger joined the local "Brichah" and led transports of Jews across the Polish–Czech border in the area of Krosno where he knew the paths. According to Berger: the "Brichah" was a secret organization dedicated to send all Jews of Eastern Europe to Palestine. The work was difficult, dangerous and illegal.

The members of the organization were ex–partisans, camp survivors, discharged soldiers from the Jewish brigade and discharged soldiers from the Polish and Russian armies like Berger himself. He remained with the organization for some time and then was replaced by another volunteer. Berger himself was sent to one of the D.P. camps in Italy where he remained for several years. He eventually reached the USA.

The Brichah was very active and thousands of Jews were escorted across the Czech-Polish borders. Entire Polish regions became devoid of Jews. The repatriation of Polish citizens from the Soviet Union became a tricle. Individual Jews still faced grave dangers heading to the Polish-Czech borders as the tombstone indicates.

The number of Jews crossing the borders decreased steadily as the number of Jews declined drastically in Poland. With the end of the Spichalsky-Tzuckerman agreement, the Polish government closed all borders but continued to grant exit visas to Jews wanting to leave the country. The Polish Brichah organization slowly dismantled the organization in Poland as the government tightened control of the borders. The Krosno office was closed, the officials left the city, and all the Krosno Jews were gone. A community of about 3,000 Jews disappeared within such a short period of time. Thus ended Krosno's Jewish history.

May they rest peacefully wherever they rest.

[Page 214]

Chapter VIII
Krosner Jews in the World

Many Krosner Jews reached the German and Austrian D.P. camps in the American zones of occupation. They formed small cells of former natives of Krosno and vicinity. They memorialized the day of the Krosno selection and comforted each other through this difficult period in their lives. Most of them wanted to go to Palestine but the British would not let them go there. Some wanted to go to the USA but the doors were closed. So the refugees sat in the D.P, hoping to leave Germany and Austria. Many of them joined the illegal ships like the "Exodus" and tried to reach the shores of Palestine.

The American landesmanschften of Krosno–Jedlicz was very active on behalf of the Krosner Jews who were locked in the D.P.camps. They organized financial aid, food packages and medical supplies for the Krosner and Jedliczer Jewish refugees.

Krosno– Korczyna Landesmanschaften in the Holy Land

The Krosno– Korczyna society was also active on behalf of their landsman. They helped the needy refugees that came to the country. They also provided guidance and help to the newcomers to the country. The Palestinian organization worked closely with the American office in coordinating some assistance projects. There were other former Krosner cells in the free world. All of these groups kept in touch with each other and tried to provide some help to the needy Jews of Krosno.

Below is a list of members that the late Baruch Munz, a native of Krosno, secretary of the Israeli landesmanschaften provided us with.

Names of Jewish survivors who signed up for membership in the Krosno–Jedlicz society in Israel following World War II. The list also includes Jews from Korczyna and the surrounding area. Baruch Munz who was the secretary of the society was kind enough to provide us with the list of members. The names were written in Yiddish letters that makes it difficult to transfer them to the Latin alphabet. Please excuse any misspellings or distortions of the names. The list does not record Krosno survivors in Israel who were not members of the society.

AHERNBERG	Pinhas
AKERMAN	Rivka
AKSELRAD	Wolf
AKSELRAD	Yaacov
AKSELRAD	Yossef
ALENBERG	Leora
ALTBACH	
ALTER	Yehoshua
AMIDROR	Arie nee Teplitzki
AMIDROR	Tzila
AMIR	Israel nee Spitz
ATLAS	Aron
BART	Genia nee Oling
BART	Yaacov
BECK	Mania nee Flapan
BEIL	Avraham
BELLER	Henoch
BELZER	Nathan
BELZES	Gite nee Stessel
BEN MENACHEM	Itzhak nee Gross
BER	Avraham
BERG	Eliyahu nee Montag
BERGER	Benyamin
BERGER	Malka
BILBERG	Yaacov
BLICHFELD	Mrs
BOBKER	Hirsh
BOBKER	Yehezkel
BORENSTEIN	Arieh
BRAND	Herman
BRAND	Mania

BRAND	Menahem
BRAND	Tzvi
BRUDER	Pinhas
BUKSBAUM	Rachel nee Zeller
BUKSBAUM	Shia
BUTNER	Benyamin
DAN	Idel
DAVID	Mrs
DIM	Mrs
DOLONSKI	nee Freund
DOMINITZ	Lea
DORF	David
DRENGER	Hava
EHRENREICH	Leib
EHRENREICH	Yehezkel
EICHENHORN	Zishe
EISEN	Yaacov
EISENBERG	Gershon
EISENSTEIN	Berta nee Akselrad
ELLOWICZ	Elhanan
ELLOWICZ	Eliezer
ELLOWICZ	Esther
ENGEL	Yehoshua
ENGEL	Hannah nee Plant
ENGELHARD	Yossef
ENGELHARD	Shlomo
ERRENREICH	Lea nee Wolf
ERRENREICH	Yehiel
FARBER	David
PRESSER	Moshe
PRESSER	Pinhas
FARBER	

FEBER	Eric
FERNHAL	Fella nee Dim
FESSEL	Elimelech
FESSEL	Moshe
FESSEL	Yaacov Itzhak
FESSEL	Yeshiahu
FINK	Yossef
FINMAN	Esther
FISHEL	Shimon
FOGEL	Hanna
FOGEL	Nachman
FOGEL	Shlomo
FRANK	Rivka
FREUND	Hava
FREUND	Naftali
FREUND	Shlomo
FREUND	Shmuel
FRIEDMAN	Avraham
FRISHMAN	Eti nee Keren
FRISHTIK	
FUHRER	Ben Zion rabbi
GEBLINGER	Tzvi
GELLER	Mrs
GERTNER	Moritza
GERTNER	Zalman
GINT–LEWINSKI	
GLEICHER	Mrs nee Shoenfeld
GOLDBERG	Itzhak
GOLDBERG	Merom
GOLDHERZ	Anne
GOLDMAN	S.
GOLOSHITZ	David

GORDON	Malka nee Weissman
GREEN	Yaacov
GREEN	Hanoch
GREENBAUM	Henka nee Zuckerman
GREENBAUM	Kalman
GROSS	Haim Itzhak
GUTWEIN	Meir
HAK	Moshe
HALPERON	Shniwitz
HEFFNER	Atara
HEILER	Alcie nee Shtiefel Sala
HEITLER	Zishe
HEITLER	Zoshe nee Dom
HELPER	Zeev
HERBLOCK	Eliezer
HERBSTMAN	Shlomo
HERBSTMAN	Shlomo
HERBSTMAN	Yaacov
HERBSTMAN	Yaacov
HERZLOCK	D.
HIRSHFELD	Shmuel
HIRSHFIELD	Buki
HIRSHPRINGER	Leon
HOLLOSCHUETZ	Yochewed
HOLLOSCHUETZ	David
HOLLOSCHUETZ	Gutwein
HOLLOSCHUETZ	Menahem
HOROWITZ	Michael
HOROWITZ	Shlomo
HOROWITZ	Yehiel
IKONIT	Miriam
JAKUBOWICZ	Mirian

KANNER	Meir
KANNER	Mordechai
KANNER	Yehuda
KARMI	Itzhak
KATZ	Nafthali
KATZ	Nahum
KATZ	Nissan
KATZ	Yehoshua
KATZ	Yosef
KAUFMAN	Shmuel
KIMEL	Avraham
KINDERMAN	Aron
KINDERMAN	Menahem
KIZELSTEIN	Menahem
KLAGSBALD	Moshe
KLAGSBALD	Yehezkel
KLEINMAN	Tzvi
KLEINMAN	Yaacov
KOLANDER	Rivka nee Freund
KONRAD	Helena
KRIGER	Michael
KRILL	Lea nee Bilberg
KRILL	Yanka
KRILL	Shlomo
KUFLICK	Arieh
KUFLICK	Leib
LANDAU	Yaacov
LANDSTEIN	Risha nee Freund
LANG	Avraham
LANG	Yossef
LAUFER	Frida
LEIZER	Yehiel

LEMPEL	Dr.
LEVANINI	Zeev
LIEBER	A.
LIEBSKIND	Maximilian
LIPINER	A.
LIPSHITZ	Yochewed nee Freund
LUZER	Yona
MALTZ	Ellen
MALTZ	Mordechai
MARGOLIS	Ella nee Holoshitz
MARGOLIS	Itzhak
MARGOLIS	Michal
MARGOLIS	Moshe
MARGOLIS	Moshe
MARGOLIS	Yaacov
MARGOLIS	Yossef
MARKUS	Tircza
MAYEROWICZ	Lea
MAYEROWICZ	Tzvi
MAYEROWITZ	Lena
MEISELS	Gila
MELAMED	David
MELBAUER	
MELLER	Hanoch
MENDEL	Pinhas
MENDELOWICZ	
MILLER	Hess
MINSTER	Dina nee Kleinman
MINSTER	Shmuel
MONTAG	Moshe
MONTAG	Yosef
MUNTZ	Avraham

MUNTZ	Baruch
NACHTIGAL	Elisheva nee Weissman
NACHTINGAL	David Dr.
NAGEL	Sima
NEIMAN	
NEISS	Shalom
NEUMAN	Menahem
NEUMARK	Rachel
NOBERT	Dov
NORD	Itzhak
NOVEMBER	Menahem
NUSSBAUM	A
NUSSBAUM	Yaacov
OFNER	Atara
ORENSTEIN	L.
ORGLER	Luba nee Kanner
OSTROWSKA	Yedwabna
PACHER	Leibish
PALANT	Avraham Dr.
PALANT	Israel
PALANT	Sabina
PALANT	Shlomo
PATAWY	Yossef
PARNESS	Yaacov
PECKER	Meir
PERLBERG	Malka
PILHARD	Hanoch
PILHARD	Zalman
PINKAS	Malka
PINKUS	Moshe
PIWIRT	Zelig
PLATNER	Avraham

PLETZEL	Binyamin
PLETZEL	Peshe
POLANSKI	Shoshana nee Fuerst
PREUSS	Menahem
PREUSS	Bronia
PREUSS	Mendel
RAB	Mrs.
RAND	Moshe nee Platner
RAUCH	Hella nee Engelhard
REICH	Yehezkel
REICHMAN	Ruzie
RINGEL	Hinda
RITTER	Heika nee Breitowicz
ROSNER	Reuven
ROSNER	Meir
ROSNER	Moshe
ROSNER	Reuven
ROSNER	Yehoshua
ROTH	Debka nee Margolis
ROTH	Pitha
RUBHEIZER	Rivka
RUBIN	Rivka
RUBIN	Shmuel
RUBIN	Shmuel
SCHAHAR	Itzhak
SCHAMROT	Reuven
SCHILER	Itzhak
SCHIRTZ	Mendel
SCHLANGER	Nathan
SCHPILER	Zelig Dr.
SCHPRINGER	Leon
SCHTERN	Esther nee Bobker

SHAHAR	Yaacov
SHAVIT	Yair nee Beim Zishe
SHPIGELMAN	Safran
SPITZ	
STAWY	Yossef
TABIZEL	Avraham
TABIZEL	Meir
TEPLICKI	Abraham
TEPLICKI	Cesia
THALER	Pinhas
THALER	Hava
TITOV	Genia
TRENCZER	Dwora
TRENCZER	Markus
TRENCZER	Moshe
TRENCZER	Yeshayahu
TZIPORI	Naphtali
UNGER	Leib
UNGER	Malka
URLBAUM	David
URLBAUM	Yehoshua
WALD	Merom
WALLACH	Aron
WALTER	
WEINBERGER	Ephraim
WEINKRANTZ	Rachel nee Kanner
WEINMAN	Hanna nee Taubenfeld
WEINSTEIN	Gershon
WEINSTEIN	Itzhak
WEISMAN	Itzhak
WEISS	Sara nee Green
WEISS	Sarah

WEISSMAN	Hava
WEISSMAN	Menahem
WEISSMAN	Yossef
WESTREICH	Yosef
WILK	Hella
WILNER	Dov
WILNER	Shimon
WILNER	Tzvi
WINERSKI	
WOLF	Avraham
ZALTZ	Moshe
ZAHLER	Yehoshua
ZELLER	Frida
ZEIDMAN	Henka
ZIGEL	Mrs.
ZILBERMAN	Meir
ZOHAR	Al
ZOHAR	Stucia nee Stein
ZOHAR	Yvonne nee Koenig
ZUCKERBERG	
ZUCKERMAN	Miriam

The list does not differentiate between Jews of Krosno who came before the war to Palestine and those that survived the Shoah or were in the Soviet Union during the war.

בערב זה יחליטו הנוכחים אם להמשיך
בקיום עצרת הזכרון לבני עירנו.

אם אתך יכול להשתתף בעצרת, נא להודיע
בכתב בהקדם האפשרי לכתובת :

ברוך מינץ
רמת-גן
ארלוזורוב 63,
או לטלפן ל: 03-738987.

ארגון יוצאי קרוסנו
קורטצינה והסביבה בישראל

במלאת 35 שנה (תשי"ב-תשל"ח) להשמדת
קדושינו-יקירינו בידי הקלגסים הנאצים
ימח שמם תתקיים אי"ה ביום שני, ערב י'
בטבת תשל"ח (19.12.1977) בשעה 6
בערב.

עצרת זכרון

באולם "שאלתיאל", רח' לוינסקי 82,
תל-אביב ע"י התחנה המרכזית.

הנך מתבקש להודיע על העצרת לכל יוצאי
עירנו והסביבה.

האולם פתוח משעה 5 בערב.

Letter to the members of the Krosno–Korczyna society in Israel

The association held annual memorial services for the Korczyner Jews who were murdered in Belzec, Szebnie and Auschwitz–Birkenau. Social gatherings were also held. As the membership aged and members passed away, the association slowly came to a halt. Above is one of the last letters to the members of the society in Hebrew.

The letter addressed to the members of the Krosno–Korczyna society states that there would be a memorial meeting on Monday, December 19, 1977 at 6 P.M. at the "Shaltiel" hall, 82 Levinski Street in Tel Aviv, near the central bus station.

The members are asked to inform their friends of the meeting. The hall would be open at 5.P.M.

At the memorial meeting, we would decide whether to continue the annual memorial meetings. If you would not be able to attend the meeting please notify us as soon as possible. Baruch Munz, Ramat Gan. 63 Orlozoroff Street or call 03–738987

The memorial service was held on the 10 day of the month of Tevet that corresponds to December 19 in 1942. This day is referred to in Israel as the "Kaddish Day." The Rabbinat of Israel has set this date to say the kaddish for the Shoah victims since we do not know exactly which day they perished. We do not know exactly when most of the Krosner Jews were murdered, so the memorial ceremony was held on the 10th day of the month of Tevet.

One of the projects that the society began was to ask all the members of the association to submit family names of those that perished in the Shoah. Some families complied and presented the names. Many others failed to reply or replied incomplete answers. Below is one of the better listings of the members that perished.

Letter in Hebrew listing the members of the First family in Krosno

Below is the translation of the Hebrew letter
7/2/1978

These were the late dear members of my
family who perished in the Shoah.
Jews of the city of Krosno.

My late father; Shmuel First
My late mother; Haya First– Shlanger
My late brothers; Awraham Ezriel Lemel,
Elimelech, Shiya, Yehonathan First.
My late sisters; Sarah and Hannah First.
My late aunt and uncle Rachel and Baruch
Pineles
My late aunt Sara Zissel and her daughter
Ester and son.

I am a member of the First family.

Signed
Shoshana (Roiza) Polanski.
My maiden name was First.

[Page 227]

Chapter IX
The Executors

The Gestapo team of the Jaslo district that included the city of Krosno These so–called officials were actually the murderers who were responsible for the deaths of thousands of Jews in the district of Jaslo. They made the area "Judenrein" or clear of Jews.

The poster of the war criminals was displayed at the police station of Jaslo following World War II. Max Findling visited the place where he was incarcerated during the war and saw the poster. He photographed the poster that showed most of the Gestapo men in Jaslo. The document is presently displayed at the local museum.

**Dr. Walter Gentz,
Kreishauptman,
of the Jaslo district**

Walter Gentz was born in Dusseldorf, Germany in 1907. He pursued his academic studies in the legal field, especially finances. He joined the Nazi party in 1928. He was awarded a doctorate in law. He advanced rapidly within the ranks of the Gestapo. In 1940, Dr. Gentz was appointed finance inspector of the Jaslo district in Galicia that included the hamlets of Zmigrod and Osiek In 1941, he was appointed "kreishauptman" district leader of the Jaslo district that included Jaslo, Gorlice, Krosno, and Zmigrod. He immediately began a process of Germanization of the city of Jaslo. He was determined to change Jaslo into a German city. He brutally persecuted Jews throughout his district. He participated in all actions aimed at the Jewish population in his district. He actively participated in the selection of Jews in Zmigrod. His sadistic behavior to innocent Jews is beyond description. Following the war, he managed to find work in Germany until he was arrested and brought to trial with some of his assistants. During the trial in Ansberg, Germany, he committed suicide in March of 1969.

Ludwig Losackers, S.S. Shturmbanfuhrer.
Wilhelm Raschwitz, was a "hauptsturmfuhrer" or chief of the Gestapo office in Jaslo from 1941 to 1943. He was killed in battles with the partisans.
Ludwig Rommies
Salzer, obersharfuhrer
Paul Baron, scharfuhrer
Laubenthal Augustin
Walter Matheus
Albert Krischook
Theodor Drzyzga
Helmut Menz

Karl Hauch
Erich Kuschke
Leopold Backer
Franz Zalser
Anton Neuman
Gunter Gutsche
Ernest Meber
Wilhelm Schumacher

Oscar Baecker was a Gestapo official of the Jaslo district but worked mostly in Krosno where he was nicknamed the "Terrible Phantom." He appeared from nowhere and killed Jews without even talking to them. He was arrested in Germany and brought to trial. The jury found him guilty of killing a Jewish girl, a Jewish mother with her two children, and an old rabbi. The court dismissed the additional charge of complicity in killing 3,000 Jews by sending them to the concentration camps where they perished. He was condemned to life imprisonment.

Schmatzler – Hauptshturmfuhrerr, head of the Krosno Gestapo. Was caught and brought to Justice in Poland. He was executed.

Von Davier –Obershturmfuhrer, was Schmatzler's assistant in Krosno.

Stentzler – Untershturmfuhrer mostly in Krosno.

Some of these officials were arrested and brought to trial. Most of them received light sentences.

[Page 231]

Chapter X
Sztern and Steiner families in Krosno

Szymon Sztern was born about 1877. The family moved to Krosno from Stanisławów. Szymon is recorded as being a member of the "Gmilat Chesed", or cooperative Jewish banking outfit in Krosno. His wife Chaja died about 1915. He was registered by the Judenrat census in 1941 as a locksmith. He lived on the Podwale Street in Krosno. His trade saved him from starvation for the Germans needed skilled workers. He even escaped the first major selection of Jews in Krosno that eliminated about 80% of the Jews of the city that were sent to the death camp of Belzec. There were no survivors of this transport. He was shot in the front of his house during the last round up of Jews of Krosno in December of 1942.

Chaja Rubin Sztern was married to Szymon Sztern. She died about 1915 in Krosno. Szymon never remarried. They had three children:

Majer Sztern born in 1906 in Krosno. He was drafted into the Polish Army in 1923 and served until 1925. He then married Chaja, also born in 1909 and they gave birth to Chaim in 1936 in Krosno. Majer left Krosno as many other Jewish males did for fear of the Germans. He crossed the newly established border between Germany and Russia, a mere 20 kilometers from Krosno. He expected to return home as soon as things settled down. He was then seized by the Soviets and sent to the gulags of Russia in Siberia. The Russian–Polish agreement released all Polish citizens from the Russian camps. He enlisted in the Polish Army under the leadership of general Berling that was formed in Russia. This army fought alongside the Russian army until Berlin.

With the end of the war in 1945, Majer was discharged and returned to Krosno to look for survivors. He saw a pretty dismal picture. There were hardly any Jews in the city and those few who did return soon left the place. They had no desire to start rebuilding their lives in Krosno. They usually opted to move west and leave Poland. After a short stay in the city, Majer joined one of the groups of surviving Jews who headed west. They crossed the border to Czechoslovakia and then to Austria. Finally he reached the American zone in Berlin where he took up residence in the D.P. or displaced camp named Dupel Center. He met and married Hadassah Brothlieb. Majer took a course and graduated as a locksmith in a training center that was organized by the IRO (International Refugee Organization). He graduated the course in October of 1946. He then joined the camp police force at the DP camp, Duppel Center, UNRRA Lager 597 in Berlin where he remained from 1946–1948. They gave birth to a son called Eli in Berlin. They moved to Israel where Majer found work in the port of Haifa. He worked there from 1948–1952. The daughter Frima was born in Haifa. The family returned to Germany and lived in the D.P. camp of Fohrenwald where he filled out papers for Brazil on November 19th 1953. The family reached Brazil. Majer divorced his wife and later married Rosa of Rumanian descent.

Chaja Sztern survived the first action in Krosno and was rounded up with the second action and sent to the ghetto of Rzeszow in December of 1942. Conditions were terrible and epidemics spread like wildfire. The Germans shot many sick people in the ghetto and many others died of starvation, hunger, and disease. Chaja was shot by the Germans in the Ghetto of Rzeszów.

Chaim Sztern, the son of Majer and Chaja Sztern, was shot by the Germans in the ghetto of Rzeszów together with his mother.

Hadassah Sztern nee Brothlieb was born in 1922 in Lublin, Poland. She survived the war. Her entire family perished in the Majdanek death camp. She married Mayer Sztern following the war. She and Majer Sztern were divorced in Brazil.

Eli Sztern, son of Majer and Hadassah Sztern nee Brothlieb, was born on the December 4th 1947 at the Krankenhaus Hubertus in Berlin, American zone of Germany. He married and had a daughter named Marina 1990.

The Sztern family in Krosno in 1937

Szymon Sztern holding his grandson Chaim Sztern
Next to Szymon Sztern sits Cesia Steiner nee Sztern with her husband Cudik Steiner
Standing from right to left: Cudik's cousin, Chana Sztern, Majer Sztern, and wife Chaja Sztern

Frima Sztern, daughter of Majer and Hadassah Sztern nee Brothlieb, was born on January 8th 1951 in Haifa, Israel. She married Isaac Gevircman in San Paolo, Brazil in 1973. They gave birth to Sergio born in 1977 and Patricia in 1979.

Their children were Mari Helena, Ingrid Irene and John Willy.

- Mari Helena gave birth to Dag in 1965 and Jon in 1969
- Ingrid Irene gave birth to Pal in 1971
- John Willy gave birth to Elin in 1973 and Erik in 1980

Hannah Sztern

Hannah Sztern was born in 1912 in Krosno to Szymon and Chaja. She attended Polish schools and spoke fluent Polish. She worked as a seamstress under the German occupation of Krosno. Hannah appears on the Judenrat census list of June 1941 in Krosno as a seamstress. She worked in one of the clothing factories of Krosno and was saved from deportation to the death camp of Belzec. But she realized the hopelessness of the Jewish situation in Krosno and began to talk to her non–Jewish coworkers about a hiding place. One of them, Mrs. Pudelko, replied in the affirmative and Hannah Sztern moved discreetly to her place and remained there for several days. Mrs. Pudelko then smuggled her out of the city of Krosno to the countryside. Aryan papers were forged for her and she began to live as a non–Jew. Her papers stated that she was Maria Josefa Suska born on June 27th 1918.

Someone recognized her and informed the Gestapo. The latter arrived but Hannah was one step ahead of them. She returned to Mrs. Pudelko, who hid her in a cellar for some time until things settled down a bit. New identity papers had to be forged and she was moved to the city of Jaslo. Here she was detained by a German roadblock that arrested Poles and sent them to Germany to work. She reached the camp of Luneburg. At the labor camp she befriended a Norwegian forced worker named Henry and they became very attached. She also had three Polish girl friends, Irka and Stasia from Warsaw, and Maria from Nowy Sacz. They were very close and worked together in a shoe factory. The four girls maintained contact with each other long after the war. Hannah never told them that she was Jewish. She told them that she was from Krosno, her parents had passed away, and that the church placed her brother and sister in different orphanages. She also stated that she worked at the church in order to pay for her stay. Contacts between the family members had long ceased and with the turmoil of the war the confusion was hopeless. With the liberation of the camp, Henry and Hannah returned to Norway where they were married and gave birth to three children. She died on June 4th 1986 in Norway.

**Hannah Sztern as a seamstress in
her workshop in Krosno during the war**

**Jadwiga and Jan Pudelko saved Hannah Sztern
in the war**

Cesia Sztern was born on March 23rd 1916 in Krosno. She married Cudik Steiner in Krosno on December 5th 1937. She survived the Auschwitz and Stuthoff concentration camps. She met her husband and they resumed life. They left Poland and lived in Linz, Austria, and then in Hof/Saale in Germany, American zone of occupation. They registered to go to Paraguay with the Joint Organization in Munich, Germany, but President Truman expanded the list of refugees who could enter the USA. The couple decided to go to the United States. They left from Bremerhaven, Germany on the ship named "General Stewart" on August 8th 1949. The ship docked in New York City on September 4th 1949. They never had children. They were naturalized on December 4th 1954. He later opened a laundry. They retired to Florida where Cesia or Sylvia died on July 6th 1986 in Boca Raton, Florida.

Moses Joseph Steiner lived in Dukla with his wife Scheindel Leichter–Steiner. They gave birth to Cudik Steiner.

Date   7,10.49   Emigr. List
Name   S T E I N E R, Cudyk   File F-6-1222/BR
BD   37 y.   BP   Poland   Nat Polish/Jew.
Next-of-Kin   Rel:
Source of Information IRO Intern.Mov.Office Bremen-Grohn
Last kn. Location Bremerhaven   Date
CC/Prison   Arr.   lib.
Transf. on   25.8.49 emigr. to   USA on USAT"General Stewart"
Died on   in
Cause of death
Buried on   in
Grave   D. C. No.
Remarks Destin: C/oH.Steiner (HIAS) 73-13 67th Drive Middle
Kou. tole Nr. 223 Village Lt. N.Y.

Cudik and Cesia Steiner are going to the USA aboard the military transport ship "General Stewart."

Cudik Steiner, was born on November 5th 1911 in Jedlicze near Krosno. His father was Moses Joseph Steiner and his mother was Scheindel nee Leichter– Steiner. He moved to Krosno where he married Cesia Sztern. He was also a locksmith. He was recorded as using the facilities of the "Gmilat Chesed" or non–profit fund of the Jewish community of Krosno. He was recorded on the census of the Judenrat of 1941 in Krosno. He survived all roundups due to his trade as a locksmith. He was sent to the Rzeszow Ghetto in 1942 and from there to the Plaszow concentration camp near Krakow. He was then transferred to the death camp of Mathausen where he arrived on August 10th 1944. He was liberated and returned to Poland to find no relatives in Krosno. He traveled to Warsaw where he registered with the central organization of Polish Jews in Warsaw located at 5 Szeroka Street in the section of Praga –Warszawa. The date was August 1945. He recorded his address as living in Linz, Austria. Apparently, he met his wife who also survived the war. In January 1946 moved to the Hof/Saale D.P. camp. He was registered with the Jewish aid organization in the camp. He was scheduled to go to Paraguay but the list to America was opened by President Truman. The couple decided to go to the States. They left from Bremerhaven, Germany on the "General Stewart" ship on August 8th 1949. The ship docked in New York City on September 4th 1949. They were greeted by a HIAS representative and the family of Hersh Steiner. The family however had to travel to Wisconsin as the paper stated and this they did. They continued their journey to Sheybogen, Wisconsin. Here they passed legal clearance and then decided to leave the place and return to New York where the family secured a place at Middle Village, 7313–75th Drive, Queens, New York. He started to work as a chicken plucker, then opened a laundry store. They never had children. They were naturalized on December 4th 1954. He later opened a grocery. They retired to Florida where Cesia or Sylvia died in 1985.

Cudik married Pauline Steiner.

Cudik Steiner had a brother who made it to Argentina where he lived until his death in 1986.

Pauline Steiner nee Sommer was a native of Krosno. She was born on May 29th 1917. She came to the United States and married Cudik Steiner in Boca Raton, Florida, on April 28th 1988.

Hersh Steiner was born in Dukla in 1888. He came to the United States on September 18th 1913, from Hamburg. He worked as a presser. Due to World War I he could not bring his family. His wife Eva came to the United States in 1920 and joined her husband. They petitioned the US on behalf of Cudik Steiner and Cesia Steiner. They also appeared as witnesses on the naturalization papers. Hersh Steiner died in 1974. He was related to Cudik Steiner.

Eva Steiner was born in Dukla, Galicia Poland, and arrived in the US on July 26th 1920 with her seven–year–old daughter, Suche Steiner, from the port of Le Havre in France.

Suche Steiner was born in 1913 in Dukla Galicia. She was the daughter of Hersh and Eva Steiner. She arrived in the USA on July 26th 1920 from the port of Le Havre in France.

Pinkas Steiner– in Dukla was the address of the nearest relative left in Poland by Eva Steiner. He must have been related to the family.

The Sztern family of Krosno

First name	Maiden name	Birth date	Died	City	Trade/Note	Father	Mother	Gender	Husband	Source	Status
Simon		1877	1942	Krosno	locksmith			M		JU/G	killed
Chaje			1915	Krosno				F	Simon	P	died
Majer		1909		Krosno		Simon	Chaje	M		JU	survived
Chaje		1909		Krosno		Simon	Chaje	F	Majer	P	Shoa
Chaim		1936		Krosno		Majer	Chaje	M		P	Shoa
Hadassah	BROTHLIEB		1922		Lublin		2nd wife	F	Majer	P	survived
Eli		1947		Berlin		Majer	Hadassah	M			
Frima		1951		Haifa		Majer	Hadassah	F			
Chane		1912		Krosno	Seamstress	Simon	Chaje	F		JU	survived
Ziwie	CESSIA		1915	Krosno		Simon	Chaje	F	Cudik	P	survived
CR Cudik		1911		Duklo							survived
CR Pauline	SOMMER						2nd wife	F	Cudik		survived

[Page 244]

Chapter XI
The Akselrads

by Batia Eisenstein nee Akselrad
Translated by William Leibner

Bendet Akselrad

Translators note: The story you are about to read was written in Hebrew by a surviving daughter, Batia Akselrad, of Bendet Akselrad and Cila Freifeld–Akselrad of Krosno. The family was well established and had extensive roots and history in Korczyna and vicinity. They contributed heavily to the Jewish community and provided leaders for the Jewish community of Korczyna and Krosno for several generations until these communities and their Jewish inhabitants were destroyed by the Germans during World War II.

Bendet Akselrad was born on April 14th 1886 and killed on July 15th 1943 at the Szebnie concentration camp in Poland. He was the head of the Jewish community in Krosno for many years and also served as the head of the Korczyna Jewish community. Cila Akselrad nee Freifeld was the wife of Bendet Akselrad. She was born in 1888 and killed in Korczyna near Krosno, Galicia, in 1943.

Batia Akselrad states: "My father was Bendet Akselrad, head of the Jewish communities of Korczyna and Krosno, Galicia, Poland. He was married to Cila Freifeld and they had five sons and a daughter. My oldest brother was Shmuel, who was born in 1909 and married to Klara Rosenberg from Debice and they had a daughter named Irenka born in 1935. My second brother was Shalom, born in 1911. The third brother Avraham was born in 1922. The fourth brother was Yehuda, born in 1924; and the fifth brother was Levy, born in 1930. I Batia Akselrad, was born on the 24th of May 1932.

"I will presently try to describe the family as far as my memories permit since I was a small youngster at the time, as my birthday indicates. The family revolved about my father, who was devoted to the community. He was a gentle person who had a great deal of patience and listened to everybody who came to the house with a problem; and the Jews of Krosno and Korczyna had many problems, mainly survival problems in a sea of anti–Semitic environment.

"As a child I loved the Jewish holidays of Purim, Passover, and Friday nights. My father always brought home dinner guests from the synagogue who joined us at the table and shared our meals. Dinners were always interlaced with conversations and discussions. To this day, people who knew my father praise him for his patience, understanding, and assistance in solving problems. These people describe to me in great detail his deeds that were unknown to me. These comments make me feel proud of my parents and family.

"They also helped me to better understand my father since the people in question dealt with him personally, while I was a mere child on the sidelines. Many influential Polish gentiles visited our home and discussed ways and means to avoid or smooth sore spots within the Krosno community between Jews and Christians. The Polish population was very anti–Semitic and the slightest incident could turn into a major riot or a pogrom, as often happened in the country. The Jews wanted to avoid confrontations at any costs and merely desired to continue with their life, which was very difficult for they were discriminated against every step of the way. Even gifted Jewish youth could only dream about positions or jobs in government or public offices. Anti–Semitism was deeply embedded amongst the Polish population and was even transferred from generation to generation with minor changes.

Cila Freifeld–Akselrad

"Father devoted most of his time to the community and considered this task to be his "raison d'etre" or essence of life. He left his various businesses in Krosno to his older sons while he devoted himself to the needs of the Jewish population. The oldest sons Shmuel and Shlomo graduated the School of Commerce and Administration and managed various family businesses. Bendet Akselrad was also a graduate of this school. Schooling was very limited to Jews and some trades or professions were closed to Jewish students; in some instances a few Jewish students were admitted as a token of Jewish presence.

"Mother also helped my father since she received the people who came to the house while father was not at home. She spoke to the visitors and made notations that were relayed to father on his arrival home. My brother and I also had important jobs for we ran to open the door whenever the bell rang. Any of the family discussions revolved around the impending war and my parents and older brothers were very perturbed by the news events of the day. I was terrified and expected the worst, especially when I heard the screechings of Hitler on the radio. I had bad feelings but did not really understand what was happening.

"The Polish–German War started in September of 1939, and my brother Shalom was immediately drafted at night and I was unable to say good–bye to him. Time passed and we heard nothing from Shalom. Then a Pole came to our house and told the family that my brother was seriously injured in his legs and was being treated at a hospital in Stanislawow, Eastern Galicia. Of course, he received a nice reward for the information. Father took Awraham and Yehuda and they left the house in the direction of the city where Shalom was supposedly convalescing. Father left the community affairs in the hands of Shmuel, his oldest son.

"They soon arrived at Stanislawow (presently in Ukraine) and discovered the hoax. Shalom Akselrad was not in the city. But they did meet many Jews from Krosno who fled to this area prior to the arrival of the Germans. The Akselrads decided to return home but Russian forces now occupied Stanislawow as part of the partition of Poland by Germany and Russia. It took some doing and they managed to reach Krosno. Here a postal card awaited him from his son Shalom who was a prisoner of war in a German camp. Shalom continued to send postal cards and in one of them he informed us that he would soon be sent home. Our joy was boundless.

"Father was very busy with the community and was assisted by his elder sons. The city of Krosno had received many Jewish refugees from many places who needed help and temporary lodgings. The Jewish economic situation in the city was very bad, for many Jewish businesses were confiscated and Jews were not permitted to circulate freely in the city.

"The situation worsened with each day. A white armband with a Star of David had to be worn; anti–Jewish rules and regulations appeared daily. The situation assumed alarming proportions and my father and brothers barely coped. They tried to help with whatever they could and the Jews needed all the help that they could get. The fact that father and my brothers spoke fluent German, for the family lived for many years in Vienna and had Austrian citizenship, gave them the ability to use the language to help the Jews of Krosno.

"The Germans refused to deal with Jews, especially those who did not speak German. Every demand had to be written and submitted to the Germans in their language. The Akselrads were busy drafting and writing all kinds of requests for the Jews of Krosno. They also had to follow up these requests and I saw my father's face when he returned with a negative answer. Although I was small, I began to hear strange words I didn't understand like concentration camps, ghetto, searches, and Gestapo. I did not understand these words but feared them for they were uttered in fright. I began to mature rapidly as children do in such special circumstances.

I was about 8 years old when one evening father came home and I saw sadness in his eyes. Mother told me that they wanted to talk to me privately. Father told me that he found a special place for me with a fine Polish family that wanted to take me to their house. He told me that they would like me very much. I listened seriously but did not really understand what was taking place. Mother packed a bag with clothing. The next evening, my brother Shalom took me to the Krukierek family. During the walk he explained to me how to behave in the new home and to be a good and obedient girl. He instructed me to listen and fulfill all the commands of the new family. He also told me that I now had a new name, Berta, that I must use. Furthermore, I must not cry or ask to return home, he said. We shall visit you when we can. Parting was very sad, I saw the tears in my brother's eyes and I barely restrained myself from crying. Still we parted sadly and I entered the new home.

The family was very happy to receive me. I saw a grandfather and a grandmother where I would remain in hiding for the duration of the entire war. My parents and my brothers occasionally visited me, except for Awraham. The latter went one day to buy bread and disappeared, not to be seen again until the end of the war.

Awraham Akselrad was picked up on the streets of Krosno by the Gestapo to fulfill their quota of needed Jews for work. They immediately transported the arrested Jews to the workplace where they remained for a long time. Awraham could not communicate with Batia or any other member of the family who remained in Krosno. During Awraham's absence, Batia went into hiding, her brothers left Krosno and her parents went into hiding. The Germans returned Awraham to Krosno shortly before the big action had sent most Jews of Krosno to the death camp of Belzec. Awraham did not see his family when he returned to Krosno since they were all in hiding. With the final liquidation of the ghetto of Krosno in December 1942, Awraham was sent to the ghetto of Rzeszow with all the remaining Jews of the city. The Akselrads continued to visit Batia. Then suddenly they stopped. The brothers moved to Warsaw using "Aryan" or non–Jewish identifications while the parents went into hiding in the industrial section of Krosno. Of course, Batia was not aware of these developments until after the war. My brother Shmuel, his wife Clara, their daughter Irenka, and Shulim Akselrad were caught in Warsaw with faked Aryan papers and were killed. Yehuda was killed while fighting the Germans near Warsaw. Levy who was hiding with his parents was stopped by police and made a run for it. He was killed in Krosno. The Akselrad hiding place was discovered and Bendet was arrested and sent to the Szebnie harsh labor camp where he was murdered. Cila Akselrad managed to escape to Korczyna where she was caught and shot in 1943. When the war ended and I saw that nobody came to Krosno to look for me, I of course assumed that nobody of the family survived the war and I was the only Akselrad survivor.

Batia Akselrad in 1946 in France

"I missed my parents and brothers and kept dreaming about them. I saw them almost every night in my dreams and was very happy, only to awaken to the bitter reality that I was alone. I was very sad since I wanted the dream to continue, but to no avail. I remained in the house with my adopted grandfather and adopted grandmother while their married son and wife went to work. I did everything I could since I tried to please everybody in the family. I was always afraid that I might be kicked out of the house. This fear lingered on and frequently prevented me from sleeping. Slowly and steadily I became attached to the Christian family and integrated myself within the family. Followed their customs and habits and became a practicing Polish Catholic youngster.

"This was also the year that I had to start school for the first time and I wanted to be like all the other children, namely Christian. I wanted to be accepted and not shunned. The family encouraged me in that direction. Presently I loved the family and was very attached to it. I went to the priest in Krosno and asked to be baptized. He was very surprised and told me that he knew my father. He asked whether there were any survivors in the family and I replied that I was the sole survivor. The priest baptized me on September 5th 1945, and that same month I started school for the first time. I was admitted to the seventh grade in the elementary school; I had to be prepared by a private teacher since I had to make up a great deal of schooling.

"I was a very diligent student and loved to go to school and to study. I made many friends and wanted to be accepted. I tried to make up for all the lost time that I was locked up. I finished elementary school and received a certificate. I was registered to continue schooling the next year. Meanwhile I enjoyed the summer recess during which time I met my friends and took trips with them.

One day, a Polish officer appeared at the house and talked to the Krukierek family but I did not pay any heed. It tuned out later that the officer was captain Yeshayahu Druckier who came to the house on behalf of my brother Awraham Akselrad. Awraham wanted to take me away from the non–Jewish home and place me in a Jewish orphanage where I would slowly return to the Jewish fold. Awraham survived the concentration camps but was in poor health. It took him a long time to recuperate. He finally managed to reach the Lubeck–Neustadt D.P. refugee camp in the British zone of occupation in Germany. He rested and regained some strength. He decided to visit Krosno and see whether there were any family survivors. The UNRRA (United Nations Relief and Rehabilitation Administration) organization arranged his transportation back to Poland as it did for thousands of other refugees returning home after the war. He reached Krosno and was very disappointed. There were a few Jews in the city living in fear of their lives. He did not recognize the city or the people. His inquiries established that his sister, Batia Akselrad survived the war with the Krukierek family. He approached the family but they refused contact. They refused to let him meet his sister. Awraham was too weak to take on the Krukierek family. He himself was still weak, confused but determined to remove his sister from the Christian home. Awraham did not have a home nor did he want to remain in Poland. He saw one solution namely to place his sister in a Jewish orphanage where she could grew up as a Jew. Awraham started to make inquiries but soon had to leave Poland since the borders were being closed. He smuggled his way back to his D.P. camp in Germany. He kept writing letters to various Jewish Polish organizations where he explained the situation. One of his letters reached the office of the chaplain of the Polish Army, Rabbi Dawid Kahane who handed the letter to captain Yeshayahu Drucker who specialized in these matters.

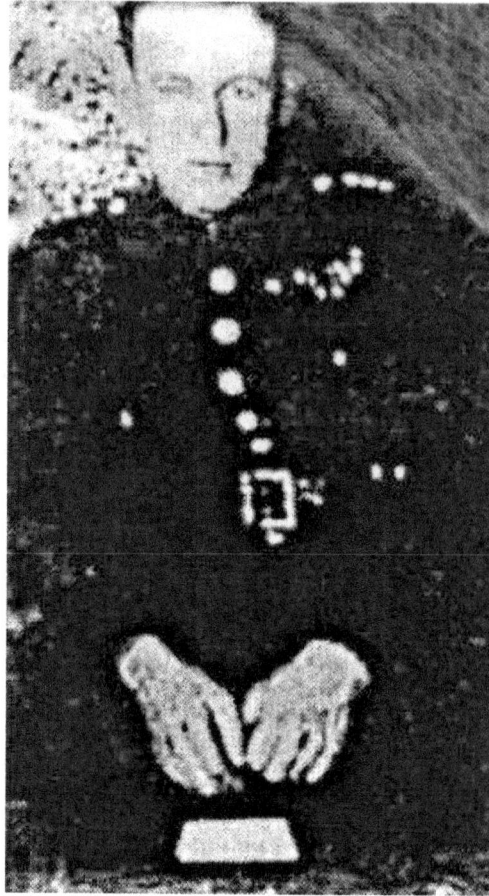

Yeshayahu Drucker

Yeshayahu Drucker began by first confirming the facts of each case and then developed a plan of action to redeem the child from the non-Jewish home. He also made it his business to travel to remote villages and hamlets to locate Jewish children. Drucker arrived in Krosno wearing his Polish army officer's uniform, riding in a Polish military car that was driven by a uniformed Polish soldier. The car and driver were supplied by Rabbi Kahane. No Pole who was confronted by Drucker could believe that he faced a Jew. He not only spoke Polish fluently but looked Polish. This was a very important attribute when Drucker talked about a Jewish child who lived with the family. Looking at Drucker in his army uniform, Krukierek assumed that the Polish government wanted the matter settled quickly. He of course answered all questions without hesitation. Yes, he said to Drucker that they have adopted Batia Akselrad during the war with her parents' permission. She is now part of the family and was even baptized into the Catholic faith. Drucker saw that the family would not surrender the child.

Drucker made several inquiries regarding the Krukierek family in the city of Krosno and was told that they were influential. Drucker decided to proceed legally against the Krukierek family. He asked Awraham Akselrad to sign a power of attorney that would enable him to begin legal proceedings. A law suit was initiated against the Krukierek family for holding a minor and refusing to return her to her biological family namely Awraham Akselrad. The court procrastinated and delayed action hoping that the matter would die with time but Drucker pursued the matter. Finally, a settlement was worked out between the parties. Batia Akselrad would stay with her brother for a period of two weeks where they would become acquainted. Since Awraham did not have a place, the decision was made that she would be placed in the Zabrze Jewish orphanage where her brother could visit her as often as he wanted. The court also decided that the entire estate of the Akselrads would be handed over to the Krukierek family except for the part that belonged to Batia Akselrad. Awraham Akselrad and Yeshayahu Drucker took possession of Batia and they all left for Zabrze.

I did not like the decision. I felt safe in my adopted environment. I went to school, to church on Sunday since I was baptized as a Catholic, and had friends. All this came to an end when Awraham and Drucker began to visit my new home and tried to talk to me. I refused to talk to them. With the court decision, I had to abide but I was angry at my brother for destroying my adopted life. At Zabrze I was watched and all my mail was censored. Many years later, I was informed by the Krukierek family that they wrote letters to me but never received a reply.

Zabrze orphanage in Silesia, Poland

I did not get along with my brother. I resented him for destroying my new home. He, on the other hand, was not able to understand my needs as a teenager. Besides, Awraham had to leave since he was granted a temporary visit to appear in the Polish court regarding my case. Awraham returned to his D.P. camp. The Zabrze home soon sent me to France with a children's transport. I reached the city of Perigueux, in the south of France where I remained for two years and then went to Israel in 1948. I attended the agricultural school "Mikveh Israel" and in 1950 joined the army. In 1953 I married and raised a Jewish family. I have two sons and 4 grandchildren. I live in a private home at Kiriat Ono and tend to my garden and flowers. I spend my time attending lectures and reading books.

Chateau Vouzon near Perigueux where Batia Akselrad–Eisentein spent her time in France until she left for Israel

My New Parents

by Batia Eisenstein (nee Akselrad)
Translated from Hebrew by William Leibner

I was born on May 5, 1932, in Krosno, Galicia, Poland. My parents were Bendet and Cila nee Freifeld Akselrad. I had five older brothers. I was the sheltered baby of the family and their worries about my well–being greatly increased with the German occupation of the town. The Jewish economic situation in Krosno went from bad to worse with each day. My parents decided to seek shelter for me with a non–Jewish family named Krukierek. Our family was well acquainted with this family whose sons worked at our sawmill in Krosno. The family responded positively to the inquiries.

My mother packed a suitcase of clothing and I packed a small suitcase of items that were dear to me. I took some notebooks, pencils, coloring pencils and some other knick–knacks that were precious to me. One evening, my brother Shulim took me to my new family. I cried all the way while my brother talked to me about behaving nicely to the family members and being obedient and respectful.

The separation was very difficult and painful. My brother tried his best at soothing my feelings by stating that the family would always be in touch and visit me at the new home. As to my question about why I had to leave the house, there was no immediate answer. Shulim merely said that the family selected a nice and safe place for me where I would be treated as a member of the family. His words gave me some confidence and I ceased crying. We then entered the new home and I was greeted warmly.

I saw a grandmother, a grandfather, and a young couple. Of course, I was very sad since I was left alone when my brother left. The new family named me Basia (a typical Polish Christian name). I cried the entire first night and was unable to fall asleep. I had a hard time adjusting to the idea that I was left alone with a new and strange family. No longer would I be able to rejoin my dear and beloved family. I rose early in the morning and went to the yard. I approached the gate and looked at the path that we used the previous night, but nobody was in sight.

I stood there and cried, hoping to see a familiar face, but no one appeared. I continued to stand or sit there for hours each day in the hope of seeing someone from the family, but in vain. I was depressed and entered the home only when grandfather called me to eat, but I had no appetite. Grandmother understood the situation and tried to alleviate my fears by saying that my old family would probably visit me during the day or tomorrow. This of course did not alleviate my depressed feelings but it showed me that someone cared.

Needless to say, I was very happy when a member of the family visited and brought a gift from the old home. They always promised to visit me as often as they could to cheer me up, for they saw my red and swollen eyes. They tried to visit often and indeed everybody visited me except my brother Avraham. We already mentioned what happened to Awraham. The family visits always ended in sadness, for I was left alone with my depressed feelings.

Suddenly my family stopped visiting me. It seemed like they vanished from the face of the earth. The year was 1943 and indeed some members of the family were caught by the Germans and killed, while others were no longer in the city. I had the feeling that I would never again see my dearly beloved family. At night I dreamed that my family visited me and I was very happy, but on awakening I realized that it was a mere dream.

I slowly became attached to the new family and became more familiar with them. They worried about me and were constantly fearful that an informer might reveal my existence to the Germans. The home of the new family was located in a rural area in the vicinity of the airport of Krosno. Still there was fear that someone might spot this young girl in the courtyard. The Krukierek family decided that the risks of being exposed were serious and took the necessary steps. They began to shift my hiding places. Sometimes I slept hidden in a straw bed in the attic. Others times I was hidden in dark places that affected my vision on seeing light.

On nice evenings, I would emerge and play a bit in the wheat field. Some evenings, grandmother would give me a basket and send me to pick potatoes. I dug the potatoes by hand in the dark so that no one would see me. I picked the big ones and left the small ones in the ground so that they would continue to grow, as grandmother Weronika instructed me to do. I would return with a basketful of potatoes and then clean them before entering the kitchen. Grandfather was pleased with the work and would always say that I earned my keep for the day and would give me an extra heavy slice of bread. I was very proud of my achievements and accepted wholeheartedly these compliments. Grandfather was rather economical with his compliments; thus I relished them when I received one.

Potatoes and cabbage was the standard food of the day for the family. Sunday was a special menu that consisted of potatoes, cabbage, and rabbit meat. The latter were raised on the farm next to the cows and roosters. At night I picked potatoes and during the day I tended to the daily household chores. I always volunteered to do extra chores in order to ingratiate myself with the family. The fear of being rejected was always on my mind. I spent a great deal of time peeling potatoes and when I did a good job, I received a slice of bread. I did all the chores with devotion for I craved attention. I wanted to be accepted. Thus, I was very busy in the house, for grandfather had a leg injury and limped, while grandmother was weak and tired easily.

In addition to the regular household chores, I also mended clothing, helped prepare the feed for the cows, and did many other kinds of work in the house. Of course, there was less work during the winter when the fields were covered with snow and then I spent my time hiding in the cowshed. The weather was freezing. I spent my time talking to the rabbits and roosters. It seemed to me that they answered but I was not sure if I heard them. I was very lonely and continued to talk to the small animals, for I had no friends.

This was a difficult period, for the Germans increased the intensity of their searches and my adopted family was seriously frightened by the new policy. They even considered throwing me out of their house. I was terrified and could not fall asleep for fear of winding up in the street. Grandmother cared a great deal for me and stated that she would assume full responsibility for my protection. Furthermore, she stated that she would leave the house if I were thrown out. Grandmother's threats worked and she saved me. She asked her son Kazek to hide me at the mill where he was a guard. The sawmill belonged to our family prior to the war but was now owned by a German named Schmidt, and Kazek watched the place. He built a hiding place and one night took me from the house in a bag of sawdust.

The hiding place was under a wooden floor amid sawdust. Kazek's brothers also worked at the mill. They all married and left the household. Only grandmother, grandfather, their married daughter Jozefa, and myself lived in the house that was near the sawmill. Kazek brought me to the hiding place and gave me instructions how to behave during the day when the Polish workers tended to their jobs. He also showed me how to position myself in the hiding place so as not to arouse suspicions. I could not sit, move, or turn in the dark hiding place. During the day it was still bearable but at night it was frightening. I kept dreaming about my killed parents and brothers; I had a premonition that they were all killed. I did not want to dream but could not help myself. The dreams continued and I always awakened to stark reality. Furthermore, rats occasionally promenaded on my body and I could not do a thing about it for there was no room for my hands to move. I was left with the terrible feeling of the creatures walking about me.

For several months I continued to sleep in sawdust under the wooden floor. Autumn was approaching and with it came the rains. Everything was wet and dreary. The cold weather became a reality. Still I had to stay in hiding during the day for fear of being spotted by a worker or by a customer who came to buy wood. Only at night could I slowly venture out. As a result of my hiding position, I could barely walk. I was depressed and the thought of ending my life frequently crossed my mind, but I was a coward. I did not divulge these thoughts to Kazek for fear of embarrassing him after all his efforts on my behalf.

Winter approached and the family decided to return me to the house. They still hid me here and there but within the house, for it was bitter cold outside.

I also became accustomed to my new Christian family and realized then that I would never return to Judaism. I no longer wanted to belong to the persecuted and humiliated Jewish people. Grandfather always told me that the Jewish people had always been persecuted throughout history. Even the Arabs were killing the Jews in Palestine. I heard and saw all these things. I saw how Jews were being persecuted while the Christian children played and had fun. I felt jealous and felt ashamed at having been born a Jew.

These thoughts persisted and became stronger as time passed. Suddenly, the roar of shells shook the entire area for we were near the Krosno airport. The Russians shelled the entire area prior to their advance and for several days the cannon fire could be heard and then there would be silence.

The area was liberated but nobody came to take me home. I started school for the first time in 1945 and was registered as a Christian student. I excelled in my studies since I devoted myself wholeheartedly to schoolwork. I was a very good student and easily made friends. I felt a certain compensation for all the years spent in terrible deprivation. I also decided to convert to Catholicism, a deed which pleased the family and gave me further security at the new home. Suddenly, my brother Awraham and his friend Yeshayahu upset all my plans. I was forced to leave the Krukierek home and was taken to the Zabrze home. The orphanage was aware of my refusal to part from the Krukierek home. Thus, I was observed closely. I never receved letters from the Krukierek family although they promised to write. Many years later I discovered hat they wrote letters that were never given to me. Of course my letters to the Krukierek family were never mailed. I felt homesick for my adopted family. The orphanage soon sent me with a transport of Jewish children to France and then to Israel where I arrived in 1948. I was sent to a school to study the Hebrew language and adopted the Hebrew name of Batia that was close to my original birth name of Berta. I stopped using the Polish name Basia. Following the army service, I married at the rabbinate. I have two married sons and four grandchildren.

I continued to write to the Krukierek family and even maintain correspondence with the grandchildren and great grandchildren of the family. Jozefa died in 2002 at the age of 92. I assisted her with whatever I could. I continue to correspond with the younger members of the family who do not even know me. But it is important for me to maintain contact with my past.

Signed **Batia Eisenstein**

Dated June 8, 2008

William Leibner loosely translated the story written in Hebrew

Awraham Akselrad
by William Leibner

**Awraham Akselrad on a visit to
Israel following the Shoah**

Awraham Akselrad, the son of Bendet and Cila Akselrad, was born in Domaradz, near Krosno, Galicia, Poland, on July 12, 1922. He was the third child in a family of six children. They lived in Krosno, although the family originated in Korczyna near Krosno. The father, Bendet Akselrad, was very involved in the Jewish community and on several occasions was elected to be the head of the Jewish community of Krosno. The family was well–to–do; Awraham received a tutorial education, and then went to a private school in Germany where he studied until Hitler came to power. He then left for Belgium where he continued his education. His father went to Belgium in 1937 and brought Awraham back to Krosno. He received tutorial help with the Polish language. Awraham then presented himself for admission to the Tkacka National Institute for Weaving in Krosno. The school rarely admitted Jews but the right pressure was applied and he was admitted to the school. The Akselrad family was involved in the weaving and linen business, and Awraham hoped to enter the family business. His studies ended with the German occupation of Krosno.

```
A K S E L R A D    Abraham              417 809
od. AXELROD
Bendet u. Cilla Freifeld               jüd.


17.7.1922 Domarac/Polen                amerik./poln.
 4.40         Ghetto Krodno
12.42 -  6.43 Reichshof
 6.43 - 12.43 ZAL Plaszow
12.43 -  5.44 ZAL Skarzysko
 5.44 -  1.45 ZAL Czenstochau
 1.45 -  2.45 Buchenwald, 2.45-4.45 Dora
 4.45 - Ende 4.45 Sachsenhausen
 1.1.47 DPL Lübeck-Neustadt, dann ausgewandert
```

Record of Awraham Akselrad during the war years.

**Abraham Akselrad's wartime employment record in Europe.
ZAL stands for Zwangs Arbeit Lager, or forced labor camp.
DPL stands for displaced people camp, or D.P., and was
established after the war to provide a temporary shelter for
the inmates of the liberated camps.The UNRRA (United
Nations Relief and Rehabilitation Administration)
organization maintained the D.P. camps**

The Germans were constantly short of workers and frequently set up check posts and detained Jews for work details. One day in April of 1940 , Awraham went out to get bread for the family and was arrested by SS men who were seizing Jews for a work detail. Apparently, he was sent to a distant work place for he did not return daily to his home as did other Jewish workers. The German labor card above explains what happened to Awraham Akselrad during the war years. He was recorded as living in the Ghetto of Krosno in April of 1940 when he was detained by the Germans. (The entry is in error. There was no ghetto in Krosno in 1940). The ghetto was established in May of 1942. Most of the Jews lived in their places of residence except for the luxury apartments that were confiscated for the use of Germans. Then there is a blank of time that would indicate various work details outside the city for he was never at home in Krosno. As a matter of fact, he is not listed in the census of Jews in Krosno conducted by the "Judenrat" in June of 1941.

The admission card of Awraham Akselrad to the Mittelbau–Dora concentration camp, a subsidiary of the Buchenwald concentration camp empire on January 21st 1945

Abraham Akselrad was eventually returned to Krosno, only to be sent by train with all the remaining Jews of Krosno to the Rzeszow Ghetto in December of 1942. The trip was a horror journey with people fainting and dying everywhere within the enclosed cattle cars. Finally, they arrived at the Rzeszow (Polish name) or Reishe (Yiddish name) or Reichshof (German name) railway station. Krosno was now officially "Judenrein" or clean of Jews, except for some hidden Jews.

With the liquidation of the Ghetto of Rzeszow, Awraham was sent to the terrible labor camp of Plaszow near Krakow. This camp was well portrayed in the movie "Shindler's List." Awraham stayed in this hell–hole for six months and even managed to survive an execution scene. His work boss, or kapo, caught him slacking on the job and decided to set an example. He selected him for execution. All inmates in Plaszow who were selected for execution were taken to one of three killing sites. The most famous was of course the hill nicknamed "Chujowa Gorka." Practically no one returned alive from this place. German military deserters were also executed on this hill. They were usually killed by a firing squad, following the reading of the verdict and the presence of a priest. Jews and later Hungarian Jews were usually killed by machine–

gun fire and their bodies burned according to Dr White, formerly Alexander Bialywlos, a survivor of Plaszow. It is estimated that 8,000 people were killed in Plaszow. Awraham Akselrad went to the hill and returned alive. Apparently, the executioners had enough for the day or some mechanical mishap. Of course, Awraham died many deaths emotionally until he returned to the barrack.

In December 1943, Awraham was sent to the Skarzysko–Kamiene concentration camp in southern Poland where thousands of Jewish slave laborers worked in the munitions factories. The workers had no protective masks or special clothing and worked with various explosive materials. Most of the exposed parts of their bodies became yellow and all workers developed all kinds of breathing problems that ended with typhoid. Furthermore, the workers were undernourished and the death rate amongst them was extremely high.

Awraham remained at this camp for about 5 months and was then taken to the Czestochowa concentration camp in Poland, where he remained until January 1945. He was then shipped to the Buchenwald concentration camp but there was no room for him and he was transported to a subsidiary camp named Mittelbau Dora located in Nordhausen, Germany. This camp produced the V1 and V2 rockets. Most of the work was done in excavated tunnels to prevent Allied bombers from affecting production. Thousands of workers died digging the tunnels due to lack of food and medicine, as well as sheer exhaustion. Awraham was lucky since he only stayed a short time in this camp. He was then marched to the Sachsenhausen death camp where he was liberated at the end of April 1945 by the Russian army.

Awraham slowly recuperated from his war experiences and began to deal in goods. There was a shortage then in Germany of everything and the black market was thriving. He accumulated some money and asked the UNRRA Organisation to transport him to Poland as they did for other Polish refugees in Germany. He soon reached Krosno. There were a few Jews in the city who lived in fear for their lives. He did not feel at home in Krosno. He made several inquiries about his family and discovered that his sister Batia Akselrad survived the war hidden by the Krukierek family. Awraham knew the Krukierek family from before the war .He approached the family and asked for the return of his sister to his custody, since she was still a minor. The family did not say yes, nor did they say no. The Krukierek family adopted delay tactics — we will discuss it, come later, the girl does not want to go.

Batia Akselrad did not want to leave her adopted family despite Awraham's pleas. He was devastated but could do very little. Besides, the Polish borders were being closed and he did not want to stay in Poland. He managed to cross the borders illegally and reached his D.P.camp in Germany. Awraham began to write letters to Jewish Polish organizations to help him regain his sister. One of the letters reached Captain Rabbi Yeshayahu Drucker. The latter investigated the situation and suggested to Awraham to take legal action to recover his sister who was a minor. Drucker filed suit against the Krukierek family and the case was settled out of court. The settlement was as follows:

Batia Akselrad would leave the Krukierek home and stay at the Zabrze Jewish orphanage for several weeks where her brother Awraham Akselrad would have free access to visit her whenever he wanted. The Krukierek family would be financially compensated by receiving all the property of the Akselrad family, except for the share of Batia Akselrad. In case Batia Akselrad returned to the Krukierek family in Krosno, the agreement would be null and void. The agreement was left in the courthouse that would enforce it.

Yeshayahu, Awraham, and his sister Batia left Krosno and headed to Zabrze. Awraham met his sister several times and talked to her about his experiences and their situations, but coolness and even a certain animosity prevailed between brother and sister. The sister wrote letters to the family but they were never posted by the home administration. Yeshayahu gave strict instructions to stop all letters from the family to Batia and to watch her from a distance. He was afraid that the family might come and return her to Krosno. Soon Batia left Poland with a transport of children to France and then to Israel. Awraham left Poland and settled at the Lubeck–Neustadt D.P., or Displaced Persons camp, in Lubeck, in the British occupied zone of Germany. But he was determined to remove his sister from the Christian home regardless of price or feelings. He wanted her placed in a Jewish home. He succeeded with the help of the Jewish religious community in Poland.

Yeshayahu Drucker promised Awraham that Batia would soon leave Poland and head to Palestine. Awraham also hoped to join her there. In reality, the British blockaded the shores of Palestine and did not permit Jews to enter the country. Some young Jews went illegally to Palestine like the "Exodus" ship passengers and were intercepted by the British. Awraham was in no condition to undertake such a trip. So he stayed in the camp with little hope to leave Germany. The JDC (American Joint Distribution Committee) and the HIAS(Hebrew Immigrant Aid Society) organizations interceded on his behalf and he obtained a visa for the USA. He left for the USA while his sister was already in Israel.

No. 7421782

Name AXELROD, Abraham *

residing at 314 W. 100th St. N.Y.N.Y.

July 17, 1922   Mar. 25, 1955
Date of birth   Date of order of admission

Date certificate issued Mar. 25, 1955   by the

U. S. District Court at New York City, New York

Petition No. 6√4 G 7 C

Alien Registration No. 7 327 753

x *Abraham Axelrod*
                    (Complete and true signature of holder)

Awraham Akselrad was officially naturalized in New York City

Awraham left the Port of Bremen, Germany, aboard a troop ship named General McRae on October 17, 1949. He arrived in New York City on October 24, 1949, and was met by a representative of the "United Service for New Americans" (this organization was created in 1946 to help new immigrants, especially Jewish immigrants, to settle in the USA. The organization merged with the HIAS organization, or Hebrew Immigrant Aid Society, in 1954). The representative told him that his papers for admission were conditional on his settling in Galveston, Texas, where he was expected and arrangements had been made for him.

Awraham was not anxious to go to Texas but had no choice in the matter since the organization had already purchased a train ticket to this destination. He therefore reluctantly left Grand Central Terminal in New York City and headed via Chicago to Galveston, Texas, where he arrived on October 26, 1949. Awraham was met by a representative who helped him settle in the city. There he started to work as a tailor and received his Social Security Number.

He later moved to New York City where he was naturalized on March 25, 1955 (Certificate Number 7421782). Awraham asked the judge to change his name to Abraham Axelrod and the judge consented. Abraham lived at 314 West 100th Street in New York City. He later moved to 212 West 91st Street. In New York City he resumed his old trade of weaving. According to a friend, he met a woman and lived with her for a while until they split. He went to Israel to see his sister and returned to New York City.

Abraham had no children and died of heart complications on January 22, 1991, in New York City. He is buried at Mount Moriah cemetery in New Jersey.

Epilogue to the Akselrad –Zajdel family of Krosno, Galicia, Poland

The Akselrad family in Krosno owned a large sawmill near the river called "Tartak Parowy" or steam sawmill. The mill employed many workers, among them members of the Krukierek family. Ignac Krukierek and his wife Weronika had six sons and a daughter who died in infancy

Ignac Krukierek worked at the oil refinery but most of his sons worked at the Akselrad establishment in Krosno in various capacities. One of the sons, Andzej Krukierek, was a very capable and skillful maintenance man. Bendet Akselrad liked this worker and promoted him on various occasions. He also entrusted him with some delicate matters that were executed without a hitch. The relationship between the two grew with time and they had absolute confidence in each other. Andzej Krukierek moved up the ladder of management and assumed an important position at the plant.

When the Germans occupied Krosno they of course "Aryanised" or seized the sawmill and practically gave it for nothing to a "Volksdeutch" or Pole of German origin named Schmidt. The latter did not interfere with the running of the mill and left it in the hands of the old management.

Bendet Akselrad, as mentioned before, was very active on behalf of the Jewish community and due to his fluency in the German language came in contact with the Gestapo and SS people in Krosno. It soon became apparent to him that Jewish survival under German occupation would become very difficult if not impossible. Harassment of the Jewish population increased daily. The pauperization of the Jewish population was obviously a designated or planned policy of the German administration. Bendet was determined to avoid the plans that the Germans had for him and the Jews of Krosno. He even became a member of the J.S.S. or Jewish Self Help Committee in Krosno that assisted poor Jews with food and money. He decided to search means and ways to obtain "Aryan" or non–Jewish papers. Easier said than done, especially for a well–known family like the Akselrads in Krosno. He entrusted the mission to his loyal and confident man Andzej Krukierek, who had an executive position at the mill and could absent himself from work whenever he needed to attend business matters on the outside.

Andzej Krukierek started to work on this matter and slowly established the necessary contacts to obtain illegal papers. This was very expensive since the danger of being caught was real and fatal if one fell in the hands of the

Gestapo. Still, Krukierek continued with his work and obtained papers under the name of Zajdel, a Polish–sounding name. The family was, however, too well–known to pass even under a different name. So a hidden place was found on the outskirts of Krosno where individual members of the Akselrad family would arrive and stay until they were shipped out of Krosno.

The Akselrads began to disappear slowly from Krosno. Andzej Krukierek traveled to Warsaw, the capital of Poland, to make the necessary arrangements such as living quarters and employment. When he settled all matters he then returned to Krosno and took a member of the family from the hiding place to the village of Polanka near Krosno, where they boarded the train for Warsaw. He took every person and escorted him in the same manner. The expenses were huge but Bendet was ready to pay any price to save his family.

The Krosno Jewish census of June 1941 indicates that the following Akselrads were still in the Krosno Ghetto: Cila Akselrad nee Freifeld; her children Shulim, Leib or Levi, and Beile or Berta. Bendet Akselrad, his son Shmuel Akselrad, his wife Klara Akselrad nee Rosenberg, and their daughter Irene, and Yehuda Akselrad were no longer in the ghetto. They had all vanished under different names. Only Bendet Akselrad, or rather Zajdel, was still in Krosno in hiding.

The other Zajdels were already in Warsaw, where they lived and worked in different places. Irene, Bendet and Cila's granddaughter who was now called Marysia Zajdel, went to school. The Zajdels of course spoke fluent Polish; most Jews in Poland did not. The next member of the family to be removed from the ghetto was Batia Akselrad.

Bendet Akselrad tried to place his youngest son, Levy, with a Polish family but it was very difficult to find a place. There was great fear amongst the local population to take in a Jewish boy. Meanwhile Shulim received papers and he too left the ghetto and reached Warsaw where he began to work. Andzej continued his work and soon Luzer Ellowicz, a friend of Shulim Akselrad, also reached Warsaw, as did Doctor Awraham Rosenberg and his wife Sara nee Wander, from Krakow. Cila Akselrad and her son Levy soon joined Bendet Akselrad–Zajdel in his hiding place. The place was located in a sawmill in the industrial section of Krosno, at a distance from the Krukierek home where Batia was hidden. Andzej Krukierek had built it especially for the Akselrad–Zajdel family.

The entire family escaped from their usual place of residence and their Jewish identity. None of the Zajdels showed up for the big round–up of Jews in Krosno on August 10th 1942, or at the final round–up of Jews on December 4th 1942, except for Awraham Akselrad who was recently returned by the Gestapo to Krosno. .Andzej Krukierek continued to provide for and protect the family in Krosno and probably helped other Jews leave the city on illegal papers.

Suddenly the Polish police came at night to the home of Ignac Krukierek where Batia Akselrad was hiding. They used flashlights and awakened the house. Batia was certain that they came for her and slid under the covers trembling with fear. The police entered the house and spoke Polish. They asked the father where his son Andzej lived and asked him to escort them to the son's place. They arrested Andzej Krukierek but left his wife Janka and their infant son Marek at home. They also sent the father back to his house. The entire family was now terrified of the consequences. Apparently someone was out to get Andzej. He was soon transferred to the Gestapo and then sent to Gestapo headquarters in Krakow where he was interrogated at the Montelupich prison. The interrogations lasted for some time and resulted in the arrest of three Poles in Krosno who disappeared. All of them worked in various civil service offices. We can definitely surmise that the arrested Poles were tortured and must have revealed some information. The Gestapo interrogators at Montelupich were known for their brutality in obtaining information.

The Gestapo soon traced Shmuel Zajdel (Akselrad) and arrested him. His daughter Marysia Zajdel (formerly Irene Akselrad) was walking with her mother Klara when she saw her father being led away. She ran to her father and blew her mother's cover. Of course, they were all arrested and interrogated according to Sara Rosenberg, sister–in–law of Shmuel Akselrad. They all perished in the Shoah.

The Gestapo then traced Shalom Zajdel and arrested him. They also grabbed Doctor Awraham Rosenberg whose daughter Klara married Shmuel Akselrad. The wife of the doctor, Sara Rosenberg managed to escape and survived the war. The Gestapo also looked for Yehuda Zajdel–Akselrad but he joined the ranks of the Polish partisans and was killed in 1943 in the vicinity of Warsaw in a fight with the Germans. Luzer Ellowicz escaped the police dragnet by leaving Warsaw. He returned to Krosno where he found a hiding place with the Polish maid that the family had prior to the war. Yadwiga, or Wisza as she was called. She took him in and hid him until the end of the war.

Andzej Krukierek remained in prison for some time; his wife was even permitted to visit him with her son and then she received a letter that he died of a heart condition. It seems strange that the Gestapo never questioned the old couple Krukierek or their sons who worked in or about the sawmill. They all knew something about Andzej's business and certainly knew that their parents were hiding a Jewish child whom they saw at the house. True, the sons never brought their families or friends to their parents' home; still the sons knew of the Akselrad family. Of course, discussions took place at the Krukierek home about the girl and the possible consequences if they were caught hiding Batia.

Meanwhile Bendet Akselrad–Zajdel became aware of the fact that Andzej has not been in touch and was missing. He had set up the hiding place and established contacts with several Poles in Krosno to provide basic necessities for the family in hiding. Bendet could not go shopping even with false papers because he was well known in town and would be recognized. So he sent his son Levy Akselrad in the evenings to pick up the family food and supplies.

**Shalom Akselrad with his little brother Leib
Akselrad and sister Batia Akselrad prior to
World War II in Krosno, Galicia, Poland**

Someone spotted the boy and denounced him. The police stopped him and asked for identification. Levy Akselrad was only aged 13 but he realized that he would not pass a personal check and that furthermore, he might be recognized as an Akselrad. He would then be arrested, questioned, and forced to reveal his parents' hiding place and then he would be shot, as was the custom when a Jew was caught in Krosno after the ghetto was liquidated.

Levy decided to take advantage of the evening and make a break for it. He ran, but the police were fast on the trigger. They fired their weapons and killed the boy. They soon discovered that he was Jewish and that someone might have also recognized the Akselrad boy. This wealthy Jewish family had vanished from Krosno without leaving a trace. Furthermore, where had he been hiding and who was with him? Obviously he was not hiding in a

Christian home since they would never dare to send a Jewish boy on errands in the streets of Krosno. So the Akselrad family had to be in the vicinity.

The Gestapo and the Polish police conducted an intensive search and located the hiding place. They entered at night and arrested Bendet Akselrad. Cila Akselrad managed to escape in her night–robe through the window into the darkness. Bendet Akselrad was sent to the Szebnie concentration camp where thousands of Jews and Russian prisoners of war were murdered. He was killed on July 15th 1943. Cila Akselrad managed to reach the apartment of Yadwiga, or Wisza, the former maid of the Ellowicz family. She gave her a dress and let her rest for awhile. Of course, the maid did not tell Cila Akselrad that she was hiding a Jew. Instead, she helped her to look for a hiding place. But the police were in hot pursuit and arrested Cila in Korczyna near Krosno. She was taken to the Jewish cemetery in Korczyna and shot. The police ordered a Polish worker to bury her and supposedly even paid him a few zlotys.

The killings of the Akselrads set in motion the entire Krukierek family. Most of them saw an opportunity to get rid of the girl and finish the family ties to the Akselrads. After all, there were no more Akselrads to deal with. The Krukierek family, of course, had assumed that Awraham Akselrad was long dead while in reality he was at the Plaszow death camp. Similar events occurred throughout Poland where Poles agreed to hide children and when their parents were deported or payments stopped, they would chase the child from the hiding place.

Batia's cousin Marylka Freifeld, born in 1932 to Yehezkel and Rusia Freifeld, was chased out from her hiding place on the deportation of her parents. Her father was a brother of Cila Akselrad nee Freifeld. The girl was killed. In another instance, Leib Freifeld, the son of Yaakov and Hinda Freifeld, was hidden by a Christian family in the vicinity of Berta Akselrad's hiding place. When the parents were deported by the Germans in Korczyna, they threw the child onto the streets where he was killed.

Of course, Batia did not know then of these events. But she felt sudden tension and her insecurity grew by the day. She became frightened by every gesture or whisper and she tried her best to be helpful throughout the house. She had the feeling that her life and destiny was on the line.

Her adopted grandmother, Weronika Krukierek, stood by her and defended her against all antagonists. She stated that she would never leave the girl and that if she had to go she would leave the house with her, according to Batia Akselrad.

As the searches for Jews intensified in Krosno, one of the Krukiereks, Kazimierz or Kazek Krukierek who was a night watchman at the sawmill, decided to build a hiding place in the mill for the girl. The place was well hidden and in the shape of a toy box where she would spend days and have freedom of movement only at night when the workers were away. Kazek took her to the sawmill and explained to her what he wanted her to do and she obeyed. Kazek brought her food every evening when he came to work but she had to lay in that box every day regardless of the weather. The sun heated the place and the rain wetted the place, but she had to remain hidden while the workers were there. Of course Kazek was there at night, but he was busy with his girl friend in their room while Batia roamed about until the workers began to arrive. Frequently she had cramps and was unable to walk after a full day of hiding in the box. Then Kazek would help her restore her circulation. Weronika Krukierek told all her neighbors that she had chased away the girl. Months passed and things settled down a bit. The cold weather set in and the Krukiereks decided to bring the girl back to the house where they built a special hiding place for her.

The Germans began to retreat and the Russian armies took the initiative and started their long liberation drives. They liberated Russia and entered White Russia, the Ukraine. Russian planes were pounding the Krosno airfield, according to Batia Akselrad. The Germans were constantly regrouping or shortening their front lines while the Russians kept advancing. Eastern Poland was soon freed and the Russians were approaching Krosno. The Germans blew up the Krosno airport as they left the city.

Krosno was liberated but nobody came for Batia Akselrad. She became convinced that she was left alone in the world except for her adopted family. Slowly she accepted her fate and integrated herself into her new environment where she felt safe. The safety was dispelled with the arrival of Awraham Akselrad.

[Page 287]

Chapter XII
The Spa Resort Iwonicz–Zdroj

Translated by William Leibner

The spa center Iwonicz–Zdroj is located south of Krosno and north of Dukla

The spa center of Iwonicz–Zdroj , better known as Iwonicz is located in the Krosno province. It is situated 16 kilometers south of the city of Krosno and 80 kilometers south of Rzeszow, Galicia, Poland. The place is located about 400 meters above sea level and surrounded by hills covered with trees. Already in 1578 it was known as a health spa. Iwonicz contained a variety of mineral waters and mud baths that helped people. The place developed and became a leading health spa center in Poland, especially Galicia. In the summer and to a certain extent in the winter, many well to do people spent their vacations in Iwonicz. Some people even built summer homes in the area. The number of health establishments kept growing. Iwonicz had a small population of about 2,000 people during the year but this number greatly increased during the summer or winter vacation seasons.

**The summer and winter resort home of the Akselrad family
in Iwonicz–Zdroj about 16 kilometers from Krosno**

In 1785 we find 18 Jews in Iwonicz and by 1921 there are 61 Jews in the hamlet. The Jews in Iwonicz were under the supervision of the Jewish community of nearby Dukla. There was a small Jewish community in Iwonicz that grew with time. According to Batia Akselrad, her father helped built the synagogue in Iwonicz where rabbis like Shmuel Fuhrer or Moshe Twerski prayed when on vacation in Iwonicz. Many hotels provided religious services within their premises for the orthodox Jews. With time, Jewish shops like butcher shops, bakeries, fish stores and restaurants opened to provide the needs of the Jewish population especially during the tourist seasons.

Many Krosno Jews spent their vacations in nearby Iwonicz, notably rabbi Moshe Twerski or the Akselrad family. Iwonicz also had Jewish families that lived permanently the hamlet amongst them the Glazier and the Lusthaus families. Edmund Lusthaus was a physician and his wife Helena studied pharmacology prior to the war. The latter were assimilated Jews who spoke only Polish. The Lusthaus family survived the war. Edmund was drafted into the Polish army and taken prisoner by the Russians in 1939, where he later joined the Polish Army that left Russia and fought with the Allies. Helena Lusthaus and her daughter, Elizabeth, managed to reach Tarnow where they had family. Mrs. Lusthaus worked as a pharmacist for the Germans and managed to obtain "Aryan" papers for herself and her daughter that saved them. They were eventually liberated by the Russian army and left Poland. The entire family met in Italy where Edmund was stationed with the Polish Army.

Here is what Dora Beinfish–Cohn, a resident of Krosno and Iwonicz, had to say about Iwonicz–Zdroj. "We lived in Krosno in a large house. My father was an engineer. The family acquired a big parcel of land from the 'Chrabia,' or Count Zatuski who owned a good part of Iwonicz but was always short of cash. The family decided to build a 44–room hotel named the 'Bristol' and 2 apartment buildings with stores on the ground floor. The entire project was finished in 1939 just before the beginning of the war. The family moved to Iwonicz."

Bended Akselrad, head of the Krosno Jewish community, drinking the mineral water at the Iwonicz spa

Strolling in the spa center of Iwonicz
From left, Bendet Akselrad, head of the Jewish community in Krosno;
Rabbi Moshe Twerski, Hassidic rabbi of Krosno; and a close follower of
the rabbi

Rabbi Moshe Twerski, second from left,
with Hasidic entourage in the resort spa of Iwonicz–Zdroj

On entering Iwonicz the Germans converted the hotel to a military hospital. They soon ordered all the Jews to leave the spa center and proceed to the Ghetto of Rymanow. The Germans forced most of the Jews of Rymanow to cross the border to the Russian–controlled part of Poland. Some Jews disobeyed the order by hiding and then reappeared in Rymanow. They were also joined by some Jews who returned from the Russian controlled areas. In August of 1942, most of the Jewish men were rounded up and sent to the concentration camp of Plaszow, near Krakow in Poland. On August 13, 1942, all the Jews of Rymanow were assembled and sent by train to the death camp of Belzec.

Dora Fishbein–Cohn survived the war due to the extensive support she received from the Zatuski family at the beginning of the German occupation. Later she was assisted and protected by Mrs. Dunajewski and the Kazarski family in the village of Wola Komborska.

Another small Jewish community was devastated without leaving a trace of Jewish existence in Europe.

[Page 294]

Chapter XIII
Bibliography

Avriel, Ehud, Open the Gates. Atheneum, New York 1975

Berger, Ronald J., Constructing a collective memory of the Holocaust. University Press of Colorado. 1995

Breitowicz, Yaacov, To Hell and Back. Survivor from Krosno, Galicia

Bauer, Yehuda, The Brichah – She' erit Hapletah 1944–1948. Jerusalem 1990

Bauer, Yehudah, Out of the ashes, Oxford 1989

Bauer, Yehudah, Flight and Rescue– Bricha New York, 1970 2000

Dobroszycki, Lucjan "Survival of the Holocaust in Poland– A Portrait based on Jewish Committee Records 1944–1947" Published by M.E. Sharpe, Armonk, New York. USA.

Cohen, Jonathan, The great Escape of Polish Jews 1946–1947, Yad Vashem

Cohen, Richard, The Avengers, A.Knopf publishing co. 2000

Fessel, Felicia, I wanted to live in Hebrew, Tel–Aviv, August 983, Israel

Garbacik J., Krosno, studia z dziejow miasta I regionu Krakow 1975, Jaslo, Oskarza, Warszawa 1973, pp39–40, 47.

Grobman, Alex. Battling for Souls. Ktav Publishing House, Jersey City, N.J

Holocaust Encyclopedia

JDC Oral history project–Gaynor Jacobson– (Greece) Tuesday 21 1981

Interview Murray Kass, Herbert Katzki

Korczyna, memorial book, New York 1967. Yiddish

Krosno–Shtetl link, JewishGen

Pinkas Hakehilot–Yad Vashem

Rączy E.: Ludność żydowska w Krośnie do 1919, Biblioteka Krośnieńska, zeszyt 9, Krosno 1995

Rączy E.: Ludność żydowska w Krośnie 1919–1939, Biblioteka Krośnieńska, zeszyt 13, Krosno 1997

Rączy E.: Ludność żydowska w Krośnie 1939–1946, Biblioteka Krośnieńska, zeszyt 15, Krosno 1999

Rosner, Leo "The Holocaust Remembered" published 1998, USA.

Shragai, Shlomo Z. Massa Hatzala , Jerusalem, 1948 Hebrew

Szulc, Tad, The Secret Alliance, Farrar, Straus and Gitroux in New York, 1991 USA

Turkov, Jonas En Pologne, après la liberation (book was written in Yiddish "Noch dem Bafraiung" and translated by Maurice Pfeffer into French), published by Kalman–Levy in 2008

Urzad Documentace A vyestrovani Zlocinu Komunismu, Policie Ceskie Republky. Czech police documents pertaining to Communist regime crimes

White Alexander Dr., formerly Bialywloss, Be a Mentsch–a legacy of the Holocaust, April 20004, Arizona, USA, Yad Vashem Archives

Zertal, Idith, From Catastrophe to Power, University of California Press, London England 1996.

Newspapers and periodicals

Gordonia–Maccabi Hatzair Archives, Hulda, 28/6
Yad Vashem Archives, JM/1572, jm/1848–1867,M–1/E990/865;
06/18,06/19, 016/337, 016/2832,021/16, 053/105–II P.154. TR.10/797 pp.11–24
YIVO Archives; ADRP 20, 21
Central Historical Archives of the Jewish People in Jerusalem; HM/7921
Central Zionist Archives; S–6/1876, S–6/2181, S–6/2196; Z–3/820, Z–4/222–23 Z–4/226–24B, Z–4/234–13,Z–4/2997–II, Z–4/3732.
Shomer Hatzair Archives, (3)84, 1,2.
American Joint Archives; Poland, CULT.REL.344a, 399.
Tagblat (newspaper) ;7/11/1912,
Hamagid; 23/6/1898.
"Hamitzpe" (newspaper); 28/8/1908, 25/6/1909
Chwila (newspaper): 8/1/191929, 17/1/1930
Chwila Wieczorna (newspaper): 15/4/1935, 15/1/1937, 29/1/1937, 28/3/1938
"Divrei Akiva" 9/4/1937, 16/4/1937
"Noar Hatzioni" (newspaper) 15/4/1935, 10/11/1935, 15/6/1936
"Nasha Walka"14/8/1938
"Nowy Dziennik" (newspaper); 1919, 1926, 1927, 1930–1932, 1934–1929.
"Slowo Mlodych" listopad 1930

William Leibner interviewed the following residents of Krosno:

Akselrad Batia
Bialywlos, Alexander
Breitowicz Herbert
Breitowicz Yaacov
Munz, Baruch
Lang, Awraham
Lang, Shimshon
Lang, Yossef
Trenczer, Yossef

[Page 298]

Chapter XIV
Krosno

by Elzbieta Raczy

The Polish historian Elzbieta Raczy did an extensive study of Jewish Krosno. She published her findings in several small publications in Polish under the name of Krosno Library. Having access to many state and city documents enabled her to describe a very fine table of Jewish life in Krosno. The wealth of historical details gives us an excellent perception of Jewish life in Krosno. We want to thank the author for her gracious permission to use her written material in our Yizkor or Memorial book for the Jews of Krosno.

The editors, graphic artists, and other involved personnel did a fine job of presenting the material in a presentable and cohesive format for which we want to thank them.

We want to thank Monika Hendry for her excellent translation of the Polish text to English.

Arrangement and editing of the material by William Leibner.

**The Krosno Library
Historical series**

**Notebook 9 [1995]
Elzbieta Raczy**
Jews in Krosno to 1919
Krosno 1995
Translated by Monika Hendry from Polish to English
Arrangement and editing by William Leibner
Editor of the series is Ewa Mankowska. Proofreader is Iwona Jurczyk.
Copyright by Museum Rzemiosla w Krosnie Krosno 1995
ISBN 83–902057–8–5
Na Okladce; I Arched galleries in Krosno [pocz XX w.] karta pocztowa.

Contents of the Chapter

The main purpose of this publication is to portray the history of the Jewish community in Krosno.

The sources available about the Jewish community in Krosno until 1919 are insufficient, fragmented and scattered. The Jewish communal archives did not survive the war. I base my research on the materials available at the Archives in Skolyszyn, the Museum of Crafts in Krosno, the Central Military Archives in Warsaw, the Jewish Historical Institute Archives in Warsaw, and the Yad Vashem Institute Archives in Israel. I also used materials from the Central Historical Archives in Lwow [Lembeg, presently Ukraine], that provided information regarding the privilege de non tolerandis Judeis {non–acceptance of Jews} given to Krosno in the 16th century.

Among the existing publications, valuable information was obtained from Kronika gmin– Encyklopedia Osad Zydowskich od zalozenia po ich zaglade w II wojnie swiatowej (Chronicle of Jewish communities– the Encyclopedia of Jewish settlements from their establishment until World War II) published in 1984 in Jerusalem and the city's monograph. The gaps were filled by testimonies of surviving former Jewish residents of Krosno. I would like to thank all of these people.

The beginnings of Jewish settlement in Krosno

Krosno's status as a royal town was the most important factor in shaping the history of the Jewish settlement there. Jewish settlements flourished mainly in the gentry–owned cities in the Sanok area. The gentry encouraged Jewish settlements mainly due to common economic interests. Jews made good administrators and tenants. Their flair in trade provided a boost to the city economy and their involvement in crafts created goods for the market.

Cities such as Lesko, Dynow, and Rymanow were in private hands and Jewish communities developed basically without restrictions.

The opposite was the case with royal towns such as Krosno (a royal town until the 18th century) where the legal status of Jews was determined by royal privileges that were secured by the city dwellers. Townspeople usually resented Jews, mainly due to their prowess in trade. In the Sanok area, there were other royal cities, among them Mrzyglod and Sanok[1]. The situation was similar in towns belonging to the church, such as Brzozow and Babice, that opposed Jewish settlements for religious reasons.

The first mention of Jews in Krosno appeared in the first half of the 15th century in an undated document by King Wladyslaw Jagiello, who allowed two brothers from Ransburg, Nachem and Lazar, to settle in Krosno[2]. They were allowed residence for three years and were free from taxes for that period[3].

Nachem was rich. In 1427–28 he extended a number of loans to Poles and Hungarians. His debtors included Mathias Mild, Hanus Olbracht, Johanes Ronchyn, and Stenczel Bone. The last one pledged to repay the money and interest to "Jew Nacham in Lancut after Christmas." Nachem's brother, Lazar, lived in Krosno much longer than three years as confirmed by a privilege given to him by Casimir Jagiellonczyk, freeing him from transport duties in the whole country. The sources do not mention when the brothers left Krosno. The permission to allow them to live in the city seems to have been an exception, as a document from 1569 states that the town never had Jewish inhabitants. Krosno, however, was not the only town in the Sanok area to exclude Jews under the so–called non–tolerandis Judeis Act [the Exclusion of Jews]. Other cities also received this type of privilege or exclusion.

A modest influx of Jews into Sanok and Mrzyglod seemed to confirm that these places removed, at least for a period of time, their restrictions on Jewish settlement. The next sources mentioned Jews in the area in about the 16th century. It was then that they emigrated from Western Europe to settle in Lesko, Sanok, Rymanow, Dukla, and other places in the area.

Above is a copy of a document, issued by the
Polish King Wladyslaw Jagellon to the Jews
Nachema and Lazare that granted them the right
to settle in Krosno

The town's royal privilege

The scarcity of references to Jews in Krosno in the second half of the 15th century indicates that there were few such residents in town. This can be directly attributed to the efforts of the local citizens against Jewish settlement. The pressure was very successful and in 1569 Jews were formally forbidden to enter Krosno with the granting of the non tolerandis Judeis Act privilege, or right of Jewish exclusion, to the city fathers. The document read: "We (the King) are informed by the residents of the whole district and the town that since its establishment, Jews had not resided and have no settlements or buildings here and they [local population] seek protection to remain free from such settlements in the town and vicinity. We regard the request as just and hereby give them a privilege that no Jew in Krosno or vicinity can buy for himself or his heirs any property. Nor are they [the Jews] allowed to establish any dwellings in the town and vicinity. They are also forbidden to sell goods that will harm the community interests..." These privileges or exclusions were reiterated subsequently several times. At the beginning of the 17th century, the town elders passed a resolution–forbidding resident to receive Jewish guests for longer than a day and to lease or rent stalls to Jews to trade or to store goods. The punishment was a fine of 30 "grzywna" (local currency)[4]. It seems that these rules were largely ignored because in documents from 1587 we read that one town mill was leased to a Jew named Leon and in 1694 there is a note about the death of Joseph Seygadlo (baptisatus addescens). So despite the explicit prohibition, Jews continued to live in Krosno[5].

Panoramic view of Krosno in 1838

Below is a document issued by King Zygmunt August in 1569 that barred Jews from residing in Krosno, the so–called non–tolerandis Judeis Act.

**Royal document granting Krosno the
right to prevent Jews from residing in
the hamlet of Krosno**

The privilege de non suscepiendis Judeis [of not hosting Jews] did not extend to Jews visiting from other towns. Fair day drew not only Jews but also tax collectors. In 1634, Cracow merchants Jakub Kozielkiewicz, Wojciech Dzieciolowski, Matias Kasprzycki, and Tomasz Grodkowicz accused Mayor Rapowicz and the council members of conspiring with a Jew, Jakub Aronowicz from Przemysl. He was supposedly a crown treasury administrator who did not exempt them from duties, although they were entitled to this as residents of Cracow.

[Page 10]

The mayor sent the most bellicose, Jakub Kozielkiewicz, to prison, and the other three were kept in Krosno until they paid the tax[6]. Jews from Dukla and Rymanow frequented Krosno fairs and competed with the town merchants. In the 17th century, demand for crafted goods dropped and contributed to the growing friction between Polish and Jewish communities. This resulted in the ordinance issued by the Krosno town board that "a robbery or killing of a Jew from Rymanow should not be punished." Rymanow Jews were also banned from entering and trading in Krosno[7].

The contacts between Jews from Rymanow and Poles from Krosno were frequent. In 1700, the Jewish elders from Rymanow, Jakub Chaimowicz, Jakub Kisiel, Jakub Jerychowicz, and Joseph Hankowski borrowed 500 zloty from Wojciech Gierlinski, a priest from the Farny church in Krosno. The collateral for the loan were: the Jewish school, the synagogue, the property, the land, the houses and shops of the leaders of the community.

It seems that from the end of 17th century until the middle of the 19th century, no new Jews settled in Krosno as there is no mention of them in the sources. Przyjaciel Ludu, a local paper, wrote on 3 November 1838: "Krosno inhabitants are involved in industry, especially trade with Hungary and can't stand starozakonnych (Jews). Local laws and long traditions prohibited Jewish settlement."

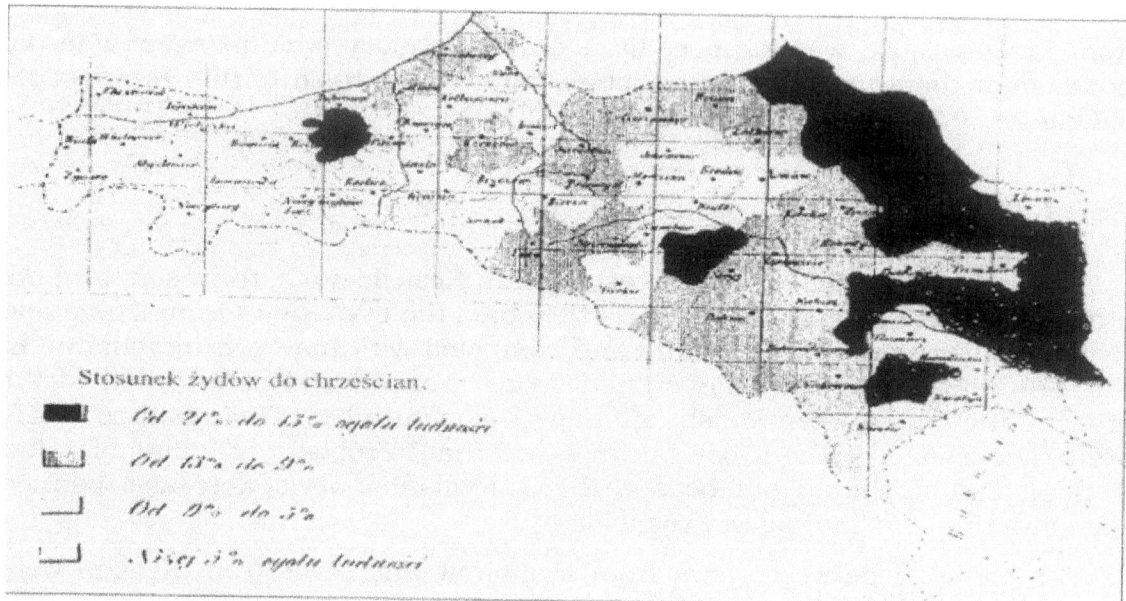

Stosunek żydów do chrześcian.

Jewish population in Galicia toward the end of the 19th century

The Jewish community in Krosno between the 19th and the 20th century

In the 19th century, Jews were first mentioned in 1851. A census of houses and properties mentioned three Jewish owners: Loje Grunspan, Mojzesz Grunspan, and Sehije Dym.

In the 1890s and the first ten years of the 20th century, the Jewish community grew very rapidly. Between 1859 and 1890, about 50 Jews settled in Krosno, and in the next ten years another 32 Jews settled there. Among them were: Jachet Balzam, Chane Bilet, Riwe Beiz, Mendel Mozes, Chaim Beck, Aprel Samuel and his wife Sara, and their children: Israel, Chaim, Estera, and Ryfka.

In 1880 Jews represented 11.6% of all Krosno's inhabitants and 28.2% in 1910. They came mainly from Dukla, Korczyna, Sanok and some from farther corners of Galicia. The growth rate of Krosno's Jewish population was the highest in all of Western Galicia.

The population of Krosno

Year	Population	Catholic	Jews	Greek Orth.
1870	2,132	2,100	26	6
1880	2,461 (2,810)	2,318 (127)	113	30
1890	2,839 (3,251)	2,454 (567)	327	58
1900	3,276 (3,310)	2,664 (961)	567	45
1910	4,353 (5,582)	3,329 (1,559)	961	63
1914	5,521	3,839	1,558	70

The numbers within the parenthesis are the numbers provided by Yad Vashem in Jerusalem, Israel.

Column 1 is Year, total population, Roman Catholics, Jews, and Greek Catholics

Column 2 represents the total population of Krosno that grew by 96.5% between the years 1870–1910. Column 3 represents the Catholic population that grew by 60.5% between the same years. Column 4 represents the Jewish population that grew between the same years by 376% . If we go by the numbers within the brackets provided by Yad Vashem, the Jewish population even grew by a much larger percentage. Column 5 represents the Greek Catholic church that grew between the same years by 17.2%

Between 1880–1910 the general population grew by 96.5%. According to religious affiliation we have recorded a growth of 60.5% of Roman Catholics, 17.2% Greek Catholics, and 376% of Jews. The rapid growth of the population was mainly due to the excellent geographic location of the town and the discovery of oil. Money and prospectors arrived in large numbers and created an economic boom. Krosno was linked to the railway in 1884. The line extended from Zagorz and Sanok to Jaslo, and provided the city with the proverbial "window to the world." Until then the only communication link was the so–called "subcarpathian trail" from Gorlice via Krosno to Sanok and Przemysl.

[Page 13]

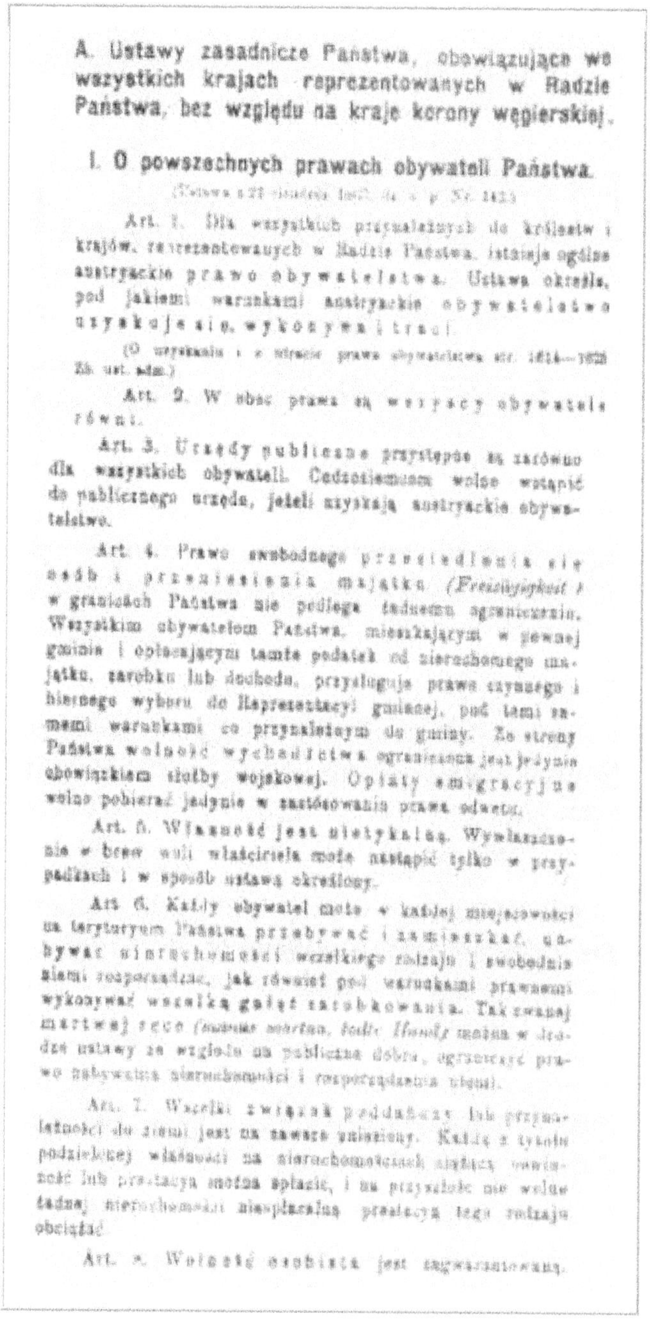

A. Ustawy zasadnicze Państwa, obowiązujące we wszystkich krajach reprezentowanych w Radzie Państwa, bez względu na kraje korony węgierskiej.

I. O powszechnych prawach obywateli Państwa.

([illegible])

Art. 1. Dla wszystkich przynależnych do królestw i krajów, reprezentowanych w Radzie Państwa, istnieje ogólne austryackie prawo obywatelstwa. Ustawa określa, pod jakiemi warunkami austryackie obywatelstwo uzyskuje się, wykonywa i traci.

(O uzyskaniu i o utracie prawa obywatelstwa str. [illegible] Zb. ust. adm.)

Art. 2. W obec prawa są wszyscy obywatele równi.

Art. 3. Urzędy publiczne przystępne są zarówno dla wszystkich obywateli. Cudzoziemcom wolno wstąpić do publicznego urzędu, jeżeli uzyskają austryackie obywatelstwo.

Art. 4. Prawo swobodnego przesiedlenia się osób i przeniesienia majątku (*Freizügigkeit*) w granicach Państwa nie podlega żadnemu ograniczeniu. Wszystkim obywatelom Państwa, mieszkającym w pewnej gminie i opłacającym tamże podatek od nieruchomego majątku, zarobku lub dochodu, przysługuje prawo czynnego i biernego wyboru do Reprezentacyi gminnej, pod temi samemi warunkami co przynależnym do gminy. Ze strony Państwa wolność wychodźtwa ograniczona jest jedynie obowiązkiem służby wojskowej. Opłaty emigracyjne wolno pobierać jedynie w zastósowaniu prawa odwetu.

Art. 5. Własność jest nietykalną. Wywłaszczenie wbrew woli właściciela może nastąpić tylko w przypadkach i w sposób ustawą określony.

Art. 6. Każdy obywatel może w każdej miejscowości na terytoryum Państwa przebywać i zamieszkać, nabywać nieruchomości wszelkiego rodzaju i swobodnie niemi rozporządzać, jak również pod warunkami prawnemi wykonywać wszelką gałęź zarobkowania. Tak zwanej martwej ręce (*manus mortua*, *todte Hand*) można w drodze ustawy ze względu na publiczne dobro, ograniczyć prawo nabywania nieruchomości i rozporządzania niemi.

Art. 7. Wszelki związek poddańczy lub przynależności do ziemi jest na zawsze zniesiony. Każdą z tytułu podzielonej własności na nieruchomościach ciążącą powinność lub prestacyę można spłacić, i na przyszłość nie wolno żadnej nieruchomości niespłacalną prestacyą tego rodzaju obciążać.

Art. 8. Wolność osobista jest zagwarantowaną.

Fragments of the constitution of 1867 that granted equality to the citizens

The Austrian government's policy also played a significant role in the growth of the Jewish population in Krosno. Until 1860, Jews were forced to maintain a separate judiciary and communal system of administration that marked the Jews as an alien element. The government also tried to restrict the number of marriages and to expel poor Jews from the country. In 1859 the restrictions were eased (on 29 November the marriage restriction was removed). The emperor also removed some rules banning Jews from certain professions and allowed them to buy land. All these measures were civil rules and did not grant citizenship or political rights to the Jews. Only on December 21st 1867, a new constitution was promulgated that granted equality among all inhabitants of Poland.

Occupations of Krosno Jew

In the 19th and the beginning of the 20th century, Jews in Krosno, as in other places in Poland, mainly engaged in trade. Crafts were weaker and catered mainly to the needs of the Jewish community. There are no records regarding Jewish bakers in the second half of the 19th century in Krosno. We know that such bakeries existed since observant Jews were not permitted to buy bread from non-Jews due to religious rules. Of course, many Jews also baked bread at home, as was the custom then. In 1906, Krosno had six bakeries that included two Jewish bakeries: Seling Findling and Chaim Oling. Sandek Fessel, Wolf Mahler, Jakub Grunspan, and Tobiasz Nagiel owned very prosperous butcher shops. Buying the right to slaughter and sell meat was quite an expensive proposition so we can assume that these butchers belonged to the richer elements of the Krosno Jewish community. Jakub Grunspan and his family owned properties in the city and around it, confirming his affluence. There are no detailed records about the butchers in the first ten years of the 20th century.

Jews were prominent in the metal industry in Krosno: Dawid Mehel, Chaim Korba, and Jakub Pinkas. Jonasz Steifel was involved in metal and tin. Jozef Flama, Dawid Tabzel, and Isaac Wielopolski were also involved in the metal industry but the sources give no details. The only brass manufacturer was Mojzesz Springer. Jewish craftsmen preferred the light industry. The Grand Guild record books from 1910–1914 mentioned tailors, shoemakers, barbers, painters, and watchmakers, footnote: watchmakers: Chaim Just, Jakub Berenger, and Benzion Montaga; barbers: Natan Zorna and Jakub Bender.

We know quite a bit about Krosno's merchants who dominated the trade in terms of the number of shops and the variety of goods that they provided. They traded in cattle, grain and other agricultural products, furs, leather, building materials, agricultural machinery, and crafted products.

The main square was the trading center. Every Monday Krosno held its weekly fair. Jews differed from the crowds with their long black "chalats" or coats. They busied themselves around the square, buying as much as possible at the lowest price. Traditionally, a drink in a tavern followed a successful transaction, and this custom was very popular. Not surprisingly, alcoholic drinks represented one of the mainstays of Jewish trade. One of the most profitable trades was the selling of spirits. Abraham Weisman and Szymon Pastor dominated the area.

**A Galician Jew
about 1899**

He won the tender in 1868 by defeating three other Jewish competitors. Jews ran the taverns throughout the Galician period. In 1867–70, the exclusive right for the sale of alcohol was granted to Sehija Dym. She paid an annual tax of 4,017 zloty. After her contract expired, Issac Herzig took over the lease. In 1872, Issac Herz, Kuna Feissel, and Szyja Dym jointly entered the alcohol market and were granted the exclusive right to sell liquor in Krosno and all the villages belonging to the town, such as Bialobrzeg and Suchodol.

Jews dominated the economic area of leases known as arrendar in the 19th and in the first half of the 20th century. The biggest group among Krosno's Jewish lessors were those who were granted the lease to collect public revenues. One of these lessors was Hersch Wasserstrum. He won the right to collect the tax on wine consumption from 1916–18. Wasserstrum agreed to pay 5,900 zloty in 12 installments for this lease. Others involved in this type of activity were Rebeka and Leja Dym. They obtained the lease in 1917 to collect the fees on alcoholic drinking production in Krosno.

Another group was made up of lessors of public buildings. In 1869, Isaac Heller and Szulima Leker leased the market place. We don't know for how long nor who took it over later. We suspect it could have been a Jew, because such leases required large sums of money and traditionally Jews contended for them. The city authorities were also eager to give them to Jews because large capital investment was needed and Jewish merchants were capable of raising these sums. Often, there were competitions amongst the Jewish merchants for these leases. In this manner, Saul Babinowicz gained the lease for the town property of Suchodol in 1867[8].

The Synagogue of Krosno in 1930

The Jewish communal organization

All Jewish communities had a certain degree of autonomy in establishing and administrating their particular needs. The latter were implemented through the offices of the gmina or kehilla, or communal center. This body of the Jewish residents carried out many roles in the community's life, mainly meeting the religious, administrative, and educational needs of the particular community.

In the second half of the 19th century, the Krosno region had two well–established Jewish communal centers: Dukla and Korczyna. Jewish inhabitants of Krosno seemed to have belonged to the one in Korczyna. Footnote 35– the Jewish communal center in Korczyna provided religious services for Krosno, Guzikowka, Bajdy, Bialobrzegi, Bonarowka, Borek, Bratkowka, Czarnorzeki, Dobieszyn, Glowinka, Jaszczew, Jedlicze, Iskrzynia, Kombornia, Krasna, Kroscienko Wyzne and Nizne, Lezany, Odrzykon, Polanka, Potok, Rzepnik, Suchodol, Swierzawa Polska, Turaszowka, Weglowka, Wojtkowka, and Wola Komborska.

Materials published in Israel state that Krosno's Jewish community belonged to Rymanow. However, this was not confirmed by our findings. The Rymanow communal center, or gmina, was established probably in the 16th century and, as such, was the oldest in Galicia. In the 19th century, Rymanow became a famous hasidic center in Poland. Its prestige might have attracted Krosno Jews to visit the famous Rabbi of Rymanow. However, when in the second half of the 19th century Jewish settlers appeared in Krosno, the Korczyna gmina provided the religious needs such as the cemetery for the Jewish inhabitants of Krosno. Thus we can conclude that the Krosno Jews

The Krosno communal organization was created on January 1st 1900. The governor of Galicia granted the request for the organization on September 12th 1899. It covered the following communities: Bajdy, Bialobrzegi, Borek, Bratkowka, Chlebna, Chorkowka*, Dlugie*, Dobieszyn, Jaszczew, Jedlicze, Koptowa and Stanowiska*, Kroscienko Nizne, Krosno, Lesniowka*, Leazny, Miejsce Piastowe*, Moderowka with Bialkowka and Budzisz, Piotrowka*, Podniebyle*, Polanka, Poraj*, Potok, Suchodol, Szczepancowa, Swierzowa Polska, Targowiska, Turaszowka, Ustrobna, Wojakowka, Wroblik Krolewski*, Zrecin*, Zarnowiec*, Zeglce* (* asterik denotes communities removed from the communal center of Dukla while others were removed from the control of the communal center of Korczyna)[10].

Each Jewish community drew up its own statutes that were then submitted to the authorities for approval. The original statutes for the Jewish community of Krosno did not survive. However, all the documents of the Galician Jewish communities were based on the government ordinance from July 6th 1894[11] that outlined the legal framework for Jewish communal organizations. Based on that regulation we can recreate, in general terms, the manner in which the communal organization of Krosno, or the kehilla, functioned. According to the ordinance, the kehilla had to meet the religious needs of its members and had to set up the necessary facilities to implement these needs. Caution had to be exercised that all steps were in accordance with the rules of the government.

A governing body ruled the Jewish community of Krosno but we do not know the names of the members due to lack of sources.

The kehilla leadership controlled all officials within the Jewish communal organization; it approved budgets and administered the finances of the organization. It supervised houses of prayer, ritual places, and charitable organizations run by the community. It also mediated in disputes among the community members through officials who headed its judiciary division. The most important official in the community organization was the head of the kehilla, or the Jewish community. He called and chaired the meetings of the governing body. He issued membership certificates, kept records of the members and communal possessions, ran the chancery, and made sure that the rules passed by the governing body were within the scope of the law. He signed all official documents and stamped them with the seal of the head of the Jewish community in Krosno. If documents were related to obligations to a third party or a matter for which an approval of the council was necessary, they had to be signed by two other members of the council and bear its explicit approval[12]. The council or governing body appointed rabbis, assessors, religion teachers, cantors, mohels or circumcisers, and shochtim or religious slaughterers. They all received regular wages from the kehilla.

Jewish Cemetery of Krosno in 1946

In 1904, the governing body selected Rabbi Samuel Ozon [Aron] Fuhrer as the Rabbi of Krosno[13]. He was highly recommended and was appointed for a probationary period of three years, which was extended for a long period of time. He was the only Krosno rabbi and remained in office until 1939. This led us to believe that the position was given to him for life.

The main duty of a rabbi was to tend to the spiritual needs of the Jewish community, supervise prayers, deliver sermons during Sabbath and other holidays, and answer questions pertaining to the faith in matters of ritual. He officiated at marriages and supervised the bathhouses and butcher shops so that they would conform to religious laws.

Each member of the community had his personal rights that included use of all the ritual, educational, and charitable facilities of the kehilla. He had a passive and active right to elect the communal authorities. Only men were granted these rights: active rights to those over 24 years old who paid annual contributions and passive rights to those Austrian citizens over 30 years old who were members of the Krosno community for at least two years[14]. The members also had duties, including obeying the authority of the kehilla and its rules, providing money for the community needs, and performing ceremonial functions when requested by the community.

Saved Jewish gravestones from the Jewish cemetery in Krosno in 1946

Krosno Jews between 1914–1918

The role of Krosno Jews in the Polish independence movement in 1914–1918 cannot be overlooked. The rising national awareness prior to World War I led the Jewish youth away from Polish national organizations, in which their participation was never high and was made up of people who considered themselves Poles but of Judaic persuasion.

Two Jews were members of the Zwiazek Strzelecki (Rifle Association) in Krosno and Mehel Rubin[15] was a representative of Jewish members of the Powiatowego Komitetu Narodowego (Regional National Committee). Three Jews were members of Polish Legions: Szymon Stilmann, who joined on September 4th 1914; Jozef Jadas, who joined an auxiliary battalion on November 9th 1914; and Maks Adermand, who joined Polish forces but later deserted[16].

Such negligible Jewish participation in the fight for Polish independence could lead one to make false assumptions, notably that the Jews opposed Polish independence. This was not the case. We must remember two things about the Jewish population: (1) the situation in Krosno was similar to other Galician towns, and (2) Jewish attitudes and ways of thinking were conditioned by the historical circumstances of the Jewish Diaspora.

The differences in language, religion, culture, and the lack of political rights until the mid–19th century led to Jewish isolationism that manifested itself in religious conservatism and Zionism. Some Jews in Krosno identified with slogans of other Jewish communities in Poland, "a nation within a nation"[17].

We can however conclude that the Krosno Jewish community supported the Polish independence movement because it took part in the celebrations of Polish national anniversaries and other important Polish events. When the Act of November 5th 1916 was announced, Jews in Krosno illuminated and decorated their houses with national symbols and Jewish craftsmen volunteered their help in preparation of equipment for the Polish legionnaires.

Material Culture of Krosno Jews

Along with the annihilation of Jewish residents, the monuments of their material culture were also destroyed. The synagogue and Jewish archives were destroyed and the only surviving trace of the Jewish community is the cemetery. It is a very precious but not quite appreciated monument. It is a source to understand the Jewish presence in the city and a monument of national memory. Germans buried murdered Jews here. The content of inscriptions on tombstones, the size and opulence of the cemetery depended on the wealth of the community. Krosno's Jewish cemetery is one of the few cemeteries that wasn't totally devastated because it was surrounded by a wall. Krosno citizens of Jewish ancestry who survived and came back in 1946 saved it from total destruction[18].

A Krosno resident, Baruch Minc living in Israel gave us information about the efforts that were made to save the cemetery after World War II. His father was involved in these efforts. According to him, the cemetery tombstones were removed by unknown people and sold to someone in Bialobrzeg who wanted to build a house and wanted the tombstones for the foundation. Thanks to prompt legal action, the tombstones were returned to their original place.

It is difficult to ascertain the credibility of this story. Oral testimonies can be subjective and imprecise. In this case, however, they sound credible and were confirmed by the pictures of the Krosno Jewish cemetery from 1946. According to the evidence, the case of the tombstones was taken to court that ruled that they should be returned to the Krosno Jewish cemetery from where they were removed. A search of the various court records in Skolyszyn, Sanok, and Jaslo yielded no results. The records may have been misplaced, discarded, or destroyed due to the low archival importance attached to them.

The cemetery is located on a slope behind the Zawodzie Park, squeezed now between private buildings. Originally it was on the fringes of the city. As with the community, it is difficult to determine when the cemetery was established. Undoubtedly, it was created some time towards the end of the 19th century. However, since Jews resided in Krosno since 1850, it is likely that they buried their dead at the Korczyna Jewish cemetery before the Krosno cemetery was established.

The matzeva, or tombstone, was a characteristic feature of the Jewish cemetery. They were lined up in rows and faced east. A wall surrounded the cemetery; at the gate there was probably a place to wash hands for those who participated in the burial ceremony. There is no trace of the water basin. The watchman's brick house is also gone. The tombstones were sandstone slabs with semicircular tops. The tops were adorned with reliefs; below them were inscriptions. Symbols and writing commemorated those aspects of life of the dead that were related to the Old Testament, his religious role or his propensity to do good deeds.

Tombstone of Samuel Lilbera who died in 1928

Tombstone of Sara, daughter of Samuel, died in 1948

The tombstone of Bernard Munz who died in 1930

It is difficult to ascertain which of the signs are symbols and which are just pure ornaments. There are about 100 tombstones at the Krosno Jewish cemetery. It is not known how many were lost, but the sunken graves with shattered reliefs and illegible writing testify that the destruction was extensive. Most tombstone writings were in Hebrew.

The tombstone of Jakub Jeszai, son of Zwij, who died in 1919, has a crown on top that probably symbolizes religious piety or the head of a family. The text reads: Here lies in eternal rests a modest and honest man devoted to God. He raised his family in good faith and respect. He rendered his soul before the age of 70[19].

The tombstone of Shmuel Lielberg, who died in 1928, reads: Here lies in eternal rest Shmuel Lielberg, a simple and honest man, a member of the Elimelach Segal family. Let his name be remembered forever.

The tombstone of Sara, daughter of Shmuel, is adorned with a candlestick, a characteristic feature of female graves. On it is written: Here rests our blessed mother Sara. Honest, she was very good to people. The daughter of Shmuel, she died in September 1936. Blessed be her memory[20].

Apart from candles, birds and flowers inform us about the life of women. The matzeva of Chaia Libenschow indicates her age. The text reads: Her life ended in her youth, only three months after she was married. She died on Saturday, 1926.

Only three gravestones are different from traditional tombstones. One lacks any symbols and the text in Polish informs us of the death of Zygmunt Heller, son of Baruch and Dora Shuman; and Ryszard Blum, son of Oscar and Lola Heller. The second one has a broken tree, a symbol of death on it and informs of the death of Hersch Kern in Hebrew and Polish. The use of Polish and laconic inscriptions including only the name and the date of death are unusual, as most gravestone writings are in Hebrew. This may be a proof that some Jews in Krosno were being assimilated.

The third gravestone is one of the most interesting at the Krosno Jewish cemetery. It belongs to Bernard Munz, who died in 1930. A stone base with a Hebrew inscription on the front is topped off with a sculpture of a broken tree. Under the Hebrew text there is an inscription in Polish informing of his birth and death.

The undertakers who tended to the burial of the dead were members of the Hevra Kadisha[21]. They were pious people who knew all the customs pertaining to religious burial. There were full members who had full rights and newly accepted members who had no rights. After a period of apprenticeship they were granted active rights that allowed them to participate in elections of the board of the Hevra Kadisha. The organization derived its income mainly from donations paid by families of the dead, from donations paid for prayers, and from fees for gravesites[22]. The kehilla authorities set the fees. In line with the general rules of Jewish communities, they could not exceed 500 zloty. The money was used to cover the expenses of poor people who could not afford burial expenses and the wages of the cemetery watchman. The latter also maintained the cemetery.

The Final Word

This work, although not exhaustive, allows us to formulate several conclusions. The Jewish settlement since the Middle Ages until the 19th century was frequently hampered by the actions of towns people who tried to protect themselves from the competition of Jewish merchants. This was the reason Krosno, like other Polish cities, received privileges forbidding Jewish settlement. These prohibitions, though frequently ignored, excluded the city from the Jewish settlement until the 19th century. Only then can we begin to talk about the history of Krosno's Jewish community.

The main source of income for Jews were leases, trade, and to a smaller extent crafts. The Jews were very active in food production and light industry. They controlled the trade in town. Jewish economic activities boosted Krosno's market through attracting the peasantry into monetary exchanges and thus spurred economic growth of the city.

World War II destroyed the Jewish community and ended the common history of Jews and Poles who lived in Krosno together, linked through a peculiar bond of closeness and animosity. Today this is all history.

Footnotes

1. M.Horn, Jews in Sanok to 1650.[W] Bulletin of the Jewish Historical Institute of Warsaw 1970,nr.76,s.4.

2. We also find several references to Jewish residents in Krosno between 1385–1427.

3. Liber cancelariae Stanislai Ciolek, J. Caro, Wien 1871, nr 30, s.67–68.

4. Gazety Lwowskiej from Lwow 1856 nr.42.

5. St. Cynarskie, op.cit. s.81

6. M. Horn, op.cit., s. 23.

7. T.A. Olszanski. Jews in the Carpathian areas. Beskid Niski–Bieszczady–Pogorze, Warszawa 1991, s.20.

8. APS, AMK, Book of records for the city of Krosno 1867–1872, Sygn.1

9. M. Koczynski, Zbior ustawyrozporzadzen adm. Krakow 1897, t.I. S.412.

10. Miejscowosci oznaczona symbolem.

11. M. Koczynski, op.cit., s.471.

12. Ibidem.

13. Kronika gmin, op.cit., s.526.

14. M. Koczynski, op.cit., s.488.

15. Archiwum Panstwowy w Krakowie, Naczelny Com.sygn.510 s.734.

16. APKr, NKN Korespondancja z Powiatow. sygn 290, s.321.

17. APKr, NKN Korespondancja z Powiatow. sygn 510, s.915.

18. Wedlug wspomnianej relacij sprawa.

19. Teksty hebraiskie zostaly przetlumamaczony.

20. Kronika gmin, op.cit., s.527.

21. Ibidem.

22. Oplaty za miejsce.

[Page 325]

Chapter XV

**The Krosno Library
Historical series**

**Notebook 13 [1997]
Elzbieta Raczy**

Jews in Krosno Between 1919–1939

**Krosno 1997
Translated by Monika Hendry from Polish to English
Arrangement and editing by William Leibner**

**Editor of the series is Ewa Mankowska.
Copyright by Museum Rzemiosla w Krosnie Krosno 1997
ISBN 83–905920–4–5
Na Okladzie:
Ucznowie szkoly hebrajskiej wraz z nauczczycielka Riwka Gross Wykonane
w latach 1927–1928. Zbiory Leah Krill Balberg.**

Contents of the Chapter

Introduction

Jewish Demographie in Krosno

The economic structure of Krosno Jews

Jewish cultural life

The Krosno kehilla

Material aspects of Jewish culture

Conclusion

Introduction

The second pamphlet also deals with the life of the Jews in Krosno. It is dedicated primarily to the life and activities of the Jews of Krosno. The lack of materials prevents us from drawing a clear and precise picture of the situation. Nevertheless, it is a fact that Jews played an important role in the life of the Krosno community and they were a part of the Polish nation.

Most of our research was based on materials that are available in Polish archives and museums. We also collected information from former Krosno Jewish inhabitants. The Yad Vashem Institute in Israel and the Jewish press that dealt extensively with Jewish problems in Poland provided an important source of information. The city of Krosno did a fine job in preserving many of the archives in chronological order up to the outbreak of World War II.

Demography of Jews in Krosno

The Jewish population in Krosno grew significantly during the wars. But the precise growth that can only be ascertained by analyzing certain statistical documents, notably the census of 1921 and the one of 1931. Based on the data of the 1921 census, Krosno had 6,887 inhabitants that included 1,725 Jews who represented 25% of the total population. According to P. Burchard,"Relics and Momentos of Jewish Culture in Poland," published in Warsaw in 1990. In Krosno in 1921, there were 6,887 inhabitants that included 4,871 Jews or 70% of the population was Jewish. With that many Jews the Jewish community would be classified as big community and according to the governmental regulations would have to be governed by a board rather than by a mere council. There are no sources that confirmed such number and those available points to a much smaller figure). This census was based on religious affiliation.

In 1931, the town had 12,125 people that included 683 Jews[1]. This census was based on the language spoken at home. Many Jews spoke Polish and therefore were recorded as Poles. Still others preferred to be recorded as Poles. The economic crisis of 1929–1935 mainly affected the countryside and hence farmers' demand for industrial products declined. Trade was one of the main occupations of Krosno's Jews and was aimed mainly at farmers. Lower demand for products was another reason for the drop in Jewish population in Krosno.

The nationality make–up of the town was well–described in 1924. Krosno's 635 houses had 6,278 residents that consisted of 5,287 Poles and 746 Jews. The rest of the population belonged to other minorities. In religious terms, Krosno had 4,474 Roman Catholics; 1,725 Jews; and 88 Greek Catholics and Russian Orthodox Church followers'[2]. The data shows that many Jews identified themselves as Poles. Still there was a sizable discrepancy in the number of Jews between the surveys.

Analyzing the census data one must remember the different criteria used. The 1921 census used the criteria of religious identity and the one ten years later that of the language spoken home. It is unknown how often Jews put down Polish as their mother tongue, which may have been influenced by their sense of loyalty to the state. The real number of Jews is probably somewhere between those who declared Hebrew [probably Yiddish since few Jews spoke

Hebrew, ed.] their mother tongue and Judaism their religion. This meant that the 1921 census was probably more objective as the nationality issue was not investigated in 1931.

The Acts of the town of Krosno listed 14,752 residents in 1938 that comprised 12,023 Christians and 2,729 Jews that represented 18.5% of the total population. Krosno's Jewish population grew mainly at the end of the thirties because of war fears. The town council noted at its meeting on 8 March 1938 that about 300 Jewish needy refugees settled annually in Krosno. They required assistance from the Jewish Committee. The high numbers of Jewish refugees were the result of the Jewish policy of the Third Reich. Germany expulsed all foreign Jews, especially Polish Jews,(ed.). The council allocated 300 zloty as assistance to needy refugees'[3].

The streets with the highest density of Jewish residents were Blich, Forteczna, Franciszkanska, Ordynacka, Pilsudskiego, Slowackiego, Sienkiewicza, and the main square. The table at the end of the pamphlet shows the distribution of Jewish residents in the town]. They created the town's commercial center. The synagogue and the ritual bath were located in the same area. This suggested that the choice of Jewish dwellings was influenced by economic and religious factors.

Jews also owned most buildings in the center of town that was resented by the Poles. Frequently the town council intervened and defused possible conflicts. In 1926 it ordered officials to publicly apologize for the words spoken during a meeting "The magistrate was disgraced again by selling property on the main square to a Jew."[4]

Fragmented sources do not permit us to establish which houses belonged to Jews in the center of town. Exact records show owners of building 5–11 on the north side of the square and building 12 on the south side. All numbers are given according to the current numeration. The building no. 5 was bought in 1890 by Hanna and Abraham Moses Ratz and belonged to the Ratz family until 1929. Then Abraham Rubinstein bought half of the house from Chaim Ratz and the other half was bought Beila and Mendel Linderberg in 1931. The first Jewish owner of the house currently numbered as 11 was Izrael Neubert who bought in 1874 and held it until 1899. Then, he probably sold Â¾ of it to Chaim Keil and Â¼ to Branla Keil and in 1900 the magistrate issued permission to Chaim Keil to repair the roof. In 1921 he gave his share to his children with each getting 3/20 of the house. In 1892 Salomon and Ita Spett bought the property at no. 12 for 10,150 zlotys and held it until 1918 when it was sold to Elias and Blima Zeller who owned it until 1957.

There were also buildings that had many owners.

This was due to inheritances. Each part of the house was frequently divided in the process of inheritance or commercial dealings. For example, the house no. 11 was subdivided several times and finally belonged to eleven owners. Many Jews were rich enough to own more than one building. Council member Joseph Ratz owned house 5 and 45 located at the square. In the 1920s Jews owned houses 7, 9, 10, 11, 12, 25, and 27. This, however, did not bear out the real housing situation of the majority of Jews of Krosno. The rich minority owned houses in the center. Most of Krosno Jews lived in small flats, usually with one or two rooms. Those able to afford a three–room flat were considered well–off. A Jewish flat was not that different from a Polish one. The determinant factor was the financial standing of the owner. A characteristic feature of a Jewish home was the mezuza (a small container with verses from the Bible written on paper [probably parchment, ed.] attached to the right side of the entrance door, observant Jews would kiss it on entering and leaving the home). The Jewish home had more pots and pans because meat and milk dishes had to be kept separated due to the kashrut laws of the Jewish religion. [Memoirs of Baruch Munz, ex–resident of Krosno, currently in Israel.]

Jewish families were usually extensive and large with many children. A one flat may house eight to 10 people. Big families were the rule among the rich and the poor. Not many families could afford to rent separate premises for their workshops. The term "workshop" denotes here anything that was used for making a living. Most artisans lived and worked in the same place. The more enterprising owners went abroad to earn money and modernized their workshops. Krosno did not have too many of these individuals. Abraham Munz was that kind of man. He started a family when he was 19 and became an independent turner. He went to work in Czechoslovakia and Germany and worked for 7 years. He earned enough money to build and equip his workshop that became quite popular and had clients from Korczyna, Miejsce Piastowe and Rymanow.

Occupational structure of the Jewish community

Krosno's Jews engaged mainly in trade and in crafts. World War I disrupted the activities of the occupational organizations. The last meeting of the board of the Great Guild was held on May 17th 1914 and it didn't resume meetings till February 24th 1919[5]. To the guild belonged most craftsmen in Krosno, both Poles and Jews. The most popular crafts among the Jews were the trades of tinsmith, tailor, and baker. The situation was similar in most places in Galicia, for example in Sanok and in Rymanow. In Sanok Jews were attracted to weaving, leather making, and baking. In Rymanow, Jews dominated the tinsmith trade, tailoring, watch making, and baking. The town had 14 bakeries and only one was Polish–owned. In 1937, Sanok had 11 bakeries that included 8 Jewish bakeries, and 37 tailor shops that included 24 Jewish stores. On the other hand, Poles there dominated the trade of blacksmith, wheel making, and carpentry. The table at the end of the pamphlet lists the Jewish craftsmen of Krosno).

The most known Jewish craftsmen in Krosno were: baker Izrael Breitowicz, tinsmith Abraham Munz, and turner Mozes Springer.[6] It is worth noting that some, including the brick laying[7] trades, did not attract Jews at all. These included stone masonry, carpentry, blacksmith, etc.

Stationary of Munz's firm in Krosno

The apprenticeship and mastery of most trades under the auspices of the Great Guild lasted 2–4 years. The terms of the contract, pay, accommodations, and living expenses were negotiated individually between teacher and student or his guardian beforehand. The parties would usually sign an agreement that was authorized by the board. Most young Jews were taught by their co-religionists, because of religious considerations. Such an arrangement made it easier for students to fulfill their religious obligations; however, there were many exceptions. Fathers tended to teach their children the trade since they could not afford to pay the tuition[8]. Teaching at home was cheaper and many workshops were family-owned and passed from generation to generation as few could afford to buy a new workshop and equip it.

From 1936–1938, masters of the Great Guild had 197 students including 27 Jews[9]. The board was in charge of executing the laws of the Guild and supervised exams, the eradication of usury, the issuance of "industrial cards" or certificates of trade, and solving disputes among masters and students. Indeed, it was forced to intervene frequently as attested by the guild books[10]. The Great Guild also supervised the production levels and timely fulfillment of orders.

An important role was played by the butchers' guild. Anyone who possessed an industrial card and managed an independent butcher shop could also become a member of the butcher guild. Many stores were Jewish-owned and belonged to the butcher guild, among them: Flisk Breitowicz, Mojzesz Breitowicz, Sander Fessel, Jakub Grunspan, Dawid Lambik, Tobiasz Nagiel, Menes Trenczew, and Mahler Wolf[11]. On 29 December 1920 the board granted "industrial cards" to Salomon Beim and Shie Kwill. On 5 January 1926 it fined Abraham Munz 10 zloty for failing to report a student. This was a breach of the rules and required a penalty.

In 1928 there were 20 butcher shops in Krosno, including 9 Jewish-owned stores.

Between 1922–1930 there were 20 students and judging by their surnames and the fact they were taught by Jewish masters, it can be concluded that they were Jewish. Jewish religion required special slaughtering procedures [schitah, ed.] and this could only be taught by fellow Jews. At the end of the1930s, all Jewish masters were expelled from the butcher guild and the great guild expelled all Jewish artisans. They later formed the Collective Israelites Guild. Jewish craftsmen tried to establish their own guild much earlier. The Great Guild was deliberating such a request at its meeting on 14 April 1932[12]. According to the minutes from the meeting, Jewish craftsmen put forward a request to leave without giving reasons. It was probably because of the growing competition among Polish and Jewish craftsmen and some of the rules might hamper Jewish activities. Jewish craftsmen may have felt tempted to form a separate guild as a way of maintaining their current economic position. But the split was avoided and the situation was defused with the help of Samuel Goldstein. He was a representative of the Jewish craftsmen and led his co–religionists to a settlement that avoided a rift of the organization[13].

The Jewish craftsmen left the Guild in 1938[14]. At the time, the anti–Semitic sentiments in Krosno began to weaken. These feelings always existed, but in 1936 they erupted in public. The anti–Semitic sentiments can be attributed to the fact that the Jews dominated the local economy and they lived in a separate and different culture. Anti–Jewish actions in Krosno were mainly limited to economic boycotts, stalking Jewish shops, anti–Jewish demonstrations that frequently resulted in broken windows in Jewish stores, and mugging Jews on the streets[15] "Nowy Dzennik," 29 December 1936). The first anti–Semitic incident took place on 25 December 1936. A group of young people led by Wieslaw Mazur and Marek Ruszkowski wrecked the local Jewish sports club Makkabi. The police estimated the financial losses at 700zl. They also broke windows in the house of Jakub Alter. The main instigator of these acts was the Guild of Christian Craftsmen that printed leaflets with slogans such as "buy only from those that help build Poland for Poles [Jews were not considered Polish citizens by this organization, (ed.)][16].

The boycott undoubtedly affected the economic life of some Jews, but the damage was much greater in the sphere of human relations between Jews and Poles and deepened the mutual distrust that already existed below the surface.

These anti–Semitic sentiments in Krosno between 1936–1938 were a reflection of the general situation in Poland. The influence of the National Democrats, a right–wing nationalist and anti–Semitic party, was growing. Big economic crisis fueled competition and social conflict. From 1935–1939, there were attempts to stop ritual slaughter, limit Jewish access to certain professions, especially law and medicine and to create specific Jewish seats in the classrooms. These measures were demanded by the National Democrats and had support in the government.

Against this background, nationalistic ideas of the National Democrats were gaining attention in certain circles of the Polish society. Jews also engaged in and dominated trade, thus providing an excellent target for hate. Krosno was an industrial and mercantile center with extensive economic links far beyond the county. Merchants attended its fairs from the Sanok, Brzozow, and Jaslo counties. Between 1920–1939, Krosno had 12 annual fairs held on the first Monday of the year and weekly ones held on Mondays. Korczyna and Dukla also had weekly fairs.

Trade was also the traditional Jewish occupation. The fairs were held in the main square of town that was small, and inconvenient. So the Town Council decided to build a new square near the train station that was completed in 1936[17]. In 1928, Krosno had 80 shops, most of them owned by Jewish residents. The table at the end shows the number of Jewish merchants and types of goods on sale.

Jewish shops in Krosno were very similar to Jewish shops in other towns. They were located in basements or on lower ground floors and frequently offered assorted goods[18]. The income was barely enough to support a family. There were of course prosperous merchants, notably Leopold Dym, Eber Englander, Majer Ellowicz, Wilhelm Hirschwald, Jozef Horowitz, and Samuel Rosshandler. Many advertised their shops in the local press[19]. There was also a petrol station opened in 1928 by Chanie Just and Diana Landau. This was the first gas station in the region and it proved very successful.

Apart from crafts and trade, Jews also managed small restaurants. Lack of sources doesn't allow us to establish the exact list of such places. Two of these restaurants must have been quite successful since the owners advertised in the press. They were M. Ider's restaurant on Staszica street and R. Dym's tavern on Franciszkanska street[20].There were three strictly kosher restaurants owned by Abraham Korn, Chanie Platner, and Golda Pastor and a ritual dairy farm set up in 1925 by Samuel Weinberger[21].

Krosno's intellectuals were concentrated in free trades, such as medicine and law. At the end of the 1920s, Krosno had 11 doctors including 3 Jews[22]. The most trusted were doctors Jakub Braumring who lived on Korczynska Street, and Jonas Stil who lived on Franciszkanska Street. Sources stress that all Jewish doctors attained very high ethical and professional levels. Throughout the 1920s and 1930s, about 30% of law offices in Krosno belonged to Jews.

Education and cultural life

Education played a very important role in the Jewish community. It was conducted in religious and secular schools, with various teaching approaches and languages. The primary level of education for boys was conducted at the cheder, a one–room school with one teacher who taught the Hebrew alphabet, prayers, and some lines of the Old Testament. Parents paid the teacher. There were many elementary cheders in Krosno. Those parents who could afford to pay the Hebrew teacher continued the education of their sons who attended the more advanced cheder. Children studied the weekly section of the Old Testament, customs, and the Talmud. The schooling lasted from 5 to 12 years of age.

Attending cheder did not free children from compulsory schooling, so many also attended secular schools. In the 1930s, Meilech Golda Fenig, living at the Podwale Street, taught at Krosno's cheder[23]. Another basic level Jewish school in the town was the Talmud–Tora, similar to the cheder. Girls could attend the "Beis Yaacow" religious school opened in 1925[24]. This school was under the influence of the Agudat Israel party [an Orthodox religious party, (ed.)]. It prepared girls for their role as Jewish wives and mothers. There was another religious Jewish school in Krosno that taught religious and secular subjects similar to the public school. The teaching language in all these institutions was Yiddish[25].

The Zionist–influenced Tarbut organization set up in Krosno in 1920 a school with Hebrew as the teaching language. It had 5 grades with 80–100 pupils[26]. In 1922, the Tarbut organisation has264 educational institutions in Poland, including 227 schools, 4 high schools and 4 technical schools. It employed 1,019 teachers and had 34,230 pupils. The school must have had difficulties in finding a permanent location because the educational authorities tried to get financial assistance. The money was provided by the town's budget of 1929[27].

Lea Krill–Balberg's report from the Hebrew school in Krosno

The amount of 500 zlotys, granted by the municipal council, was earmarked for the construction and equipment of the school's new building. It is uncertain where the rest of the funds for the construction of the school came from. Undoubtedly some of the money must have been contributed by the kehilla, and the rest by private donations. Jewish children in the area also attended secular schools and represented up to 25% of all pupils.

Krosno had four public schools and 2 high schools: for men and women, which were later transformed into the coeducational City High School and coeducational State High School. Polish schools were open six days a week, including Saturdays. In practice Jewish students did not attend school on Saturdays.

The table:[28]

Year	Class	No. of pupils	Jewish pupils	Total % share
1930/1931	IV a.b	85	16	18
1931/1932	IV a.b	41	17	41.5
1934/1935	IV a.b.c	137	30	21.9
1938/1939	IV a.b.c	130	30	23.1
1939/1940	IV a.b	79	20	25.3

Jewish youth also attended high schools in Krosno, but their numbers were small. The main barriers to study were financial difficulties, rather than religious considerations. The annual high school tuition fee averaged 240zl[29]. This prevented poor children as well as children from traders to attend high. Only children of the wealthy or owners of prosperous workshops and trading companies could afford a higher education.

Even amongst the well–to–do, it was customary to send children to learn a trade or an apprenticeship rather than academic schooling. It was much easier for Jewish children of intellectuals such as doctors, lawyers, civil servants, and teachers. These children represented a large proportion of Jewish children attending high schools. The reasons behind this were not only financial but also family tradition and high esteem in which education was held[30]. A similar feeling existed among Polish families. In Krosno's schools, Jewish children had their special religious hours of instruction. At the end of the school term, Jewish teachers would give grades and these were incorporated into the official school certificates.

The public general technical school, whose students worked during the day and studied at night, played an important role among Krosno's educational institutions. The classes were held in the evenings. This institution was not very popular among Jewish workers and craftsmen. Between 1920–1926, only 2.5% of the student body was Jewish. This would tend to indicate a low demand for this type of education among Jewish youth in Krosno and the area. The situation was similar in the 1930s. The increasing competition between Jews and Poles, and the need to upgrade skills, prompted more Jewish students to enroll at the technical school. They studied predominantly tin making, tailoring, baking, and shoe making[31].

Despite everyday problems, mainly providing for the family, cultural life thrived in Krosno's Jewish community. Reading was especially popular. Besides, the public reading room, the Jewish community had its own reading room and a library. It had 100 permanent members[32]. The most popular reading materials were Jewish.

[Yiddish] newspapers such as "Moment" (Chwila) published in Lwow, and "Nowy Dzennik" today published in Krakow[33]. Apart from Jewish issues they focused on national and world matters. There were also available media published by Jewish political organizations, such as the Zionist "Hajmat" or homeland or Polish newspapers.

Evenings were usually spent in Jewish establishments or visiting friends. The favorite pastime was playing cards or chess, accompanied by discussions about political and economic problems. The youth usually spent their free time in sport clubs, Gideon and Makkabi that had gymnastic, running and football teams[34]. The clubs frequently organized competitions between the Krosno Jewish teams and Jewish teams from neighboring towns. The Makkabi club located in the Town Square was particularly famous and popular[35]. In the evenings, it would be crowded with young members, who came to listen to the radio and meet friends.

Quite important in the town's cultural life were hobby and interest clubs. There were music and theatre clubs sponsored by Jewish youth organizations such as Brit Trumpeldor and Hanoar Haiwri[36]. The theatre club staged mainly plays by Jewish authors and used the revenue to support the Hebrew school. These performances must have been quite popular and well–acted, as they were mentioned in the Jewish press[37]. On 11 October 1930, Szalom Alejchem's drama "Scattered and Dispersed" was staged at the Krosno Co-operative. Well–acted parts included: M. Katz as the father, D. Steigbugel as the family favourite, and J. Spitz as a shadchen or matchmaker. A correspondent of Nowy Dzennik said the drama "was enthusiastically received by the Jewish community from the area. Hebrew teacher M. Szeberszteiner directed the dramas that were sponsored by one of Krosno's active Zionists. F. Trenczer and M. Szberszteiner replaced Riwka Gross who worked at the Hebrew school at the end of the 1920s.

The description of Jewish cultural life would be incomplete without mentioning social customs. Krosno's Jews differed from their Polish neighbors in a few respects, especially in terms of religion and rituals. These differences were especially marked during Jewish holidays and family celebrations.

The private life of Jews was regulated by religious rules. From birth through wedding until death, the rituals were very important. Birth was associated with the first important rite, circumcision. This happened on the eight day after the birth of a male baby. This act symbolized the joining to the Jewish community that followed the laws of God. In the 1920s, Rubin Kaufman, Rubin Peretz, Jakub Klagsbald, and Majer Ellowicz did circumcisions in Krosno[38]. The kehilla also employed a midwife, Ester Ader[39].

Another ritual was the bar mitzvah. On the first Sabbath of a boy's 13th birthday, he would be called up to the torah as an adult male. This made him, from the religious point of view, an adult fully responsible for his actions.

Other celebrations were also subject to religious rules, including weddings. Most of them were arranged by parents. Before the bride and groom stood under the Huppa or canopy, their parents would sign a pre–nuptial contract stipulating material conditions of the future union. This was most often done during the engagement, when the date of the wedding was also set. After returning home, guests were invited to a traditional meal, while the couple organized their stag and hen night. A characteristic feature of the wedding was the girl's ritual bath in the mikveh on the eve of her nuptials. This custom is still observed today. The wedding always took place in the afternoon. During the celebrations the groom was required to crush a glass with his shoe, which symbolized the destruction of the temple in Jerusalem. The ceremony was followed by a lavish banquet with the newly married eating the so–called golden soup, a symbol of marital unity. The soup was a kind of chicken soup which the couple ate from the same bowl, remembers Leah Krill–Balberg.

The social and political life of Krosno's Jewish community

After Poland regained its national independence, it issued laws that standardized the structure of Jewish communities in the country. It included a decree dated February 7th 1919 from the Head of State, an order of the President from October 14th 1927, that extended the above–mentioned law to the districts of Lwow, Krakow, Stanislaw, and Tarnopol. The text of rules that stipulated the political structure of the Jewish communities was published on April 5th 1928. These were supplemented by acts of the Ministry of Religion and Public Enlightenment from October 24th 1930 and September 9th 1931. They replaced all Austrian laws from March 21th 1890.

These were in force until World War II. The communities became legal and public corporations. They had legal status and performed mainly religious functions. All people of the Jewish faith within their area of residence were considered members. Krosno's Jewish kehilla was classified as a small community with under 5,000 members. According to the decree by the Ministry of Religion and Public Enlightenment dated December 24th 1927, the following kehillos were classified as large communities in the Lwow district: Drohobycz, Dubiecko, Jaroslaw, Lwow, Przemysl, Rawa Ruska, Rzeszow, and Sambor.

The Krosno community was headed by an eight–member council, elected every four years according to the piecioprzymiotnikow [five requirements notably, male, residence, age etc.] electoral law. Men over 25 years of age, who lived within the area for at least one year, had active voting rights. Passive voting rights were given to those over 30 years of age who had Polish citizenship.

There was a clause in the electoral rules that the electoral committee could exclude from the voting lists those who were against the Jewish faith and deny voting rights to those who were jailed or lost Polish citizenship. This new ordinance did not give equal voting rights to women but severed the connection between the voting rights and the amount of tax paid by an individual[40]. As described by one of Lwow's newspapers "Moment" from 29 April 1928, "... the current reform breaks away from the dependence of the electoral law on the amount of tax and scores of other archaic methods. (...) the community will be run by people who will treat their posts not as some ceremonial duty but as a mission to serve the Jewish people, who are able to encompass all issues concerning the community..."

The first Krosno election after the independence took place on 25 May 1924[41]. Israeli publications give 1925 as the date of the first post–World War I elections in Krosno. Polish sources, which were used in this research, do not confirm this date. ("Nowy Dzennik" from 1 June 1924 and 19 May 1925.)

The electoral campaign for the kehilla control was primarily between the Aguda, orthodox party, and an alliance of Zionist parties that formed a united democratic–Jewish list. The fight intensified and three weeks before the elections, the Zionists organized a few meetings led by M. Wieenfeld and S. Rosshlandler. The meetings unveiled the party's own program but also severely criticized the current leadership of the kehillah. The Aguda accused the Zionists of trying to set up a non–observing school and to close down the synagogue. These were not the only methods. The Aguda posted written letters by hassidic rabbis that urged Jews not to vote for the Zionist parties[42].

A week before the elections, Aguda members plastered the town with the letter from the Hassidic Rabbi of Belz asking not to elect Zionists "who want to convert Jewish children..." as reported by Nowy Dzennik," "with particular hatred they attacked the head of the Zionist block organizations, Mojzesz Wiesenfeld" –Nowy Dzennik , 1 June 1924.) The newly elected democrats were: Mojzesz Wiesenfeld, Meschulem Weinberger, Dr. Wilhelm Hirschfeld, Samuel Stiefel, Leopold Dym, and Ozjasz Hiller. Zionists and their supporters gained a majority of the council. Among the board members, half were Zionists, who created a club led by Mojzesz Wiesenfeld. Under their influence, the new budget for 1925 earmarked 600 zl for Keren Hajesod and some money for educational and cultural activities.

Fragmented documents do not allow us to reconstruct the full membership of the commune's authorities in 1924 or other years (1928 and 1936). Each Jewish kehilla had to meet religious needs of its members. Its other important function was charity, mainly for the old, sick, orphaned, and unemployed.

The first elections were based on the statutory rules from the beginning of the 20th century. From 1927, all Jewish communities in Small Poland or Galicia were governed by a new electoral ordinance. Based on this ordinance, the government called for elections in 1928. The orthodox Aguda and the Zionist parties competed for influence within the communities. Aguda supported the current legislation that stipulated that Jewish communities were religious institutions, while the Zionists tried to turn them into a cornerstone of the Jewish independent community. We must not forget that control of the kehilla gave certain economic advantages and the right to decide how to spent the budget. The 1928 election brought victory to the Zionists in most of the communities in Small Poland including Brzozow, Drohobycz, Jaslo, Rzeszow, and Sanok.)

Following World War I, Krosno's kehillah faced some serious problems. One of the most important problems was the impoverishment of the community membership and the availability of medical services. The American Joint helped financially solve some of these problems. USA Jews set up the Joint Distribution Committee after World War I. In its first years, its help was limited to meeting the immediate needs of Jews in the war–ravaged Europe. Later it focused on establishing and developing charitable institutions such as hospitals or homes for the aged. The kehillah's efforts to provide welfare assistance were supported by a number of religious and secular charities that included the Jewish Women Association, that had 70 members in the 1930s, as well as Linas Chojlim (Organization to help the sick and needy). These organizations cared for the poor, providing warm meals and the basic foodstuffs to the most needy. To achieve their goals, these committees also lobbied for support. Some money came from the kehillah's (check spelling throughout for consistency) budget and donations from wealthy Jews, some from the town's coffers.

In 1937, the town paid the Jewish Women Association 20 zloty to cover the cost of medical treatment for the poor[43]. From 1937–38, the magistrate granted Linas Chojlim coal and paid for milk for Jewish children. An important role in caring for the sick and poor played the Bikur Cholim Association that also provided medical help for the poor. It looked after 70 children for whom it tried to ensure at least one warm meal a day[44].

Jewish organizations also looked after visiting Jews, from outside the kehillah. It provided food, places to sleep, and met the spiritual needs of the visitors. One of these organizations was Hachnassat Orchim [providing for guests] that ensured that the guest had a place to stay and to observe the Shabbath. Apart from charities, Krosno also had purely cultural, professional, and cooperative associations. One of them was the non–interest credit association. The first of them, Mutual Help Cashier, was established in 1928. Between 1937–38, Malopolska (Little Poland) had 224 cooperative associations of the type of cashier. All of these offices loaned a total of 2,798,000 zlotys to the needy Jews in the area.

At the beginning, it lent 17,477 zlotys to 158 individuals[45], mainly unemployed craftsmen and merchants. Other Jewish co–operative societies included the Merchant Association and Jad Charucim (Artisan Association) set up in 1929. They played a significant role in the period of the economic crisis and the growing Polish–Jewish conflict in the second half of the 1930s. With their meager resources at their disposal, they still managed to save many Jewish workshops and shops.

In the 1920s, Krosno had several Jewish political organizations. They differed in their theoretical approach and practical ways of solving Jewish problems. Agudat Israel was an orthodox religious party. It aimed to defend religious rights of Jews, spread the faith, prevent social changes, and protect civil rights that were not in conflict with religious dogmas. It also sponsored charitable organizations by setting up religious educational and philanthropic institutions.

Available sources don't mention when Krosno's Agudat was established. Its program and activities attracted mainly religious conservatives from all levels of the Jewish community. Its leaders in the 1920s were Eber Englander and Samuel Hirschprung. The party co-operated with administrative authorities that supported it because Aguda was loyal towards the Polish State and bitterly opposed Zionism.

Growing anti–Semitism in the 1930s, and the government's policies, probably undermined this co–operation. To achieve its goals, Aguda tried to take power in the kehillot. Zionists, especially the Organization of General Zionists [middle class party, ed.] was in total opposition to the Aguda. The Zionists wanted to take control of the kehillot and turn them into secular self-governing bodies that supported a broad range of Jewish activities including support for Palestine and the emigration of Jews to the Holy Land.

The head of Krosno's Zionists was Moses Wiesenfeld; the vice–chairman was Meschulem Weinberger; and the secretary was Dr. Josef Gross. The Krosno Zionist committee also included two women. The other members of the committee were S. Hirschfeld, Dr. L. Dym, S. Rosshlander, L. Engiel, Platner, and Salomn. This party co–operated with another Zionist organization in Krosno – the moderate religious Zionist party "Mizrachi." Its leader was Samuel Rosshlandler and members and sympathizers came from among the enlightened middle– and lower–middle class.

Its policy placed it somewhere between Aguda and the General Zionists on religious matters. Mizrachi supported Zionist programs regarding emigration to Palestine but stressed the modernization of Jewish life within the religious framework. In the 1930s, Mizrachi cooperated with General Zionists in the election to the town council to diminish the influence of Agudat Israel. In the mid–war period, there were other political parties in Krosno, namely Brit Hanoar ,youth wing of the right wing Revisionist Zionist party, the Zionist Labor Party (Hitachdut), and other workers' parties. To the working party coalition also belonged the General Jewish Worker League, also known as the Bund and the Poalei Zion. An indicator of the influence of Zionist parties in Krosno is the number of their members elected as delegates to the Zionist Congress[46]. The following table shows them.

Table of Zionist elections in Krosno

Year	General Zionists	Mizrahi	Revisionists	Hitachdut	Socialist
1927	77	40	7	71	
1929	66	42		96	
1931	114	46	46		72
1935	226	73			160

Following the Zionist Congress in Basle in 1897, any Jew was considered a Zionist if he accepted the program of the Congress and paid dues, called the shekel. The purchase of shekel and 18 years of age gave the individual the right to participate in the election of delegates to the National Zionist Congress. Any Zionist aged 21 and active in the Keren Hajesod (the foundation fund) was eligible to present himself as a delegate. The election was secret and the number of delegates for each city depended on the number of shekels purchased. In 1928, Krosno had 3 delegates to the National Congress of Zionists from West Malopolska and Silesia. This was the highest number of delegates in the area. The cities of Brzozow, Korczyna, Jedlicze, and Rymanow elected only one delegate per township. Places where less than 50 shekels were sold did not elect delegates[47]. This happened in Krosno in 1925. The Krosno committee of Zionists then joined forces with those of Korczyna and helped elect Dr. Ludwik Oberlander from Jaslo as their spokesman.

At the 1928 congress of Zionists from Western Galicia and Silesia, a new executive was elected. It consisted of 7 delegates and the agenda consisted of the following items: Palestine, finances, culture, economy, and youth. The chairman of the executive was Dr. Ignacy Schwarzbart and the secretary general was Abraham Hofstatter. The Congress selected a central council of 37 delegates and a party council of 45 delegates that included Dr. Jakub Braumring from Krosno[48]. Besides national country and international Zionist conferences, there were also regional meetings. On Feb 5th 1922, there was a meeting in Sanok with delegates from 22 places including Bialigrod, Brzozow, Dukla, Korczyna, Krosno, and Rymanow.

A very important function of the Zionist organizations was the collection of funds to help create a Jewish homeland in Palestine. There were two main Zionist financial institutions. The Keren Hajesod collected money for the building of a Jewish infrastructure in Palestine and the Keren Kayemet L'Israel. The latter was created by the Zionist Congress to raise money in order to purchase land in Palestine. In Krosno, many fund–raising activities occurred in the streets of the city and were organized by the local committee of the Jewish National Fund, headed by Dr. Romm. On the 20th and the 21st of October, Commissar of the Fund, P. Teplicki, took part in the street collection for the Fund. The Aguda party planned its own fund raising campaign on the same day but following intensive negotiations, the idea was dropped. The Aguda office received some financial compensation[49].

Similar fund drives were organized in other towns, such as the one on July 13th 1930 in Iwonicz[50]. Apart from fund raising, the committee also sponsored readings about the Keren Kajemet activities in neighbouring places. The most active was Mojzesz Wiesenfeld, who frequently took part in these meetings. In June 1925, he lectured twice at the Bethmidrash [synagogue] in Dukla.

Not all towns could meet the quotas set by the Fund. The collection depended on the generosity of the residents. Krosno failed to reach the quota in 1928.[51] Here is a sample of the quotas imposed on various townships in 1928: Dukla 270zl; Krosno 11,25lzl; Rymanow 810zl; and Sanok 1,620zl. In 192,5 Krosno exceeded its quota and raised 3,000zl for Keren Hajesod and 1,300zl for Keren Kajemet. In 1920, the Fund launched a campaign of entering names in its Golden Book. Each entry also made a financial contribution to the Fund. In 1928, a campaign was launched to inscribe Poland's name in the Golden Book, in honor of the 10th year of the independence of the country. The idea was very well received in Krosno. A committee of residents was formed to collect money for that purpose. Mayor Emil Rappe oversaw it. To include Polish residents, the Zionists organized a large mass rally on the 27th December with some guests including vice–mayor M. Miasowicz. Dr. L. Oberlander from Jaslo was the main speaker[52].

Between the wars, there were a few Jewish youth organizations in Krosno. Most of them were linked to Zionist organizations. They included Hashomer Hatzair [the Young Guard], Hechalutz [Pioneer], Brit Trumpeldor Trmpeldorf Alliance], and Hanoar Haiwri [Jewish Youth] established in 1930 by Abraham Hofstatter[53] Trumpeldor was a Jewish national hero). H. Frlapan, L. Teplicki, and S. Steigbugel headed it[54]. Their members were children and Zionist youth. They taught their members different trades in preparation for their emigration to Palestine. They raised money for the National Fund and organized trips and training camps, as well as celebrations to commemorate important events and people from the Zionist movement[55].

They also paid a lot of attention to propagating Zionist principles among the Jewish youth through organizing meetings with prominent Zionist activists.

Youth organizations in Krosno were popular because of their scout character and the possibility of emigrating to Palestine. Although not many young people actually left for Palestine, these organizations gave the young a chance of self–fulfillment through focusing on the development of Jewish culture. Jewish political organizations in Krosno were very active in the elections to the Polish parliament because Jewish representatives in the highest level of power were essential in protecting the community's interests. However, because of lack of materials, we can't establish political preferences of Krosno's Jewish community and the level of engagement in the elections during the 1919–1922 period.

In the 1928 parliamentary elections, the Jewish community had six lists (including two orthodox lists, Auguda and Charajdim; two socialist lists, Bund and Poalej Zion Left) and a united Zionist block representing the various Zionist parties that called itself the National–Jewish Alliance[56]. Analysing the chances of different Jewish factions, the "New Daily" said: (is this a direct quotation?) the leaders of both orthodox parties hate each other and would drown each other in a spoonful of water. None of these lists belong to the orthodox. All the labor lists together represented only a small percentage of the population and had no chance to elect a mandate in Malopolska.[57] The Zionist block in Krosno included: the General Zionist Party, Mizrachi, Hitachdut, and Jad Charucim. Samuel Rosshlandler, the leader of Mizrachi, headed the town's election committee of the National–Jewish Alliance[58]. The Zionist block and the Non–party Block of Co–operation with the Government (BBWR) competed for the support of Jewish voters. Krosno's Mayor Krukierek was a candidate of the BBWR. Pre–election rallies and meetings were held since February 1928. The election committee of the National–Jewish Alliance on 14 Feb 1928 organized a rally led by Dr. Schreiber, an MP, and by an MP candidate of the Zionist block, Dr. L. Reich [[59]–[60]].

Present at the meeting was also the representative of Aguda, Samuel Hirschprung. On the same day, in the evening, the Zionists organized another meeting and invited the Jewish MP F. Rottenstreich, who explained the election program of the National–Jewish Alliance. The most important item on the agenda was the protection of Jewish political, cultural and economic interests, including the maintenance of proportional election. The right to employment at government institutions and the solution of the problem of Sunday as a rest day, as a result of which Jewish people were forced to take off two days incurring losses in business.

BBWR was also engaged in campaigning. On 26 February it organized a meeting with the electorate. A correspondent of Lwow's "Moment" wrote, "The chairman of the magistrate, Krukierek, who was the 3rd candidate of the Non-party Block list, invited the magistrate to visit the most prominent residents of Krosno except for the Zionists, he was convinced that as good neighbors and citizens the Zionists will vote for him anyway". However, the representatives of Krosno's Jewish residents were invited to this meeting. Josef Horovitz gave a speech on their behalf. The general Zionists were fiercely attacked at the meeting and Samuel Rosshlandle tried to defend them. He rejected an attempt to influence Jewish political representatives to support the government list. In his speech he said, "We will co–operate with Pilsudksi's government having our own people from the list 17 (National–Jewish Alliance) who understand Jewish matters"[61].

Out of 22,000 eligible voters with the right to vote for Jewish lists in the Przemysl region (including Krosno), 75% actually voted[62]. The most votes went to BBWR and the second highest to the National–Jewish Alliance. Zionists organizations formed a common election block called National–Jewish Block in Malopolska (list no. 14) for the parliamentary elections in 1930. Their candidate was Mateusz Mieses. The remaining candidates on list number 14 were: Dr. H. Rosmarin, Dr. E. Sommerstein, Dr. K. Schwartz, Dr. D. Koch, Dr. I. Nehmer, M. Reich, Ch. Eliasz, and Dr. S.Seelenfreund.

Well known Jewish community leader, Bendet Akselrad of Krosno and formerly of Korczyna succeeded by Mechel Hisrchfeld, Chaim Dym, Mechel Rubin, and Izaak Stiefel

Before the separate blocks were formed, there were attempts to form electoral alliances among Jewish the organizations. Aguda and the Zionist parties held talks in September 1930 to try to form a General Jewish National Block. Mizrachi opposed it and the talks collapsed. In the end, the Aguda formed an electoral coalition called the General Jewish Economic Block, and the candidate list was finalized on October 6th 1930. The Socialists formed the Socialist Left Block and also had their own electoral list.

At this time, Krosno residents focused on the parliamentary elections. The election committee of the Zionist block, headed by Samuel Rosshlandler, was actively participating in the electoral campaign supported by the youth organization Brit Trumpeldor. On November 2nd, they organized their first meeting with the editor of Storch publication from Przemysl, which according to the newspaper "New Daliy" was "a magnificent display of support of local Jews for the list no. 14 and its candidate 48 – Mateusz Mieses"[63]. The second meeting was organized on November 9th at the hall of the Beth Hamidrasz [synagogue] with about 100 people in attendance. Dr. Weintraub from Przemysl gave a speech. Quoting Dr. Ojasz Thon, a leading political figure in

Malopolska, he said: "When Poland goes to the polls under the banner of changing the constitution, we may be the only ones to go to vote for the fulfillment of the constitution. Still, the trophy for which Jews will go again to the polling are still the same old boring issue; actual equality in deeds and not mere words."[64] In the Przemysl region, the list of the National Jewish Block received 9,900 votes and the Socialist Left Block 137. In Krosno, out of 3,666 eligible voters, 2,780 voted. The National–Jewish Block received "New Daily," November 30th 1930, criticized the rabbi for meddling in the election and said: "Since so many rabbis and miracle makers felt the call to become political leaders, the Krosno's Rabbi, Mr. Fuhrer could not stay behind. Apart from him, also some Hassidic youth tried to rig the Jewish votes."[65]

Following these elections, the government adopted a new constitution in April 1935 that resulted in new voting rules that reduced the possibility of electing candidates. Krosno's Jewish residents lost interest in parliamentary elections[66]. The same thing occurred in most towns of Galicia.

The representatives of the three largest Jewish political organizations protected the interests of their electorate. The number of Jewish councilors and their political affiliation depended on the various elections. In the first 15 years of independence, the municipal council had 24 members. This number grew to 31 prior to World War II. Between 1919–1935, the Jewish councilors represented 6% and in 1938 only 3% of the council members[67]. The sharp decline can be attributed to the unfavorable situation toward the Jewish community at the end of the 1930s. The professional structure and the party membership of the Jewish councilors are only known for the year 1938.

Council members were primarily merchants. They consisted of one representative of the intelligentsia and one craftsman. In addition, Eber Englander, Leopold Dym, Rubin Mehel, and Samuel Steifel represented religious conservatives. Jozef Horovitz, Wilhelm Hirschwald, and Samuel Rosshlandler represented Zionists[68].

Material culture of Krosno's Jews

According to the documents, the Jewish kehilla of Krosno was formed at the end the 19th century. It built the brick synagogue at that time. Krono's map of 1851 does not show the synagogue. Rules issued in 1882 by the authorities forbade building any wooden buildings in the town center. It became the center of Jewish life in Krosno. It of served as a place of prayer, teaching, meetings and kehilla activities. It was adorned with Arcadian decorations and looked like a modest progressive synagogue. It was situated on a sloping hill at the beginning of Slowacki Street[69].

Between the wars, the synagogue was a two–story building covered with a double sloping tin roof. It is hard to establish whether the synagogue was modified during its existence. A small building next to it was a ritual poultry slaughterhouse. The upper part was the actual synagogue hall where the people prayed, men and women were separated in accordance with orthodox tradition[70]. Along the eastern wall was the holy arc where the Torahs were enclosed. A distance away stood an elevated stage or bima, a few steps above the floor. The Torah scroll was usually removed from the holy arc and carried to the bima where it was read. Following the reading, the Torah was returned to the arc. The middle level had prayer rooms[71] for different groups of people, especially smaller groups, and also a house for the caretaker. At the bottom of the building was a ritual bath.

The kehilla's administrative and judicial offices were also located in the synagogue. It had a Bet–Hamidrash or study hall where a hundred students could sit and study religious texts[72]. Some rooms were used as offices for the kehilla.

The synagogue served the Jewish community until 1941. It gave shelter to Jewish refugees who were displaced from the surrounding areas and also to single women[73]. The manager, or Szemes Silberberg, tended to the synagogue to the end. When the Krosno Jews were deported and the remainder locked up in the ghetto in 1942, the synagogue was converted to a warehouse by the Germans. Then in 1943, the Germans shot the last hiding Jews of Krosno within the building. The building survived World War II[74] and was subsequently dismantled by the residents of Krosno. Presently, there is no trace left of the synagogue.

Distribution of the residences of Krosno according to religion

Table of Jewish residents in Krosno in relation the total population
Source of information: APS, AMK, city records for the years 1936–1938, sygn 43

Name of street	Number of Christian residents	Number Jewish residents
Blich	12	32
Cmentarna	22	–
Forteczna	151	102
Franciszkanska	12	110
Kolejowa	96	9
Korczynska	165	37
Kosciuszki	95	16
Krakowska	79	26
Lewakowskiego	93	33
Lwowska	90	6
Lukasiewicza	283	45
Ogrodowa	58	36
Olejarska	150	16
Ordynacka	15	45
Pawla	3	4
Pierackiego	319	30
Pilsudzkiego	131	211
Plac 3–go Maya	37	–
Podwale	42	62
Pojezuicka	31	7
Polna	213	3
Rozna	3	5
Rynek strona pol,	92	218
Rynek strona pol,	50	75
Sienkewicza	24	50
Skargi	12	1
Slowackiego	29	129

Staszica	80	34
Szewska	13	–
Szkolna	2	17
Tkacka	43	10
Walslebna	45	2
Wislocza	22	19

Table of Jewish masters and apprentices in Krosno
Source: MRzK, membership in the Major Guilds, sygn. Arz–38, sygn. Arz–23

Trade	Jewish masters in 1919–1930	Jewish apprentices in 1919–1942
Plumbing	Ch. Korb, L. Altman, O. Bertenfeld, L. Altman, A. Korba, I. Rosenfeld, S. Bein, J. Flam, D. Tabizel, I. Wielopolski, R. Munz	H. Korb, W. Lozowski, J. O. Altman, M. Munz, I. Altman, J. Korba, L. Bertenfield, A. Lindsberg, L. Kupfermen, J. Rosenfeld, M. Rosenfeld, Ch. Szyja
Shoe parts	J. Ratz, J. Rotke	M.S alz , N. Amsterdam, S. Wagshal
Conditors	J. Konig	M. Konig, S. Margulies
Hats	B. Kondes	A. Kondes
Barbers	J. Bodnara, S. Seiden, N. Pinkus	H. Janas
Tailoring	M. Gelb, J. Berger, O. Turek, A. Hauber, R. Fischber, S. Goldstein, Ch. Standfeld, S. Rothe, D. Fischbein, A. Lindenberg, A. Steiner, J. Knustlinger, F. Rozmer, S. Rothe	J. Rosenfeld, O. Berger, R. Pinkas *, J. Gutler, O. Berger, S. Diamant, M. Wolf, F. Gebel, S. Berger, A. Lobel, J. Turek, M. Goldstein, S. Turek, J. Salz, W. Leiter, P. Mandel*
Furrier	M. Schlanger	Ch. Schlanger
Painting	M. Garfunkel	L. Silberberg
Brass	M. Springer, L. Altman	J. Ozias, D. Springer, Ch. Munz, Altman
Baking	I. Breitowicz, J. Szyja, Ch. Konig, B. Krieger, H. Muller, H. Gross	F. O. Bergman, Ch. Entner L. Lupnik, J. Kriegel, A. M. Breitowicz, D. Tralez, E. Leib
Carpentry	Ch. Balaban, S. Zeman	

Glaziers	M. Bialywloss, Ch. Horowitz	I. Springer, M. Haller, S. Horowitz
Locksmith	D. Fruchman	M. Konig, A. Malz, M. Felbaum, Czemerys, J. Fruchman
Turnery	M. Springer, L. Altman	I. Springer
Brooms	H. Edelheit	J. H. Sperber
Watch industry	J. Tepper, A. Lobe, K. Wiedor	A. Apt, D. Leib, S. Steimetz

* denotes a woman

Table of Jewish merchants in Krosno, in the 1920s
Source: Address book of merchants in Galicia, Krakow, 1931

Type of business	Number of merchants
Haberdashery	15
Construction Materials	4
Cattle	1
Sugar	2
Timber	2
Luxury Goods	11
Eggs	1
Women's Hats	1
Colonial Produce	2
Kitchen Utensils	7
Flour	2
Furniture	2
Dairy Products	2
Naphtha	4
Shoes	9
Heating Materials	1
Fruits	1
Sundry Goods	52
Pipes	1

Table of the Number of Jewish students and their percentage in the Krosno High School

Year	Number Jewish	Total

	of pupils	pupils	% share
1925/1926	423	31	7.3
1930/1931	495	36	7,2
1934/1936	456	23	5.0
1937/1938	360	11	3.1

Table of Jewish students at the Kopernik school in Krosno. Year book

Year of Graduation	Initial and Surname
1919	P. Stilman*
1920	———
1921	I. Oling, J. Omachel, M. Spat, D. Berel
1922	A. Lindenberg, R.Weistreich
1923	———
1924	M. Altman, M. Kinderman, A. Scheiner
1925	———
1926	———
1927	N. Weinberger, I. Goldberger, J. Siegel, S. Perkis, H. Wiesefeld
1928	H. Altman, J. Dym, M. Weinberger
1929	Ch. Altholz, Ch. Margules
1930	J. Fink, J. Laufer
1931	S. Neuss, A. Steigbugel
1932	M. Schertz, Ch.Fries*, I. Krill* G. Platter
1933	M. Kleinman, B. Fischbein
1934	M. Goldberg, J. Stiefel, S. Stiefel
1935	———
1936	———
1937	———
1938	M. Steinvrocher*, E. Stein*, D. Steinbucher
1939	M. Salomon, A. Chorowitz

* asterisk denotes a woman

Table of Jewish councilors in Krosno between the wars

Year	Number of Councilors	Jewish Councilors	Names of Jewish of Councilors
1919	24	5	Abraham Dym, Baruch Juda, Baruch Presser, Chaim Dym, Eber Englander
1925	24	4	Abraham Dym, Baruch Presser, Eber Englander, Jozef Ratz
1935	24	4	Leopold Dym, Izaak Stiefel, Jakub Baumring, Wolf Hirschfeld
1938	31	10	Eber Englander, Samuel Rosshandler, Bronislaw Kleiner, Jozef Horowitz, Abraham Munz, Izaak Stiefel, Leopold Dym Rubin Mehel, Samuel Stiefel, Wilhelm Hirschwald

Conclusion

The archival materials regarding the Jewish community of Krosno are very scant and can't serve as a base to evaluate the life and activities of Jews in the town between the wars. Jews represented almost 20% of Krosno's population and were an integral part of the town's population. They focused on economic, cultural, and educational activities. They engaged in trade and crafts, and catered to the needs of the town and villages in the area. Many Jews were involved in textiles and leather trades and none in carpentry or smithing.

A large number of Krosno's Jews were poor and the kehilla and charitable organizations provided needed social assistance. The crisis of 1929–1935 lowered people's purchasing power and unemployment, and had a profound impact on the Jewish community as most members were casual workers or lived from trade. The boycott of Jewish shops initiated by professional Christian organizations as a way to reduce competition also had an adverse impact on the Jewish population. Economic difficulties forced Jewish people to set up credit co–operatives to help those most needy[113].

Krosno had many Jewish political parties, with the most influential being the Agudat Israel and the General Zionists. Krosno's Jews took an active part in the political and economic life of the town. Despite their different religion and culture they considered themselves residents of Krosno and that feeling survived among the survivors today.

Footnotes

1. The State Archives in Skolyszyn, the Acts of the Town of Krosno, the list of people belonging to the town of Krosno. Jewish names in original writing, sygn 47.

2. red J. Garbacik, Krosno studia... Krakow 1973, t.II, s.48

3. red J.Garbacik, op.cit.s.49

4. APS,AMK, Ksiega posiedzen Rady Mejzkiej z lat. 1921–1927 sygn 28

5. Muzeum Rzemiosla w Krosnie uchwal Cechu...t.II,sygn ARZ60

6. Baruch Munz's testimony.

7. MRzK, Ksiega wpisowa ucznikow... t I_IV, sygn K.W Arz 61

8. Ibidem

9. Ibidem

10. MRzK, Ksiega Uchwal Cechu, Wielkiego... t I_IV, sygn K.W Arz 61

11. MRzK, Stowarzys. Rzeznikow I Masazrzy, Ksiega z lat 1910–1926.

12. MRzK, Ksiega Uchwal... sygn ARZ60

13. Ibidem

14. red J.Garbacik, op.cit.s.66

15. Nowy Dzienik 29 Dececmber 1936

16. Commercial information, The Chrisdtion Merchants Assoc. 1938, s.2–4

17. red J.Garbacik, op.cit.s.72

18. Ksiega Adresowa Malepolski, Krakow 1929

19. Glos Krosnienski nr.1. 1928

20. Ibidem

21. APS,AMK, Ksiega posiedzen... sygn 28

22. Ksiega Adresowa,op.cit. Nowy Dzenik.1 Kwiecien 1925

23. Urzad Stanu Cywil... z lat. 1930–1938

24. Yad Vashem

25. Kronika gmin...t.III, S.526

26. Yad Vashem

27. red J.Garbacik, op.cit.s.64

28. Archiwum Panstwowe w Przemyslu, Ksiega spisowa skoly

29. St. Mauersbberg, Komu szluzba szkola Lodz 1988, s.49

30. Lack of information

31. APP, Vocational information in Krosno..sygn 17

32. Yad Vashem

33. Nowy Dzienik

34. Baruch Munz's testimony.

35. Nowy Dzienik, 29 December 1936

36. Nowy Dzienik 18 October 1930

37. Nowy Dzienik 11 October 1930

38. USC w Krosnie,Metriki z lat 1925–1942

39. Ibidem

40. Chwila from Lwow, 1928

41. Nowy Dzenik April 1st 1924 and May 19th 1935

42. Nowy Dzienik, October 1st 1924

43. APS,AMK, Ksiega protokolow...z lat 1935–1937 sygn 40

44. Yad Vashem

45. Kronika gmin... op.cit., s.527

46. Yad Vashem

47. Nowy Dzienik, September 30th 1928

48. Nowy Dzienik, November 7th 1928

49. Nowy Dzienik, October 30th 1930

50. Nowy Dzienik,July 20th 1930

51. Nowy Dzienik,July 20th 1930

52. Nowy Dzienik,July 20th 1930

53. Ibidem

54. Ibidem

55. Ibidem

56. Nowy Dzienik, February 1928

57. Ibidem

58. Chwila marca 1st 1928

59. Chwila marca 28th 1928

60. Ibidem

61. Ibidem

62. W. Wierzbieniec, Spolecznosc zydowska Przemysla...Rzeszow 1996,s.160

63. Nowy Dzienik, November 10th 1930

64. Ibidem

65. Statystyka Polski, seria C, z. 4, Warszawa 1935

66. Nowy Dzienik, November 30th 1930

67. APS,AMK, Ksiega posiedzen... sygn 42

68. Ibidem

69. Baruch Munz's testimony.

70. Baruch Munz's testimony.

71. Ibidem

72. Nowy Dzienik, November 9th 1930

73. Kronika gmin... op.cit., s.527

74. Commission investigating crimes committed against the Polish nation.
    Charge sheet against Oskar Becker,sygn 1893/71, t.II, relacja Hilary Zajac.

Chapter XVI

The Krosno Library
Historical Series

Notebook 15 [1999]
by Elzbieta Raczy

Jews In Krosno Between 1939–1946

Krosno 1999

Translated by Monika Hendry from Polish

Arrangement and Editing by William Leibner

Editor of the series is Ewa Mankowska.
Copyright by Museum Rzemiosla w Krosnie Krosno 1999
ISBN 83–905920–7–x

Cover. Reproduction of painting entitled "Krosno" by Zwi Majerowicz.

Contents of the Chapter

Zwi was born in Krosno in 1911. He left the city in 1929 to study in Berlin. He then left in 1934 for Palestine. He resided in Haifa until 1974. He represented Israel at the Biennale of Venice and San Paolo. His works can be classified as lyrical realism in Israeli painting. His paintings can be viewed at private collections throughout the world.

Introduction

This chapter represents the third and last part of the series about the history of Jewish inhabitants of Krosno. It is intended to portray the fate of Krosno's Jews during World War II. The material is based on the documents found at the archives of Yad Vashem Institute in Jerusalem, the Jewish Historical Institute in Warsaw, and the Main Commission for Investigating Crimes committed against the Polish Nation in Warsaw where there are records of the trials of former Krosno Gestapo officials. We also used materials from the museum of Auschwitz–Birkenau, mainly death certificates of the inmates of the camp.

An important source of information were the living testimonies of the surviving witnesses and the documents they possessed, notably certificates of detention in Soviet prisons, letters from relatives written during the occupation, and lists of survivors. Additional information about Krosno Jews was provided by the works of: Martin Gilbert's "The Atlas of the Holocaust," Artur Eisenbach's "Nazi policy of annihilation of Jews," Simon Datner's "55 days of Wermacht in Poland," and Jozef Garbacik's and Stanislaw Cynarski's "Jaslo accuses: Nazi crimes in the Jaslo region during 1939–45."

Full reconstruction of events in Krosno is not easy. Scarce sources make chronology difficult. Conflicting witness accounts complicate the establishment of certain facts.

The work covers the period from 1939 to 1946. It not only portrays the process of extermination of Krosno Jews but also attempts to show briefly what happened to those who survived the nightmare of World War II.

The Occupation

On the evening of Sept 8th 1939, detachments of the XIV Wermacht Army led by General Wilhelm List entered Krosno[1]. This marked the beginning of the town's occupation. At first the army administered the town. In October of 1939, the civil organs assumed these tasks. In Jaslo, the German authorities set up a council that covered Krosno. The Jaslo region covered the following counties: Gorlice, Jaslo, Krosno, part of Sanok with Rymanow, and part of Strzyzow.

This division was undoubtedly influenced by the fact that oil deposits were located in the area. Oil was an important raw material for the war industry and was given special attention by the occupiers. In the autumn of 1939, General Governor Hans Frank toured the region. On October 15th 1939, a special Krosno county was established. The highest number of Jews were in the following places: Brzozow, Domaradz, Dukla, Dynow, Jasliska, Jasienica Rosielna, Korczyna, Krosno, and Rymanow. Michael Zuzik, who remained in office until August 15th 1942, headed the Krosno County. His replacement Dr. Heinisch remained in office until the end of the German occupation of the city[2].

Following the army's occupation of Krosno, a German security police group arrived and was stationed at Ordynacka Street at first and then at Czajkowskiego Street that was then called Hermann Goringstrasse. The permanent staff consisted of Ludwik von Davier, Gerhard Sacher, Paul Stenzel, and Oskar Backer. Gustav Schmatzler headed the group from October 1940 until the spring of 1944[3]. Gustaw Schmatzler was born on January 17th 1895 in Neudorf. He finished 6 years of primary education. In 1943 he joined NSDAP. Schmatzler was arrested in 1945 and tried in a special court in Rzeszow. On October 8th 1945, he was sentenced to death for crimes committed in Krosno. The sentence was carried out.

Oskar Backer was born in Grodek Jagiellonski in a family of German colonists. From September 1939 until spring 1944, he was a member of Krosno's Gestapo branch, acting as a translator. Backer was arrested in January 1945 in Germany and sentenced by a German court to prison. He was released in 1946 but tried again in 1973 in Bonn, Germany. He was found guilty of six murders during the occupation and sentenced to life. His further fate is unknown.

With the first days of the war, the Jewish population of Krosno and nearby areas started to move. Most town residents looked for better conditions to survive the Nazi invasion and moved to Polish areas in the East that bordered the Soviet Union and Romania[4]. These were mostly people with certain financial means. Many found themselves after September 17th 1939 under Soviet occupation. This included a certain number of Krosno's Jews who left the town in response to a Polish government radio announcement calling on all men able to serve in the army to withdraw to the eastern regions of Poland and join the Polish army there.

Many of them returned to their hometowns when they learned of the Soviet aggression. With the cessation of military operations, the Jewish exodus from Krosno stopped to a large extent. There were still occasional escapes, mainly by young people who crossed the San River to the Soviet side. They were prompted by the terror and restrictions imposed by the Nazis on the Jewish residents of Krosno. Some escapees crossed the river with the help of Jewish authorities in border towns. The Germans tacitly approved these policies since they were interested in reducing the Jewish population in the occupied areas of Poland. Testimony by Josef Weisman, former resident of Krosno, presently resides in Israel. This was the reason for the popularity of border towns such as Sanok and Dynow. For many escapees, the attempts to find shelter there ended tragically in the early days of the occupation[5]. The archives of the Jewish Historical Institute, 301/4681, account by Sacher Grunbaum.

A few days after entering Dynow, the Nazis killed about 170 Jews taken from homes or caught in the streets. Some of them were Jews from Krosno. The victims were buried on the spot. In the spring of 1940, the Krosno's kehilla obtained permission to exhume the murdered bodies and buried them at the Jewish cemetery of Dynow.

The situation was completely different on the Soviet side of the border. Illegal crossing landed many in Soviet prisons. Then they were moved deep into Russia. Ultimately this fate befell most of the former Polish citizens who were not native to the areas that the Russian Army occupied in Poland.

Photo 1. Map of Krosno area under German administration as of October 1st 1941

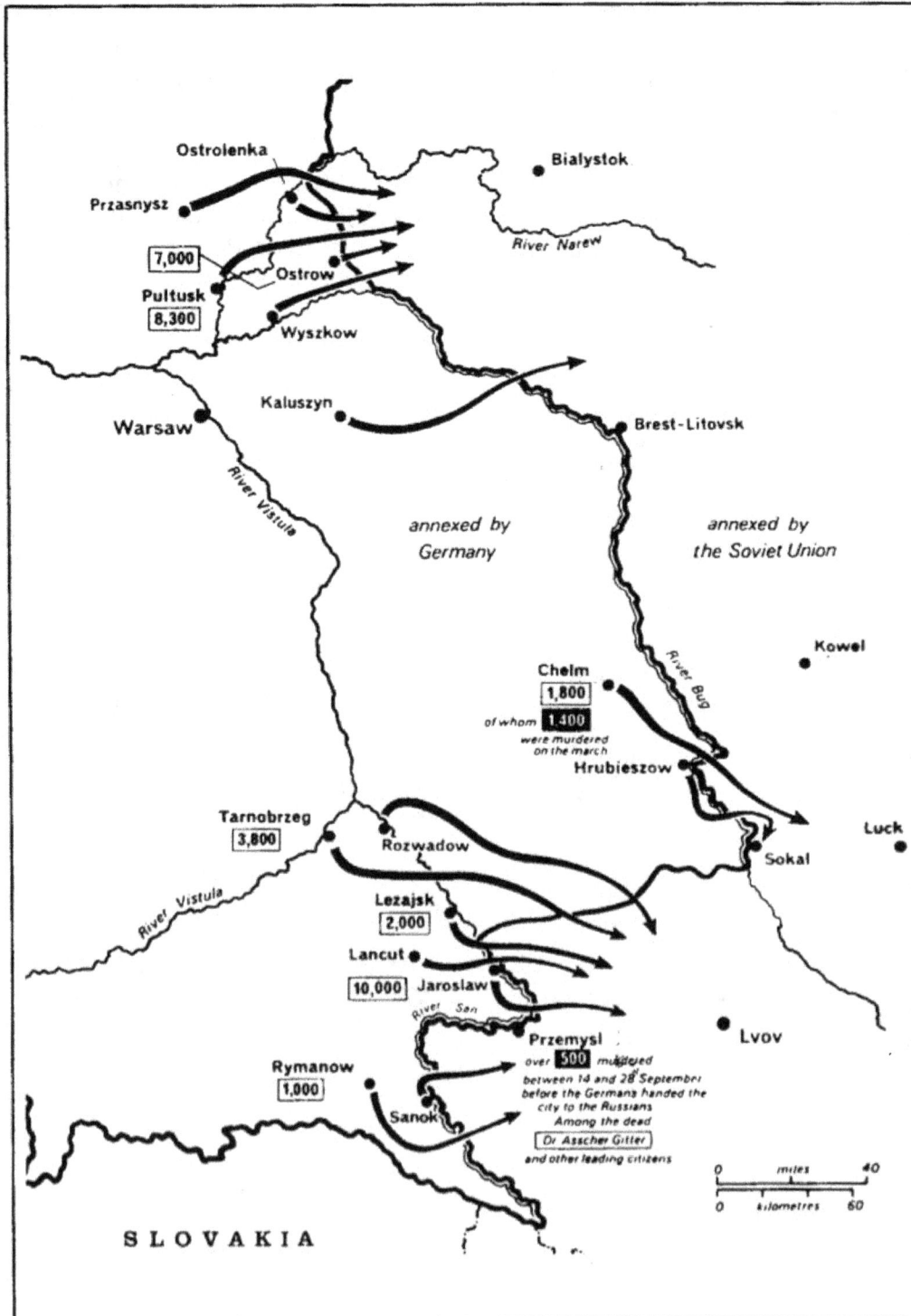

**Photo 2. Border between German occupied Poland and Russian occupied Poland
in 1939. Main crossing areas of Jews from German occupied areas to Soviet
occupied areas**

Krosno Jews in the Soviet Union

Most Jews deported to the interior of the Soviet Union were those who refused Soviet Union citizenship and declared their willingness to return to their hometowns. Most of them were deported in the spring and summer of 1940. The routes of deportations of Krosno's Jews led to the northern parts of the European part of the Soviet Union, the White Sea region, the Far East – Jakuck and to northern and eastern parts of Kazakhstan. The detailed account of routes and destinations of all transports is now impossible.

It is also difficult to establish the exact number of deported Polish citizens from the Krosno area. According to estimates, there may have been about several hundred people; these facts were established from subjective materials – memoirs and accounts of witnesses. We have not been able to obtain original NKWD documents. Among a few first–hand accounts of deportations, the best known is the fate of the transport from Sambor, Eastern Poland, and today Ukraine. It left the city on June 28th 1940 and contained a number of Krosno and Krosno area Jews. According to Krosno's Jews, the transport included 24 people of the following families: Breitowicz, Engelhard, Flapan, Munz, and North.

One witness recalls, "At 2:30 A.M somebody knocked. We were not sleeping. We were anxiously awaiting these unwelcome visitors. An NKWD soldier entered. We started packing. At 4 A.M trucks came. They loaded us aboard the trucks, 45 people with luggage per truck. Unbearably hot. Doors were kept closed. Noise, screams, cries; we didn't know what was happening, what awaited us, where were being taken." Perla Munz, Memoirs. An unpublished diary of a former Jew of Krosno written during her stay in the Soviet Union. Original provided by her son, Baruch Munz.

The destination was the region of Jakuck, east of the river Judoma. In the area, according to a popular saying, "the rules were set by the taiga [or snowforest area between the tundra and the steppe] and executed by the bear." Memoirs of Baruch Munz (the author's recollection).

They reached the place after 3 months of traveling. The route led by railway via Lwow to Irkutsk, then by boat across the rivers Aldan, Lena, and Judoma. The last leg of the journey was a 25–km hike on foot. Many weak deportees died in this transport due to overcrowding, lack of hygiene and food. After using up their own food supplies, not many could afford to buy food. For example a bunch of wild onions growing along the rail tracks cost 2 roubles, an egg 3 roubles, and a liter of milk up to 14 roubles.

Work and existence of those taken in the Sambor transport did not differ much from the situation of those deported to the Far East and North of Russia. Primitive dwellings, crowded living conditions, difficult physical work clearing forests, and harsh climate conditions that frequently reached minus 60degrees centigrade quickly drained the deportees. The main problem was hunger. The rations were small and of poor quality. The prisoners had to bring their own food to the camp. Thus they were forced to carry bags weighing 20–30kg for distances of up to 25km. In the slang of the camp, they were referred to as the "Polish horses." Memoirs of Baruch Munz.

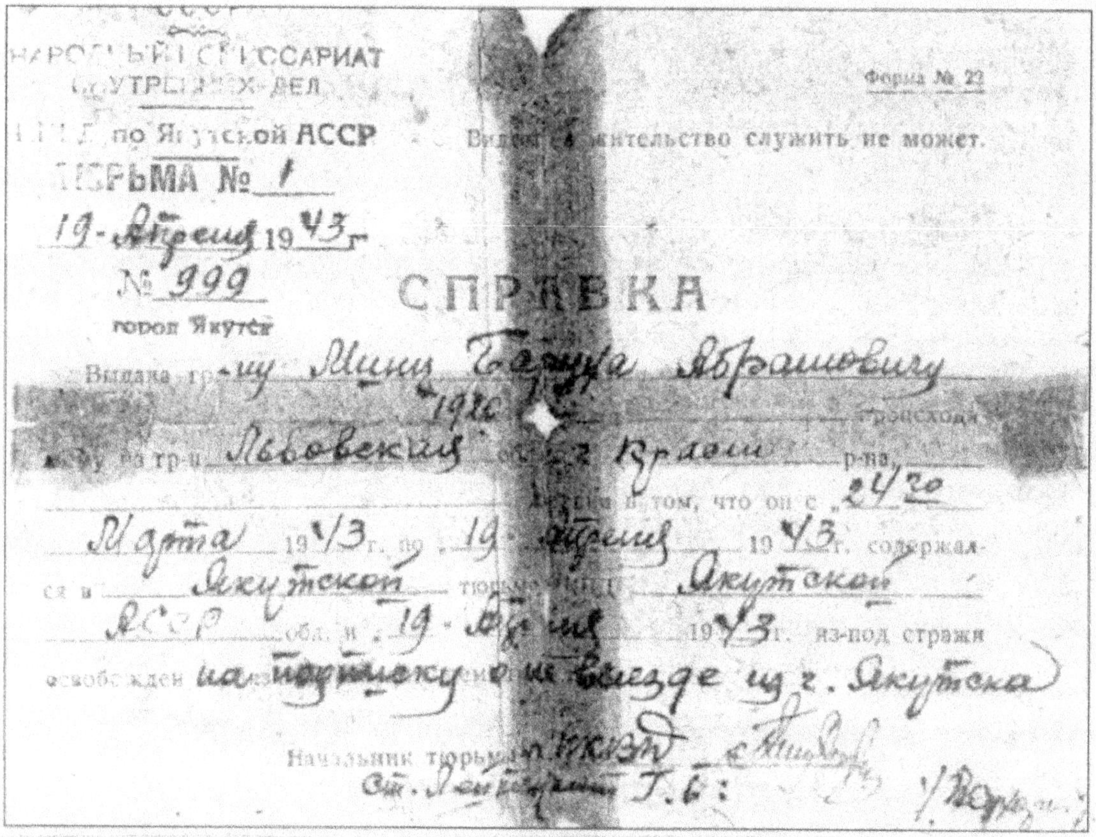
ССАРИАТ
по Якутской АССР
ТЮРЬМА № 1
19 43 г.
№ 999
город Якутск

Форма № 22

Вид на жительство служить не может.

СПРАВКА

Photo 3: **A photocopy of a document about the imprisonment of the Krosno Jew, Baruch Munz after his second refusal to accept Soviet citizenship**

(Baruch Munz's collection)

The signing of the Polish–Soviet agreement in July 1941, and the amnesty for the forcibly displaced Poles announced in August of the same year, changed the status of the imprisoned and enabled them to leave the detention camps. Krosno Jews left the camps and moved to big cities or west and south into the Soviet Union. There they obtained jobs or entered high schools and universities. Among those who graduated from Soviet Union Universities was Marian Flapan. He was deported with other Krosno Jews to the Soviet Union and after the amnesty, he entered university. He graduated in medicine and specialized in oncology. After his return to Poland he settled in Jaworze. He left for Israel probably in the 1960s.

The year 1943 brought another change in the situation of Polish citizens in the Soviet Union. The Soviet government changed its policy of 1941 regarding the nationality of the deportees and attempted to force them to adopt Russian citizenship. Krosno's Jews responded in many ways. Some accepted Soviet passports under the pressure of the authorities or the police, while others refused.

Many deportees, however, ended up in Soviet jails again for their repeated refusals. Some even paid with their lives for this decision. The refusals were not a result of any special sentimental attachment to the Polish State. Rather, they stemmed from worries that a Russian passport would jeopardize any chances of leaving the Soviet Union that in turn would close the doors to any further hopes of emigrating to Palestine, West Europe, or the US. Perla Munz, Memoirs. Baruch Munz's account.

In 1943, the Association of Polish Patriots (ZPP) took over matters concerning the deportees in the Soviet Union. At the end of April 1943, Russia permitted the formation of a new Polish army and the government freed most prisoners, including those not freed under the amnesty of 1941. The amnesty did not apply to those Krosno Jews who were caught crossing the border illegally and charged with spying. They were jailed in Soviet prisons. Memoirs of Josef Weisman.

This prompted another migration to the western areas of the Soviet Union.

One of the witnesses remembers his stay in the Soviet Union: "Why did God punish us so much? Is there another hell possible? We are living in hell in our own lifetime." However the situation of those under the Nazi occupation was far more tragic. Perla Munz, Memoirs.

The Jewish administrative authorities in Krosno and the Jewish Social Self–help Organisation

The Germans appointed a Judenrat to oversee the Jewish community, as in other towns of Poland. The Jundenrat was an administrative institution. It was set up to carry out the orders of the Gestapo. The Nazi authorities determined the scope, the structure and the personnel of the Judenrats. The Krosno Judenrat was formed in the early 1940 and consisted of former kehilla members. The chairman was Jehuda Engel. A representative of Jewish Social Self–help Organization from Krakow described him in the following words: "The chairman of the local Jewish Council [of Krosno] stands out among all chairmen of Jewish councils in the General Gubernia. He is short but with a very expressive face and absolutely disinterested. He sent the amount of 5,000 zlotys that he received for writing petitions to the authorities with all accounts to the kehilla's treasury. He is a man of principles and very socially orientated.[6] From documents of the Jewish Social Self–help Organization.

The chief of the Jewish council developed quite a strong system of power over his subordinates. Like all chairmen, he was forced to cooperate with the Nazi authorities. The occupant tolerated only those who complied with his orders. Jehuda Engel must have suited the Nazis since the sources don't mention changes regarding the head of the Judenrat in Krosno. He took credit for all concessions negotiated from the Nazis. His deputy was Mosze Kleiner and members included: Mojzesz Wiesenfeld, Samuel Rosshlandler, and Jakub Baumring. The Judenrat was headed by members of Krosno's financial and cultural elite. The author describes them in greater detail in her work "Jews in Krosno in between the wars." The structure of the Krosno's Judenrat changed. Krosno's Judenrat fell under the jurisdiction of the Regional Jewish Council in Jaslo, headed by Jakub Goldstein. In December 1940 there were 16 Judenrats in the Jaslo region, notably: Biecz, Bobowa, Brzostek, Dukla, Jalso, Jedlicze, Frysztak, Gorlice, Jodlowa, Kolaczyce, Korczyna, Krosno, Olpiny, Osiek, Rzepiennik Strzyzewski, and Zmigrod.

On 10 September 1941, a new Krosno county was established which resulted in wider authority for the Judenrat of Krosno. Soon it was renamed the Jewish County Council of Krosno. It gained authority over Judenrats in the new county of Krosno. Krosno's Judenrat supervised Judenrats in Brzozow, Dukla, Dynow, Domaradz, Jedlicze, Korczyna and Rymanow. Brzozow's Judenrat was headed by Mojzesz Knobelbarth, Dukla's by Szymon Stoff, Jedlicze's by Szymon Friss and Rymanow's by Herman Spira.

The Krosno Judenrat had the following departments: Social Security, Education, Labor, Public Cleaning Services, and Health. The departments supervised commissions that were formed according to the changing needs of the residents. In January 1942, the Judenrat appointed a hygiene commission headed by Moses Wiesenfeld due to the rising mortality among local Jews. Members of this commission were mainly in charge of sanitation and burying the dead at the Jewish cemetery.

The Judenrat was housed in a building in the square until July 1942, when it moved to building no. 15 on Franciszkanska Street.[7] Jewish Newspaper, July 9th 1942. The Newspaper was started in Cracow, Poland on July 23rd 1940. One has to be cautious interpreting information it printed and needs to remember that the paper was inspired by the Nazi authorities that controlled it. Also, the reports submitted by Jewish authorities to the paper often did not reflect real situations. Some information in the newspaper was substantiated by archival documents. These issues were discussed in greater depth in Marian Fuks' "Life in ghettos in GG based on the Jewish Newspaper." The Judenrat moved its headquarters because of the establishment of Krosno's ghetto that comprised the Franciszkanska Street. In December of 1942, the Jewish ghetto was finally liquidated.

With the approval of the Nazi authorities, the Krosno Judenrat opened a branch of the Jewish Social Self–help Organization in Krosno. The members of the local committee of the Jewish Social Self–help Organization (JSSO) were: Jakub Baumring, Mojzesz Wiesenfeld, Samuel Rosshlandler, Bendet Akselrad, and Mendel Bialywlos. In the beginning of 1940, the Germans started to form a social welfare organization for the General Gubernia, or the parts of Poland that were not annexed to any other country. On May 29th 1940, they approved the statute of the Supreme Welfare Council (NRO) that included the Polish Main Welfare Council, the Ukrainian Welfare Council, and the Jewish Social Self–help Organization. The headquarters were in Krakow and the Jewish Social Self–help Organization supervised many branches. The organization was disbanded on July 29th 1942.

In November of 1941, the Krosno committee of the Jewish Social Self–help Organization [JSSO] created a County Care Committee headed by Samuel Rosshlandler. It was enlarged on June 25th 1942 and included Berich Henoch Abrahamson, Melech Rubin and Mozes Ettinger who worked as messengers and collectors. The Germans disbanded this organization on November 12th 1942.

There were frequent squabbles between the head of the Judenrat and the JSSO mainly due to the overlapping of some of their activities. Already at the first meeting of the delegates, sharp disagreements appeared. Jehuda Engel blocked the opportunities for the JSSO to expand into welfare, sanitation, legal services, and childcare. A representative of JSSO wrote in his report of November of 1940 to the chairman of Judenrat: "In this way he reduced the branch to a committee distributing our subventions"[8]. Another disagreement regarded the building that the JSSO received from the Judenrat. The building contained a shelter for the displaced run by Szemes Silberger, a shelter for old and single women and an activity center for orphans. In the end, after a four–week trial period they were taken over by the County Care Committee (KOP)[9].

The most important problem faced by the Judenrat in the early days of its existence was care and food for the Jewish people. In December of 1939, as a result of robberies and confiscations of Jewish property, most Krosno's Jews became impoverished. The situation was aggravated by the fact that the town received 500 Jewish deportees from other parts of Poland. The Judenrat appealed for help on December 22nd 1939. According to the head of the Judenrat, Yehuda Engel, this was the first appeal of its type in the area of the General Gubernia. The appeal was for warm clothes.

As the war progressed the food situation worsened tragically for the Krosno Jewish population.

Aufruf

Zum bevorstehenden Winter benötigen wir für cirka 400 unbemittelte und verarmte Juden unserer Gemeide sowie für bisher in Krosno angekommene etwa 500 ausgesiedelte Glaubensgenossen warme Überkleider, Kleider, Wäsche, Schuhwerk etc.

In jedem bürgerlichen und wohlhabenden Hause befinden sich überflüssige oder entbehrliche Kleidungsstücke, die wir dringend benötigen.

Auch Du, jüdischer Rassegenosse, nachdem Du alle Deine Schränke und Rumpelkammer auf das genauste durchgesehen hast, wirst feststellen, dass Du eine ganze Menge solcher Kleidungsstücke nicht mehr trägst, oder entbehren kannst, und unnützerweise dem Mottenfrass und dem Verderben aussetzst und verwahrst.

Wir appellieren eindringlichst an Dich, gebefähiger Rassegenosse: Bringe uns sofort, alle irgendwie entbehrliche Kleidungsstücke und überreiche sie uns mit sichtlicher Freude, in dem Bewusstsein, einem Glaubensgenossen in dieser schwierigen Notzeit helfen zu wollen.

Schlage alle Rekorde und Erwartungen, komme als erster mit dem grössten Sack voll.

Beweise! dass Du keinen Stein, sondern ein edles, verständiges Herz im Leibe strägst.

Beweise! dass Du den Ernst und die Not der Zeit kennst und zu helfen mit Leib und Seele gewillt bist.

Beweise! dass Du es verstehst, dass es nicht Dein Verdienst ist, ein Günstling des Schicksals zu sein, dass es nicht der Witwen und Waisen Verschulden ist, vom tragischsten Geschick getroffen zu werden, und dass Du selbst morgen schon auf milde Gaben angewiesen sein könntest.

Beweise! dass man Dich nicht erst durch Verordnungen zur Hülfeleistung veranlassen muss, dass Du vielmehr auch aus eigenem Entschluss und freiwillig Dein zweites Hemd einem hungernden und frierenden Bruder und Schwester zu verschenken fähig bist.

Krosno, den 22. 12. 1939.

Die Jüdische Gemeinde
gez. ENGEL

Photo 4: The text of the appeal for help by the Krosnoer Judenrat with the arrival of many Jewish refugees from other parts of Poland

The food rations distributed by the Germans were very low and food coupons were issued irregularly. For example, in the nearby hamlet of Korczyna, people received food coupons for the first time in December 1941. They were mainly for bread and sugar and only for children under 10 years of age and the elderly over 60. This forced the Jewish community to look for other ways of obtaining food. The most obvious option was to buy on the free market, or rather the black market, but fewer and fewer people could afford the prices. The Jews ran out of cash and precious things that could be exchanged for food. Therefore the authorities had to provide supplies in many different forms.

Thanks to the efforts of the Judenrat and JSSO, a People's Kitchen was formed in Krosno. This type of kitchen also existed in Brzozow, Dukla, Jedlicze, Korczyna, and Rymanow. At first it provided all meals free of charge. However as the economic situation worsened due to the impoverishment of the Jewish population, the number of recipients grew while the resources of the Jewish Council steadily declined. The Jewish Council's income was made up of fees and donations of the town's residents and a subsidy from Krakow. Impoverishment and decreasing subsidies meant fewer services for the people.

Starting August 1941, the Judenrat limited the number of breakfasts and charged for lunches. In March of 1942 lunch cost 40 groszy. Other towns in the county faced similar problems. The Kitchen in Brzozow faced several financial difficulties. In October of 1941, the town had 1,007 Jews and the kitchen issued 4,862 portions to 187 people during this month. Lack of subsidies in 1942 led to a significant decrease in the number of meals. The same situation existed in Rymanow. In May of 1942, its kitchen issued only 300 lunches a month. Jedlicze's kitchen was set up in September of 1941 but quickly run out of money and was shut down. It was reopened in March of 1942 and thanks to the subsidies from the JSSO it issued 4,500 meals a month. In June of 1942, the kitchen in Dukla issued 500 meals, which was far below demand. The town had at the time 1,600 Jews including 300 refugees. The situation in Korczyna was the best. Its kitchen served 14% of the population, issuing 3 meals a day.

It is hard to estimate how many people could afford to pay for this kind of lunch that most of the time consisted of a bowl of soup with very low calorie content. The main ingredients of the meals were brukiew or beet derivatives and potatoes.

The fat content of such meals was very modest. Assuming that portions were standardized, in August of 1941, one portion distributed by the kitchen contained 4.1g of fat. Jewish authorities and organizations did their best to help the poorest. They appealed to the head office of the JSSO in Cracow for financial and material assistance and in response received some money and food that were distributed among the poorest. Cracow benefited from donations from the US Red Cross and the Committee to Help Jews. The donations were distributed to different branch offices. On September 12th 1940, Krosno received 100 kg of peas and 100 kg of grains, on November 18th 1942, Krosno received 500 packages of soup – out of 3,400 that were available in Cracow. This, however, did not meet the needs. The November contribution was reduced to one meal per ghetto resident.

In April of 1941, 318 people received help. Judenrat distributed 3,450 zlotys and 673 kilograms of matza.[10] The table at the end shows some names of people who in April of 1941 received help from the Judenrat and JSSO in Krosno. Korczyna had 700 Jews in December of 1941 and the town's Judenrat spent 17,686 zlotys in that year on social welfare. The kitchen received 12,085 zlotys and other services 5,169 zlotys. Jedlicze had 512 Jews in July of 1942, including 210 deportees. Its Judenrat spent 5,893 zlotys and 72 grosze on social services in the first seven months of that year. The poorest also received basic foodstuffs in the beginning of every month. However this help was a drop in a sea of demand.

Verband der jüd. Handwerker
Związek Rzemieślników Żyd.
K r o s n o.

Jewish association of artisans in
Krosno in 1942

About 1,000 people needed assistance in Krosno. The situation was worsening. In

August of 1942, the Judenrat was able to allocate only 2,885 zlotys for the needy in the ghetto. About 1,110 zlotys from that sum went to the displaced people. Spending on food supplements and medicines was also reduced. In April of 1942, 200 zlotys was spent on medicines and in July half of that figure. The Judenrat's main function, however, was to carry out tasks imposed by the Gestapo. These included compilation of lists of people for deportation, who most of the time came from the poorest social strata or had no connections within the Krosno's Judenrat.[11]

Indirect Extermination – Forced Labor

Following the Wermacht's entry to Krosno, Jews were forced to perform all sorts of tasks. They were also beaten and humiliated. Most often they were caught off the streets and used as labor. In December of 1939, the Gestapo decided that all Jewish residents of Krosno aged between 14 and 60 must perform public work. The occupant treated the General Gubernia as a labor reservoir. Forced labor was classified as a duty for Poles and a compulsion for Jews. The difference between the two was in the conditions and payment for work as both were enforced brutally. Judenrats were obliged to supply workers and labor departments to assign tasks. They included street cleaning services, rubbish disposal, cleaning of toilets and German houses. On average about 140 people performed these tasks daily. The number of the employed differed from town to town. In Korczyna in 1942, all men within the age bracket were employed. In Jedlicze in the same period, only 70 out of 512 workers were employed. A similar situation existed in Rymanow. To keep the town's streets passable in the winter, Judenrats in Dukla and Korczyna supplied some extra people.[112] In January of 1942, Korczyna supplied 40 men a day to clear the snow from the streets of Krosno. Judenrats themselves paid these laborers.

In 1942, Krosno's Judenrat spent on these services 20,000 zl.[113] The real value of the monthly pay was low. The prices were rising continuously and some of the pay went to pay membership dues of the Jewish Council that was helpful when trying to avoid deportations. A lot of money was spent on salaries of clerks. The monthly salary of the head of Krosno's Judenrat was 400 zl. Whenever possible, the Judenrat also tried to feed those employed by distributing some bread, marmalade, and sugar. The quantities were miniscule, in view of the type of labor and widespread hunger.

Jews were also employed in the quarry in Dukla and in military factories. The quarry employed Jews from all over the area. Dukla itself provided about 200 workers in 1942.

The workers were beaten and treated brutally. In the Dukla quarry a Volksdeutch, Karol Marcinkowski, who was even more brutal than the Nazis, supervised Jewish workers.[114] The military factories employed in autumn of 1942 more than half of all the Jews in the Krosno area.[115] The table shows the number of Jews from Krosno and the region employed (by type of work) in November 1942.

Some Jews worked on German farms. They had chances of obtaining extra food, but at the risk of beatings that sometimes even resulted in death. To all these work details the Jews went frequently without shoes and appropriate clothes. In the autumn of 1942, every second Jew in Krosno had no shoes and to meet demand in that year about 500 pairs were needed according to Judenrat estimates. In its report, the Judenrat's board wrote, "The laborers wear out shoes very quickly and it is impossible to repair them. The 100 pairs we received are beyond repair and the wooden clogs are also very weak and useless after a month of use". [16]

Some Jews worked in crafts, which was the main occupation after trade of Krosno's Jews between the wars. This was a result of the occupant's policy. Directives sanctioned the policy by General Governor Hans Frank. They included one issued on November 15th 1939 about confiscation of Polish state properties, and two issued on January 24th 1940 about confiscation of private property and about the duty to report all Jewish property in the General Gubernia. There were also directives about monetary transactions and about curfew. Both forbade Jews from trade dealings and limited their contacts with producers and clients in other towns.

Looting, seizures, and restrictions resulted in shop closures and the impoverishment of Krosno's Jews. Despite this, until mid–1941, most Jewish artisans worked in their own trades. This is confirmed by witness accounts. "In 1941, I left Jaslo for Krosno because the Gestapo there was nicer to Jews. [17] In Krosno, together with dentist Wandenstein from Cracow we opened a clinic." A representative of JSO gives a similar testimony from Cracow who was in Krosno in the autumn of 1941: "When one travels across the town one can see Jewish shops on both sides of the street without commissar boards." [18] Commissar boards were formed by the Germans in order to take over Jewish manufacturing, trading, and service facilities.

[Page 18]

Undoubtedly this policy was pursued to prevent the total elimination of Jews from trade and crafts that would harm local economy and German interests. Memories of Icchak Goldberg, formerly of Krosno now in Israel.

Only at the end of 1941 did the Nazi authorities start the process of full "aryanization" of the economy. They implemented draconian rules that were strictly adhered to and quickly and dramatically worsened the situation of the Jewish population. They deprived the Jews of the means to earn a living and to exist. To fully utilize Jewish labor, Nazi authorities formed a collective called Jewish Craftsmen Association (JCA) on February 1st 1942 with Leopold Altman as chairman. [19] Jewish Newspaper –March 13rd 1942. These kinds of collectives were formed in the entire area occupied by the Nazis. On July 31st 1942, Jewish Work Collective was formed in Jaslo. It included the following trades: leather, textiles, timber, metal, paper, and brush. The leather section gathered shoemakers, slipper makers, and bootmakers. Until the end of January 1942, Krosno's Jewish Craftsmen Association was a branch of Jaslo's Chamber of Craftsmen. The association covered all towns in the county and such trades as clothing, shoemaking, and metal trades. Its main function was to distribute raw materials supplied by the authorities and to coordinate work. With help from JCA, a shoemaker team was formed in Brzozow and later in Dukla. They had three sections: underwear, tailoring and shoemaking, and employed 25 women.

Slave–like work in workshops gave the employed a false sense of security. Until mid–1942, the Jews were not subjected to deportations. To save from bankruptcy those few Jews who were still working in the second half of 1942, the Judenrat decided to grant them financial assistance in the form of Interest–free Loans from a fund established for that purpose on June 25th 1942[20]. The funds were raised among Jewish inhabitants of Krosno and the region. However its resources were very limited because of widespread poverty. In 1942, it lent 4,920 zl. to 33 people, mainly merchants and craftsmen who were members of the Judenrat. The fund was closed in the winter of 1942 when the Jewish quarter was liquidated.

Besides forcing Jews to work in their local areas of residence or nearby, the German authorities also sent Jews to labor camps. There were a few camps in the Krosno region. On August 25th 1942, one such camp was set up in Krosno proper and was under the jurisdiction of the command center of Luftwaffe.[21] There were two camps in Dukla. Both were set up in August of 1942 and liquidated in November and December of 1942. They employed an average of 310 people. Inmates worked in nearby quarries and building the road from Barwinek to Nowy Zmigrod for the companies of Artur Walde – Breslau and Emil Ludwig – Munchen. From 1940 until August 1944 there was a big labor camp at Szebnie. About 80% of 130 men and 30 women in the camp were Krosno Jews. The figures are supplied by Leopold Blech. They were mainly craftsmen employed as carpenters while women worked in the kitchen and laundry. They were on the verge of starvation fed only 100g of bread and a bowl of soup a day. There were some in the camp who ate quite well. Those included inmates who were employed in the administration of the camp, skilled master craftsmen, and doctors.[22] The supervisor was Leib Langsam from Gorlice and the doctor was Tadeusz Lass from Cracow. Money and contacts with Poles allowed them to get extra food, medicines, and clothes, making their existence much more bearable. There is no data about mortality in the camp, but certainly diseases were widespread because of hard work (from 7 A.M. until 5 P.M.), poor nutrition, and overcrowding. Inmates lived in two barracks that were divided into a few rooms, each housing about 12 people.

From the winter of 1942 this was the only official place in Krosno where one could find Jews. The camp was liquidated on January 1st 1944 and the inmates were shipped to the death camp of Belzec and other places[23] according to Franciszek Selz.

Photo 5. The first on the right is Moshe Szebersziner who comes from Gorlice. He was the Hebrew teacher at the Hebrew school in Krosno. According to unverified sources he died at the death camp of Plaszow [Leah Krill–Bleiberg photo collection]

Direct extermination

From the first days of the German occupation of Krosno, there were cases of Jews being murdered in the city and its vicinity. The first such crime was committed by a detachment of the Wermacht that shot 12 Jews from Jaslo and Krosno in the forest of Warzyce soon after entering the area.[24] In the forest of Warzyce near Krosno, the Germans killed Jews and Poles brought from prisons in Jaslo and Frysztak, from camps in Szebnie, and ghettos in Iwonicz, Jaslo, and Krosno. That moment marked the beginning of humiliation and degradation for the Krosno Jews. Goods and equipment of workshops were confiscated. Frequently the value exceeded 10,000–15,000 marks according to S. Polanski, currently living in Israel.

However, these events could be considered calm when compared with the events of 1942. Witnesses remember the period as calm: "In October 1939 I returned to Krosno. Jews were relatively well off at that time financially but morally they felt terrible"[25]. Helen Steifel came back to Krosno from Truskawiec in 1941: "The situation of Jews I saw in Krosno could be considered 'idyllic' compared with other places"[26].

Terror against Jews intensified in the winter of 1941. In December, under the threat of death they were forced to surrender all their furs and warm clothes because the German army needed them. The collection process was brutal and a few people were killed including an unknown man and 26–year-old Tonia Turst who was shot in the back in the street[27].

Mass debasement also started at the time. In December of 1939, there were 500 Jews in Krosno who were evicted from areas incorporated into the Reich. The Jewish Council appealed for assistance to absorb these refugees[28]. In the autumn of 1941, mass evictions started in the Jaslo region. On November 19th 1941, the first 100 people were taken from Krosno to Rymanow.

They were allowed to take with them all "movable" possessions[29]. The largest wave of evictions came in the summer of 1942. This was the prelude to the 'Final Solution' in the Krosno area. In July of 1942, most people were settled in the ghettos of Brzozow, Dukla, Jedlicze, Korczyna, and Rymanow[30] The evictions resulted in migration of people: 550 to Brzozow, 500 to Dukla, 170 to Jedlicze, 160 to Korczyna, and 600 to Rymanow. The first months of 1942 brought more victims among Krosno Jews. The Gestapo murdered 10 people and hardly a week went by without an execution. Nobody was safe. The summer of 1942 opened the bloody finale in the history of Jews of Krosno.

The directive of the central authorities of the General Gubernia from October 1940 put restrictions on Jewish settlements and served as a base for establishing isolated Jewish districts. At first it didn't have a significant impact on the Krosno County. The first practical step towards the ghetto establishment in the Jaslo region was the order issued by the Gestapo dated August 7th 1941 forbidding the free movement of Jews in the whole region. This was followed by the decision to set up Jewish districts in most towns of the Jaslo area and the selection of their residents. The first such selection in Krosno took place on August 10th 1942[31]. The Judenrat, under the threat of death, ordered all Jews to gather at the market place. Each Jew was allowed 10kg of luggage. This order prompted panic among people. A witness remembers: "This was like the day of reckoning. Krosno was so far spared such actions but we knew from the experience of other towns that this meant death"[32]. Fewer than half of Krosno Jews showed up on the square. The members of the Gestapo, notably Oskar Backer, Ludwig von Davier, and Gustaw Schmaltzer carried out the selection.

Most of the selected Jews of Krosno were taken to the death camp of Belzec and some to the Rzeszow Ghetto. The old, sick, and children were driven by truck to the forest near Brzozow and shot there by the SS and Ukrainian police. Those who stayed were given registration cards. The Germans murdered many of those who tried to hide and their bodies were buried at the Jewish cemetery. In charge of burial were two Jewish undertakers, Jozef Korba and Szyja Altman. Helping them was a Pole, Andrzej Janas.

It is difficult to establish the number of victims of the first selection. Those shot in the town numbered about 50. The exact number of the murdered is not known. Among them were: Karol Nussbaum, Benjamin Girch 37 years old, Marcus Glutz 35, Joseph Leib Urtem 27, and Samuel Hein 72.

Photo 6. Several Jewish women from Krosno prior to World War II. The first on the left is Hanka Friess from Zrencina, who studied in Krosno. She survived the war during the occupation. On the right is Pepka Breitowicz, a resident of Krosno, who perished during the war. In the center is Maria Haber, a resident of Krosno, who also perished during the war

[Lea Krill–Bleiberg photo collection]

Photo 7. The Jewish deportations from Western Galicia to the death camp of Belzec in 1942

To catch the hidden Jews in Krosno, the Gestapo issued two registration appeals. Only a small number responded to the first appeal and all received registration cards. This encouraged those in hiding and many more responded to the second appeal. This time the outcome was tragic for the majority who were rounded up and sent to the death camp of Belzec. Only a few received the promised registration cards.

On the day of the first selection, a Jewish district was established in Krosno. The date is given according to Jewish survivor testimonies. Polish witnesses state that August 6th 1942 was the selection date. The "Jewish Daily" states that on July 8th 1942, "Jewish merchants were moved to the Jewish Housing District." Krosno's ghetto was so called "rudimentary" and hence was small encompassing only one street in the town – Franciszkanska.

Sienkiewicza and Spoldzielcza streets demarked the Krosno Ghetto along Franczkanska Street. A brick wall surrounded the ghetto and the two entrances were fenced with barbwire. One entrance was from Sienkiewicza Street and the other one through the church of the Franciscans. There were 12 multi-story buildings in the ghetto crowded with 600 people[33]. This overcrowding resulted in a tragic housing situation that improved with time as people were murdered. A small number of Jews managed to avoid being locked up in the ghetto. They were rich people who could afford to pay high "ransom" to the Gestapo. The Weisenbergs and the Tiszlers lived outside the ghetto. Unfortunately they shared the fate of the majority of Jews. The Tiszlers were murdered in December of 1942 in their house and buried there. The Weinbergers survived the liquidation of 1942 paying for it in gold. The Gestapo shot them a few months later[34].

Those locked up behind the ghetto walls were without means. The best-off were county officials and the families that resided prior to the war on the Franciszkanska Street. The last ones avoided displacement. The worst-off were people from other places in the region who constituted the majority of ghetto residents. The latter were forced to leave their possessions in their original place of residence and were taken to completely alien surroundings. This had psychological implications and many suffered apathy and depression. Some tried to adapt by setting up small workshops and shops in the gates of buildings, some tried to buy food selling their last possessions.

The residents of Franciszkanska did not have medical care. The ghetto had only a small first-aid station and dental-aid room. The doctors employed there had no tools or supplies to try to control the spread of disease.[35] The doctors included Baumring, Rosenberg, and the dentist Wandstein. The first two were long-term residents of Krosno. Jakub Braumring was shot while being taken to a camp. The fate of the others is not known.

Somehow the ghetto avoided an epidemic. The most widespread were diseases of alimentary canal, respiratory diseases including Tuberculosis, and circulatory diseases. They were due to heavy work, poor housing, lack of hygiene and clothing, hunger, and worries about loved ones. The official daily food rations were one slice of bread and a small amount of soup.

On December 4th 1942, the Nazis started to liquidate the ghetto of Krosno.[36] By December 1942, the Nazis liquidated most of the ghettos in the Krosno county. This was due to the order issued by Reichsfuhrer SS Heinrich Himmler on July 19th 1942, demanding that all Jews within GG (General Gubernia) must be liquidated by the end of the winter of 1942.

With cries and beating the Jews were gathered in the square on Franciszkanska Street, formed into columns, and marched to the train station. One witness remembers: "I saw people led from the ghetto. The Nazis were rushing so fast that they did not even allow the victims to dress properly. There were children walking without shoes or proper clothes, which shows how hurried they were."[37] Witness Helena Kenig.

They were taken to the Rzeszow Ghetto and settled in the so-called west ghetto, earmarked for those unable to work and deported to other places[38]. Hunger and diseases had bumper crops, especially typhoid. There are no data about the number of dead among the Krosno deportees. We can assume that there were many. The deported were always the worst off.

In the autumn of 1943, the majority of those from Krosno who survived and others were taken to Belzec and Szebnie, and from there after 4 months to Auschwitz– Birkenau. The transport from Szebnie of 4,237 people arrived in the camp on November 5th 1943[39] The table at the end lists Krosno Jews who died in Auschwitz–Birkenau in 1942–1943.[40] After the selection at the ramp, 952 men and 396 women were taken to the camp. The rest (2,889 people) were gassed on arrival.

Despite the meticulous plan for the ghetto liquidation and the surprised timing, some people managed to hide or escape during the march to the station. Some survived. The Gestapo searched the abandoned Jewish district and found a few people whom they shot at the monastery wall[41]. A group of escapees found a week after the liquidation of the ghetto was handled with special brutality[42]. All were taken onto the street and the seven children who were among them were shot in front of their parents. The parents were taken into a building that was on fire. Those who escaped during the march were more difficult to find. An appeal that was issued stating that if they reported voluntarily, they would be spared. They were all shot dead. The hunt for hidden Jews lasted until March 1943[43].

The locations of the last mass killings of the Jewish residents of Krosno were the synagogue, the wall of the Franciszkanow church, and the building itself that housed the Gestapo offices and a prison. Krosno prison was set up in 1939. It was located at Czajkowskiego Street. From July until December 1942, it held about 120 Jews. They were fed starvation rations that consisted of a chunk of bread and 50g of margarine per day per person.

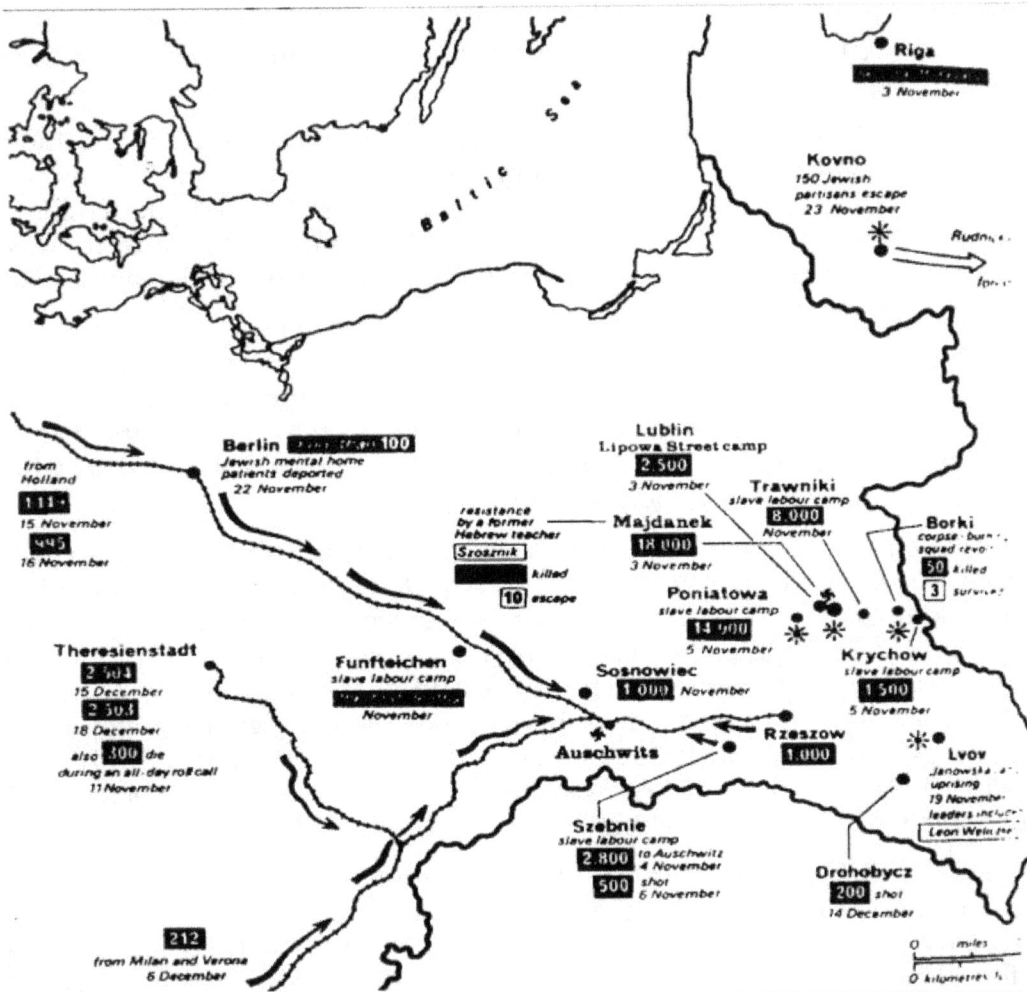

Photo 8. Deportations of Jews from Rzeszow and Szebnie during November and December of 1943

When the ghetto was liquidated, all Jewish prisoners were deported. Young ones were taken to the Szebnie camp, children and the old to nearby forests where they were shot. Of course, they were robbed of their possessions prior to being murdered, and those who resisted were shot immediately.

Realizing that deportations from the ghetto meant death, many people tried to escape but only a few succeeded. The Nazi authorities made it impossible for Jews to leave closed districts by issuing inhumane orders. These include the directive of the General Governor on October 15th 1941 who imposed the death penalty on Jews escaping from the ghetto and anyone who helped them. (The issue is elaborated in Szymon Datner's "Nazi crimes on ghetto escapees: Threats and 'legal' orders towards Jews and cooperating Poles" – the Bulletin of the Jewish Historical Institute, Warsaw 1970, no. 75.) Poles from Krosno and the surrounding area helped them. In the village of Zrecin, Polish residents hid seven Jewish ghetto escapees for 2 years: Mark Bergman, Romek Bergman, Rubin Bergman, and the family of Ignacy Lipner. Later Haskiel Morgenstein and Breitowicz joined them. Hunger forced them to wander and search for food. Only Morgenstein returned, the gendarmes shot his friend. The others survived the war[44].

Many Jews tried to avoid being taken to the ghetto. First they tried to hide by themselves, usually in attics or cellars of their own houses, workshops, or shops. As the liquidation plan unfolded these hideouts proved insufficient. Thus they were forced to seek help. A lucky few had some money and friends among the Poles. For them hiding, getting fake documents, and leaving the town or joining the partisans was easier.

To hide one Jew, Poles had to be very resourceful and brave. They also needed cooperation of others. A typical example is the story of Stefan Stiefel and his family. At first he was hiding in a shed of a Polish friend and then, wearing the robes of a priest, left Krosno. The priest, Chodorski–Kedra, who sheltered him in his own house, helped him.

He introduced Steifel to his neighbors as a priest who escaped from the Poznan area. As a result of his persecution by the Germans, he suffered a nervous breakdown and therefore was unable to conduct mass. The priest managed to get "Aryan" papers (false identity papers) for him in the name of Stefan Szymanski. Steifel used them until the end of the war, first in Cracow, then in Tarnopol where he settled with the help of Jadwiga Niepokoj from Krosno. Jadwiga Niepokoj also helped to hide his two sisters Helena and Sala, and their father Samuel, who at first was hiding in the house of a Krosno man whose surname we could not establish.[45]

This man was the first to offer his help, sheltering Samuel in his cellar[46]. When offered money for his efforts he said, "I will not take any money for helping to save the life of Samuel Steifel"[47]. When the Gestapo summoned him, he found a new hideout for Samuel with the Sochanski family. Here he remained sheltered until the end of the war along with 3 other Jews.

Jan Niedzielski from Lutcza also helped to hide Krosno Jews. He hid Herman Stercel and put him in touch with the partisans after Herman obtained his Aryan papers.

Herman survived the war in a detachment of the Home Army (AK) under the command of Edward Kurcon as Henryk Pieniowski, Polish officer, a POW[48]. In April of 1942, a Krosno engineer named Blazejowski sheltered Helena Kenig and her child[49]. The family helped them get Aryan papers and travel to Warsaw. She survived the war. These were the lucky few. The worst off were children. Many lost their parents and they wandered the streets looking for help most often from their compatriots who worked for the kehilla as they would have most resources. Unfortunately, their generosity left much to be desired. The most infamous, etched deep in the memory of Krosno Jews, was the head of the Judenrat in Jedlicze, Szymon Fries[50].

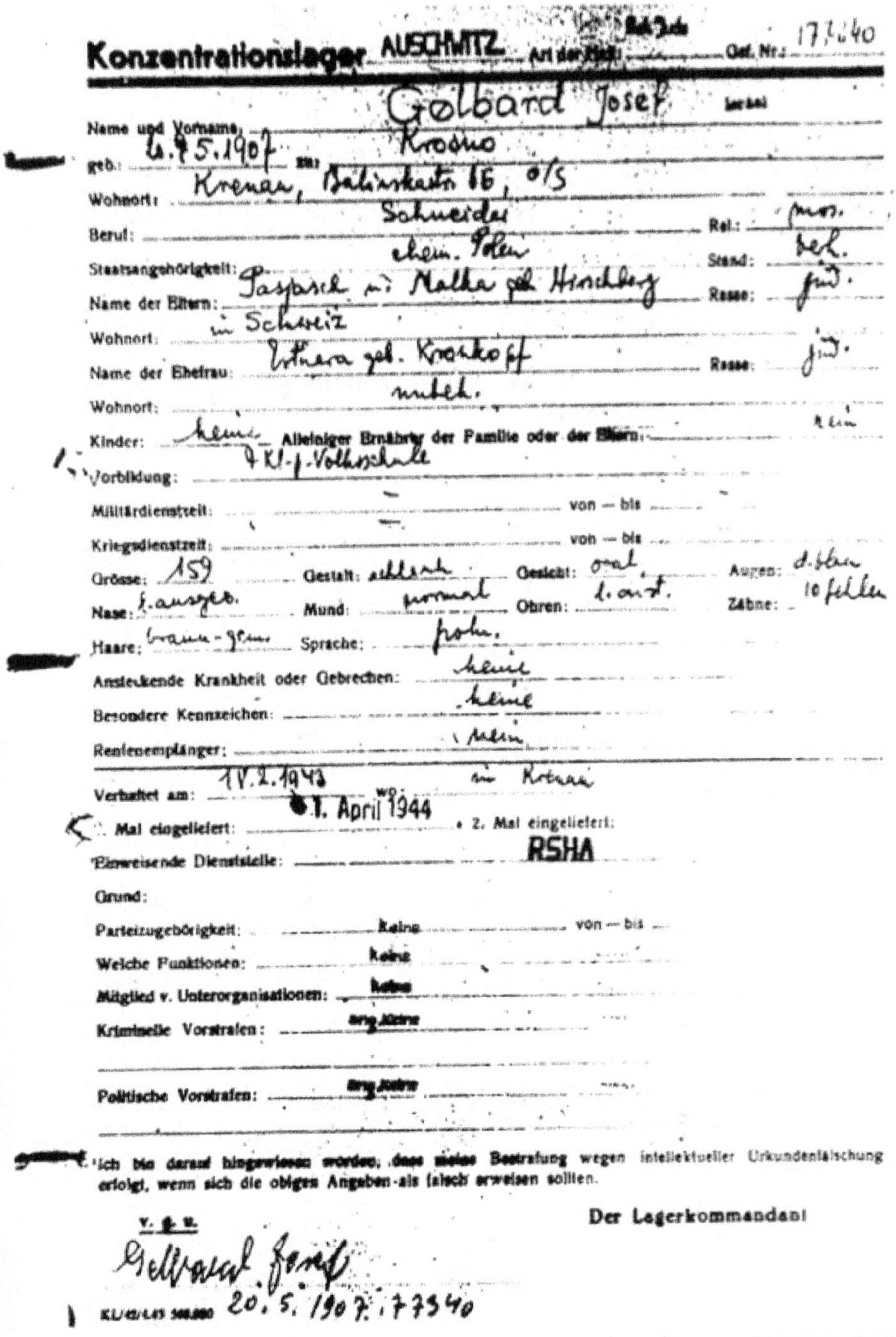

Konzentrationslager AUSCHWITZ Art der Haft: Sch. Jude Gef. Nr.: 177340

Name und Vorname: Golbard Josef Israel

geb.: 20.5.1907 zu: Krosno

Wohnort: Krenau, Balinskastr. 16, O/S

Beruf: Schneider Rel.: mos.

Staatsangehörigkeit: ehem. Polen Stand: verh.

Name der Eltern: Jaspasch u. Malka geb. Hirschberg Rasse: jüd.

Wohnort: in Schweiz

Name der Ehefrau: Esthera geb. Krochkopf Rasse: jüd.

Wohnort: unbek.

Kinder: keine Alleiniger Ernährer der Familie oder der Eltern: nein

Vorbildung: 4 Kl. Volksschule

Militärdienstzeit: — von — bis

Kriegsdienstzeit: von — bis

Grösse: 159 Gestalt: schlank Gesicht: oval Augen: d.blau

Nase: l. ausgeb. Mund: normal Ohren: l. abst. Zähne: 10 fehlen

Haare: braun-grau Sprache: poln.

Ansteckende Krankheit oder Gebrechen: keine

Besondere Kennzeichen: keine

Rentenempfänger: nein

Verhaftet am: 17.2.1943 wo: in Krenau

1. Mal eingeliefert: 1. April 1944 2. Mal eingeliefert:

Einweisende Dienststelle: RSHA

Grund:

Parteizugehörigkeit: keine von — bis

Welche Funktionen: keine

Mitglied v. Unterorganisationen: keine

Kriminelle Vorstrafen: angebl. keine

Politische Vorstrafen: angebl. keine

Ich bin darauf hingewiesen worden, dass meine Bestrafung wegen intellektueller Urkundenfälschung erfolgt, wenn sich die obigen Angaben als falsch erweisen sollten.

v. g. u. Der Lagerkommandant

Golbard Josef

20.5.1907. 177340

Photo 9. Registration card of Josef Golbard from Krosno at Auschwitz–Birkenau death camp

Orphaned children often turned to Poles for help. It is hard to establish the exact number of people who risked their own lives and those of their families in order to save strangers. Many remain unknown as they perished along with those they were trying to save, denounced by their Polish neighbors or even fellow Jews. Survivors confirmed these facts. Rena Kant from Jedlicze stated after the war: "I looked for help from Polish peasants. I slept in their house, they fed me....I was sheltered by a Pole but he did not want me to disclose his surname"[51].

The Balance of Losses

The population chart illustrates the situation of Krosno Jews. The result of the Nazi policies was the declining birth and the growing death rates.

The table below shows the grim statistics. The table doesn't give a full set of data for births and deaths and it is difficult to establish if the numbers are complete because it is not known whether all newborns were registered. The same applies to the registration of the deaths that may have not been recorded especially in 1942.

Period	Number of deaths	Number of births
1940	35 no data for Jan and Feb	26
1941	43 no data for March	18
1942	22 no data for June–December	7 [Jul–Dec out]
1943–4	no information	no information

Between 1941–1942, 56 people married in Krosno. Akiba Hermeling, who temporarily replaced Krosno's rabbi Ozon Leib Furher who was murdered by Gestapo man Oskar Backer, married them The exact date of the death of the rabbi is not known. Witnesses say Oskar Backer killed him in 1942. There are two versions of events. According to the first, he was murdered in the last selection of people from the ghetto in December of 1942. According to the other version, he was shot on the street.[52] The only information we actually have of the period is a census conducted by the Judenrat in June of 1941. At the time, Krosno had 2,072 Jews consisting of 1,181 women, 885 men, 172 people above the age of 60, 395 children below the age of 12; and 84 babies.

Presenting the balance of losses among Krosno's Jewish population, a few factors have to be noted. As a result of the Nazi policy, only some original Jewish residents remained in Krosno. Many were deported or emigrated to the East. At the same time, there was an influx of Jewish people from other areas, including escapees from various ghettos in the region.

All these factors create difficulties in estimating the Jewish population of Krosno. In the first three years of occupation, Krosno's Jewish population shrunk from the pre–war level by 25% as a result of deportations, escapes, death from starvation, disease, and murders. In 1942, most of the Jewish residents were eliminated, and Krosno's population shrunk further. A census in 1946 showed there were 13,873 people in Krosno.[53] the results should be evaluated carefully. Movements of people following the war changed the figure rapidly.

With the extermination of Krosno's Jewish residents, we need to note those who survived World War II. They were mainly those transported by the Russians to the Soviet Union. We know that a few survived Soviet labor camps and settled later in Israel.

They make up a small percentage of Krosno Jews. Among those who returned after the war, only a few contemplated starting a new life in Krosno. The majority returned in the hope of finding relatives or getting some information about them. Some who felt a need to settle old real or imaginary scores stayed for longer. One witness describes his revenge on Poles in the following way: "After the Russians came I joined NKWD. I wanted to take revenge on the Poles who denounced my siblings. I worked for the NKWD for 18 months. During that time I avenged not only my family but many other Jews."[54] During the occupation, Herman Stelcer lost all his family: his parents and 6 siblings. Poles sheltered two of them but because of denunciations they were murdered. He himself survived the war thanks to help from Poles.

Many returning Jews also hoped to find lost children who survived the war while entrusted to Polish families. Zionist centers attached enormous importance to the emigration of Jewish children. The Joint among others did the financing. This was not simple. Children brought up by Poles frequently did not remember their relatives and did not know their origins. They developed close relationships with their guardians. These ties were hard to break. If financial compensation did not appeal to the Poles, the cases usually went to court where the children were returned to their families. Then, they often ended up in Jewish orphanages in the western and northern parts of Poland.

There are a few known cases from Krosno that ended in this manner. About 20 children recovered their Jewish identity, among them Berta Akselrad, the daughter of the former head of the kehilla in Korczyna and Krosno, and some children from the Fogel, Majerowicz, Montagu, and Nussbaum families. Berta Akselrad was growing up in a Polish family under the name of Barbara. In 1946, a court ordered that she be returned to the Jews. She was then placed in a Jewish orphanage in Zabrze. From there, via France, she went to Palestine. A boy from the Nussenbaum family who lost all his relatives in the war followed a similar route. At first he was sheltered by Poles, then ended up in an orphanage in Miejsce Piastowe. On court orders he was handed over to Jews.

Krosno Jews were released from prisons and Nazi camps, and those returning from the Soviet Union, settled in the western parts of Poland mainly in lower Silesia.

Those linked to the Zionist movement before the war picked up their work in the revived organizations that focused on facilitating emigration to Palestine.

At first the Polish authorities did not meddle in these kinds of activities. This policy changed at the end of the 1940s. In 1949, 12 Jews were arrested and jailed by the Polish security services in Wroclaw and Wlabrzych; Memories of Baruch Munz. Among them were a few from Krosno. At first they were charged with espionage but, then in the course of court proceedings, their death sentences were overturned. The espionage charges were dropped and they were sentenced to one year for belonging to illegal organizations whose membership they denied anyway.

Those who settled in lower Silesia were just waiting for a chance to leave Poland. Most of Krosno Jews emigrated legally. But because this route entailed long waits, some opted for illegal means. It is hard to estimate how many left Poland legally or illegally. Some were captured at the border and sentenced to jail, especially those who tried to cross the borders at the end of the 1940s. Before autumn 1946, it was not difficult to cross the Polish border illegally. Only from the end of 1946 were illegal emigrants handled in a stricter manner. The problem is elaborated in Natalia Aleksiun–Madrzak's "Illegal emigration of Jews from Poland" in a bulletin of Jewish Historical Institute, Warsaw 1996, no. 4. P. 34.

Not all Jews who were left Krosno aimed at settling in Palestine. Some wanted to go to the US or Western Europe, where they saw opportunities to make a living with the help of their relatives who already resided there. Changes of decision as to where to settle permanently were usually made after leaving Poland. The decisions were influenced by hearsay or media information about the situation of Jews in the relevant country. One witness describes his motives behind choosing Israel as his place of permanent residence in the following way: "I felt too old to start my life anew carrying two humps: one on the front as a 'greenie' among US Jews who called new immigrants this way and the other on the back, as a Jew among strangers."

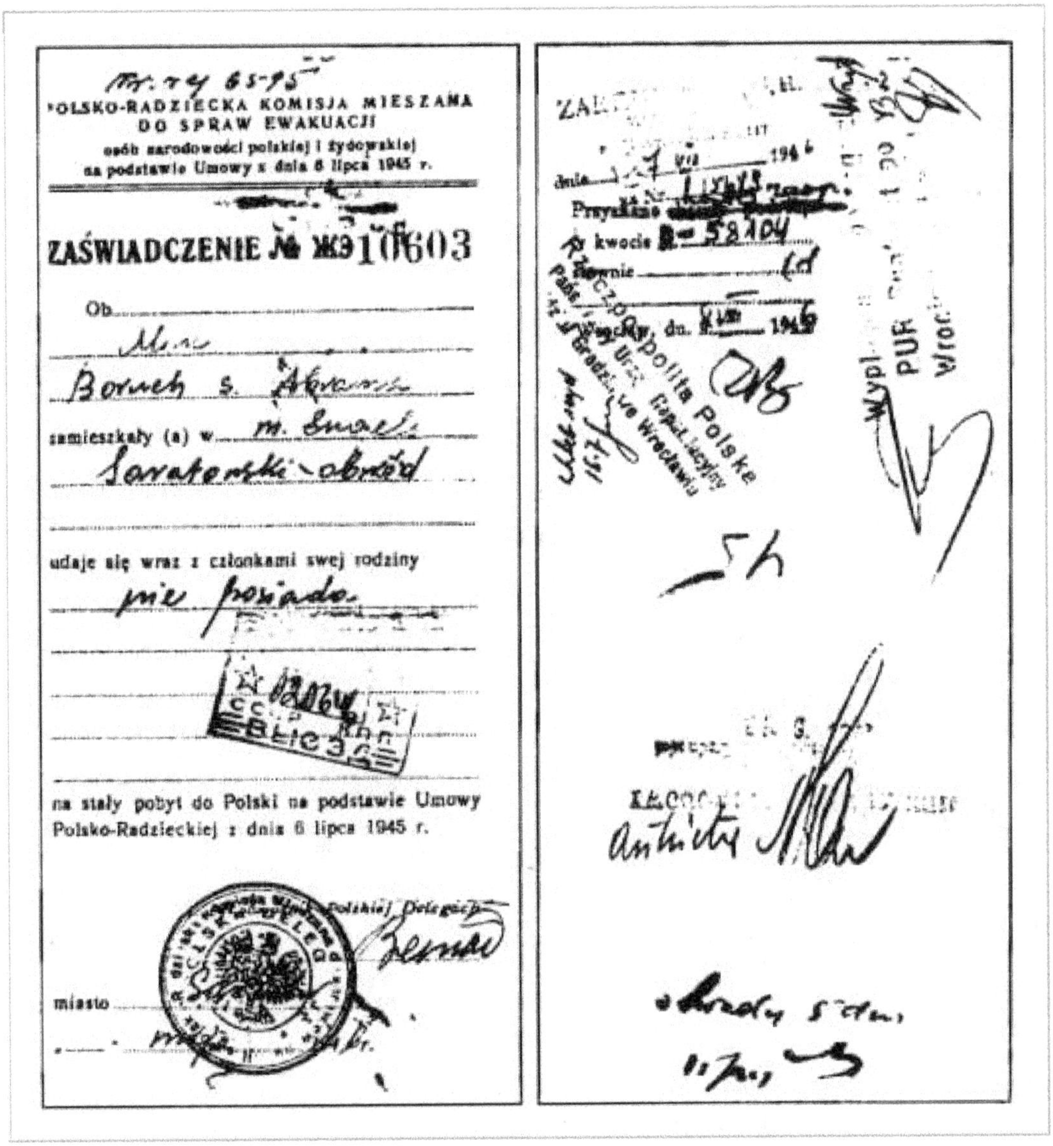
POLSKO-RADZIECKA KOMISJA MIESZANA
DO SPRAW EWAKUACJI
osób narodowości polskiej i żydowskiej
na podstawie Umowy z dnia 6 lipca 1945 r.

ZAŚWIADCZENIE №

Ob.

zamieszkały (a) w

udaje się wraz z członkami swej rodziny

nie posiada

na stały pobyt do Polski na podstawie Umowy Polsko-Radzieckiej z dnia 6 lipca 1945 r.

miasto

Przyjęto

kwocie

Słownie

Rzeczpospolita Polska

PUR

Photo 11. Document permitting Baruch Muntz to leave the Soviet Union following the end of the war. Front and back of the document

Conclusion

The story of Krosno's Jews during World War II is no different from that of other Polish Jews, since the Germans aimed to eliminate all the Jews. In contrast to the Nazis, the Russian government did not consider Polish Jews a separate nation nor did it adopt special policies towards them. They were considered foreign nationals and deported to the depths of the Soviet Union.

The German policy of extermination was carried out in two stages. Indirect extermination included robbery, eliminating Jews from social and economic life, and forced labor. Direct extermination meant murder. All these stages affected Krosno Jews. The only difference was that the first stage was relatively peaceful in Krosno and lasted much longer than in other places. The tragic finale of the history of Krosno Jews started with the day of the first selection in August of 1942 and ended on December 4th 1942 when the ghetto was liquidated.

Photo 12. Polish and 4 Jewish girls from Krosno, uncertain date. First on the left is Hanka Friess, who survived the war. The fourth on the left is Leja Krill, who left for Palestine in 1934. The fifth on the left is Gena Platner, who was in Russia during the war. The first on the right was Blima Fischbein, who perished during the war

From more than 2,500 Jews in Krosno before the war, only a few survived. Their attitudes towards life in post-war Poland were no different from those of other Polish Jews. Many did not see any place for themselves in the country regardless of the current situation and treated their return as a stepping-stone towards resettling in Palestine or the USA. Still others left due to the political system that was being established in Poland. A handful of Polish Jews decided to stay in Poland.

Free Krosno kitchen output

IA

Breakfast	226	210	203	216	210	180	190	198	206
Lunch	220	206	201	215	209	178	189	197	200
Dinner	—	—	—	—	—	—	—	—	—

IB

Breakfast	198	186	200	206	190
Lunch	196	182	200	204	191
Dinner	—	—	—	—	—

Tables IA and IB describe the number of breakfasts and lunches distributed by the Krosno kitchen during the month of August of 1941. The tables do not include the days that there were no meals.
Source: AZIH, Acta ZSS, sygn 4924

Table II types and amounts of products used by the kitchen in August 1941.

II

Products	Quantity in kilos or liters
Onions	8 kilos
Sugar	7 kilos
Bread	14 kilos
Beans	116.5 kilos
Eggs	67
Grains	95 kilos
Matza	673 kilos
Milk	155 liters
Meat	30 kilos
Salt	18 kilos
Coffee substitute	22.5 kilos
Potatoes	400 kilos

Source: AZIH, Acta ZSS, sygn 4924

III

Last and first name	Money in zlotys	Kilos of matza
Alter, Jakob	28	2
Breitowicz, Lea	25	5
Buchsbaum, Sala	25	5
Lipner, Feiga	20	4
Fessel, Lipa	40	8
Fischbein, Genia	20	4
Geller, Feiwell	20	4
Heferling, Blime	28	2
Nord, Hirsch	25	5
Holloschuetz, Berta	25	4
Pinkas, Mendel	28	2
Langbaum, Mozes	25	5
Liberman, Hirsch	20	4
Lehrer, Leiser Josef	30	6
Lehrer, Wolf	50	10
Mandel, Jakob	20	4
Mostowicz, Chaja	30	6
Riedel, Gitel	25	5
Sitzer, Isaak	25	5
Stiefel, Chaim	25	5
Wehrmann, Ida	25	5
Wrobel, Bernard	25	5

Table III Lists of people who received the Judenrat's biggest assistance in April 1941.
Source: AZIH,Acta ZSS, sygn 4924

Table IV

Name of establishment	Number employed
Krosno Airport	About 100
AVI, HUV	About 100
Farms	About 110
Tank camp	About 30
Road work	About 70
Crafts	About 80
Factories in Kombornia	About 50
Quarry in Dukla and factory in Rymanow	About 320

Table IV Places of work and number of employed Jews in November 1941.
Source: AZIH, Acta ZSS, sygn 4924

Table V

Occupation	First and last name	Birth date	Birth place	Residence	Killed on
Clerk	Baruch Berglass	9.12.1901	Korczyna	Holland	26.09 1942
Clerk	Szlama Simon Berger	2.07 1920	Krosno	Krosno	29.07 1942
	Lea Sara Fischer	7.03 1905	Korczyna	Krosno	26.02 1943
	Daughter Chaima and Sary Margules				
	Beila Gebel	1889?	Korczyna	Krosno	26.02 1943
	Daughter of Mehel and Rosy Kuref				
Worker	Dora Hersohn	27. 02 1908	Korczyna	Krosno	7.03 1943
	Daughter of Moshe and Bajlli Gebel				
Seamstress	Sara Hersohn	15.03 1915	Krosno	Krosno	1.03 1943
	Daughter of Jakob and Dory Hersohn				
Carpenter	Jozef Jakubowicz	5. 11 1920	Krosno	Paris	4.07 1942
Worker	Jozef Kaufman	28.09 1918	Krosno	Antwerp	30 08 1942
Butcher	Abraham Kircher	14.05 1899	Korczyna	Bruxelles	10. 01 1943
Farmer	Lazar Kirschner	14 05 1893	Korczyna	Slovakia	5.01 1943
Clerk	Israel Lieber	2. 08 1892		Krosno	16.08 1942
Photographer	Mendel Rozenzweig	19.08 1890	Dukla	France	16. 10 1942
Cook	Leser Kohn	1.4 1908	Dukla	France	11.07 1942
Tailor	Szyja Trenczer	8.08 1897	Krosno	Antwerp	6. 01 1943
Seamstress	Rachel Wiener	7.07 1903	Krosno	Tarnow	6.01 1943
	Daughter of Jakob and Dory Pinkas				

Jews from Krosno, Korczyna, and Dukla who died in the death camp of Auschwitz–Birkenau in 1942–1943. Cause of death was not given. To hide the real cause of death, documents often gave fictitious diseases etc.

Source: The National Museum of Auschwitz, Politische Abteilung, Sterbebucher, 1, 1/2, 1/3, 4/1, 7/2, 8/2, 8/3, 10/1, 10/3, 15/3, 18/1, 22/3, 25/1, Death lists of Auschwitz, Munich–New Providence–London–Paris, 1995, t.2–3

The list of Jews from the Krosno area who moved to Israel after the war based on the list owned by Baruch Munz.
The list doesn't include people who are only mentioned by surname without a first name.
[The list only includes people who registered in the Krosner association in Israel.]

Aichton Zisle	Firer Ben Zion	Krill Lea	Rozner Mosze
Aisen Jakow	First Szoszana	Krill Szlomo	Rozner Meir
Akerman Riwka	Flapan Maria	Kufic Arie	Rozner Ruben
Akselrad Berta	Freud Jochewet	Lang Abraham	Rowheizer Riwka
Akselrad Josef	Freud Szmuel	Lang Josef	Rubin Szmuel
Akselrad Wolf	Freud Baftali	Laufer Frida	Rubin Riwka
Atlas Aron	Fris Menachem	Leiser Jona	Stiefel Hela
Arzenberg Gershon	Goldberg Icchak	Leiser Jechial	Szachar Jakow
Baim Zisle	Grin Henoch	Liber Aron	Szlanger Natan
Bail Avraham	Grin Sara	Lipszic Jochewet	Szerf Mendel
Balser Nachem	Grinbaum Kalman	Majerowicz Lea	Szpringer Leon
Bart Genia	Gross Icchak	Majerowicz Zwi	Szpringer Dawid
Ber Avraham	Hak Mosze	Maiz Mordechai	Tabish Abraham
Berger Benjamin	Hak Szlomo	Manster Szmuel	Teplicki Cesia
Bnedar Pinchas	Herbsman Szlomo	Margules Mechel	Teplicki Lewi
Bobker Ester	Herbsman Jakow	Margules Josef	Trenczer Mosze
Brand Zwi	Hirschfield Zofia	Margules Icchak	Trenczer Jeshajahu
Brandt Menachem	Holoshitz Menache	Margules Mosze	Unger Leib
Bursztein Arie	Horowitz Jehial	Melamed Dawid	Unger Malka
Dominitz Lea	Kac Jehoshua	Mendel Pinchas	Weisman Chawa
Dominitz Sonia	Kac Naftali	Montag Josef	Weisman Josef
Dorf Dawid	Kaner Rachel	Munz Adolf	Weisman Menach
Dranger Chaja	Kaner Luba	Munz Baruch	Walach Aron

Dym Zofia	Kaufman Leib	Munz Nechema	Wald Miriam
Ehrich Dawid	Kaufman Szmuel	Nachtigel Eliazer	Weinberger Efraim
Ellowicz Eliazer	Kiwiel Avraham	Nachtigel Dawid	Weinster Gershon
Elrenberg Pinchas	Kisenstein Menach	Nagel Sima	Weinster Icchak
Engelhardt Szlomo	Kinderman Menah	Nais Aron	Wilner Zwi
Engelhardt Josef	Klagsbald Mosze	Neimarch Rachel	Wolf Abraham
Erenreich Jecheskel	Klein Jakow	Nord Icchak	
Erenreich Leib	Kleinman Dian	Nord Marie	
Erlbaum Jehoshua	Kleinman Josef	Nowember Menach	
Faber Arie	Kleinman Zwi	Nussbaum Jakow	
Feltkard Henoch	Koner Jehuda	Ofner Atara	
Feltkard Zalmen	Koner Maier	Oling Genia	
Fesel Mosze	Koner Mordechai	Orenstein Leib	
Fink Hela	Kriger Michal	Reich Jecheskiel	

Footnotes

1. Andzej Dashkiewicz, Z dziejow ruchu oporu... Krakow 1973,t.II,s.185

2. Jozef Garbacik,Stanislaw Cynarski, Jaslo oskarza...Warszawa, 1973,s.26

3. Glowna Comisja Badania zbrodnip–co...sygn 85,t.I–III [dalej GKBZ IPN

4. Yad Vashem Archives, Relacje, sygn 1270 Helene Stiefel's testimony

5. Jewish Historical Institute, sygn 301/4681, testimony of Sachar Grunbaum

6. AZIH, Akta Zydowskiej Samopomocy Spoleczenej[dalej AZSS] sygn 4924

7. Gazeta Zydowska, July 9th 1942

8. AZIH, AZSS, sygn 4924

9. Ibidem

10. AZIH, AZSS, sygn 4924

11. AIYV, sygn, 1270 testimony of Helen Stiefel

12. Gazetat Zydowska, May, 20th 1942

13. Gazetat Zydowska, May, 20th 1942, AZIH,ZSS, sygn 4924

14. AZIH,IPN, sygn 301/3448 testimony of Rubin Bergman

15. AZIH,ZSS, sygn 4924

16. AZIH,ZSS, sygn 4924

17. AZIH,IPN, sygn 301/1093 testimony of Leopold Blech

18. AZIH,ZSS, sygn 4924

19. Gazeta Zydowska, March 13th 1942

20. Gazeta Zydowska, July 15th 1942

21. GKBZ IPN, Anicta Sadu Grodziekiego, sygn 16D [DALEJ asg]

22. GKBZ IPN, Anicta Sadu Grodziekiego, sygn 16D

23. GKBZ IPN, sygn 25, testimony of Franciszek Selz

24. Szymon Datner, ...55 dni Wehrmachtu w Polsce, Warszawa 1967,s.477

25. AZIH,IPN, sygn 301/2832 testimony of Helena Konig

26. AZIH,IPN, sygn 1270 testimony of Helena Stiefel

27. GKBZ IPN, Anicta Sadu Grodziekiego, sygn HS93/71

28. AZIH,ZSS, sygn 4924

29. Gazeta Zydowska, November 19th 1941

30. Gazeta Zydowska, July 8th 1942

31. AIYV, sygn 1270,testimony Hele Stiefel

32. Ibidem

33. GKBZ, IPN Ankieta. Obozy... sygn 58, t.1 [dalejAOG]

34. GKBZ, Akta proc... sygn HS93/71, T.I. Testimony Andzej Janas

35. Gazeta Zydowska, July 8th 1942

36. Kronika gmin, op.cit., t.III, s.522

37. AZIH,IPN, sygn 301/2832 testimony of Helena Konig

38. Stanislaw Parandowski, Zaglada Zydow rzeszo... Warszawa 1988, nr.I–2,s.98

39. Danuta Czech, Kalendarz wydarzen w KL Auschwitz, PMO 1992, s. 521

40. Ibidem

41. GKBZ, IPN,Akta proc... sygn HS93/71, t.II. Testimony Hilary Zajac

42. Ibidem

43. GKBZ, IPN,Akta proc... sygn HS93/71, t.II. Testimony Franciszek Zajder

44. AZIH,IPN, sygn 3421 testimony of Andzej Czajkwski

45. AIYV,sygn 3421, testimony of Sala Heiler, nee Stiefel

46. Ibidem

47. Ibidem

48. AIYV,sygn 672, testimony of Herman Stelcer

49. AZIH,IPN, sygn 301/2832 testimony of Helen Konig

50. AZIH,IPN, sygn 301/1373 testimony of Rena Kant

51. AZIH,IPN, sygn 301/1373 testimony of Rena Kant

52. Kronika gmin,op.cit., s.521

53. Statystika Polski, Seria D. z.1

54. AIYV,sygn 672, testimony of Herman Stelcer

The Krosno synagogue between the wars
Back Cover of the book

Chapter XVII
List of Jews in Krosno prior and during World War II

Compiled by William Leibner

Sources

B	Business directory
G	Gmilat Hessed fund for needy Jews in Krosno
J	Judenrat list established by the Judenrat in 1941 in Krosno
L	Association of former residents of Krosno in Israel
P	Private letters, documents & interviews
R	Elzbieta Raczy, historian, author of essays on Krosno
S	Jewish Self Help Committee during the war
Y	Yad Vashem files
YI	Yizkor list provided by survivors

Krosno, Poland Yizkor Book

Family name(s)	First name(s)	Maiden name	Birth date	Trade (German)	Trade (English)	Father's name	Mother's name	Gender	Name of spouse	Sources	Disposition (location where killed or spent war years)
ABRAHAM	Rosa		1914	Stickerin	embroider [female]			F		[J]	
ABRAHAM	Sara		1891					F		[J], [G]	
ABRAHAM	Moses		1921	Arbeiter	worker			M		[J]	
ABRAHAMSOHN	Berisch		1888	Beamter	clerk			M		[J]	
ABRAHAMSOHN	Feige Leie		1886					F		[J]	
ABRAHAMSOHN	Chaim		1923	Glaser	glazier			M		[J]	
ABRAHAMSOHN	Salomon		1908	Kürschner	furrier			M		[J]	
ABRAHAMSOHN	Chane		1909					F		[J]	
ABRAHAMSOHN	Wella		1935					F		[J]	
ABRAHAMSOHN	Dora		1939					F		[J]	
ACKERMAN	Riwka							F		[R]	survived
ADAM	Ita					Jakob		F		[Y]	Belzec
ADER	Jakob		1877	Friseur	barber			M		[J], [G]	
ADER	Ester		1880	Hebamme	midwife			F		[J]	
ADER	Benjamin		1906	Friseur	barber			M		[J]	
ADER	Hene		1917					F		[J]	
ADER	Sara		1939					F		[J]	
ADER	Pene		1910					F		[J]	
ADER	Lola		1915					F		[J]	
ADER	Sara		1917					F		[J]	
ADERMAND	Maks							M		[R]	

Surname	Given name	Year	Occupation	Occupation	Father	Sex	Source	Fate
AFTERGUT	Salomon	1893	Kaufmann	merchant		M	[J]	
AFTERGUT	Sala	1892				F	[J]	
AFTERGUT	David	1923	Elektrotechniker	electrician		M	[J]	
AHENBERG	Pinkas					M	[L]	survived
AICHTON	Zisie					M	[R]	survived
AKERMAN	Riwka					F	[P]	
ALENBERG	Leora					F	[L]	survived
ALPEROWICZ	Wolf	1855				M	[P]	USA
ALTBACH	Sender	1873				M	[J]	
ALTBACH	Helene	1877			Shimon	F	[J],[Y]	Majdanek
ALTBACH	Aharon					M	[Y]	
ALTBACH	Shimon	1900				M	[Y]	Auschwitz
ALTBACH	Ester	1914				F	[J]	
ALTER	Jakob	1881	Arbeiter	worker	Shimon	M	[J], [Y], [S], [G]	perished
ALTER	Fishel	1918			Jakob	M	[J], [Y]	perished
ALTER	Sime	1920			Jakob	F	[J], [Y]	perished
ALTER	Hiel				Jakob	M	[J], [Y]	Russia
ALTER	Osias	1923	Arbeiter	worker		M	[J]	
ALTER	Yehoshua					M	[L]	survived
ALTHOLZ	Isaac	1879				M	[P]	survived
ALTHOLZ	Moses	1899	Uhrmacher	watchmaker		M	[J]	
ALTHOLZ	Debora	1902				F	[J]	
ALTHOLZ	David	1928	Arbeiter	worker		M	[J]	
ALTHOLZ	Zila	1931				F	[J]	

Krosno, Poland Yizkor Book

Surname	Given name	Other name	Year	Occupation (Ger.)	Occupation (Eng.)	Father	Mother	Sex	Extra	Source	Fate
ALTHOLZ	Ch.			Student	student			M		[R]	
ALTHOLZ	Shmulik							M		[P]	survived
ALTMANN	Leib		1878	Klempner	plumber			M		[J], [Y]	perished
ALTMANN	Sara		1886			Meyer		F	Leib	[J], [Y]	perished
ALTMANN	Tzvi		1906					M		[J], [Y]	perished
ALTMANN	Moses		1907	Bäcker	baker	Leib	Sara	M		[J], [Y]	perished
ALTMANN	Osias		1908	Klempner	plumber	Leib	Sara	M		[J], [Y]	perished
ALTMANN	Hirsch		1909			Leib	Sara	M		[J], [Y]	perished
ALTMANN	Mania		1911			Leib	Sara	F		[J], [Y]	perished
ALTMANN	Itzhak		1912			Leib	Sara	M		[J], [Y]	perished
ALTMANN	Chune		1917	Monteur	fitter	Leib	Sara	M		[J], [Y]	perished
ALTMANN	Poje		1919			Leib	Sara	F		[J], [Y]	perished
ALTMANN	Ciwia		1917			Shlomo		F		[J], [Y]	perished
ALTMANN	Sala		1900	Lehrerin	teacher [female]			F		[J]	
ALTMANN	Shyja			Leichenbestatter	undertaker			F		[R]	
ALTMANN	L			Klempner	plumber			M		[R]	
ALTMANN	Leopold			Drechsler	lathe turner			M		[R]	
ALZOHAR		STEIN						F		[P]	survived
AMIDROR	Arie	TEPLITZKI						M		[L]	survived
AMIDROR	Tzila							F		[L]	survived
AMIR	Israel	SPITZ						M		[L]	survived
AMSTER	Dawid		1900			Israel		M		[Y]	Majdanek
AMSTER	Dewora		1908			Mordechai		F		[Y]	Auschwitz
AMSTERDAM	Chaim		1889	Kaufmann	merchant			M		[J], [G]	
AMSTERDAM	Regina		1889					F		[J]	

Surname	Given name	Occupation	Year	Occupation			Sex			Fate
AMSTERDAM	Gerson	Arbeiter	1911	worker			M		[J]	
AMSTERDAM	Ester		1913				F		[J]	
AMSTERDAM	Naftali	Schäftemacher	1923	upper shoe maker			M		[J]	
ANTENER	Chaim		1898		Ben		M		[Y]	Treblinka
ANTENER	Khinia		1933		Chaim		M		[Y]	Treblinka
APELSTEIN	Sala		1911				F		[J]	
APFEL	Guetl		1896				F		[J]	
APFEL	Menashe		1908		Dawid		M		[Y], [G]	Belzec
APFEL	Toba		1912		Moshe		F		[Y]	perished
APFEL	Renia				Shimon		F		[Y]	perished
APFELBAUM-BEER	Mendel	Friseur	1898	barber			M		[J]	
APFELBAUM-BEER	Frieda		1908				F		[J]	
APFELBAUM-BEER	Rosa		1929				F		[J]	
APFELBAUM-BEER	Leib		1930				M		[J]	
APFELBAUM-BEER	Samson		1934				M		[J]	
APFELBAUM-BEER	Schmaje		1939				M		[J]	
APRIL	Samuel						M		[R]	
APRIL	Sara		1864		Samuel		F	Samuel	[J], [G]	
APRIL	Chaim				Samuel	Sara	M		[R]	
APRIL	Israel				Samuel	Sara	M		[R]	

Surname	Given name	Alt/Married name	Year	Occupation	Occupation	Father	Mother	Sex	Spouse	Source	Status
APRIL	Ryfka					Samuel	Sara	F		[R]	
APRIL	Estera					Samuel	Sara	F		[R]	
APT	A.			Uhrmacher	watchmaker					[R]	
ARGAND				Uhrmacher	watchmaker					[P]	
ARON	Ite		1865					F		[J]	
ARONOWICZ	David		1908	Arbeiter	worker			M		[J], [S]	perished
ARZENBERG	Gershon							M		[R]	survived
ASHKENAZI	Chana		1895			Shmuel		F		[Y]	perished
ASHKENAZI	Lea		1926			Mendel		F		[Y]	
ATLAS	Aron							M		[L]	survived
ATLAS	Salomon		1864					M		[J]	
AUSSENBERG	Menasche		1911	Arbeiter	worker			M		[J], [S]	
AUSSENBERG	Regina		1913					F		[J]	
AUZNER	Bela		1906			Mordechai		F		[Y]	perished
AWNER	Chana							F		[S]	
AKSELRAD	Schulim					Schulim		M		[P]	
AKSELRAD	Bendet		1886					M		[YI]	perished
AKSELRAD	Zile	FREIFELD	1880			Leib		F	Bendet	[JJ], [Y]	perished
AKSELRAD	Shmuel		1909			Bendet	Zile	M		[Y]	perished
AKSELRAD	Klara	ROSENBERG				Bendet		F	Shmuel	[P]	perished
AKSELRAD	Erenka		1935			Shmuel	Klara	F		[Y]	perished
AKSELRAD	Shalom		1911	Beamter	clerk	Bendet	Zile	M		[J]	perished
AKSELRAD	Awraham		1922			Bendet	Zile	M		[P]	survived
AKSELRAD	Yehuda		1924			Bendet	Zile	M		[P]	
AKSELRAD	Lewi		1930			Bendet	Zile	M		[JJ], [Y]	perished

Krosno, Poland Yizkor Book

AKSELRAD	Bertha	1932			Bendet	Zile		F	[P]	survived
AKSELRAD	Rivka	1938			Munio		Shmuel	F	[Y]	perished
AKSELRAD	Rivka	1935			Shmuel			F	[Y]	perished
AKSELRAD	Meshulam	1911			Bendet	Zile		M	[Y]	perished
AKSELRAD	Shimshon				Schulim			M	[Y]	perished
AKSELRAD	Helene	1900			Shimshon			F	[Y]	perished
AKSELRAD	Beile	1932						F	[J]	perished
AKSELRAD	Moses	1928						M	[J]	
AKSELRAD	Chaim	1927	Arbeiter	worker				M	[J]	
AKSELRAD	Luser Lipe	1907	Arbeiter	worker				M	[J], [S], [G]	
AKSELRAD	David	1934						M	[J]	
AKSELRAD	Chaim	1935						M	[J]	
AKSELRAD	Jochwet	1937						F	[J]	
AKSELRAD	Chawe	1884						F	[J]	
AKSELRAD	Leie	1919						F	[J]	
AKSELRAD	Ester	1923						F	[J]	
AKSELRAD	Fradel	1926						F	[J]	
AKSELRAD	Jsaak	1930						M	[J]	
AKSELRAD	Tobias	1890	Kaufmann	merchant				M	[J], [S]	
AKSELRAD	Hadassa	1903						F	[J]	
AKSELRAD	Feiga	1901			Alexander			F	[Y]	Treblinka
AKSELRAD	Yaacov							M	[L]	survived
AKSELRAD	Yossef Bend							M	[L]	survived

Krosno, Poland Yizkor Book

Surname	Given Name	Surname	Year	Father	Mother	Sex	Spouse	Status	Notes
AKSELRAD	Chana					F	Yossef Bend		
AKSELRAD	Rochel			Yossef Bend	Chana	F			
AKSELRAD	Izak					M		[G]	
AKSELRAD	Wolf					M		[R]	survived
AKSELRAD	Lipe					M		[P]	
FESSEL	Rachel					F	Lipe	[P]	
FESSEL	Alexander					M		[P]	
AKSELRAD	Lipe					M		[P]	
FESSEL	Rachel					F	Lipe	[P]	
FESSEL	Alexander					M		[P]	
AKSELRAD	Hinde Git	AKSELRAD		Lipe	Rachel	F	Alexander	[P]	
EISENBERG	T					M		[P]	
EISENBERG	Rickel	AKSELRAD				F		[P]	
AKSELRAD	Hershel			Lipe	Rachel	M	Hershel	[P]	
AKSELRAD	Ciwia Lea	KALB				F		[P]	
AKSELRAD	Ides			Lipe	Rachel	F		[P]	
AKSELRAD	Yossef Bendet		0.1888	Lipe	Rachel	M	Yossef Bendet	[P]	
AKSELRAD	Chana	HAUSNER	1890	Yossef Bendet		F		[P]	
AKSELRAD	Lipe		1908	Yossef Bendet	Chana	M		[P]	
SHEINOWITZ	Malka		1910	Yossef Bendet	Chana	F		[P]	
SHEINOWITZ						M		[P]	
SHEINOWITZ	Rachel	AKSELRAD	1911	Yossef	Chana	F		[P]	

Surname	Given name		Year	Occupation		Father	Mother	Sex		Code	Fate
SHEINOWITZ	Miriam	SHEINOWITZ				Bendet	Rachel	F		[P]	
AKSELRAD	Mechel					Yossef Bendet	Chana	M		[P]	
AKSELRAD	Moshe Liebe					Yossef Bendet	Chana	M		[P]	
AKSELRAD	Dora					Yossef Bendet	Chana	F		[P]	
AKSELRAD	Sara Reila					Yossef Bendet	Chana	F		[P]	
AKSELRAD	Esther Lea					Yossef Bendet	Chana	F		[P]	
BALABAN	Ch			Zimmermann	carpenter			R		[P]	
BALSAM	Jachet							F		[R]	
BALSER	Beer							M		[P]	
BALSER	Rozka		1917			Meir		F		[Y]	perished
BARD	Dawid		1907			Avraham		M		[Y]	perished
BAREL	F.			Student	student			R			
BART	Genia	OLING						F		[L]	survived
BART	Yaacov							M		[L]	survived
BARTH	Faiga		1907			Haim		F		[Y]	perished
BARTH	Josef		1860					M		[J]	
BARUCH	Perl		1883					F		[J], [S]	
BAUMANN	Markus							M		[G]	
BAUMANN	Berta		1910	Köchin	cook [female]			F		[J]	
BAUMANN	Kalman Wolf							M	Jakob	[P]	
BAUMRING	Anna		1904					F		[J]	

Krosno, Poland Yizkor Book

Surname	Given	Maiden	Occupation	Year	Occupation			Sex		Source	Fate
BAUMRING	Theodor			1934		Jakob	Anna	M		[J]	
BAUMRING	Gina			1939		Jakob	Anna	F		[J]	
BAUMRING	Jakob		Arzt	1895	doctor, town council			M		[J], [G]	perished
BECK	Chaim							M		[R]	
BECK	Mania	FLAPAN						F		[L]	survived
BEER	Moses		Kutscher	1902	coachman			M		[J]	
BEER	Zila					Moses		F	Moses	[P]	
BEER	Nechemia						Zila	M		[P], [G]	
BEER	Bella	KATZ						F	Nechemia	[P]	perished
BEER	Zila					Nechemia	Bella			[P]	survived
BEER	Sara			1906				F		[J]	
BEER	Henoch			1933				M		[J]	
BEER	Hinde			1936				F		[J]	
BEER	Marjem			1939				F		[J]	
BEER	Izrael							M		[G]	
BEER	Mendel							M		[G]	
BEER	Hersz		Schneiderin		tailoress			M		[R]	
BEER	Solomon			1862				M		[P]	USA
BEER	Solomon		Schuhmacher		shoemaker			M		[B]	
BEER	Jacob		Holzarbeiter		woodworker			M		[B]	
BEIGEL	Salomon		Arbeiter	1893	worker			M		[J], [Y]	perished
BEIGEL	Chaje			1884				F	Salomon	[J], [Y]	perished
BEIGEL	Moses		Arbeiter	1923	worker	Salomon	Chaje	M		[J], [Y]	perished
BEIGEL	Naftali		Arbeiter	1924	worker	Salomon	Chaje	M		[J], [Y]	perished
BEIGEL	Ester			1927		Salomon	Chaje	F		[J], [Y]	perished

								survived
BEIL	Avraham					M	[L]	
BEIL	Benzion	1892				M	[J], [S]	
BEIL	Abisch	1930				M	[J]	
BEIL	Mendel	1925				M	[J]	
BEIL	Rachel	1923				F	[J]	
BEIL	Nathan					M	[S]	
BEILES	Henoch	1889	Arbeiter	worker		M	[J]	
BEILES	Minna	1886	Schneiderin	tailoress		F	[J], [G]	
BEIM	Moses Jakob	1920	Angestellter	employee		M	[S]	
BEIM	Josef	1893	Arbeiter	worker		M	[J]	
BEIM	Perl	1893				F	[J]	
BEIM	Rachel	1920				F	[J]	
BEIM	Mendel	1925	Arbeiter	worker		M	[J]	
BEIM	Golde	1927				F	[J]	
BEIM	Berta	1895				F	[J]	
BEIM	Ester	1922				F	[J]	
BEIM	Feige	1925				F	[J]	
BEIM	Suessmann	1928	Elektrotechniker	electrician		M	[J]	
BEIM	Salomon	1898	Klempner	plumber	Suessmann Toni	M	[J]	
BEIM	Samuel				Zalman	M	[P]	
BEIM	Henoch				Samuel	M	[P]	
BEIM	Aron				Samuel	M	[P]	
BEIM	Moshe				Samuel	M	[P]	
BEIM	Henia				Samuel	F	[P]	
BEIM	Rysia				Samuel	F	[P]	

Krosno, Poland Yizkor Book

Surname	First name	Maiden/Married name	Birth	Occupation	Occupation	Father	Mother	Sex	Spouse	Category	Status
BEIM	Shlomo					Zalman		M		[P]	
BEIM	Siuna					Shlomo		F		[P]	
BEIM	Rysia					Shlomo		F		[P]	
BEIM	Moshe					Shlomo		M		[P]	
BEIM	Meilech					Zalman		M		[P]	
BEIM	Berish					Zalman		M		[P]	
BEIM	Dobka					Berish		F		[P]	
BEIM	Zalman					Berish		M		[P]	
BEIM	Riwke					Zalman		F		[P]	
BEIM	Chane		1924					F		[J]	
BEIM	Salomon		1927	Arbeiter	worker			M		[J]	
BEIM	Jsrael		1870					M		[J], [G]	
BEIM	Tziwia		1893					F	Jsrael	[P]	
BEIM	Zishe					Jsrael	Tziwia	M		[P]	
BEIM	Toni-Tova	WALLACE	1894			Yechiel	Hannah	F	Zishe	[P]	
BEIM	David		1920	Kutscher	coachman	Zishe	Toni	M		[J]	perished
BEIM	Jakob		1921	Arbeiter	worker	Zishe	Toni	M		[J]	survived
BEIM	Adele							F	Jakob	[P]	
BEIM	Helen					Zishe	Toni	F			survived
BEIM	Josef		1920	Arbeiter	worker	Zishe	Toni	M		[J]	
BEIM	Hinde	FREUND	1923					F	Josef	[J]	survived
BEIM	Sal					Zishe	Toni	M		[P]	
BEIM	Zalman					Jsrael	Tziwia	M		[P]	
BEIM	Salke		1923	Schäftemacher	upper shoe maker	Zalman		M		[J]	survived
BEIM	Zishe		1928			Zalman		M		[J]	survived

Krosno, Poland Yizkor Book

Surname	2nd Name	Given Name	Birth	Occupation (German)	Occupation (English)	Father/Spouse	Mother	Sex	Region	Status
BEIM		Regina	1905					F	[J]	
BEIM		Nathan	1890	Klempner	plumber			M	[J]	
BEIM		Sala	1908					F	[J]	
BEIM		Samuel	1925	Arbeiter	worker			M	[J]	
BEIM		Siegmund	1926	Arbeiter	worker			M	[J]	
BEIM		Rachel	1929					F	[J]	
BEIM		Benzion						M	[G]	
BEIZ		Riwe						F	[R]	
BELLER		Henoch						M	[L]	survived
BELZER		Nathan						M	[L]	survived
BELZES	STESSEL	Gite						F	[L]	survived
BELZYCKI		Pinkas	1890	Uhrmacher	watchmaker			M	[J]	
BELZYCKI		Feige Leie	1890					F	[J]	
BELZYCKI		Jsaak	1912	Elektrotechniker	electrician			M	[J]	
BEN MENACHEM	GROSS	Itzhak						M	[L]	survived
BENDER		Jakub		Friseur	barber			M	[R]	
BENDER		Pinhas						M	[R]	survived
BENKENDORF		Rosa-Rosalia	1907	Koch	cook			F	[J, [S]	
BER		Avraham						M	[L]	survived
BER	MONTAG	Mendel						M	[G]	
BERG		El.						M	[L]	survived
BERGER		Jakob	1872	Schneider	tailor			M	[J]	survived
BERGER		Miriam	1876			Jakob		F	[P]	perished
BERGER		Helene	1897			Jakob	Miriam	F	[P]	
BERGER		Francis	1900			Jakob	Miriam	F	[P]	

Krosno, Poland Yizkor Book

Surname	Given name		Year	Occupation	Occupation	Father	Mother	Sex		Code	Fate
BERGER	Berta		1902				Jakob	Miriam	F		[P]	survived
BERGER	Eleanor		1904			Jakob	Miriam	F		[P]	USA
BERGER	Rose		1906			Jakob	Miriam	F		[P]	USA
BERGER	Yaacov	RIEGER						M		[P]	perished
BERGER	Reisel		1893			Lazar	Pearl	F	Jakob	[J], [Y]	Belzec
BERGER	Moses		1912	Schneider	tailor	Jakob	Reisel	M		[J], [Y]	perished
BERGER	Osias		1915	Schneider	tailor	Jakob	Reisel	M		[J], [Y]	perished
BERGER	Mechel		1921	Schneider	tailor	Jakob	Reisel	M		[J], [Y]	survived
BERGER	Shlomo		1919			Jakob	Reisel	M		[P]	survived
BERGER	Berta					Jakob	Reisel	F		[P]	survived
BERGER	Benyamin							M		[L], [G]	survived
BERGER	Malka		1921					F		[L]	survived
BERGER	Hinda							F		[P]	USA
BERGLAS	Baruch		1900					M		[R]	Auschwitz
BERGMAN	Mark							M		[R]	
BERGMAN	Romek							M		[R]	
BERGMAN	Rubin							M		[R]	
BERGMAN	Jos			Bäcker	baker			M		[R], [B]	
BERGMAN	Josef			Schmied	blacksmith			M		[B]	
BERGNER	Samuel		1909					M		[P]	
BERGNER	Sabina							F	Samuel	[P]	
BERKOWICZ	Hirsch Beer							M		[S]	
BERLINSKI	Sara		1916	Angestellte	employee			F		[J]	
BERLINSKI	Dine		1906					F		[J]	
BERMANN	Lisa		1917	Hausmädchen	housemaid			F		[J]	

Krosno, Poland Yizkor Book

335

BERTENFELD	O.			Klempner	plumber			M	[R]
BERTENFELD	L.			Klempner	plumber			M	[R]
BIALYWLOS	Mendel		1891	Glaser	glazier	Avraham		M	[Y]	Auschwitz
BIALYWLOS	Leie	PLATNER	1896			Chaim		F	[J], [Y]	perished
BIALYWLOS	Mirjam-Mania		1922	Angestellte	employee	Mendel	Leie	F	[J], [Y]	perished
BIALYWLOS	Alexander-Send		1923	Glaser	glazier	Mendel	Leie	M	[J]	survived
BIALYWLOS	Salomon-Shlomo		1925	Glaser	glazier	Mendel	Leie	M	[J], [Y]	perished
BIALYWLOS	Chaim-Heniek		1931			Mendel	Leie	M	[J], [Y]	Auschwitz
BIEDER	Adolph			Schuhhändler	shoe dealer			M	[Y]	perished
BIEDER								F	[Y]	perished
BIEDER	Zigfried		1901			Adolph		M	[Y]	perished
BIEDER	Wilhelm		1902			Adolph		M	[Y]	perished
BIEDER	Admund		1917			Adolph		M	[Y]	perished
BIEDERMANN	Liepe		1886	Arbeiter	worker			M	[J], [S]
BIEDERMANN	Malke		1886					F	[J]
BIEDERMANN	Zile		1914	Verkäuferin	saleswoman			F	[J]
BIEDERMANN	Poje		1915					F	[J]
BIEDERMANN	Sara		1920	Modistin	dressmaker [female]			F	[J]
BIEDERMANN	Hirsch		1925	Arbeiter	worker			M	[J]
BIEDNAR	Adolf				goods merchant			M	[R]
BIGAJER	Chaim		1915	Schneider	tailor			M	[J]

Krosno, Poland Yizkor Book

Surname	Given name	Year	Occupation (German)	Occupation (English)	Father	Sex	Code	Fate
BIGAJER	Reisel	1916			Moshe	F	[J], [Y]	perished
BIGAJER	Aron	1941				M	[J]	
BILBERG	Yaacov					M	[L]	survived
BILET	Chana					F	[R]	
BILET	Chana					F	[R]	
BINDER	Meir				Wolf	M	[Y]	perished
BINDER	Rivka	1924			Meir	F	[Y]	perished
BIRAN	Chiel					M	[P]	survived
BIRAN	Esther				Chiel	F	[P]	survived
BIRAN	Blime					F	[P]	survived
BIRNER	Iroslav				Leib	M	[Y]	perished
BIRNER	Leopold				Itzhak	M	[Y]	perished
BIRNKRAUT	Sabine	1903				F	[J]	
BIRNKRAUT	Efraim	1912	Bäcker	baker		M	[J]	
BIRNKRAUT	Ester	1939				F	[J]	
BIRNKRAUT	Rachel	1907	Verkäuferin	saleswoman		F	[J]	
BIRON	Marcus		Schneider	tailor		M	[B]	
BLADY	Samuel	1913	Monteur	fitter		M	[J]	
BLASER	Eliasz		Kürschner	furrier		M	[R]	
BLAU	Moses	1904	Schirmmacher	umbrella maker		M	[J]	
BLAU	Rosa	1897			Dan	F	[J]	
BLAU	Adele	1938				F	[J]	
BLECHNER	Moshe	1893				M	[P]	USA
BLEICHFELD	Hermann	1879	Bauer	farmer		M	[J], [S]	
BLICHFELD						M	[L]	survived

Krosno, Poland Yizkor Book

Surname	Given	Maiden	Year	Occupation		Name 1	Name 2	Sex	Name 3	Code	Status
BLUM	Oscar							M		[R]	
BLUM	Lola	HELLER						F	Oscar	[R]	
BLUM	Ryszard					Oscar	Lola	M		[R]	
BLUMBERG	Shmuel							M		[P]	
BLUMENFELD	Berisch		1894	Kaufmann	merchang			M		[J]	
BLUMENFELD	Berta		1898			Yossef		F		[J]	perished
BLUMENFELD	Salomon		1920	Arbeiter	worker	Dov		M		[J]	perished
BLUMENFELD	Abraham		1922	Angestellter	employee	Dov		M		[J]	perished
BLUMENFELD	Naftali		1927	Arbeiter	worker			M		[J]	
BOBKER	Yehezkel							M		[L]	survived
BOBKER	Miriam							F	Yehezkel	[P]	perished
BOBKER	Ester		1903			Yehezkel	Miriam	F		[J]	perished
BOBKER	Mendel		1928			Yehezkel	Miriam	M		[J]	survived
BOBKER	Dobcze					Yehezkel	Miriam	F		[P]	perished
BOBKER	Frieda					Yehezkel	Miriam	F		[P]	perished
BOBKER	Hersh							M		[L]	survived
BOBKER	Markus		1901	Handelsgehilfe	clerk			M		[J], [G]	
BOBKER	Moses							M		[G]	
BOBKER	Mordechai							M		[P]	
BOCIAN	Pinkus		1903	Schneider	tailor			M		[J], [S]	
BOCIAN	Chaje		1907			Pinkus		F	Pinkus	[J]	
BOCIAN	Jente		1932			Pinkus	Chaje	F		[J]	
BOCIAN	Hirsch		1933			Pinkus	Chaje	M		[J]	
BODNARA	J			Friseur	barber			M		[R]	
BODNER	Chaskel		1877			Jakob		M		[J]	

Krosno, Poland Yizkor Book

Surname	Given name	Maiden	Year	Occupation	Occupation	Sex	Code	Notes
BODNER	Abraham		1878			M	[J]	
BODNER	Blime		1877			F	[J]	
BODNER	Stuessl		1915			F	[J]	
BODNER	Chaje		1940			F	[J]	
BODNER	Blueme		1917	Friseuse	coiffeuse	F	[J]	
BODNER	Regina		1914			F	[J]	
BODNER	Chaim					M	[G]	
BODNER	Menashe				vegetables	M	[R]	
BODNER-LECH	Benjamin		1912	Schneider	tailor	M	[J]	
BODNER-LECH	Scheindel		1912			F	[J]	
BODNER-LECH	Marjem		1937			F	[J]	
BOGEN	Kalmen		1885	Buchbinder	bookbinder	M	[J], [G]	
BOGEN	Nuchim		1909	Buchbinder	bookbinder	M	[J], [G]	
BOGEN	Ascher		1915	Arbeiter	worker	M	[P]	shot in 1942
BOGEN	Chaje Eidel		1880			F	[J], [S]	
BOGEN	Eidel		1880			F	[J]	
BOGEN	Chaim		1907	Schuster	shoemaker	M	[J]	
BOGEN	Hirsch		1910	Musiker	musician	M	[J]	
BOGEN	Schlama		1923	Arbeiter	worker	M	[J]	
BOGEN	Ben Zion					M	[P]	
BOGEN	Chana	HERZFELD				F	[P]	
BORENSTEIN	Arie					M	[L]	survived
BORGENICHT	Simon		1922	Schuster	shoemaker	M	[J]	
BORKOWSKI	Jsaak		1894	Schuster	shoemaker	M	[J]	
BORKOWSKI	Feige		1900			F	[J]	

Surname	Given name		Year			Sex		Source	Fate
BORKOWSKI	Chane		1920			F		[J]	
BORKOWSKI	Dine		1923			F		[J]	
BORKOWSKI	Abraham	Schuster	1927	shoemaker		M		[J]	
BRAND	Ester		1888			F		[J]	
BRAND	Mordche		1931			M		[J]	
BRAND	Hermann					M		[L]	survived
BRAND	Tzvi					M		[L]	survived
BRAND	Mania					F		[L]	survived
BRAND	Menachem					M		[L]	survived
BRANDER	Yossef					M		[P]	
BRANDER	Mindel		1900		Shmuel	F		[Y]	perished
BRANDSTATTER	Wolf			clothing merchant		M			
BRAUS	Sonia		1912		Avraham	F		[J], [Y]	perished
BRAUS	Stephan		1937		Leon	M		[J], [Y]	perished
BREITOWICZ	Mechel	Fleischer		butcher		M		[B]	
BREITOWICZ	Freidel	LEHRER				F	Mechel		
BREITOWICZ	Moshe				Mechel	M	Freidel	[P]	perished
BREITOWICZ	Shprintse					F	Moshe	[P]	died 1915
BREITOWICZ	Isidor	ISRAEL	1899		Moshe	M	Shprintse		survived in USA
BREITOWICZ	Jenny					F	Isidor		survived in the USA
BREITOWICZ	Sam		1902		Moshe	M	Shprintse		survived in USA
BREITOWICZ	Fanny					F	Sam		survived

Surname	Given	Other surname	Year	Occupation	Occupation	Father	Mother	Sex	Spouse		Fate
BREITOWICZ	Abraham		1904	Fleischer	butcher	Moshe	Shprintse	M		[J]	killed
BREITOWICZ	Helen	THALER	1908					F	Abraham	[P]	perished
BREITOWICZ	Hirsch		1935			Abraham	Helen	M		[P]	perished
BREITOWICZ	Ester		1937			Abraham	Helen	F		[P]	perished
BREITOWICZ	Janka		1939			Abraham	Helen	F		[P]	perished
BREITOWICZ	Jsaak		1905	Fleischer	butcher	Moshe	Shprintse	M		[P]	Belzec
BREITOWICZ	Esther	STRAUBING	1906					F	Jsaak	[P]	Belzec
BREITOWICZ	Abraham		1938			Jsaak	Esther	M		[P]	Belzec
BREITOWICZ	Rachel		1940			Jsaak	Esther	F		[P]	Belzec
BREITOWICZ	Jana		1941			Jsaak	Esther	F		[P]	Belzec
BREITOWICZ	Jacob		1910			Moshe	Shprintse	M		[P]	USA
BREITOWICZ	Jeannette	LUKS	1915					F	Jacob	[P]	USA
BREITOWICZ	Herb		1936			Jacob	Jeannette	M		[P]	USA
BREITOWICZ	Celia		1911			Moshe	Shprintse	F		[P]	deceased
BREITOWICZ	Ete		1913			Moshe	Shprintse	F		[P]	survived
BREITOWICZ	Lena		1889					F	Moshe	[P]	2nd wife, Belzec
BREITOWICZ	Aron		1914	Fleischer	butcher	Moshe	Lena	M		[P]	Belzec
BREITOWICZ	Bronka	KORB	1915					F	Aron	[P]	Belzec
BREITOWICZ	Stella		1940			Aron	Bronka			[P]	Belzec
BREITOWICZ	Chaim		1916			Moshe	Lena	M		[P]	deceased
BREITOWICZ	David		1918			Moshe	Lena	M		[P]	survived
BREITOWICZ	Fradel		1923	Buchhalterin	bookkeeper [female]	Moshe	Lena	F		[P]	Belzec
BREITOWICZ	Kreindel		1925	Schneiderin	tailoress	Moshe	Lena	F		[P]	Belzec
BREITOWICZ	Gitel		1927			Moshe	Lena	F		[P]	Belzec

Krosno, Poland Yizkor Book

Surname	Given name	Year	Occupation (German)	Occupation (English)	Relative	Relative	Sex	Relative	Source	Fate
BREITOWICZ	Hanka	1929			Moshe	Lena	M		[Y], [G]	Belzec
BREITOWICZ	Israel		Bäcker	baker	Dawid		F		[Y]	
BREITOWICZ	Moses	1906	Bäcker	baker	Israel		M		[JJ], [Y]	Treblinka
BREITOWICZ	Adka	1912			Israel		F	Israel	[Y]	Treblinka
BREITOWICZ	Chane	1927			Israel		F		[JJ], [S]	
BREITOWICZ	Pepi	1910			Baruch		F		[J]	
BREITOWICZ	Ete	1912			Baruch		F		[J]	
BREITOWICZ	Hene	1918					F		[J]	
BREITOWICZ	Chane	1867					F		[J]	
BREITOWICZ	Leib	1900	Fleischer	butcher			M		[JJ], [G]	
BREITOWICZ	Rachel	1905					F		[J]	
BREITOWICZ	Naftali	1936					M		[J]	
BREITOWICZ	Rosa	1938					F		[J]	
BREITOWICZ	Ester	1903					F		[J]	
BREITOWICZ	Schifre	1931					F		[J]	
BREITOWICZ	Rosa	1934					F		[J]	
BREITOWICZ	Chaje	1906					F		[J]	
BREITOWICZ	Mendel	1892					M		[P]	survived
BREITOWICZ	Chaim						M		[G]	
BRIESS	David	1909	Arbeiter	worker			M		[J]	
BRINGS	Lola	1886			Nehemia		F		[J]	
BRONFELD	Yaakow						M		[P]	
BRUCK	Mendel		Getreidehändler	grain dealer			M		[B]	
BRUDER	Benyamin	1872			Kiwe		M		[Y]	perished

Krosno, Poland Yizkor Book

Surname	Given name	Maiden	Year	Occupation	Occupation		Sex	Code	Survived
BRUDER	Pinhas						M	[L]	survived
BRUDER	Dawid			Schankwirt	innkeeper		M	[B]	
BRUDESHEWSKI	Noach						M	[P]	
BRZEZINSKI	Sische		1892	Arbeiter	worker		M	[J]	
BRZEZINSKI	Ryfke		1889				F	[J]	
BRZEZINSKI	Josef		1923	Arbeiter	worker		M	[J]	
BRZEZINSKI	Abraham		1924	Arbeiter	worker		M	[J]	
BRZEZINSKI	Aron		1930				M	[J]	
BRZIZLOWSKI	Mislaus						M	[S]	
BUCH	Levy David		1902	Schneider	tailor		M	[J]	
BUCH	Ester		1903	Schneiderin	tailoress	Zissel	F	[J], [Y]	
BUCHOLTZ	A			Arzt	doctor		M	[B]	
BUCHSBAUM	Sara-Sala		1903				F	[J], [S]	
BUCHSBAUM	Freide		1927				F	[J]	
BUCHSBAUM	Ete		1929				F	[J]	
BUCHSBAUM	Aron		1930				M	[J]	
BUCHSBAUM	Feiwel		1931				M	[J]	
BUCHSBAUM	Kinder						M	[S]	
BUCHSBAUM	Rachel	ZELLER					F	[L]	survived
BUCHSBAUM	Shia						M	[L]	survived
BURSTANOWICZ	Hirsch		1898	Arbeiter	worker		M	[J], [S]	
BURSTANOWICZ	Rachel		1902				F	[J]	
BURSTANOWICZ	Rosa		1924	Schneiderin	tailoress		F	[J]	
BURSTANOWICZ	Jakob		1926	Arbeiter	worker		M	[J]	
BURSTANOWICZ	Jonas		1928				M	[J]	

Surname	Given name	Year/Place	Occupation (Ger.)	Occupation (Eng.)	Father	Mother	Sex	Spouse	Nat.	Fate
BURSTANOWICZ	Sische	1931					M		[J]	
BURSTANOWICZ	Moses	1934					M		[J]	
BUTNER	Benyamin						M		[L]	survived
CAARES	Sabina						F		[G]	
CHAJES	Mendel	1909	Schäftemacher	upper shoe maker			M		[J]	
CHAJES	Berta	1909					F		[J]	
CHAJES	Schlama	1941					M		[J]	
CHEMERYS			Schmied	locksmith			M		[R]	
CHOROWICZ	B		Student	student			M		[R]	
CISER	Selig		Bäcker	baker			M		[B]	
CITRONENBAUM	Shmaryahu	Jaslo			Leib	Liba	M		[P]	
CITRONENBAUM	Sara	1910			Shmaryahu		F		[Y]	perished
DAN	Idel						M		[L]	survived
DAWID	Wolf						M		[P]	perished
DAWID	Sprinze	1880					F	Wolf	[J], [S]	perished
DAWID	Rosa	1903			Wolf	Sprinze	F		[J]	perished
DAWID	Freide	1915	Lehrerin	teacher [female]	Wolf	Sprinze	F		[J]	perished
DAWID	Rachel	1909	Schneiderin	tailoress	Wolf	Sprinze	F		[J]	perished
DAWID	Markus	1920	Tischler	carpenter	Wolf	Sprinze	M		[J]	perished
DAWID	Israel				Wolf	Sprinze	M		[P]	perished
DAWID	Avraham				Wolf	Sprinze	M		[P]	perished
DAWID	Lea	1922	Angestellte	employee	Wolf	Sprinze	F		[J]	perished
DAWID	Mechel	1863	Metallarbeiter	metalworker			M		[J], [G]	perished

Krosno, Poland Yizkor Book

DAWID	Sabine	1861				F		[J]
DAWID	Hinde	1905				F		[J]
DAWID	Luser	1932				M		[J]
DAWID	Sala	1913				F		[J]
DAWID	Pinkas	1897				M		[P], [G]
DAWID	Sara	1896				F		[J]
DAWID	Jochewet	1925				F		[J]
DAWID	Neche	1927				F		[J]
DAWID	Chane	1930				F		[J]
DAWID	Ester	1936				F		[J]
DAWID	Berel	1901	Metallarbeiter	metalworker		M		[J]
DAWID	Suessl	1930				M		[J]
DAWID	Anita	1935				F		[J]
DAWIDOWICZ	Mendel	1898	Glaser	glazier		M		[J]
DAWIDOWICZ	Marjem	1911				F		[J]
DAWIDOWICZ	Brandel	1935				F		[J]
DAWIDOWICZ	Chane	1941				F		[J]
DENN	Meilech		Kohlenarbeiter	coal miner		M		[R]
DENN	Shrincza	KLEINER			Meilech	F	Meilech	
DENN	Chaja Pearl	1905			Shrincza	F		
DENN	Abraham	1906	Handelsgehilfe	clerk		M		[J]
DENN	Selde	1905				F		[J]
DENN	Leib	1935				M		[J]
DENN	Pinkas	1936				M		[J]
DENN	Wolf	1893	Arbeiter	worker		M		[J], [G]

Krosno, Poland Yizkor Book

Surname	Given name	Year	Occupation	Occupation	Father	Mother	Sex	Spouse	Source	Status
DENN	Leie	1891					F		[J]	
DENN	Jsaak	1925	Arbeiter	worker			M		[J]	
DENN	Sprinze	1869					F		[J]	
DENN	Berel	1901					M		[J]	
DENN	Zelman						M	Zelman		deceased
DENN	Cywie						F			deceased
DENN	Meilech				Zelman	Cywie	M			died 1925
DENN	Mendel						M		[P]	
DEUTSCH	Dawid	1920			Alim		M		[Y]	perished
DEUTSCH	Frida	1900			Moshe		F		[Y]	perished
DIAMANT	Kalmen	1887	Kaufmann	merchant			M		[J], [G]	
DIAMANT	Pessel	1886					F		[J]	
DIAMANT	Chaje	1916					F		[J]	
DIAMANT	Sime	1922					F		[J]	
DIAMANT	Rachel	1924					F		[J]	
DIAMANT	Mindel	1926					F		[J]	
DIAMANT	Sara	1929					F		[J]	
DIAMANT	Leib	1931					M		[J]	
DIAMANT	S		Schneider	tailor			M		[R]	
DIAMANT	Mechel						M		[P]	
DICK	Beile	1879					M		[J], [Y]	perished
DICK	Marie	1909			Dawid		F		[J], [Y]	perished
DILLER	Josef	1907	Bademeister	bath attendant	Simha	Freidel	M		[J]	
DILLER	Chaje	1900					F		[J]	

Krosno, Poland Yizkor Book

Surname	Given name		Year	Occupation (Ger.)	Occupation (Eng.)	Father	Sex		Code	Fate
DILLER	Feige		1924				F		[J]	
DILLER	Jsaak		1926	Arbeiter	worker		M		[J]	
DILLER	Uri		1929				M		[J]	
DILLER	Pessel		1935				M		[J]	
DILLER	Saul		1909	Angestellter	employee		M		[J]	survived
DOLONSKI		FREUND					M		[L]	survived
DOM	Bashe						F		[P]	
DOM	Jehudith						F		[P]	
DOMINITZ	Moses				fabrics		M		[B]	
DOMINITZ	Perla		1891			Moshe	F		[Y]	Auschwitz
DOMINITZ	Lea						F		[L]	survived
DOMINITZ	Sonia						F		[R]	survived
DOMINITZ	Kalmen						M		[P]	
DORF	Menashe						M		[Y]	perished
DORF							F	Menashe	[Y]	perished
DORF	Hirsh		1925			Menashe	M		[Y]	perished
DORF	Yaacov		1927			Menashe	M		[Y]	perished
DORF	Ben Zion		1930			Menashe	M		[Y]	perished
DORF	Ester		1935			Menashe	F		[Y]	perished
DORF	Chaja		1899			Ben Zion	F		[Y]	perished
DORF	Mendel						M		[G]	
DORF	Dawid		1921			Mendel	M		[Y], [L]	survived
DERSCHEWITZ	Chaje		1890				F		[J]	
DERSCHEWITZ	Naftali		1920	Sattler	saddler		M		[J]	
DERSCHEWITZ	Chawa						F		[P]	

Surname	Given name	Year			Father	Sex	Code	Status
DRENGER	Hava					F	[L]	survived
DUNKEL	Majer	1865		goods		M	[J], [G], [R]	
DUNKEL	Luser	1911	Arbeiter	worker		M	[J]	
DUNKEL	Eisig	1916	Arbeiter	worker		M	[J]	
DWIDNER	Helena	1912			Moshe	F	[Y]	
DYM	Avraham		Stadtrat	town council		M	[R]	
DYM	Anna	1880			Moshe	F	[Y]	perished
DYM	Chaim		Stadtrat	town council		M	[R]	
DYM	Berish	1892	Kaufmann	merchant	Chaim	M	[Y]	Auschwitz
DYM	Shimon	1888			Chaim	M	[Y]	Belzec
DYM	Leib	1889	Fleischer	butcher	Chaim	M	[Y]	perished
DYM	Yaacov	1909			Pinhas	M	[Y]	perished
DYM	Moses	1910			Pinhas	M	[Y]	Belzec
DYM	Leopold		Arzt	town council, doctor		M	[R]	
DYM	Leja			spirits		F	[R]	
DYM	Rebeca			spirits		F	[R]	
DYM	Szyja			spirits		M	[R]	
DYM	Nushek					M	[P]	perished
DYM	Szyfra		Krämer	grocer		F	[B]	
DYM			Arzt	doctor			[P]	deceased
DYM	Zofia						[P]	
EDELHEIT	Blueme	1916				F	[J]	
EDELHEIT	Moses	1937				M	[J]	

Surname	First Name	Year	Occupation (German)	Occupation (English)	Other	Sex	Code	Fate
EDELHEIT	Hirsch	1887	Bürstenmacher	brush maker		M	[J]	
EDELHEIT	Golde	1894				F	[J]	
EDELHEIT	Beile	1925				F	[J]	
EDELHEIT	Berel	1930				M	[J]	
EDELHEIT	Menahem				Reuben	M	[Y]	perished
EDELHEIT	Rubin					M	[G]	
EHRENBERG	Hadassa	1902				F	[J]	
EHRENBERG	Majer	1935				M	[J]	
EHRENPREIS	Jakob	1898				M	[J], [S]	
EHRENREICH	Jakob					M	[G]	
EHRENREICH	Chana					F	[S]	
EHRENREICH	Ester	1912				F	[J]	
EHRENREICH	Leib					M	[L]	survived
EHRENREICH	Yehezkel					M	[L]	survived
EHRLICH	Chaskel	1934				M	[J]	
EHRLICH	Alter	1888	Eierpacker	egg-packer		M	[J]	
EHRLICH	Scheindel	1886				F	[J]	
EHRLICH	Sara	1916	Schneiderin	tailoress		F	[J]	
EHRLICH	Rachel	1920				F	[J]	
EHRLICH	Chane	1923	Schneiderin	tailoress		F	[J]	
EHRLICH	Leib	1924	Darmputzer	cleaner		M	[J]	
EHRLICH	Leie	1929				F	[J]	
EHRLICH	Simon					M	[S]	
EHRLICH	Elhanan					M	[P]	
EICHHORN	Regine	1922	Angestellte	employee		F	[J]	

Surname	Given name	Year	Occupation	Occupation	Father	Sex		Status
EICHHORN	Netti	1920	Angestellte	employee		F	[J]	
EICHHORN	Zishe					M	[L]	survived
EINHORN	Feiwel	1907	Arbeiter	worker		M	[J]	
EINHORN	Ester	1909				F	[J]	
EINHORN	Hinde	1939				F	[J]	
EINHORN	Rubin	1904	Arbeiter	worker		M	[J]	
EINHORN	Ester	1902				F	[J]	
EINHORN	Rische	1931				M	[J]	
EINHORN	Hudes	1932				F	[J]	
EINHORN	Hirsch	1935				M	[J]	
EINLEGER	Jhuda	1887	Angestellter	employee		M	[J]	
EINLEGER	Leie	1898				F	[J]	
EINLEGER	Rita	1932				F	[J]	
EINREDER	Mottel	1880	Arbeiter	worker		M	[J], [S]	
EINREDER	Leie	1888				F	[J]	
EISEN	Jhuda	1922	Bäcker	baker		M	[J]	
EISEN	Yaacov					M	[L]	survived
EISENBERG	Itzhak Yaacov					M	[P]	USA
EISENBERG	Leibish	1901			Itzhak Yaacov	M	[P]	USA
EISENBERG	Gershon				Itzhak Yaacov	M	[P]	USA
EISENBERG	Rivka				Itzhak Yaacov	F	[P]	USA
EISENBERG	MIndel				Itzhak Yaacov	F	[P]	USA

Surname	Given	Alt	Year	(German)	Occupation	Father	Sex	Source	Fate
EISENBERG	Saul		1887	Perückenmacher	wigmaker		M	[J]	
EISENBERG	Liebe		1890				F	[J]	
EISENBERG	Menachem		1928				M	[J]	
EISENBERG	Benjamin		1920			Avraham	M	[J], [Y]	perished
EISENBERG	Ben Zion		1922			Avraham	M	[J], [Y]	perished
EISENBERG	Yossef		1924			Avraham	M	[J], [Y]	perished
EISENBERG	Gershon						M	[L]	survived
EISENBERG	Simcha			Baumeister	builder		M	[R]	
EISENBERG	Izaac			Früchteverkäufer	fruit seller		M	[R]	
EISENSTEIN	Berta	AXELRAD					M	[L]	survived
ELENBERG	Rosa		1925				F	[J]	
ELLOWICZ	Saul		1879			Itzhak	M	[J], [Y], [G]	perished
ELLOWICZ	Chaim		1890			Itzhak	M	[Y]	perished
ELLOWICZ	Luser		1907	Arbeiter	worker		M	[J]	survived
ELLOWICZ	Esther						F	[L]	survived
ELLOWICZ	Elieazar						M	[L]	survived
ELLOWICZ	Itzhak				fabrics		M	[B]	
ELLOWICZ	Majer		1872		fabrics	Itzhak	M	[J], [Y], [G]	Belzec
ELLOWICZ	Simche		1871				M	[J]	
EMER	Machcia	KROSNO				Yunes	F	[Y]	Belzec
EMER	Jacob						M	[P]	survived
ENGEL	Jhuda		1896	[J]		Chaim	M	[Y]	Belzec
ENGEL	Mirjam		1899				F	[J]	
ENGEL	Jhudith		1926				F	[J]	

Krosno, Poland Yizkor Book

Surname	First name	Other name	Year	Occupation (German)	Occupation (English)	Name	Sex	Language	Survived
ENGEL	Helene		1901				F	[J]	
ENGEL	Dawid						M	[S]	
ENGEL	Yehoshua						M	[L]	survived
ENGEL	Hannah	PALANT					F	[L]	survived
ENGELHARDT	Moses		1916	Handtaschenmacher	handbags maker	Tzwi	M	[J], [Y]	
ENGELHARDT	Sabine		1863				F	[J]	
ENGELHARDT	Jsaak		1909				M	[J], [G]	
ENGELHARDT	Chaje		1912				F	[J]	
ENGELHARDT	Chane		1936				F	[J]	
ENGELHARDT	Chawe		1937				F	[J]	
ENGELHARDT	Mendel		1879				M	[J], [G]	
ENGELHARDT	Marjem		1878				F	[J]	
ENGELHARDT	Benzion		1901	Kaufmann	merchant		M	[J]	
ENGELHARDT	Chaje		1901				F	[J]	
ENGELHARDT	Rachel		1922				F	[J]	
ENGELHARDT	Ester		1924				F	[J]	
ENGELHARDT	Leib		1930				M	[J]	
ENGELHARDT	Ryfke		1888				F	[J]	
ENGELHARDT	Yossef						M	[L]	survived
ENGELHARDT	Shlomo						M	[L], [G]	survived
ENGELHARDT	Hena	FRUHMAN					F	[P]	survived
ENGELHARDT	Haim		1875				M	[P]	
ENGELHARDT	Ojser						M	[G]	
ENGELHARDT	Shulem						M	[P]	

Krosno, Poland Yizkor Book

ENGELHARDT	Leica					F	[P]
ENGLAENDER	Eber		Ratsmitglied	councilor		M	[R]
ENGLAENDER	Hirsch	1895	Kellermeister	cellarer		M	[J]
ENGLAENDER	Malke	1890				F	[J]
ENTNER	Abraham	1907	Bäcker	baker		M	[J]
ENTNER	Regina	1898				F	[J]
ENTNER	Ch		Bäcker	baker		M	[R]
ENTNER	Malke	1932				F	[J]
ENTNER	Hene	1934				F	[J]
ENTNER	Simon	1937				M	[J]
ENTNER	Leie	1902				F	[J]
ENTNER	Hene	1930				F	[J]
ENTNER	Berisch	1931				M	[J], [G]
ENZWEIG	Sische	1903	Arbeiterin	worker [female]		M	[J], [S]
ENZWEIG	Chaim Aron	1933				M	[J]
EPSTEIN	Berisch	1891	Arbeiter	worker		M	[J]
EPSTEIN	Rachel	1888				F	[J]
EPSTEIN	Chume	1916				M	[J]
EPSTEIN	Guetl	1918				F	[J]
EPSTEIN	Israel	1921	Schäftemacher	upper shoe maker		M	[J]
EPSTEIN	Ida	1923				F	[J]
EPSTEIN	Zile	1925				F	[J]
EPSTEIN	Nuchim	1927	Arbeiter	worker		M	[J]
EPSTEIN	Benjamin	1930				M	[J]

Surname	Given name		Year	Occupation		Name 1	Name 2	Sex	Code	Fate/Place
ERLBAUM	Josef		1883	Angestellter	employee			M	[J]	
ERLBAUM	Suessl		1884					F	[J]	
ERLBAUM	Tonka		1913	Näherin	seamstress			M	[J]	survived
ERLBAUM	Yehoshua							M	[R]	
ERREICH	Jsaak		1928	Schneider	tailor			M	[J]	survived
ERRENREICH	Leib	WOLF						M	[R]	survived
ERRENREICH	Lea							F	[L]	survived
ERRENREICH	Yehiel							M	[L]	survived
ERTEL	Abisch		1907	Arbeiter	worker			M	[J]	
ERTEL	Hene		1903					F	[J]	
ERTEL	Rosa		1907					F	[J]	
ERTEL	Shprintze							F	[P]	
ETTINGER	Moses		1893	Handelsgehilfe	clerk			M	[J], [G]	Krosno
ETTINGER	Malke		1896				Moses	F	[J], [Y]	Krosno
ETTINGER	Scheindel		1924					F	[J]	
ETTINGER	Debora		1928					F	[J]	
FABER	Feiga					Moshe		F	[Y]	perished
FABER	Hadassah		1929			Meir		F	[Y]	perished
FABER	Rachel		1929			Meir		F	[Y]	perished
FABER	Arie							M	[R]	survived
FABIAN	Samuel							M	[P]	
FABIAN	Pearl						Samuel	F	[P]	
FABIAN	Jacob					Samuel	Pearl	M	[P]	
FABIAN	Marian					Samuel	Pearl	M	[P]	
FABIAN	Morey					Samuel	Pearl	M	[P]	

Krosno, Poland Yizkor Book

FALLMANN	Hirsch	1876			M	[J]	
FARBER	David				M	[L]	survived
FASS	Bluma	1892			F	[P]	
FASS	Israel				M	[P]	
FAST	Mechel		Schokoladenhersteller	chocolate manufacturer	M	[P]	
FEBER	Eric				M	[L]	survived
FEILHARDT	Anna	1894			F	[J]	
FEILHARDT	Rosa	1922			F	[J]	
FEILHARDT	Lola	1923			F	[J]	
FEILHARDT	Ete	1927			M	[J]	
FEILHARDT	Jozek	1918		Elieazar	M	[Y]	Plaszow
FEIN	Jakob	1899	Sockenstricker	sock knitter	M	[J]	
FEIN	Liebe	1898			M	[J]	
FEIN	Chawe	1925			F	[J]	
FEIN	Wolf	1929			M	[J]	
FEIN	Ester	1934			F	[J]	
FEIT	Leib	1921	Schneider	tailor	M	[J]	
FEITELBAUM	Chaim		Gerber	skinner	M	[R]	
FELBAUM	M.		Schmied	locksmith	M	[R]	
FELCZER	Mordche-Markus	1888	Kantor	cantor	M	[J], [S]	
FELCZER	Czarne	1884			F	[J]	
FELCZER	Ite	1931			F	[J]	
FELCZER	Chane	1923			F	[J]	
FELCZER	Mindel	1924			F	[J]	

Surname	Given		Occupation	Year	Occupation	Alt. name	Sex	Code	Fate
FELCZER	Chiel		Arbeiter	1925	worker		M	[J]	
FELDER	Samuel			1900		Dawid	M	[Y]	Belzec
FELDER	Samuel			1900		Zeev	M	[Y]	perished
FELDMAN	Ester			1902		Yaacov	F	[Y]	Belzec
FELIK	Dina					Yirmi	F	[Y]	perished
FELIK	Rachel			1921		Moshe	F	[Y]	perished
FELNER	Machle			1886			F	[J]	
FENIG	Chawa						F	[G]	
FENIK	Golde			1897			F	[J]	
FENIK	Feige			1928			F	[J]	
FENIK	Simon			1930			M	[J]	
FENIK	Chaim			1932			M	[J]	
FENIK	Wele			1934			F	[J]	
FENSTER	Salomon		Schneider	1906	tailor		M	[J]	
FENSTER	Debora			1907			F	[J]	
FENSTER	Moses			1936			M	[J]	
FERNHAL	Ella	DIM					F	[L]	survived
FESSEL	Zile		Schneiderin	1915	tailoress		F	[J]	
FESSEL	Chane		Schneiderin	1920	tailoress		F	[J]	
FESSEL	Jhuda		Arbeiter	1907	worker		M	[J, S]	
FESSEL	Rosa			1907			F	[J]	
FESSEL	Wolf			1933			M	[J]	
FESSEL	Hinde			1876			F	[J]	
FESSEL	Wolf		Arbeiter	1927	worker		M	[J]	
FESSEL	Sara			1932			F	[J]	

Krosno, Poland Yizkor Book

Surname	Given name	Year	Occupation (Ger.)	Occupation (Eng.)	Father	Mother	Sex	Spouse	Code	Status
FESSEL	Liepe						M		[S]	
FESSEL	Isac				Alexander		M		[Y]	perished
FESSEL	Yaacov Itzha						M		[L]	survived
FESSEL	Khune			spirits			M		[R]	
FESSEL	Sender		Fleischer	butcher			M		[R]	Russia
FESSEL	Itzhak		Kürschner	furrier	Sender		M		[P]	Russia
FESSEL	Feige[Felicia]						F	Itzhak	[P]	survived
FESSEL	Wolf/William	1927			Itzhak	Feige	M		[P]	survived
FESSEL	Dina [Daniela]	1932			Itzhak	Feige	F		[P]	survived
FESSEL	Shmuel				Sender		M		[P]	Russia
FESSEL	Moshe				Sender		M		[L]	Russia
FESSEL	Yeshiahu				Sender		M		[L]	Russia
FESSEL	Elimelech				Sender		M		[L]	Russia
FESSEL	Feige	1906			Sender		F		[J]	
FESSEL	Rachel	1915	Verkäuferin	saleswoman	Sender		F		[J]	
FESSLER	Peretz						M		[G]	
FEUERLICHT	Samuel						M		[G]	
FEUERLICHT	Anna	1898					F		[J]	
FEUERLICHT	Feige	1921	Verkäuferin	saleswoman			F		[J]	
FEUERLICHT	Marjem	1925					F		[J]	
FEUERLICHT	Hinde	1926					F		[J]	
FEUERLICHT	Jakob	1875	Eierpacker	egg-packer			M		[J]	
FEUERLICHT	Sprinze	1878					F		[J]	
FEUERLICHT	Zipora	1914					F		[J]	

Surname	Given name		Year	Occupation				Sex		Code	Fate
FINDLING	Selig							M		[R]	
FINDLING	Jdes		1905					F		[J]	
FINDLING	Jakob			Bäcker	baker	Usher		M		[Y]	Auschwitz
FINK	Leon							M		[P]	
FINK	Klara		1879					F	Leon	[J], [G]	perished
FINK	Israel					Leon	Klara	M		[Y], [G]	perished
FINK	Helene		1915			Leon	Klara	F	Joseph	[J]	survived
FINK	Jossef					Leon	Klara	M		[L]	survived
FINK	Miriam	BLUM						F	Jossef	[P]	survived
FINK	Menek					Leon	Klara	M		[P]	perished
FINK	Michael		1910					M		[Y]	perished
FINK	Chana		1917			Shmerl		F	Israel	[Y]	perished
FINK	Israel		1920	Student	student	Israel	Chana			[P]	survived
FINK	Esther							F		[L]	survived
FINMAN	Ojzer		1887	Arbeiter	worker	Lemel		M		[J]	
FIRESS	Malke		1887			Leizer		F		[J], [Y]	Belzec
FIRESS	Josef		1915	Zuschneider	cutter			M		[J], [Y]	perished
FIRESS	Ester		1917					F		[J]	
FIRESS	David		1914	Schäftemacher	upper shoe maker			M		[J]	
FIRESS	Nathan		1930			Shmuel		M		[Y]	perished
FIREST	Sarah		1928			Shmuel		F		[Y]	perished
FIRST	Toni		1913			Israel		M		[Y]	perished
FIRSZT	Genia		1903					F		[J], [S]	
FISCHBEIN	Bronislowa							F		[P]	survived

Surname	Given	Maiden	Year	Occupation	Occupation	Name	Name	Sex	Code	Fate
FISCHBEIN	Dora		1936					F	[P]	survived
FISCHBEIN	Eva							F	[P]	perished
FISCHBEIN	Franca							F	[P]	perished
FISCHBEIN	Fishek							M	[P]	perished
FISCHBEIN	Leib		1934					M	[J]	
FISCHBEIN	Isaak		1937					M	[J]	
FISCHBEIN	Marjem		1940					F	[J]	
FISCHBEIN	Jetti		1895					F	[J]	
FISCHBEIN	Adolph		1905			Avraham		M	[Y]	
FISCHBEIN	Alte							F	[P]	survived
FISCHBEIN	Regina			Schreiner	carpenter			F	[R]	
FISCHBEIN	Dawid			Schneider	tailor			F	[R]	
FISCHBEIN	A.R.			Schneider	tailor			M	[R]	
FISCHBER	Shimon							M	[L]	survived
FISCHER	Chaim							M	[R]	
FISCHER	Sary	MARGULES				Chaim	Sary	F	[R]	Chaim
FISCHER	Lea Sara		1905					F	[R]	Auschwitz
FISCHER	Rosalia		1920					F	[P]	Auschwitz
FISCHLER	Josef		1930					M	[J]	
FISCHLER	Wolf							M	[G]	
FISCHLER	Tzwi							M	[P]	
FISCHLER	Yaakow							M	[P]	
FISHLICH	Awraham							M	[P]	
FITTER	Jozef			Klempner	plumber			M		
FLAM	Fima							M		

Surname	Given name		Year			Father	Mother	Sex	Spouse	Code	Notes
FLAM	Luser		1867	Musiker	musician			M		[J], [G]	Married 1904
FLAPPAN	Rachel	KALB	1884					F	Luser	[J], [Y]	Married 1904
FLAPPAN	Chaja Riwka		1909			Luser	Rachel	F			deceased
FLAPPAN	Frania		1910			Luser	Rachel	F		[J]	
FLAPPAN	Malka		1911			Luser	Rachel	F			deceased
FLAPPAN	Hella		1912					F		[J]	
FLAPPAN	Feige		1914					F		[J]	
FLAPPAN	Avraham					Haim		M		[Y]	Rzeszow
FLATNER	Moses							M		[G]	
FLICK	Feiga							F		[S]	
FLICK	Chaja		1923			Moshe		F		[Y]	perished
FLICK	Nachman							M		[L]	perished
FOGEL	Tziporah							F	Nachman	[P]	perished
FOGEL	Avraham					Nachman	Tziporah	M		[P]	perished
FOGEL	Bella							F	Avraham	[P]	perished
FOGEL	Nachman					Avraham	Bella	M		[P]	perished
FOGEL	Feige					Avraham	Bella	F		[P]	perished
FOGEL	Mina					Avraham	Bella	F		[P]	perished
FOGEL	Michal					Avraham	Bella	F		[P]	perished
FOGEL	Yossef					Avraham	Bella	M		[P]	perished
FOGEL	Haim					Avraham	Bella	M		[P]	perished
FOGEL	Josef		1878					M		[J]	
FOGEL	Chaje		1883					F		[J]	

Krosno, Poland Yizkor Book

FOGEL	Freide	1923	Näherin	seamstress		F	[J]	
FOGEL	Shlomo				M	[L]	survived
FOGEL	Edi				M	[R]	
FOGEL	Rivka		store		F	[L]	survived
FRANK	Josef				M	[G]	
FRANK	Frieda				F	[P]	survived
FRENKEL	Sender				M	[P]	
FRENKEL	Itzhak				M	[P]	
FRENKEL	Jsaak	1917	Schäftemacher	upper shoe maker	M	[J]	
FRAUWIRTH	Ryfke	1916			F	[J]	
FRAUWIRTH	Ite	1912			F	[J]	
FRAUWIRTH	Beile	1911			F	[J]	
FRAUWIRTH	Chaskel	1899	Angestellter	employee	M	[J]	
FREIFELD	Marjem	1932		Chaskel	F	[J]	
FREIFELD	Renia			Chaskel	F	[Y]	Korczyna
FREIFELD	Rosa	1903		Yaacov	F	[J]	
FREIFELD	Lajbek			Yaacov	M	[Y]	Korczyna
FREIFELD	Siolek			Yaacov	M	[Y]	Korczyna
FREIFELD	Chaim	1883	Arbeiter	worker	M	[J]	
FREIREICH	Feige	1892			F	[J]	
FREIREICH	Rachel	1872		Menashe	F	[J], [Y]	
FRENKEL	Bela	1904		Aron	F	[Y]	
FRENKEL	Berel	1897	Arbeiter	worker	Moshe	M	[J], [Y]	Belzec
FREUND	Elimelech	1877		Moshe	M	[Y]	Belzec
FREUND	Naphtali				M	[L]	survived

Surname	Given Name	Other Surname	Occupation	Occupation (Eng.)	Year	Father	Mother	Sex	Other Name	Code	Notes
FREUND	Shmuel							M		[L], [G]	survived
FREUND	Chane				1920	Shmuel		F		[J], [Y]	Auschwitz
FREUND	Majer				1877			M		[J]	
FREUND	Debora				1873			F		[J]	survived
FREUND	Yochewed							F		[R]	
FREUND	Adele				1914			F		[J]	
FREUND	Beile				1906			F		[J]	
FREUND	Hava							F		[L]	survived
FREUND	Betzalel Bar	TAUB			1859			M		[J], [S]	
FREUND	Miriam		Gerber	skinner		Betzalel B	Miriam	F	Betzalel	[P]	
FREUND	Moses	FRIEDMAN				Moses	Miriam	M	Moses	[G], [B]	survived
FREUND	Miriam					Betzalel B	Miriam	F		[L]	survived
FREUND	Hinda	HINDZIA				Betzalel B	Miriam	F		[P]	
FREUND	Ryfka									[P]	
FREUND	Zissel									[P]	
FREUND	Ben Tzion					Betzalel B	Miriam	M	Ben Tzion	[P]	
FREUND	Roselle					Ben Zion		F		[P]	
FREUND	Ruth					Ben Zion		F		[P]	
FREUND	Moshe							M	Moshe	[P]	
FREUND	Risha					Moshe		F		[P]	
FREUND	Meir						Risha	M		[P]	
FREUND	Esther					Meir		F		[P]	
FREUND	Eidel					Meir		F		[P]	
FREUND	Salomon		Arbeiter	worker	1911	Meir		M		[J], [L],	

Krosno, Poland Yizkor Book

362

Surname	Given name		Year		Occupation			Sex	Source	Notes
FREUND	Yaakow					Moshe	Risha	M	[G]	
FREUND	Pesha					Yaakow		F	[P]	
FREUND	Ita					Yaakow		F	[P]	
FREUND	Henia					Yaakow		F	[P]	
FREUND	Rivka					Yaakow		F	[P]	
FREUND	Mania					Yaakow		F	[P]	
FREUND	Leib					Yaakow		M	[P]	
FREUND	Chana		1898			Yossef		F	[Y]	perished
FRIDLER	Jakob		1870					M	[JJ], [S]	
FRIED	Ziwie		1884					F	[J]	
FRIED	Elieazar							M	[G]	
FRIED	B			Apotheker	druggist			M	[B]	
FRIEDMANN	Chaim									
FRIEDMANN	Sarah	PLATNER								
FRIEDMANN	Manes		1890	Uhrmacher	watchmaker	Pinhas		M	[JJ], [Y], [G]	Belzec
FRIEDMANN	Leie		1895					F	[J]	
FRIEDMANN	Pinkas		1923	Arbeiter	worker			M	[J]	
FRIEDMANN	Abraham		1924	Arbeiter	worker			M	[JJ], [L]	survived
FRIEDMANN	Chiel		1926	Arbeiter	worker	Menahem		M	[JJ], [Y]	
FRIEDMANN	Naftali		1929	Arbeiter	worker			M	[J]	
FRIEDMANN	Chaskel		1931			Menahem		M	[JJ], [Y]	
FRIEDMANN	Hinde		1933			Menahem		F	[JJ], [Y]	
FRIEDMANN	Luser		1905	Arbeiter	worker			M	[J]	
FRIEDMANN	Mendel		1906	Angestellter	employee			M	[JJ], [G]	

Surname	Given name	Other name	Year	Occupation	Occupation	Name	Name	Gender	Fate	Code
FRIEDMANN	Brandel		1901					F		[J]
FRIEDMANN	Samuel		1903	Schuster	shoemaker			M		[J]
FRIEDMANN	Eva		1899					F		[J]
FRIEDMANN	Freide		1930					F		[J]
FRIEDMANN	Leah		1900			Chaim		F		[Y]
FRIEDMANN	Ite							F		[S]
FRIEDRICH	Tille		1892					F		[J]
FRIESS	Ester		1917	Schneiderin	tailoress			F		[J]
FRIESS	Rosa		1920					F		[J]
FRIESS	Jsrael		1923	Schuster	shoemaker					[J]
FRIESS	Adele		1936					F		[J]
FRIESS	Dora		1934					F		[J]
FRIESS	Regina		1914					F		[J]
FRIESS	Menachem							M	survived	[R]
FRIESS	Ch.			Student	student			F		[R]
FRIESS	Feige		1899					F		[J]
FRISCH	Rachel		1920	Näherin	seamstress			F		[J]
FRISCH	Chaje		1921					F		[J]
FRISCH	Dine		1925					F		[J]
FRISCH	Eti	KERN						F	survived	[L]
FRISCHMAN	Yossel							M		[P]
FRISHTIK	Leib				wood merchant			M		[B]
FROSS	Chaim		1880	Kaufmann	merchant	Chaim		M	perished	[J]
FRUHMANN	Sara		1884			Sara	Chaim	F	perished	[J], [G]

Krosno, Poland Yizkor Book

FRUHMANN	Hena				Chaim	Sara	F		survived
FRUHMANN	Ceena				Chaim	Sara	M		
FRUHMANN	Itzik				Chaim	Sara	F		
FRUHMANN	Malka		1910		Chaim	Sara	F	[P]	shot
FRUHMANN	Dawid		1912	Schmied	locksmith	Chaim	Sara	M	[Y]	Auschwitz
FRUHMANN		SPINDLER					Dawid	F	[P]	perished
FRUHMANN	Michael				Dawid		M	[P]	Auschwitz
FRUHMANN	Joseph			Schmied	locksmith	Chaim	Sara	M	[P]	survived
FRUHMANN	Sara		1917		Chaim	Sara	F	[Y]	Auschwitz
FRUHMANN	Hanka				Chaim	Sara	F	[P]	survived
FRUHMANN	Moshe-Moniek				Chaim	Sara	M	[P]	survived
FRUHMANN	Mark				Chaim	Sara	M	[P]	survived
FRUHMANN	Israel		1913	Friseur	barber			M	[J]	
FUCHS	Osias		1919	Angestellter	employee			M	[J]	
FUERST	Samuel		1896	Kaufmann	merchant			M	[J], [Y]	perished
FUERST	Chaje		1890				Samuel	F	[J], [Y]	perished
FUERST	Abraham		1920	Arbeiter	worker	Shmuel	Chaje	M	[J], [Y]	perished
FUERST	Meilech		1921	Arbeiter	worker	Shmuel	Chaje	M	[J], [Y]	Auschwitz
FUERST	Shija-Osias		1923	Arbeiter	worker	Shmuel	Chaje	M	[J], [Y]	Auschwitz
FUERST	Hannah		1925			Shmuel	Chaje	M	[J]	perished
FUERST	Sara		1926			Shmuel	Chaje	F	[J]	perished
FUERST	Yonathan				Shmuel	Chaje	M	[P]	perished
FUERST	Nissen		1928					M	[J]	
FUERST	Henoch		1930					M	[J]	
FUERST	Israel-Jacub						M	[G]	

Krosno, Poland Yizkor Book

Surname	Given name		Year	Occupation		Father	Mother	Sex	Spouse	Source	Fate
FUERST	Aron Leib		1902	Arbeiter	worker			M		[J], [S]	
FUHRER	Beile		1901					F		[J], [S]	
FUHRER	Abraham		1928					M		[J]	
FUHRER	Jsaak		1931					M		[J]	
FUHRER	Mirel		1934					F		[J]	
FUHRER	Gitla							F		[J], [S]	
FUHRER	Samuel	JORALKA	1875	Rabbi	rabbi	Zelig		M		[Y]	shot in 1942
FUHRER	Sara		1869					F	Samuel	[P]	perished
FUHRER	Salomon					Samuel	Sara	M		[P]	perished
FUHRER	Ruchel					Samuel	Sara	F		[P]	perished
FUHRER	Ben Zion							M		[L]	survived
FUHRER	Malke		1912					F		[J]	
FUSS	Leie		1937					F		[J]	
FUSS	Berisch		1878			Hirsh		M		[J], [Y]	
FUSS	Feige		1878					F		[J]	
FUSS	Pessel		1913					F		[J]	
FUSS	Brandel		1914					F		[J]	
FUSS	Sender							F			
FUSS	Abraham							M		[G]	
FUTTER	Marjem		1906					F		[J]	
GABLINGER	Dine		1924	Hausmädchen	housemaid			F		[J], [S]	
GABRYLEWICZ	Leie		1900	Schneiderin	tailoress			F		[J]	
GAERTNER	Feige		1902	Schneiderin	tailoress			F		[J]	
GAERTNER	Sara		1906	Schneiderin	tailoress			F		[J]	

Krosno, Poland Yizkor Book

Surname	Given Name	Maiden	Occupation (Ger.)	Year	Occupation (Eng.)	Relation 1	Relation 2	Sex	Relation 3	Fate	Source
GAERTNER	Chana		Kaufmann		merchant			F			[R]
GAERTNER	Frimet		Näherin	1907	seamstress			F			[J]
GALON	Liebe			1933				F			[J]
GALON	Ite			1934				F			[J]
GALON	M		Maler		painter			M			[R]
GARFUNKEL	Salomon		Krämer		grocer			M			[B]
GARTNER	Moishe		Schneider	1870	tailor	Simcha		M		perished	[Y]
GEBEL	Chaja			1897		Yaacov		F		perished	[Y]
GEBEL	Michael			1910		Moishe		M		perished	[Y]
GEBEL	Mechel			1920		Moishe		M		perished	[Y]
GEBEL	Moses		Schneider	1874	tailor			M			[J]
GEBEL	Mehel							M	Mehel		[R]
GEBEL	Rosy	KUREF						F			[R]
GEBEL	Beile					Mehel	Rosy	F		Auschwitz	[J], [G]
GEBEL	Fischel		Schneider	1915	tailor			M			[J]
GEBEL	Tzvi							M		survived	[L]
GEBLINGER	Mendel							M			[G]
GELANDER	Osias		Angestellter	1894	employee			M			[J]
GELB	Pessel			1896				F			[J]
GELB	Dora			1922				F			[J]
GELB	Aron		Arbeiter	1924	worker			M			[J]
GELB	Salomon		Krankenschwester	1876	nurse			M			[J], [S]
GELB	Debora			1894				F			[J]
GELB	Josef							M			[P]
GELB	Brandl			1886				F			[P]

Surname	Given name	Birth	Occupation (German)	Occupation (English)	Hebrew name	Sex	Source	Fate
GELB	Chaim					M	[G]	
GELB	Sara	1912				F	[J]	
GELBART	M		Schneider	tailor		M	[R]	
GELD	Feiwel					M	[S], [G]	
GELLER	Dawid	1890			Henoch	M	[Y]	Buchenwald
GERBER	Pinkas	1884	Kaufmann	merchant		M	[J]	
GERLICH	Brandel	1882				F	[J]	
GERLICH	Sara	1911	Verkäuferin	saleswoman	Pinhas	F	[J], [Y]	perished
GERLICH	Osias	1881	Kaufmann	merchant		M	[J], [G], [R]	
GERLICH	Hinde	1881				F	[J]	
GERLICH	Mathias	1910	Arbeiter	worker		M	[J]	
GERLICH	Chaje	1911	Schneiderin	tailoress		F	[J]	
GERLICH	Brandel	1913	Verkäuferin	saleswoman		F	[J]	
GERLICH	Pinkas	1918	Angestellter	employee		M	[J]	
GERLICH	Moritza					M	[L]	survived
GERTNER	Zalman					M	[L]	survived
GERTNER	Benjamin					M	[L]	survived
GINT-LEWINSKI		1905					[R]	shot
GIRCH	Jacob			clothing merhant		M	[B]	
GISER	Ben Zion	1896			Avraham	M	[Y]	perished
GISINGER	Golda	1906			Ben Zion	F	[Y]	perished
GISINGER	Dawid					M	[S]	
GITLER	Lina	1887			Meier	F	[Y]	perished

Krosno, Poland Yizkor Book

Surname	Maiden name	Given name	Year	Occupation (German)	Occupation (English)	Father	Mother	Sex	Other	Code	Fate
GLASNER		Abraham	1886	Kaufmann	merchant	Mendel		M		[J]	perished
GLEICHER		Beile	1885					F	Abraham	[J]	
GLEICHER		Ete	1914	Angestellte		Avraham	Beile	F		[J]	
GLEICHER		Jehuda	1911			Avraham	Beile	M		[Y]	perished
GLEICHER	SCHOENFIEKD	Taube						F		[L]	survived
GLEICHER		Taube						F		[S]	
GLOWINSKI		Taube	1899					F		[J]	
GLOWINSKI		Chaje	1919	Schneiderin	tailoress			F		[J]	
GLOWINSKI		Max	1903	Privatbeamter	government official			M		[J]	
GLUECK		Regina	1910			Avraham		F		[J], [Y]	perished
GLUECK		Baruch	1934			Manek		M		[J], [Y]	perished
GLUECK		Markus	1907	Arbeiter	worker			M		[J]	
GLUECK		Guetl	1907					F		[J]	
GLUECK		Regina	1935					F		[J]	
GLUECK		Markus	1907							[R]	shot
GLUTZ		Samuel	1910	Arbeiter	worker			M		[J]	
GOETZ		Sara	1903					F		[J]	
GOETZ		Chane	1936					F		[J]	
GOETZ		Meschulim	1940					M		[J]	
GOETZ		Leib		Fischkonservierer	fish preserver					[J]	
GOETZLER		Feige						F		[J]	
GOETZLER		Jsrael						M		[J]	
GOETZLER		Payssach								[R]	
GOLDBARD	HIRSHBERG	Malka								[R]	
GOLDBARD		Joseph	1907	Schneider	tailor	Payssach	Malka	M		[R]	

Krosno, Poland Yizkor Book

Surname	Given		Year	Occupation	Occupation	Name	Sex	Joseph	[R]	Status
GOLDBARD	Ester						F			
GOLDBARD	Peisech	KRONKOPF					M		[J]	
GOLDBERG	Eugene		1924			Nathan	M		[Y]	perished
GOLDBERG	Herman		1878			Itzhak	M		[Y]	perished
GOLDBERG	Israel		1875			Itzhak	M		[Y], [G]	perished
GOLDBERG	Israel		1878			Schaja	M		[Y]	perished
GOLDBERG	Sarah		1888			Yunes	F		[Y]	perished
GOLDBERG	Sheindel		1885			Yunes	F		[Y]	
GOLDBERG	Itzhak						M		[L]	survived
GOLDBERG	Merom			Student	student		M		[L]	survived
GOLDBERG	Chiel		1903	Arbeiter	worker		M		[J], [S]	
GOLDFARB	Reisel		1904				F		[J]	
GOLDFARB	Moses		1929				M		[J]	
GOLDFARB	Ester		1938				F		[J]	
GOLDFARB	Abraham		1940				M		[J]	
GOLDFARB	Moses		1873				M		[J], [S]	
GOLDFINGER	Rosa		1880				F		[J], [G]	
GOLDFINGER	Chaje		1920				F		[J]	
GOLDFINGER	Simon		1916	Goldschmied	goldsmith		M		[J]	
GOLDFINGER	Jetti		1910				F		[J]	
GOLDFINGER	Zile		1916				F		[J]	
GOLDFINGER	Dawid					Moses	M		[Y]	perished
GOLDFINGER	Genia		1914			Moses	F		[J], [Y]	perished
GOLDFINGER	Anne						F		[L]	survived
GOLDHERZ	Moses		1898	Chauffeur	driver		M		[J], [S]	

Krosno, Poland Yizkor Book

GOLDMANN	Selde		1902			F	[J]
GOLDMANN	Leie		1921			F	[J]
GOLDMANN	Zlate		1929			F	[J]
GOLDMANN	Sara		1884			F	[J]
GOLDMANN	Ester		1887			F	[J]
GOLDSTEIN	Haim					M	[P]
GOLDSTEIN	Anna		1904	Schneiderin	tailoress	F	[J]
GOLDSTEIN	Mechel		1905	Kaufmann	merchant	M	[J]
GOLDSTEIN	Leie		1904			F	[J]
GOLDSTEIN	Naftali		1930			M	[J]
GOLDSTEIN	Abraham		1933			M	[J]
GOLDSTEIN	Yehiel		1905		Yom	M	[Y] perished
GOLDSTEIN	Samuel			Schneider	tailor	M	[P], [R]
GOLDSTEIN	Mayer				Samuel	M	[P] perished
GOLDSTEIN	Reisel		1914	Arbeiterin	worker [female]	F	[J] perished
GOLDSTEIN	Debora		1917	Stickerin	embroiderer [female] Samuel	F	[J] perished
GOLDSTEIN	Matel		1923	Stickerin	embroiderer [female] Samuel	F	[J] perished
GOLDSTEIN	Israel					M	[G]
GOLDSTEIN	Mathilde					F	[P]
GOLDSTEIN	David					M	[L] survived
GOLOSCHITZ	Sara		1874			F	[J], [S]
GORA	Malka	WEISSMAN				F	[L] survived
GORDON	Isaak			Schankwirt	innkeeper	M	[B]

Surname	Given	Alt. name	Year	Occupation (DE)	Occupation (EN)	Father	Mother	Sex	Spouse	Origin	Status
GORKIEL	Benjamin		1892	Arbeiter	worker			M		[J], [G]	
GOTTLIEB	Eva		1895			Alter		F		[J]	
GOTTLIEB	Schifre		1924	Schneiderin	tailoress			F		[J]	
GOTTLIEB	David		1895					M		[J]	
GRAEBER	Feige		1895					F		[J]	
GRAEBER	Zierl		1926					F		[J]	
GRAEBER	Moses		1935					M		[J]	
GRAEBER	Salomon		1892	Angestellter	employee			M		[J]	
GRAJOWER	Feige		1898					F		[J]	
GRAJOWER	Sara		1922					F		[J]	
GRAJOWER	Jakob		1928					M		[J]	
GRAJOWER	Mechel		1932					M		[J]	
GRAJOWER	Chane		1939					F		[J]	
GRAJOWER	Sonia							F		[P]	survived
GRAJOWER	Esther							F		[P]	survived
GRAU	Yaacov							M		[L]	survived
GRIN	Hanoch							F		[L]	survived
GRIN	Henka	ZUCKERMAN						F		[L]	survived
GRINBAUM	Kalman							M		[L]	survived
GRINBAUM	Aaron							M		[P]	survived
GRINSHPAN	Dawid							M		[P]	survived
GRIFFEL	Sali							F	Dawid	[P]	survived
GRIFFEL	Max					Dawid	Sali	M		[P]	survived
GRIFFEL	Igo					Dawid	Sali	M		[P]	survived
GRIFFEL	Miron					Dawid	Sali	M		[P]	survived

Krosno, Poland Yizkor Book

Surname	Given name	Year	Occupation	Occupation	Father	Mother	Sex	Code	Fate
GRIFFEL	Josef		Arzt	doctor			M	[R]	
GROSS	Wilhelm	1939					M	[J]	
GROSS	Ryfke						F	[J]	
GROSS	Chaim	1889	Bäcker	baker			M	[J], [G]	
GROSS	Ite	1898					F	[J]	
GROSS	Sala	1919					F	[J]	
GROSS	Pepe	1921					F	[J]	
GROSS	Chaim	1923	Arbeiter	worker			M	[J], [L]	survived
GROSS	Leib	1927	Arbeiter	worker			M	[J]	
GROSS	Malke	1929					F	[J]	
GROSS	Jsaak	1931					M	[J]	
GROSS	Neche	1934					F	[J]	
GROSS	Feige	1936					F	[J]	
GROSS	Ryfke	1939	Lehrer	teacher			F	[J]	
GROSS	Sime	1917	Schneiderin	tailoress			F	[J]	
GROSS	Oscar						M	[P]	survived
GROSS	Josef	1920	Schneider	tailor			M	[J]	
GROSS	Freide	1932			Yossef		F	[J], [Y]	
GRUEN	Marjem	1938					F	[J]	
GRUEN	Guetl	1868			Aron		F	[J]	
GRUEN	Wolf	1903	Angestellter	employee	Aron	Guetl	M	[J]	perished
GRUEN	Sala	1903			Aron	Guetl	F	[J]	perished
GRUEN	Aron	1872			Motel		M	[J]	perished
GRUEN/Grin	Haja	1877			Mendel		M	[Y]	Sobibor
GRUEN/Grin	Moses	1878					M	[J], [S]	perished

Surname	First name	Year	Occupation (German)	Occupation (English)	Other	Sex	Code	Note
GRINSHPAN	Ryfke	1878				F	[J]	
GRINSHPAN	Feiwel	1916	Schneider	tailor		M	[J]	
GRINSHPAN	Jakob	1864	Fleischer	butcher		M	[J], [G]	
GRINSHPAN	Guetl	1868				F	[J]	
GRINSHPAN	Kalman	1903			Jacob	M	[Y]	Auschwitz
GRINSHPAN	Getzel	1910	Arbeiter	worker		M	[J]	
GRINSHPAN	Joel	1909	Angestellter	employee		M	[J], [S]	
GRINSHPAN	Jente	1912				F	[J]	
GRINSHPAN	Meilech	1937				M	[J]	
GRINSHPAN	Gene	1922				F	[J]	
GRINSHPAN	Hanah	1877				F	[P]	USA
GRINSHPAN	Jozef		Metallarbeiter	metal worker		M	[R]	
GRINSHPAN	Mendel		Arbeiter	worker		M	[J]	
GRINSHPAN	Moshe					M		
GRINSHPAN	Aron					M		
GRUESS	Suessl					F	[J]	
GRUESS	Chune					M	[J]	
GRUESS	Mortko		Schankwirt	innkeeper		M	[B]	
GRUN	Chawa					F	[G]	
GRUN	Mirla		Schankwirt	innkeeper		F	[B]	
GRUNSPAN	Max			fashions		M	[B]	
GRUNSPAN	Flora	1898				F	[J]	
GUETER	Chaje	1925				F	[J]	
GUETER	Sara	1923				F	[J]	
GUETER	Regina	1903				F	[J]	

Krosno, Poland Yizkor Book

GURKE	Henoch				1929		M	[J]	
GURKE	J	Schneider	tailor				M	[R]	
GUTLER	Chaja			Zelig	1905		F	[Y]	Belzec
GUTMAN	Cirel			Yehuda			F	[Y]	Korczyna
GUTWEIN	Nissan			Yehuda			M	[Y]	Korczyna
GUTWEIN	Meir						M	[L]	survived
GUTWEIN	Moses				1876		M	[J], [G]	
GUZIK	Debora				1879		F	[J]	
GUZIK	Esther			Zinwel	1913		F	[Y]	Belzec
GUZIK	Jakob	Arbeiter	worker		1910		M	[J]	
GUZIK	Feige	Näherin	seamstress		1912		F	[J]	
GUZIK	Markus	Arbeiter	worker		1901		M	[J]	
GUZIK	Regina				1897		F	[J]	
GUZIK	Shaya						M	[Y]	perished
GUZIK	Rachel	Arbeiter	worker	Shaya	1924		F	[J], [Y]	perished
GUZIK	Simon			Shaya	1925		M	[J], [Y]	perished
GUZIK	Poje			Shaya	1927		F	[J], [Y]	perished
GUZIK	Doba			Shaya	1930		F	[J], [Y]	perished
GUZIK	Faya			Shaya			F	[J], [Y]	perished
GUZIK	Jakob			Shaya	1933		M	[J]	
GUZIK	Josef	Arbeiter	worker		1886		M	[J], [G]	
HABER	Rachela				1886		F	[J]	
HABER	Malke	Strickerin	tricotatrice	Yehezkel	1920		F	[J]	
HABER	Gela			Itzhak	1902		F	[J], [Y]	perished
HABER	Elieazar				1925		M	[Y]	Auschwitz

Surname	Given name		Year	Occupation (German)	Occupation	Given name 2	Sex	Source	Fate
HABER	Yossef		1870				M	[J]	
HACK	Wolf Beer		1888				F	[J]	
HACK	Adele						M	[J], [L]	survived
HACK	Moses		1911	Arbeiter	worker		M	[J]	
HACK	David		1924	Arbeiter	worker		F	[J]	
HACK	Ester		1924				M	[R]	survived
HACK	Shlomo						F	[J]	
HACK	Sara Taube		1909						
HADNER	Sara						M	[J]	
HAENDLER	Eduard		1940				M	[J], [Y]	perished
HAENDLER	Jsrael		1877			Avraham	M	[J]	
HAFERLING	Leib		1908	Angestellter	employee		F	[J]	
HAFERLING	Rosa	ZAFERN	1882				F	[J]	
HAFERLING	Sime		1922				M	[J]	
HAFERLING	Baruch		1920	Arbeiter	worker		F	[J]	
HAFERLING	Sara		1933				M	[J]	
HAFERLING	Moses		1902	Schuster	shoemaker		F	[J], [S]	
HAFERLING	Blueme		1902				F	[J]	
HAFERLING	Hinde		1932				M	[J]	
HAFERLING	Jsrael		1883	Drucker	printer		M	[J]	
HAFTEL	David		1895	Kaufmann	merchant		F	[J], [Y]	perished
HALBERSTAMM	Rachel		1899			Yossef	F	[J]	
HALBERSTAMM	Beile		1929				M	[J]	
HALBERSTAMM	Osias		1936				M	[J]	
HALBERSTAMM	Naftali		1938						

Krosno, Poland Yizkor Book

Surname	Given	2nd name	Year	Occupation (Ger.)	Occupation (Eng.)	Name	Name	Sex	Source	Fate
HALBERSTAMM	Jakob		1868					M	[J], [G]	
HALBERSTAMM	Dawid									
HALPERN	Dora		1898					F	[J]	
HALPERN	Gene		1923					F	[J]	
HALPERN	Freidel							F	[Y]	Korczyna
HALPERN	Mendel		1910					F	[Y]	Korczyna
HALPERN	Osias							M	[S]	
HALPERN	Sheinwitz							F	[L]	survived
HALPERN	Chane		1908					F	[J]	
HAMMER	Ruth		1931					F	[J]	
HAMMER	Luise		1908					F	[J]	
HAMMER	Nathan							M	[P]	survived
HAMMERMANN	Izaac H.			Gerber	skinner			M	[R]	
HARES	Liebe		1912	Arbeiter	worker			F	[J]	
HASHNIK	Kalmen									
HASENFELD	Rosa		1915	Arbeiter	worker			F	[J]	
HASENFELD	Kalman								[P]	
HASHNIK	A			Schneider	tailor			M	[R]	
HAUBER	Sara		1873	Arbeiter	worker			F	[J]	
HAUSNER	Jakob		1903					M	[J]	
HAUSNER	Moses		1912	Arbeiter	worker			M	[J]	
HAUSNER	Yehuda-Idel							M		
HAUSNER	Beile nee+B2032	PLATNER	1906	Verkäuferin	saleswoman	Mordechai	Yehuda	F	[J], [Y]	perished
HAUSNER	Heinrich					Moshe		M	[Y]	perished
HAUSNER	Chane		1925	Schneiderin	tailoress	Moshe		F	[J], [Y]	perished

HAUSNER	Zile		1877			F	[J]
HAUSNER	Rosa		1903			F	[J]
HAUSNER	Moses		1939			M	[J]
HAUSNER	Wolf		1882			M	[J], [S]
HAUSNER	Meilech		1915	Arbeiter	worker	M	[J]
HAUSNER	Chaim		1920	Arbeiter	worker	M	[J]
HAUSNER	Yudel					M	[YI] perished
HAUSNER	Beile					F Yudel	[YI] perished
HAUSNER	Izrael			Gerber	skinner	M	[R] survived
HEFERLING	Atara					F	[L]
HEFFNER	Isid			Konditor	confectioner	M	[B]
HEGGEN-BERGER	Isidor			Krämer	grocer	M	[B]
HEGGEN-BERGER	Alcie	SCHTIEFEL				F	[L] survived
HEILER	Samuel		1870				[R] shot
HEIN	Reisel		1879			F	[J]
HEINBERG-KARP	Moritz		1904	Arbeiter	worker	M	[J]
HEINBERG-KARP	Martin		1921	Arbeiter	worker	M	[J]
HEINBERG-KARP	Zishe					M	[L] survived
HEITLER	Zoshe	DORN				F	[L] survived
HEITLER	Zofia						[P]
HEITLER	Zofia	DYM					[P] survived
HEITLER	Erwin					Zofia	[P] survived
HEITLER	Moses		1906	Glaser	glazier	M Avraham	[J], [Y] perished

Surname	Given name	Other name	Year	Occupation	Occupation	Father	Mother	Sex	Spouse	Code	Status
HELLER	Rachel	KLAGSBAD	1914			Jakob		F	Moses	[J], [Y]	perished
HELLER	Guetl		1940			Moses	Rachel	F		[J]	perished
HELLER	Ryfke		1940			Moses	Rachel	F		[J]	perished
HELLER	Baruch							M		[R]	
HELLER	Dora							F	Baruch	[R]	
HELLER	Zygmunt					Baruch	Dora	M		[R]	
HELLER	Hersz				vegetables			M		[R]	
HELLER	Ozjasz				community leader			M		[P]	
HELLER	Zeev							M		[L]	survived
HELFER	Esther	KATZ						F	Zeev	[P]	
HELFER	Israel					Zeev	Esther			[P]	
HELFER	Tziporah					Zeev	Esther			[P]	
HELFER	Akiba		1895	Beamter	official			M		[J]	
HEMERLING	Ryfke		1894					F	Akiba	[J]	
HEMERLING	Feige					Akiba	Ryfke	F		[P]	perished
HEMERLING	Hirsch		1922	Arbeiter	worker	Akiba	Ryfke	M		[J]	
HEMERLING	Leie		1927			Akiba	Ryfke	F		[J]	
HEMERLING	Taube		1930			Akiba	Ryfke	F		[J]	
HEMERLING	Pessel		1933			Akiba	Ryfke	F		[J]	
HEMERLING	Elieazar							M		[L]	survived
HERBLOCK	Leib		1887			Menashe		M		[Y]	Buchenwald
HERBSTMANN	Betzalel		1905			Moshe		M		[Y]	Russia
HERBSTMANN	Feige		1904					F		[J]	
HERBSTMANN	Rachel		1929					F		[J]	
HERBSTMANN	Dora		1934					F		[J]	

Krosno, Poland Yizkor Book

Surname	Given name	Alt. name	Year	Occupation	Occupation	Name	Name	Sex	Name	Source	Fate
HERBSTMANN	Abraham		1937					M		[J]	
HERBSTMANN	Malke		1907					F		[J]	
HERBSTMANN	Feige		1936					F		[J]	
HERBSTMANN	Leie		1878		store			F		[J], [G], [R]	
HERBSTMANN	Shlomo							M		[L]	survived
HERBSTMANN	Yaacov							M		[L]	survived
HERBSTMANN	Chana		1920			Mordechai		F		[Y]	perished
HERCKO	Dawid					Yehiel		M		[Y]	Auschwitz
HERCKO	Shlomo					Yehiel		M		[Y]	Auschwitz
HERCKO	Chaim					Yehiel		M		[Y]	Auschwitz
HERCKO	Rivka		1876			Moshe		F		[Y]	
HERMAN	Judith		1912			Israel		F		[Y]	Plaszow
HERMAN	Israel Ber							M			
HERMAN	Moshe							M			
HERSON	Baili	GEBEL						F	Moshe		
HERSON	Dora					Moshe	Baili	F		[R]	Auschwitz
HERSON	Jakob		1892	Arbeiter	worker	Avraham		M		[J], [Y]	Belzec
HERSON	Dora	HERSOHN	1898			Moses		F	Jakob	[J], [Y], [R]	Auschwitz
HERSON	Sara		1925	Schneiderin	tailoress	Jakob	Dora	F		[J], [Y], [R]	Auschwitz
HERSON	Helene					Jakob		F	Jakob	[Y]	perished
HERSON	Abraham		1924	Schneider	tailor			M		[J]	
HERSON	Chaje		1927					F		[J]	
HERSON	Yossef							M		[P]	

Krosno, Poland Yizkor Book

Surname	Given Name	Other Name	Year	Occupation	Translation	Father	Mother	Other	Sex	Code	Notes
HERTZIGER	Kalmen								M	[P]	
HERTZLICH	Henoch		1864						M	[J]	
HERZFELD	Hersh								M	[P]	shot in 1942
HERZFELD	Sima Beile	WEINBERGER						Hersh	F	[P]	
HERZFELD	Chaja Ruchel					Hersh	Sima Beile		F	[P]	
HERZFELD	Wolf					Hersh	Sima Beile		M	[P]	
HERZFELD	Chawa		1890			Hersh	Sima Beile		F	[Y]	perished
HERZFELD	Sura					Hersh	Sima Beile		F	[P]	
HERZFELD	Reisel					Hersh	Sima Beile		F	[P]	
HERZFELD	Yeheskel					Hersh	Sima Beile		M	[P]	
HERZFELD	Riva					Hersh	Sima Beile	Yeheskel	F	[P]	
HERZFELD	Chana					Hersh	Sima Beile		F	[P]	
HERZFELD	Peshe					Hersh	Sima Beile		F	[P]	
HERZFELD	Leah					Hersh	Sima Beile		F	[P]	
HERZFELD	Moses			Weinhändler	vintner				M	[B]	
HERZIG	Isaac		1871		spirits				M	[R]	
HERZIG	Osias		1877	Mützenmacher	capper				M	[J]	
HERZIG	Rachel							Osias	F	[J]	
HERZIG	Blima					Yehoshua			F	[Y]	perished

Surname	Given name	Year					Sex		Source	Fate
HERZIG	Sender	1901	Arbeiter	worker	Yehoshua		M		[J], [Y]	perished
HERZIG	Chane	1906			Mordechai		F	Sender	[J], [Y]	perished
HERZIG	Neche	1936			Sender	Chane	F		[J]	
HERZIG	Chaskel	1907	Mützenmacher	capper	Yehoshua		M		[J], [Y]	
HERZIG	Rosa	1919					F		[J]	
HERZIG	Hella	1939					F		[J]	
HERZIG	Sabine	1883					F		[J]	
HERZIG	Dora	1913					F		[J]	
HERZIG	Hersh						M		[P]	survived
HERZIG					Hersh		F		[P]	perished
HERZIG	Leib				Hersh		M		[P]	survived
HERZIG	Reuven						M		[P]	survived
HERZIG	Yehuda						M		[P]	
HERZIGER	Yossef									
HERZLICH	Kalmen W						M		[R]	
HERTZOG	Ozjasz									
HERTZOG	Yehuda									
HERTZOG	Henry						M		[P]	survived
HILLER	Malke	1899					F		[J]	
HIRSCH	Mechel		Eierverkäufer	egg merchant			M		[B]	
HIRSCHFELD	Isaac	1889			Isaac		M		[J], [Y]	perished
HIRSCHFELD	Leib	1905	Bäcker	baker			M		[Y]	Belzec
HIRSCHFELD	Shmuel						M		[L]	survived
HIRSCHFELD	Mojzesz		Tischler	carpenter			M		[R], [B]	
HIRSCHFELD	Buki						M		[L]	survived

Krosno, Poland Yizkor Book

Surname	Given Name	Maiden Name	Birth Year	Occupation	Occupation (Ger.)	Father	Sex	Source	Fate
HIRSCHFELD	Wilhelm-Wolf			doctor	Arzt		M	[R]	
HIRSCHFELD	Zosha						F	[P]	
HIRSCHFELD	Leon						M	[L]	survived
HIRSCHPRINGER	Simon			grocer	Krämer		M	[B]	
HIRSCHPRUNG	Simche			religious			M	[R]	
HIRSCHPRUNG	Chaskel						M	[P]	
HIRSCHPRUNG	Chaim						M	[P]	USA
HOCHEISER	Hinda	BERGER					F	[P]	USA
HOCHEISER	Yaakow						M	[P]	survived
HOCHSTEIN	Ita	KINDERMAN					F	[P]	survived
HOCHSTEIN	Bernard						M	[P]	survived
HOCHSTEIN	Sarah					Simche	F	[P]	
HODNER	Jakob		1875	butcher	Fleischer		M	[J]	
HODYS	Jda		1881				F	[J]	
HOFFMANN	Mendel		1932				M	[J]	
HOFSTAEDTER	Avraham			youth activities			M	[R]	
HOFSTAEDTER	Chane		1915				F	[J]	
HOLFERLING	Israel								
HOLLAENDER	Joseph		1888			Hersh	M	[J], [Y]	perished
HOLLOSCHUETZ	Feige		1920			Josef	F	[Y]	Belzec
HOLLOSCHUETZ	Jidys		1922			Josef	F	[Y]	perished
HOLLOSCHUETZ	Debora		1931			Josef	F	[Y]	perished
HOLLOSCHUETZ	Shmuel		1880			Hersh	M	[J], [Y]	perished
HOLLOSCHUETZ	Taube		1892			Shmuel	F	[Y]	Belzec

Surname	Given	Maiden	Year	Father	Mother	Sex	Spouse	Code	Status
HOLLOSCHUETZ	Etel		1895	Shmuel	Taube	F		[Y]	perished
HOLLOSCHUETZ	Iser		1906	Shmuel	Taube	M		[Y]	perished
HOLLOSCHUETZ	Ezra			Shmuel	Taube	M		[P]	perished
HOLLOSCHUETZ	Bila			Shmuel	Taube	F		[P]	perished
HOLLOSCHUETZ	Moshe			Shmuel	Taube	M		[P]	perished
HOLLOSCHUETZ	Chaskel		1937			M		[J]	
HOLLOSCHUETZ	Berta		1888			F		[J], [S]	
HOLLOSCHUETZ	Ester		1933			F		[J]	
HOLLOSCHUETZ	Jsaak		1869			M		[J]	
HOLLOSCHUETZ	Sara		1875			F		[J]	
HOLLOSCHUETZ	Yochewed					F		[L]	survived
HOLLOSCHUETZ	Dawid					M		[L]	survived
HOLLOSCHUETZ	Menachem					M		[L]	survived
HOLLOSCHUETZ	Michael					M		[L]	survived
HOLLOSCHUETZ	Gitel					F		[L]	survived
HOLLOSCHUETZ	Yossef					M		[P]	
HOLTZER	Yossef								
HOLTZER	Itzhak					M		[P]	
HOLTZER	Rivka	FREUND		Betzalel B	Miriam	F	Itzhak	[P]	
HOLTZER	Fanny					F		[P]	
HOLTZER	Gusti					M		[P]	
HOLTZER	Meno					M		[P]	
HOLTZER	Mira		1907			M		[J]	
HONIGSTOCK	Alice		1929			F		[J]	

Krosno, Poland Yizkor Book

Surname	Given name	Year	(German)	Occupation	Name	Name	Sex	Sources	Note
HONIGSTOCK	Kalmen	1887	Fleischer	butcher	Abraham		M	[JJ], [Y], [G]	perished
HORNIK	Beile	1922	Photograph	photographer	Kalman		F	[JJ], [Y]	perished
HORNIK	Mirel	1929			Kalman		F	[JJ], [Y]	perished
HORNIK	Feige	1893			Samuel		F	[JJ], [Y]	perished
HORNIK	Abraham	1924	Arbeiter	worker			M	[J]	
HORNIK	Moshe	1892			Yossef		M	[JJ], [Y]	perished
HOROWITZ	Chaje	1900			Yossef		F	[JJ], [Y]	perished
HOROWITZ	Moshe	1904			Yossef		M	[Y]	perished
HOROWITZ	Ben Zion	1890	Angestellter	employee			M	[J]	perished
HOROWITZ	Sarah	1892				Benno	F	[Y], [G]	perished
HOROWITZ	Moses	1924	Arbeiter	worker	Ben Zion	Sarah	M	[J]	perished
HOROWITZ	Benno	1878	Angestellter	employee			M	[J]	
HOROWITZ	Avraham	1925			Moshe		M	[Y]	perished
HOROWITZ	Rafael	1916	Angestellter	employee			M	[J]	
HOROWITZ	Norbert	1922	Konditor	confectioner			M	[J]	
HOROWITZ	Eva	1912	Schneiderin	tailoress	Tzvi		F	[JJ], [Y]	perished
HOROWITZ	Golde	1907	Schneiderin	tailoress			F	[J]	
HOROWITZ	Hirsch						M	[JJ], [S]	
HOROWITZ	Guste						M	[J]	
HOROWITZ	Netti	1912	Schneiderin	tailoress			F	[J]	
HOROWITZ	Moses	1915	Tapezierer	paperhanger			M	[J]	
HOROWITZ	Shmuel				Asher		M	[Y]	Korczyna
HOROWITZ	Michael						M	[L]	
HOROWITZ	Shlomo						M	[L]	
HOROWITZ	Yehiel						M	[L]	

Surname	Given name		Year	Occupation	Occupation	Sex	Code	Fate
HOROWITZ	Josef				fashions	M	[B]	
HOROWITZ	Eliasz				food	M	[R]	
HOROWITZ	Fishel	Zeev	1895			M	[Y]	perished
HOSK	Chaim		1891	Mützenmacher	capper	M	[J]	
HUDES	Ester		1890			F	[J]	
HUDES	Abraham		1919	Arbeiter	worker	M	[J]	
HUDES	Aron		1921	Mützenmacher	capper	M	[J]	
HUDES	Berisch		1926	Arbeiter	worker	M	[J]	
HUDES	Reisel-Renia		1912			F	[J], [S]	
HUTTNER	Leib		1936			M	[J]	
HUTTNER	M				restaurant	M	[R]	
IDER	Miriam					F	[L]	survived
IKONIT	Elias		1886	Fleischer	butcher	M	[J], [S]	
IMMERLING	Akiwa							
INFELD	Hinde		1887			F	[J]	
INFELD	Pinkas		1921	Metzger	butcher	M	[J]	
INFELD	Josef		1923	Schneiderin	tailoress	M	[J]	
INFELD	Josef					M	[R]	
JADAS	Brandel		1907			F	[J]	
JAKUBOWICZ	Salomon		1901	Arbeiter	worker	M	[J], [S]	
JAKUBOWICZ	Sala		1924			F	[J]	
JAKUBOWICZ	Beile		1925			F	[J]	
JAKUBOWICZ	Rafael		1904	Klempner	plumber	M	[J]	
JAKUBOWICZ	Beile	Jakob	1902			F	[J], [Y]	Belzec
JAKUBOWICZ	Sala	Raphael	1930			F	[J], [Y]	perished

Krosno, Poland Yizkor Book

Surname	Name		Year	Occupation (German)	Occupation	Father	Mother	Sex	Source	Fate
JAKUBOWICZ	Marjem		1937			Raphael		F	[JJ], [Y]	Belzec
JAKUBOWICZ	Miriam							F	[L]	survived
JAKUBOWICZ	Zila		1917			Raphael		F	[J]	perished
JAKUBOWICZ	Jozef		1920	Tischler	carpenter			M	[R]	Auschwitz
JAKUBOWICZ	Mendel		1895	Arbeiter	worker	Avraham		M	[JJ], [Y], [G]	perished
JAMEL	Chane	KROSNO	1897			Berish		F	[JJ], [Y]	perished
JAMEL	Ryfke		1920	Verkäuferin	saleswoman			F	[J]	perished
JAMEL	Leie		1923	Schneiderin	tailoress			F	[J]	
JAMEL	Leib		1925	Monteur	fitter			M	[J]	
JAMEL	Markus		1928					M	[J]	
JAMEL	Chaim		1931					M	[J]	
JAMEL	Rosa		1933					F	[J]	
JAMEL	H			Friseur	barber			M	[R]	
JANAS	Feiwel		1895	Lehrer	teacher			M	[J]	
JERUCHIM	Leie		1894					F	[J]	
JERUCHIM	Simon		1921	Arbeiter	worker			M	[J]	
JERUCHIM	Aron		1923	Arbeiter	worker			M	[J]	
JERUCHIM	Chawe		1928					F	[J]	
JERUCHIM	Malke		1929					F	[J]	
JERUCHIM	Shragai Zew	JERUCHIM						M	[P]	
JERUCHIM	Leah					Shragai Zew		F	[P]	
JERUCHIM	Shimon					Shragai Zew	Leah	M	[P]	
JERUCHIM	Aaron					Shragai Zew	Leah	M	[P]	

Surname	Given	Year			Father	Mother	Sex	
JERUCHIM	Sarah				Shragai Zew	Leah	F	[P]
JERUCHIM	Chawa				Shragai Zew	Leah	F	[P]
JERUCHIM	Mala				Shragai Zew	Leah	F	[P]
JERUCHIM	Osias	1906	Bauer	farmer			M	[J]
JOSEFOWICZ	Toni	1916					M	[J]
JOSEFOWICZ	Leib	1938					M	[J]
JOSEFOWICZ	Baruch						M	[R]
JUDA	Hene	1910					F	[J]
JUDENHERZ	Jocheweth	1915					F	[J]
JUDENHERZ	Jakob						M	[S]
JUDENHERZ	Chania		Tankstellenwart	gas station keeper			F	[R]
JUST	David	1896	Angestellter	employee	Chaim		M	[J], [Y]
JUST	Guetl	1897					F	[J]
JUST	Sabine	1922	Strickerin	tricotatrice			F	[J]
JUST	Amalie	1925					F	[J]
JUST	Naftali	1928	Öllieferant	oil supplier			M	[J]
JUST	Perl	1899					F	[J]
JUST	Dobe	1934					F	[J]
JUST	Chaje Ete	1929					F	[J]
JUST	Jakob	1898	Angestellter	employee			M	[J]
JUST	Sala	1904					F	[J]
JUST	Debora	1929					F	[J]

Krosno, Poland Yizkor Book

Surname	First Name	Year	Occupation	Occupation			Sex	Source
JUST	Naftali	1932					M	[J]
JUST	Hirsch	1881	oil supplier	Öllieferant	Naftali		M	[J], [Y]
JUST	Feige	1885					F	[J]
JUST	Tille	1916					F	[J]
JUST	Abraham	1913	worker	Arbeiter			M	[J]
JUST	Don	1894	merchant	Kaufmann	Naphtali		M	[J], [Y] perished
JUST	Ryfke	1895					F	[J]
JUST	Chaje	1921	saleswoman	Verkäuferin			F	[J]
JUST	Rische	1925					F	[J]
JUST	Rachela	1876				Yaacov	F	[J], [Y]
JUST	Baruch	1911	worker	Arbeiter			M	[J]
JUST	Leib	1910	worker	Arbeiter			M	[J]
JUST	Osias	1882	merchant	Kaufmann			M	[J]
JUST	Kreindel	1893					F	[J]
JUST	Malke	1916					F	[J]
JUST	Chaim		teacher	Lehrer			M	[R]
JUST	Moses	1902	shoemaker	Schuster			M	[J]
KACHAN	Ester	1902					F	[J]
KACHAN	Rosa	1923					F	[J]
KACHAN	Jakob	1925	worker	Arbeiter			M	[J]
KACHAN	Sara Ryfke	1928					F	[J]
KACHAN	Frimet	1930					F	[J]
KACHAN	Jsaak	1939					M	[J]
KACHAN	Moses	1874					M	[J]
KALB	betzlel							

Krosno, Poland Yizkor Book

Surname	Given name	Year	Occupation	Occupation	Name 1	Name 2	Name 3	Sex	Source	Notes
KALB	Adele	1890						F	[P]	
KALB	Leie	1870						F	[J]	
KALB	Ascher	1878						M	[J]	died 1942
KALB	Chaje	1881						F	[J]	
KALB	Rachel	1904						F	[J]	
KALB	Schulim	1905	Arbeiter	worker	Ascher			M	[J], [Y]	died 1922
KALB	Baruch	1918			Ascher			M	[Y]	
KALB	Samuel Bee				Josef	Feige		M		died 1922
KALB	Chaya Rivka						Samuel B.	F		deceased
KALB	Leibish	1900			Samuel B.	Chaya R.		M		deceased
KALB	Samuel	1910	Schuster	shoemaker				M	[J]	
KALB	Sarah	1899						M	[P]	
KALB	Zishe							M	[P]	
KALB	Lipa							M	[P]	
KALMENSOHN	Freide	1912						F	[J]	
KALMENSOHN	lipa									
KAMPEL	Aron	1904	Bäcker	baker	Avigdor			M	[J], [Y]	perished
KANAREK	Chaje	1907						F	[J]	
KANAREK	Viktor	1936						M	[J]	
KANAREK	Ester	1931						F	[J]	
KANAREK	Sara	1864						F	[J], [S]	
KANNER	Moshe									
KANNER	Chawe	1908	Schneiderin	tailoress				F	[J]	
KANNER	Meilech	1895	Arbeiter	worker				M	[J], [S]	
KANNER	Leie	1895						F	[J]	

Krosno, Poland Yizkor Book

KANNER	Sali	1926	Arbeiter	worker			F	[J]	
KANNER	Chaje	1929					F	[J]	
KANNER	Leib	1900	Arbeiter	worker			M	[J], [S]	
KANNER	Rosa	1908					F	[J]	
KANNER	Fischel	1933					M	[J]	
KANNER	Fradel	1870					F	[J], [S]	
KANNER	Ewa	1916			Moshe		F	[Y]	perished
KANNER	Simcha	1914			Aron		M	[Y]	perished
KANNER	Meir						M	[L]	survived
KANNER	Mordechai						M	[L]	survived
KANNER	Yehuda						M	[L], [G]	survived
KANNER	Chaskel						M	[G]	
KANNER	Avraham				Itzhak		M	[Y]	perished
KARFIOL	Itzhak						M	[L]	survived
KARMI	Golde	1895					F	[J], [S]	
KARSCH	Chaim Wolf	1885	Angestellter	employee			M	[J]	
KATZ	Zile	1893					F	[J]	
KATZ	Mates	1908			Chaim		M	[Y]	Russia
KATZ	Chane	1910			Chaim		F	[J], [Y]	perished
KATZ	Sala	1907					F	[J]	
KATZ	Hene	1914					F	[J]	
KATZ	Suessmann	1875					M	[J]	
KATZ	Zishe						M	[P]	perished
KATZ	Chaje	1882				Zishe	F	[J]	perished
KATZ	Bella				Zishe	Chaje	F	[P]	perished

Surname	Given name	Maiden/alt name	Year	Occupation	Occupation	Father	Mother	Sex	Spouse	Religion	Notes
KATZ	Klara		1892					F		[J]	
KATZ	Mathias		1912	Arbeiter	worker			M		[J]	
KATZ	Osias		1910	Angestellter	employee			M		[J]	
KATZ	Sara		1908					F		[J]	
KATZ	Zwi		1936					M		[J]	
KATZ	Sime		1940					F		[J]	
KATZ	Ettel		1865					F		[J]	
KATZ	Leie		1894	Angestellter	employee			F		[J]	
KATZ	Neche		1900					F		[J]	
KATZ	Feige		1925					F		[J]	
KATZ	Guetl		1929					F		[J]	
KATZ	Naphtali							M		[L]	survived
KATZ	Nissan							M		[L]	survived
KATZ	Jossef							M		[L]	survived
KATZ	Raphael							M		[G]	
KATZ	Israel Dow							M		[P]	
KATZ–HERMANN	Ryfke	FREUND	1881					F	Israel Dow	[J]	Name is crossed out on list
KATZ–HERMANN	Nahum					Israel Dow	Ryfke	M		[P]	survived
KATZ	Lea	JUST						F	Nahum	[P]	
KATZ	Shshana					Nahum	Lea	F		[P]	
KATZ	Nathan					Israel Dow	Ryfke	M		[P]	survived
KATZ–HERMANN	Yehoshua					Israel Dow	Ryfke	M		[P]	survived
KATZ	Bracha	ZUCKERMAN						F	Yehoshua	[P]	

Krosno, Poland Yizkor Book

KATZ	Shmuel			Yehoshua	Bracha	M	[P]	
KATZ	Shulamit			Yehoshua	Bracha	F	[P]	
KATZ	Esther			Israel Dow	Ryfke	F	[P]	survived
KATZ-HERMANN	Miriam			Israel Dow	Ryfke	F	[P]	survived
KATZ-HERMANN	Ita			Israel Dow	Ryfke	F	[P]	perished
KATZ-HERMANN	Shendele			Israel Dow	Ryfke	F	[P]	perished
KATZ-HERMANN	Hirsch Leib	Uhrmacher	1917	watchmaker			[J]	perished, name is crossed out in list
KATZ-HERMANN	Josef		1918	Avraham		M	[Y], [R]	Auschwitz
KAUFMAN	Shmuel	Kantor		cantor		M	[L]	survived
KAUFMAN	Ruben Peretz					M	[G], [R]	
KAUFMAN				Ruben Peretz		M	[P]	
KAUFMAN	Paula			Ruben Peretz		F	[P]	survived
KAUFMAN	Leib					M	[R]	survived
KAUFMAN	Haim					M	[R]	
KEIL	Branla				Haim	F	[R]	
KEIL	Anna		1901			F	[J], [S]	
KEIL	Feige		1931			F	[J]	
KEIL	Neche		1929			F	[J]	
KEIL	Leie		1926			F	[J]	
KEIL	Abraham	Friseurgehilfe	1924	barber assistent		M	[J]	
KEIL	Symche		1914	Aron		M	[Y]	perished

Krosno, Poland Yizkor Book

Surname	Given name	Year	Occupation (German)	Occupation (English)	Father	Sex	Source	Note
KENNER	Tzipora	1911			Dawid	F	[Y]	perished
KEREN	Yona	1913			Dawid	M	[Y]	perished
KEREN	Robert		Öllieferant	oil supplier		M	[B]	
KERN	Leie	1871				F	[J]	
KERN	Baruch	1912	Arbeiter	worker		M	[J]	
KERN	Mala	1909	Verkäuferin	saleswoman		F	[J]	
KERN	Taube	1926				F	[J]	
KERN	Anna	1892				F	[J]	
KERN	Awraham					M	[P]	
KERN	Mozes	1915			Yona	M	[Y]	Tarnow
KERNER	Tonia	1912			Yona	F	[Y]	Tarnow
KERNER	Machla	1888				F	[J]	
KERNKRAUT	Fischel	1925	Arbeiter	worker		M	[J]	
KERNKRAUT	Yehoshua					M	[P]	
KERNKRAUT	Moshe	1892			Yehoshua	M	[Y]	perished
KIESELSTEIN	Sala	1891				F	[J], [S]	
KIESELSTEIN	Chaje	1923				F	[J]	
KIESELSTEIN	Chiel	1922	Arbeiter	worker	Elieazar	M	[J], [Y]	perished
KIESELSTEIN	Dora	1890				F	[J]	
KIESELSTEIN	Moses	1892	Spediteur	shipper	Yehoshua	M	[J], [Y], [G]	perished
KIESELSTEIN	Samuel	1916	Arbeiter	worker	Moshe	M	[J], [Y]	Rzeszow
KIESELSTEIN	Chane	1923	Schneiderin	tailoress	Moshe	F	[J], [Y]	perished
KIESELSTEIN	Mendel	1925	Arbeiter	worker		M	[J]	
KIESELSTEIN	Zile	1926			Moshe	F	[J], [Y]	

Krosno, Poland Yizkor Book

Surname	Given name	Other name	Birth	Occupation	Occupation	Father	Mother	Sex	Spouse	Source	Fate
KIESELSTEIN	Menachem							M		[L]	survived
KIESELSTEIN	Chaim Zeew							M		[P]	
KIESELSTEIN	Emalia	JOHANS	Jaslo					F	Chaim Zeew	[P]	
KIESELSTEIN	Taube		1937					F		[J]	
KIJOWSKI	Avraham							M		[L]	survived
KIMEL	Itzhak Wolf							M		[G]	
KIMEL	Zierl		1865			Yonas		F		[J], [Y]	Belzec
KINDERMANN	Perl		1909	Angestellte	employee			F		[J]	
KINDERMANN	Menachem							M		[L]	survived
KINDERMANN	Aron							M		[L]	survived
KINDERMANN	Izaac			Eisenhändler	ironmonger			M		[R]	
KINDERMANN	N.			Student	student			M		[R]	
KINDERMANN	Mendel				linen			M	Hanah	[B]	Krosno
KINDERMANN	Hanah	ATLAS						F	Mendel	[P]	
KINDERMANN	Margula					Mendel	Hanah	F		[P]	
KINDERMANN	Hersz			Öllieferant	oil supplier	Mendel	Hanah	M	Fradel	[R]	
KINDERMANN	Fradel							F	Hersz	[P]	
KINDERMANN	Srul					Hersz	Fradel	M		[P]	Jaslo
KINDERMANN	Hanah					Hersz	Fradel	F		[P]	Russia
KINDERMANN	Awraham					Mendel	Hanah	M	Sala	[P]	Russia
KINDERMANN	Sala	FRIEDEMAN						F	Awraham	[P]	Russia
KINDERMANN	Ides							F			
KINDERMANN	Yaakow		1894			Mendel	Hanah	M		[P]	perished
KINDERMANN	Ida	ATLAS	1892					F		[P]	perished
KINDERMANN	Rechel		1922			Yaakow	Ida	F		[P]	perished

Surname	Given name	Year	Occupation	Occupation	Father	Mother	Sex	Spouse	Code	Fate
KINDERMANN	Ita				Mendel	Hanah			[P]	Russia
KINDERMANN	Dawid				Mendel	Hanah		Lea	[P]	Russia
KINDERMANN	Lea							Dawid	[J]	
KINDERMANN	Moses	1899	Friseur	barber			M		[J]	
KIRES	Ester	1904					F		[J]	
KIRES	Ida	1900					F		[J]	
KIRSCHNER	Georg	1925	Schäftemacher	upper shoes maker			M		[J]	
KIRSCHNER	Mirel	1929					F		[J]	
KIRSCHNER	Avraham	1899					M		[R]	Auschwitz
KIRSCHNER	Lazar	1893					M		[R]	Auschwitz
KIRSCHNER	Eber	1902	Mohel	mohel	Yaacob		M		[J], [S], [Y], [G], R	perished
KLAGSBALD	Yehezkel	1902					M		[L]	survived
KLAGSBALD	Amalie						F	Yehezkel	[J]	
KLAGSBALD	Freide	1925			Yehezkel	Amalie	F		[J], [Y]	perished
KLAGSBALD	Debora	1927			Yehezkel	Amalie	F		[J], [Y]	perished
KLAGSBALD	Rachel	1929			Yehezkel	Amalie	F		[J]	
KLAGSBALD	Guetl	1935			Yehezkel	Amalie	F		[J]	
KLAGSBALD	Moshe						M		[L]	survived
KLAGSBALD	Samuel			goods			M		[R]	
KLEIN	Jakob						M		[R]	survived
KLEIN	Jakob	1878					M		[J]	
KLEINBERGER	Yaacov									
KLEINBERGER	Berta	1878					F		[J]	

Krosno, Poland Yizkor Book

Surname	Given name	Year	Occupation (German)	Occupation (English)	Father	Sex	Code	Note
KLEINBERGER	Bronislaw		Ratsmitglied	town councilor		M	[R]	
KLEINER	Mayer		Getreidehändler	grain dealer		M	[B]	
KLEINER	Mendel	1885	Arbeiter	worker		M	[J]	
KLEINER	Malke	1897				F	[J]	
KLEINER	Leie	1926				F	[J]	
KLEINER	Pauline	1930				F	[J]	
KLEINER	Moses	1893	Angestellter	employee		M	[J]	
KLEINER	Ella	1898				F	[J]	
KLEINER	Samuel	1923	Uhrmacher	watchmaker		M	[J]	
KLEINER	Feige	1926		speech		F	[J]	
KLEINER	Jakob m M.	1863		farm products		M	[JJ], [G]	
KLEINER	Jhuda	1901				M	[J]	
KLEINER	Mariano	1918			Bronislaw	M	[Y]	Lemberg
KLEINER	Tynia	1903			Henoch	M	[Y]	Lemberg
KLEINER	Salomon	1909	Arbeiter	worker		M	[J]	
KLEINMANN	Lipa					M	[P]	
KLEINMANN	Adele	1908			Lipa	F	[JJ], [Y]	perished
KLEINMANN	Leie	1913	Schneiderin	tailoress	Lipa	F	[JJ], [Y]	perished
KLEINMANN	Sara	1918	Schneiderin	tailoress	Lipa	F	[JJ], [Y]	perished
KLEINMANN	Blueme	1937				F	[J]	perished
KLEINMANN	Chane	1938			Shlomo	F	[JJ], [Y]	perished
KLEINMANN	Pepi	1911	Arbeiterin	worker [female]	Itzhak	F	[J]	
KLEINMANN	Ester	1901			Moshe	F	[JJ], [Y]	perished

KLEINMANN	Mendel	1935			M		[J], [Y]	perished
KLEINMANN	Henia	1912		Itzhak	F		[Y], [G]	perished
KLEINMANN	Tzvi				M		[L]	survived
KLEINMANN	Yaacov				M		[L]	survived
KLEINMANN	Josef				M		[R]	survived
KLEINMANN	M		Student	student	M		[R]	
KLEINMANN	Sara	1880			F		[J]	
KLOTZ	Itzhak				M		[P]	
KLOTZ	Rachel	1854			F		[J]	
KLUCZKOWSKI	Abraham	1886			M		[J]	
KLUCZKOWSKI	Chaje	1886			F		[J]	
KLUCZKOWSKI	Brandel	1926	Schneiderin	tailoress	F		[J]	
KLUCZKOWSKI	Kalman				M		[G]	
KNOBEL	Chaim David	1913	Arbeiter	worker	M		[J]	
KNOBLOCH	Reisel	1909		Moshe	F		[J], [Y]	Jaslo
KNOBLOCH	Jsaak	1899	Arbeiter	worker	M		[J], [S], [G]	
KNOPF	Chaje	1904			F		[J]	
KNOPF	Naftali	1932			M		[J]	
KNOPF	Debora	1934			F		[J]	
KNOPF	Haim		Konditor	confectioner	M		[J]	
KOENIG	Leie	1880			F	Haim	[J]	
KOENIG	Jsaak	1904	Konditor	confectioner	Chaim	Leie	M	[J], [Y]	perished
KOENIG	Hella	1906		Chaim	Leie	F		[J], [Y]	perished
KOENIG	Moses	1908	Konditor	confectioner	Chaim	Leie	M	[J], [Y]	perished

Surname	Given	Other	Year	Occupation	Occupation			Sex	Source	Status
KOENIG	Chaje		1910			Chaim	Leie	F	[J]	perished
KOENIG	Ruth		1937			Chaim	Leie	F	[J]	survived
KOENIG	Rivka	FREUND						F	[L]	survived
KOENIG	Chaim									
KOLANDER	Berel		1893	Arbeiter	worker			M	[J]	
KOLBER	Basche		1898					F	[J]	
KOLBER	Baruch		1933					M	[J]	
KOLBER	Ester		1936					F	[J]	
KOLBER	B			Mützenmacher	capper			M	[R]	
KONDES	A			Mützenmacher	capper			M	[R]	
KONDES	Samuel		1892	Arbeiter	worker			M	[J]	
KONINSKI	Helene		1897					F	[J]	
KONINSKI	Siegmund		1920	Drucker	printer			M	[J]	
KONINSKI	Ignaz		1923	Arbeiter	worker			M	[J]	
KONINSKI	Leiser							M	[S]	
KONRAD	Helene							F	[Y]	survived
KOPFZUCKER	Fishel							M	[S]	
KOPITO	Sala		1910					F	[J]	
KORB	Hirsch		1889	Klempner	plumber			M	[J]	
KORB	Leie		1889					F	[J]	
KORB	Brandel		1921					F	[J]	
KORB	Stella		1940					F	[J]	
KORB	Abraham		1897	Klempner	plumber			M	[J], [S]	
KORB	Reisel		1905					F	[J]	
KORB	Berta		1932					F	[J]	

KORB	Malke		1864			F	[J]
KORB	Brandel		1905	Angestellte	employee	F	[J]
KORB	Tamara		1937			F	[J]
KORB	Chaim			Klempner	plumber	M	[R]
KORBA	Josef			Bestatter	undertaker		[R]
KORBA	Guetl		1878			F	[J]
KORNITZER	Regina		1893			F	[J]
KORNREICH	Anna		1914			F	[J]
KORNREICH	Sabine		1895	Näherin	seamstress	F	[J]
KORNREICH						M	[P]
KORNREICH	Zeisel	FREUND			Betzalel B	Miriam	F	[P]
KORNREICH	Seinwel		1923	Schäftemacher	upper shoes maker	Zeisel	F	[J]
KORNREICH	Feige		1925			Zeisel	F	[J]
KORNREICH	Sara		1926			Zeisel	F	[J]
KORNREICH	Alte					F	[G]
KORNREICH	Feige		1873			F	[J]
KRANZ	Berel		1897	Schuster	shoemaker	M	[J]
KRANZ	Eva		1896			F	[J]
KRANZ	Hinde		1928			F	[J]
KRANZ	Jsaak		1932			M	[J]
KRANZ	Basche		1936			F	[J]
KRANZ	Josef					M	[G]
KRANZ	Hene		1910			F	[J]
KREISBERG	Naftali		1908	Lehrer	teacher	M	[J]

Krosno, Poland Yizkor Book

Surname	Given name	Year	Occupation	Occupation	Name	Name	Sex	Relation	Source	Fate
KRESCH	Ete	1910					F		[J]	
KRESCH	Ziwie	1939					F		[J]	
KRESCH	Feiwel	1941					M		[J]	
KRESCH	B		Bäcker	baker			M		[R]	
KRIEGEL	J		Bäcker	baker			M		[R]	
KRIEGEL	Baruch	1881	Bäcker	baker			M		[YI]	Krosno
KRIEGER	Sara	1890			Naphtali		F	Baruch	[YI], [Y]	Krosno
KRIEGER	Brandel	1907			Baruch	Sara	F		[J]	Krosno
KRIEGER	Meilech	1918	Angestellter	employee	Baruch	Sara	M		[YI]	Krosno
KRIEGER	Hirsch	1929			Baruch	Sara	M		[YI]	Krosno
KRIEGER	Shifra				Baruch	Sara	F		[YI]	Krosno
KRIEGER	Jakob	1936			Baruch	Sara	M		[YI]	Krosno
KRIEGER	Jsaak	1936					M		[J]	
KRIEGER	Charles	1905	Bäcker	baker	Mordechai		M		[J], [Y]	perished
KRIEGER	Marjem	1940					F		[J]	
KRIEGER	Rosa	1913					F		[J]	
KRIEGER	Suessl	1931					F		[J]	
KRIEGER	Markus	1934					M		[J]	
KRIEGER	Anna	1938					F		[J]	
KRIEGER	Josef	1903	Tischler	carpenter			M		[J]	
KRIEGER	Rosa	1904					F		[J]	
KRIEGER	Jsrael	1939					M		[J]	
KRIEGER	Michael						M		[L]	survived
KRIEGER	Yehoshua		Bäcker	baker	Yehuda		M		[J], [Y]	perished
KRIELLER	Baruch									

Surname	First name		Year	Occupation (German)	Occupation (English)	Name	Sex	Source	Fate
KRILL	Lea						F	[L]	survived
KRILL	L	BILBERG					F	[R]	
KRILL	Yanka						F	[L]	
KRILL	Shlomo						M	[L]	
KRILL	Hersh						M	[L]	
KRILL	Reisel						F	[P]	
KRILL	Simche		1914	Weißbinder	house painter		M	[J]	
KUDLER	Markus		1921	Arbeiter	worker		M	[J]	
KUDLER	Irene		1920	Verkäuferin	saleswoman		F	[J]	
KUDLER	Feige		1929				F	[J]	
KUDLER	Frieda		1896				F	[J]	
KUDLER	Guetl		1921	Kontoristin	book keeper [female]		F	[J]	
KUDLER	Jakob		1907	Zuschneider	cutter		M	[J]	
KUCZIBORSKI	Moniek						M	[P]	survived
KUENSTLINGER	Leie		1905				F	[J]	
KUENSTLINGER	Leib		1883	Kaufmann	merchant		M	[J], [Y]	survived
KUFLIK	Ester		1880				F	[J]	
KUFLIK	Leie		1919				F	[J]	
KUFLIK	Arieh						M	[L]	survived
KUFLIK	Ryfke		1898				F	[J]	
KUPPERMANN	Etsche		1927				F	[J]	
KUPPERMANN	L			Klempner	plumber		M	[R]	
KUPPERMANN	Fryda		1891			Aron	F	[Y]	Belzec
KURZ			1870			Shimshon	F	[Y]	Auschwitz

Krosno, Poland Yizkor Book

Surname	Given	Year	Occupation	Occupation		Sex	Source	Town
KURZ			Tischler	carpenter		M	[B]	
KURZ	Henryke	1864				F	[J]	
KURZER	Siegmund	1904	Uhrmacher	watchmaker		M	[J]	
KURZMANN	Rosa	1912				F	[J]	
KURZMANN	Shie		Fleischer	butcher		M	[R]	
KWILL	Ester	1919				F	[J]	
LACHNER	Feige	1882	Arbeiterin	worker [female]		F	[J]	
LAMBERG	Ides	1917				F	[J]	
LAMBERG	Feige					F	[S]	
LAMBERG	Elieazar					M	[YI]	Korczyna
LAMBIG	Dawid					M	[YI]	Korczyna
LAMBIG	Lea					F	[YI]	Korczyna
LAMBIG	Haim					M	[YI]	Korczyna
LAMBIG	Herzke	1886	Arbeiter	worker		M	[J]	
LAMBIK	Ryfke	1886				F	[J]	
LAMBIK	Samuel	1923	Arbeiter	worker		M	[J], [S]	
LAMBIK	Mordche	1921	Arbeiter	worker		M	[J]	
LAMBIK	Rosa	1904				F	[J]	
LAMBIK	Brandel	1923				F	[J]	
LAMBIK	Simon	1925	Klempner	plumber		M	[J]	
LAMBIK	Israel	1932				M	[J]	
LAMBIK	Samuel	1897	Arbeiter	worker		M	[J]	
LAMBIK	Yehiel					M	[P]	
LAMM	Yehiel				Chaim			
LAMM	Hinda	1885				F	[Y]	perished

Surname	Given name	Year	Occupation	Occupation	Father	Sex	Source	Status
LAMM	Menachem	1880			Chaim	M	[Y]	perished
LAMM	Shia	1896			Berl	M	[Y]	perished
LAMM	Pearl					F	[G]	
LAMM	Chaim					M	[G]	
LAMM	Samuel	1901	Fleischer	butcher		M	[J]	
LAMM	Fanni	1906				F	[J]	
LAMM	Osias	1933				M	[J]	
LAMM	Rafael	1937				M	[J]	
LAMM	Gershon	1939				M	[J]	
LAMM	Berel	1872				M	[J]	
LAMM	Malke	1874				F	[J]	
LAMM	Josef	1904	Arbeiter	worker		M	[J]	
LAMM	Chaim					M	[P]	
LAMM	Tile	1883				F	[J]	
LANDAU	Dine	1878				F	[J]	
LANDAU	Sindel	1882	Kaufmann	merchant		F	[J]	
LANDAU	Schifre	1909			Meir	F	[J], [Y]	perished
LANDAU	Osias	1913	Verkäufer	salesman		M	[J]	
LANDAU	Chane	1917				F	[J]	
LANDAU	Mechel	1920	Arbeiter	worker		M	[J]	
LANDAU	Samuel	1907	Arbeiter	worker		M	[J]	
LANDAU	Feige	1907				F	[J]	
LANDAU	Sara	1935				F	[J]	
LANDAU	Moses	1938				M	[J]	
LANDAU	Chaim	1940				M	[J]	

Surname	Given name		Year			Father	Mother	Sex		Notes	Fate
LANDAU	Ryfke		1911	Hilfslehrerin	supply teacher [female]	Itahak		F		[J], [S], [Y]	Rzeszow
LANDAU	Leiser		1918			Meir		M		[Y]	Belzec
LANDAU	Tzvi		1910			Sender		M		[Y]	perished
LANDAU	Yaacov	LANDAU						M		[L]	survived
LANDAU	Feivel			Krämer	grocer			M		[G]	
LANDAU	Leah	HERZFELD						F	Feivel		
LANDAU	Leo							M		[G]	
LANDAU	Feige		1906	Näherin	seamstress			F		[J]	
LANDGARTEN	Risha							F		[L]	
LANDSTEIN	Chaim				clothing			M		[P]	Russia
LANG	Feiga reisel						Chaim	F		[P]	Russia
LANG	Avraham					Chaim	Feiga Reisel	M		[Y]	survived
LANG	Seril					Chaim	Feiga Reisel	F		[P]	
LANG	Shimon		1908			Chaim	Feiga Reisel	M		[Y]	perished
LANG	Henia									[P]	perished
LANG	Shimshon					Chaim	Feiga Reisel	M		[P]	Israel
LANG	Sime		1912			Chaim	Feiga Reisel	F		[J]	perished
LANG	Josef		1916	Angestellter	employee	Chaim	Feiga Reisel	M		[J]	survived
LANG	Shprincze		1918			Chaim	Feiga Reisel	F		[P]	survived
LANG	Moses		1870					M		[J], [S]	

Krosno, Poland Yizkor Book

Surname	Given	Year	Occupation (German)		Occupation (English)	Father	Mother	Sex	Code	Notes
LANGBAUM	Moshe							F	[J]	
LANGBAUM	Chane	1871						M	[B]	
LANGBAUM	Josaphat		Wirt		innkeeper			F	[L]	survived
LASKOWSKI	Frida	1889						F	[J]	
LAUFER	Berta							F	[J]	
LAUTMANN	Leiser	1900	Tischler		carpenter			M	[J], [S]	
LEHRER	Tali							F	[J]	
LEHRER	Leie	1905						F	[J]	
LEHRER	Feige	1934						F	[J]	
LEHRER	Helene	1936						M	[J]	
LEHRER	Chaim	1937						M	[J]	
LEHRER	Aron	1941						M	[S]	
LEHRER	Wolf							M	[J]	
LEHRER	Majer	1913	Arbeiter		worker			F	[J]	
LEHRMANN	Ziwie	1939						M	[R]	
LEHRMANN	D		Uhrmacher		watchmaker			M	[R]	
LEIB	E		Bäcker		baker			M	[J], [S]	
LEIB	David	1892	Schneider		tailor			F	[J]	
LEIBEL	Rosa	1900						M	[J]	
LEIBEL	Levy	1932						F	[J]	
LEIBEL	Ete	1937						M	[Y]	Bergen Belsen
LEIBEL	Josef	1911				Aron		M	[J]	
LEIBEL	Wolf	1880						M	[P]	survived
LEIBEL	Jakob	1906				Ephraim	Shprincze			

Krosno, Poland Yizkor Book

Surname	Given name	Year	Occupation (German)	Occupation (English)	Father	Mother	Sex	Spouse	Source	Notes
LEIBNER	Seril	1905			Chaim	Feiga	F	Jakob	[P]	survived
LEIBNER	William	1936			Jakob	Seril	M		[P]	survived
LEIBNER	Yehuda	1938			Jakob	Seril	M		[P]	survived
LEIBNER	Anschel		Wirt	innkeeper			M		[B]	
LEICHT			Tischler	carpenter			M		[B]	
LEICHTBERG	Jhuda	1882					M		[J], [S], [G]	
LEICHTBERG	Regina	1892			Yaacov		F		[Y]	Lemberg
LEICHTBERG	Ete	1886					F		[J]	
LEICHTBERG	Chaim	1912					M		[J]	
LEICHTBERG	Baruch	1916			Avraham		M		[Y]	perished
LEIDNER	Dawid	1912			Avraham		M		[Y]	perished
LEIDNER	Naphtali						M		[P]	
LEHRER	Regina	1876					F		[J]	
LEINER	Arthur	1912	Kürschner	furrier			M		[J]	
LEINER	Rosa	1916	Pelznäherin	fur seamstress			F		[J]	
LEINER	Chaim	1901	Kaufmann	merchant			M		[J]	
LEINER	Luise	1902					F		[J]	
LEINER	Aron	1898	Kaufmann	merchant			M		[J]	
LEISER	Sala	1896					F		[J]	
LEISER	Ides	1927					F		[J]	
LEISER	Chaim	1930					M		[J]	
LEISER	Yechiel						M		[L]	survived
LEISER	Jona						M		[R]	survived
LEISER	W		Schneider	tailor			M		[R]	

Surname	Given Name	Maiden	Birth Year	Occupation (German)	Occupation (English)	Father	Mother	Sex	Spouse	Category	Notes
LEITER	Rachel		1891	Arbeiterin	worker [female]			F		[J]	
LEMBERG	Marjem		1896	Arbeiterin	worker [female]			F		[J]	
LEMBERG				Arzt	doctor			M		[L]	survived
LEMPEL	Wolf Beer		1885	Lehrer	teacher			M		[J]	
LERNER	Reisel		1890					F		[J]	
LERNER	Golde		1913	Friseuse	coiffeuse			F		[J]	
LERNER	Hirsch		1914	Taschenmacher	bag maker			M		[J]	
LERNER	Moses		1916	Arbeiter	worker			M		[J]	
LERNER	Schaje		1917	Arbeiter	worker			M		[J]	
LERNER	Chaje		1923					F		[J]	
LERNER	Jakob		1925		clothes			M		[J], [B]	
LERNER	Meilech		1927	Arbeiter	worker			M		[J]	
LERNER	Simon		1930					M		[J]	
LERNER	Shlomo							M		[P]	
LERNER	Malka	KATZ						F	Shlomo	[P]	
LERNER	Miriam					Shlomo	Malka	F		[P]	
LERNER	Ruth					Shlomo	Malka	F		[P]	
LERNER	Nathan		1921	Elektromonteur	electrician			M		[J]	
LESSIG	Zeev							M		[L]	survived
LEVANINI	Jacob					Leib		M		[Y]	Korczyna
LEWAJ	Regina					Dawid		F	Jacob	[Y]	Majdanek
LEWAJ	Chaje		1924					F		[J]	
LICHOLAT	Ryfke		1896					F		[J]	

Surname	Given name	Alt. name	Year	Occupation	Occupation (Eng.)	Name 1	Sex	Name 2	Code	Fate
LIEBER	Moses		1925	Arbeiter	worker		M		[J]	
LIEBER	Feige		1929				F		[J]	
LIEBER	Samuel		1922	Angestellter	employee		M		[J]	
LIEBER	Hinde		1886				F		[J]	
LIEBER	Chaje		1925	Schneiderin	tailoress		F		[J]	
LIEBER	Jakob		1888	Lehrer	teacher		M		[J], [S]	
LIEBER	Aron						M		[L]	survived
LIEBER	Izrael		1892				M		[R]	Auschwitz
LIEBER	Berish						M		[P]	
LIEBER	Tzwi						M		[P]	
LIEBER	Hirsch		1906	Arbeiter	worker		M		[J], [S]	
LIEBER	Anshel									
LIEBERMANN	Ilona-Rosa		1906				F		[J], [S]	
LIEBERMANN	Jsrael		1929				M		[J]	
LIEBERMANN	Ascher		1933				M		[J]	
LIEBERMANN	Maximilian						M		[L]	survived
LIEBERMANN	Alois			Öllieferant	oil supplier		M		[P]	died 1932
LIEBERMANN	Fredericke						F	Alois	[P]	perished
LIEBERMANN	Otto			Öllieferant	oil supplier	Alois	M	Fredericke	[P]	survived
LIEBERMANN	Stella	SCHACHER					F	Otto	[P]	survived
LIEBERMANN	Eva	EUGENIA	1931			Otto	F	Rosner	[P]	survived
LIEBERMANN	Luiza	BROOK				Otto	F	Brook	[P]	survived
LIEBESKIND	Luba		1916			Avraham	F		[Y]	perished
LILJING	Abraham		1904	Schneider	tailor	Emanuel	M		[Y]	perished
LINDENBERG	Mendel						M		[R]	perished

Krosno, Poland Yizkor Book

Surname	Given		Year				Sex			Status
LINDENBERG	Beila						F	Mendel	[R]	
LINDENBERG	A			Klempner	plumber		M		[R]	
LINDENBERG	Giza					elieazar	F		[Y]	perished
LION	Ludwig					Yossef	M		[Y]	perished
LION	Feige		1875				F		[J]	
LIPINER	Pepi		1912				F		[J]	
LIPINER	Rosa		1914				F		[J]	
LIPINER	Siegmund		1913	Arbeiter	worker	Naphtali	M		[J], [Y]	perished
LIPINER	Ester		1918	Koch	cook		F		[J]	
LIPINER	Ignac						M		[R]	
LIPMERA	Josefine		1896				F		[J]	
LIPPNER	Ferdinand		1885	Beamter	official		M		[J], [S]	
LIPPNER	Olga-Feiga		1898				F		[J]	
LIPPNER	Yochewed	FREUND					F		[Y]	survived
LIPSCHITZ	Samuel						M		[P]	
LITTMAN	Israel						M		[P]	
LITTMAN	Basche		1903				F		[J], [S]	
LITWOK	Chaim		1895	Arbeiter	worker		M		[J]	
LITWOK	Samuel		1932				M		[J]	
LITWOK	Feiwel		1902	Sockenstricker	socks maker		M		[J]	
LIZEWSKI	Leie		1903				F		[J]	
LIZEWSKI	Chaim		1928				M		[J]	
LIZEWSKI	Chane		1931				F		[J]	
LIZEWSKI	A			Uhrmacher	watchmaker		M		[R]	
LOBE	A			Schneider	tailor		M		[R]	

Krosno, Poland Yizkor Book

Surname	Given name	Year	Occupation	Occupation (trans.)	Other	Sex	Code	Notes
LOBE	Ite	1915				F	[J]	
LOEBEL	Sabine	1919	Modistin	milliner [female]		F	[J]	
LOEBEL	Chaim Leib	1940				M	[J]	
LOEBEL	Rachel	1922	Modistin	milliner [female]		F	[J], [S]	
LOEBEL	Chane	1929				F	[J]	
LOEBEL	Eva	1892				F	[J]	
LOEBEL	Abraham	1914	Schneider	tailor		M	[J]	
LOEBEL	Zindel					M	[P]	
LONDON	Feibish					M	[P]	
LONDON	Wolf		Klempner	plumber		M	[R]	
LOZOWSKI	Mendel					M	[P]	
LUDENBERG	Misiek					M	[P]	survived
LUFT	L		Bäcker	baker		M	[R]	
LUPNIK	Sara	1912			Elimelech	F	[Y]	perished
LUST	Elias	1894	Klempner	plumber		M	[J], [S]	
LUSTIG	Sara	1898				F	[J]	
LUSTIG	Rachel	1925				F	[J]	
LUSTIG	Matel	1930				F	[J]	
LUSTIG	Osias	1933				M	[J]	
LUSTIG	Yona	1900				M	[L]	survived
LUZER	Dora				Meir	F	[Y]	Zwickau
LWOWSKI	Aron	1894	Arbeiter	worker		M	[J], [S]	
MAENNER	Chaje	1905				F	[J]	
MAENNER	Markus	1931				M	[J]	

MAENNER	Jsrael		1933			M	[J]	
MAENNER	Jsaak		1941			M	[J]	
MAENNER	Hirsh					M	[S]	
MAGEL	Elieazar	RIVKA				M	[YI]	Korczyna
MAHLER	Haya				Elieazar	F	[YI]	Korczyna
MAHLER	Moses		1904	Fleischer	butcher	M	[J]	
MAHLER	Sala		1910		Getzil	F	[J], [Y]	Belzec
MAHLER	Manes		1935		Moshe	M	[J], [Y]	perished
MAHLER	Leiser		1890	Bäcker	baker	M	[J]	
MAHLER	Regina		1900			F	[J]	
MAHLER	Hirsch		1923	Bäcker	baker	M	[J]	
MAHLER	Genia		1896			F	[J]	
MAHLER	Hirsch		1923	Arbeiter	worker	M	[J]	
MAHLER	Rafael		1902	Fleischer	butcher	M	[J]	
MAHLER	Marjem		1916			F	[J]	
MAHLER	Nissen		1940			M	[J]	
MAHLER	Shimon		1896			M	[P]	
MAHLER	Avraham					M	[G]	
MAHLER	Wolf			Fleischer	butcher	M	[R]	
MAHLER	Simon				Simon	M	[P]	
MAHLER	Eva					F	[P]	
MAHLER	Yeshayahu		1895	Kaufmann	merchant	Shaya	M	[J], [Y]	Warsaw
MAJEROWICZ	Leie		1898			F	[J]	
MAJEROWICZ	Eva		1924		Yeshayahu	M	[J], [Y]	perished
MAJEROWICZ	Marjem		1926			F	[J]	perished

Krosno, Poland Yizkor Book

Surname	Given name	Year	Occupation	Occupation		Sex	Code	Status
MAJEROWICZ	Sala	1932				F	[J]	
MAJEROWICZ	A		Schlosser	locksmith		M	[R]	
MALTZ	Ellen					F	[L]	survived
MALTZ	Mordechai					M	[L]	survived
MALTZ	Mindel	1885				F	[J]	
MALZ	Leie	1917				F	[J]	
MALZ	Jochweth	1922	Schneiderin	tailoress		F	[J]	
MALZ	Pinkas	1906	Schneider	tailor		M	[J], [S]	
MANDEL	Dora	1910				F	[J]	
MANDEL	Chaim	1935				M	[J]	
MANDEL	Sprinze	1938				F	[J]	
MANDEL	Jakob	1877	Schuster	shoemaker		M	[J], [S]	
MANDEL	Ryfke	1877				F	[J]	
MANDEL	Debora	1910				F	[J]	
MANDEL	Pessel	1915	Näherin	seamstress		F	[J]	
MANDEL	Shmuel					M	[R]	survived
MANSTER	Mendel	1886	Lehrer	teacher		M	[J], [S]	
MARCHEWKA	Chume	1894				M	[J]	
MARCHEWKA	Basche	1924	Schneiderin	tailoress		F	[J]	
MARCHEWKA	Schulim	1927	Arbeiter	worker		M	[J]	
MARCHEWKA	Scheindel	1930				F	[J]	
MARCHEWKA	Jsaak	1932				M	[J]	
MARCHEWKA	Leie	1936				F	[J]	
MARCHEWKA	Selig	1898	Expedient	dispatch clerk		M	[J]	
MARFELD	Hadassah	1897				F	[J]	

Surname	Given name	Maiden name	Birth	Occupation		Father	Sex	Codes	Fate
MARFELD	Samuel		1928				M	[J]	
MARFELD	Chaje		1930				F	[J]	
MARFELD	Selde		1936				F	[J]	
MARFELD	Ella nee	HOLLOSCHETZ					F	[L]	survived
MARGULES	Itzhak						M	[L]	survived
MARGULES	Michael						M	[L]	survived
MARGULES	Moshe						M	[L]	survived
MARGULES	Yaacov				materials		M	[L], [R]	survived
MARGULES	Yossef						M	[L]	survived
MARGULES	Moses		1900	Angestellter	employee	Chaim	M	[J], [Y], [G]	perished in Buchenwald
MARGULES	Eva		1905				F	[J]	
MARGULES	Moses		1885	Expedient	dispatch clerk	Yossef	M	[J], [Y]	perished
MARGULES	Ester		1888				F	[J]	
MARGULES	Matel		1912			Moshe	F	[J], [Y]	perished in Majdanek
MARGULES	Pessel		1927				F	[J]	
MARGULES	Mehel		1886		products		M	[J], [G]	
MARGULES	Reisel		1875				F	[J]	
MARGULES	Hirsch		1875			Yossef	M	[P]	shot in 1942
MARGULES	Malke		1908			Chaim	F	[J], [Y]	perished
MARGULES	Chaim		1877				M	[J]	
MARGULES	Sara		1878				F	[J]	
MARGULES	Amalie		1911			Chaim	F	[J], [Y]	perished
MARGULES	Jochweth		1912				F	[J]	

Krosno, Poland Yizkor Book

MARGULES	Anna	1910		Mechel	F		[J], [Y]	perished in Krakow
MARGULES	Markus	1903	Arbeiter	worker	Chaim	M	[J], [Y]	perished
MARGULES	Salomon	1901	Konditor	confectioner	Hirsh	M	[J], [Y]	perished
MARGULES	Minna	1902			Chaim	F	[J], [Y]	
MARGULES	Josef	1939				M	[J]	
MARGULES	Hinde	1890				F	[J]	
MARGULES	Kalmen					M	[G]	
MARGULES	Machcia					F	[G]	
MARGULES	Ch		Student	student		M	[R]	
MARGULES	Israel		Eierverkäufer	egg merchant		M	[B]	
MARGULES	Aaron					M	[P]	
MARIN	Aaron							
MARIN	Tircza					F	[L]	survived
MARKUS	Chana					F	[G]	
MAROKA	Eliasz					M	[R]	
MATZNER	Tzvi					M	[L]	survived
MAYEROWICZ	Lena					F	[L]	survived
MAYEROWICZ	Sarah					F	[P]	Moniek
MAYEROWICZ	Manka	1916			Wolf	F	[Y]	perished
MAZER	Moshe					M	[P]	
MEBEL	Dawid		Metallarbeiter	metalworker		M	[R]	
MEBEL	Dawid							
MEHEL	Rubin		Ratsmitglied	councilor		M	[R]	
MEHEL	Avraham		Metallarbeiter	metalworker		M	[R]	
MEILECH	Menachem					M	[P]	

Surname	Given name	Extra name	Year	Occupation	Name 1	Sex	Name 2	Code	Status
MEILECH	Yehoshua					M		[P]	
MEILECH	Aron					M		[G]	
MEINER	Mala		1904			F		[J, [S]	
MEISELES	Sala		1926			F		[J]	
MEISELES	Chaje		1906			F		[J]	
MEISELES	Feige		1914			F		[J]	
MEISELES	Gila					F		[L]	survived
MEISELES	Lazar					M		[G]	
MEISELS	Jsrael		1898	Angestellter	employee	M		[J]	
MEISLICH	Frimet		1908			F		[J]	
MEISLICH	Guetl		1929			F		[J]	
MEISLICH	Ryfke		1931			F		[J]	
MEISLICH	Jhuda		1934			M		[J]	
MEISLICH	David					M		[L]	survived
MELAMED	Rachela					F		[G]	
MELAMED	Awraham Cha					M		[P]	
MELAMED	Israel Hersh					M			deceased
MELAMET	Rachela	KALB				F	Israel		Married 1924. Deceased
MELAMET	Salomon				Israel	M	Rachela		died 1916
MELAMET	Sussel		1925		Israel	F	Rachela		deceased
MELAMET	Leie		1912			F		[J]	
MELAMET	Hersh					M			deceased
MELAMET	Rachel	DENN				F	Hersh		deceased

Krosno, Poland Yizkor Book

Surname	Given name	(Kleinman)	Year	Occupation	Occupation	Father	Mother	Sex	Code	Status
MELAMET	Pinkas		1918			Hersh	Rachel	M		deceased
MELAMET	Beile Ester		1921			Hersh	Rachel	F	[J]	
MELAMET	David		1923	Arbeiter	worker	Hersh	Rachel	D	[J]	
MELAMET	Suessl		1925					F	[J]	
MELAMET	Matel		1904			Reuven		F	[Y]	Belzec
MELAMET	Majlech			Kürschner	furrier			M	[B]	
MELLER	Shprintze							F	[P]	
MELLER	Sprinze		1870					F	[J]	
MELLER	Henoch							M	[L]	survived
MELLER	Shmuel		1886					M	[P]	
MELTZER	Jakub							M	[G]	
MENDEL	Pinchas		1910			Yaacov		M	[Y], [L]	
MENDEL	Moses							M	[R]	
MENDEL								M	[L]	survived
MENDELOWICZ	Aron							M	[G]	
MENNER	Rachela							F	[G]	
METZGER	Alte Chane		1898					F	[J]	
MILLER	Chiel		1933					M	[J]	
MILLER	Hess							M	[L]	survived
MILLER	Avraham							M	[P]	
Mintz	Awraham									
MINC	Sara		1907			Avraham		F	[Y]	perished
MINC	Dina	KLEINMAN						F	[L]	survived
MINSTER	Shmuel							M	[L]	survived
MINSTER	Tziona							F	[P]	

Krosno, Poland Yizkor Book

Surname	First name	Year	Occupation	Occupation	Father	Mother	Sex	Codes	Fate
MISTROWSKI	Chaje-Clara	1903	Maniküristin	manicurist			F	[J], [S]	
MOHR	Malke	1884			Naphtali		F	[J], [Y]	perished
MONHEIT	Feige	1914					F	[J]	
MONHEIT	Samuel	1919	Handelsgehilfe	clerk			M	[J]	
MONHEIT	Naftali	1922	Handelsgehilfe	clerk			M	[J]	
MONHEIT	Mechel	1924					M	[J]	
MONHEIT	Benzion						M	[P]	
MONTAG	Sima					Benzion	F	[Y], [G]	perished
MONTAG	Sara				Benzion	Sima	F	[P]	perished
MONTAG	Rivka				Benzion	Sima	F	[P]	deceased
MONTAG	Lea				Benzion	Sima	F	[P]	deceased
MONTAG	Nehema				Benzion	Sima	F	[P]	
MONTAG	Gittel				Benzion	Sima	F	[P]	
MONTAG	Golda				Benzion	Sima	F	[P]	
MONTAG	Yaacov Shija				Benzion	Sima	M	[P]	died 1929
MONTAG	Josef	1911	Rohproduktenaufkäufer	seller of raw products	Ben Zion	Sima	M	[J], [Y]	Mathausen
MONTAG	Moshe						M	[L], [G]	survived
MONTAG	Mindel	1917			Asher		F	[J], [Y]	perished
MONTAG	Ete	1940					F	[J]	
MONTAG	Yossef						M	[L]	survived
MONTAG	Benjamin	1904	Kaufmann	merchant			M	[J]	
MORGENSTERN	Minna	1904			Avraham		F	[J], [Y]	perished in Krosnice
MORGENSTERN	Schifre	1930					F	[J]	

Surname	Given name	Year	Occupation (German)	Occupation (English)	Name	Sex	Source	Fate
MORGENSTERN	Sara	1936				F	[J]	
MORGENSTERN	Blanka	1910	Angestellte	employee		F	[J]	
MORGENSTERN	Ascher	1849				M	[J]	
MOSES	Rachel	1849			Avraham	F	[J], [Y]	Belzec
MOSES	Wolf	1875	Angestellter		Asher	M	[J], [Y]	Belzec
MOSES	Abraham	1885	Angestellter	employee	Asher	M	[J], [Y]	Belzec
MOSES	Chane	1880				F	[J]	
MOSES	Sala	1888				F	[J]	
MOSES	Suessl	1927				F	[J]	
MOSES	Josef		Buchbinder	bookbinder		M	[B]	
MOSKOWICZ	Chaje	1898			Itzhak	F	[J], [S], [Y]	perished
MOSKOWICZ	Hinde	1909				F	[J]	
MOSKOWICZ	Ester	1910	Zahnärztin	dentist [female]		F	[J]	
MOSKOWICZ	Nischl	1913				M	[J]	
MOSKOWICZ	Moses	1914	Schuster	shoemaker		M	[J]	
MOSKOWICZ	Ite	1918	Angestellte	employee		F	[J]	
MOSKOWICZ	Ilona	1933				F	[J]	
MOSKOWICZ	Moses	1932				M	[J]	
MOSKOWICZ	Pinkas	1930			Meir	M	[J], [Y]	perished
MOSKOWICZ	Josef	1925			Meir	M	[J], [Y]	perished
MOSKOWICZ	Benzion	1897	Arbeiter	worker		M	[J]	
MUEHLRAD	Chane	1899				F	[J]	
MUEHLRAD	Saul	1927	Arbeiter	worker		M	[J]	
MUEHLRAD	Kalmen	1928				M	[J]	

Surname	Given	Year	Occupation	English	Father	Mother	Sex	Code	Status
MUEHLRAD	Chaim	1929					M	[J]	
MUEHLRAD	Reisel	1931					F	[J]	
MUEHLRAD	Guetl	1933					F	[J]	
MUEHLRAD	Moses	1935					M	[J]	
MUEHLRAD	Sime	1936					F	[J]	
MUEHLRAD	Jsaak	1938					M	[J]	
MUEHLRAD	Chawe	1939					F	[J]	
MUEHLRAD	Jsrael	1941					M	[J]	
MUEHLRAD	Schaje	1911	Zuschneider	cutter			M	[J]	
MUEHLRAD	Debora	1937					F	[J]	
MUENZ	Rubin	1892	Klempner	blumber			M	[J], [G]	perished
MUENZ	Rosa	1910			Rubin		F	[J]	perished
MUENZ	Majer	1922	Klempner	blumber	Rubin	Rosa	M	[J]	perished
MUENZ	Eisig	1924	Klempner	blumber	Rubin	Rosa	M	[J]	perished
MUENZ	Abraham	1936					M	[J]	
MUENZ	Avrahaam		Ratsmitglied	councilor			M	[L]	
MUENZ	Pearl				Avrahaam		F	[L]	survived
MUENZ	Regina				Abraham	Pearl	F	[P]	survived
MUENZ	Sara	1907	Näherin	seamstress	Abraham	Pearl	F	[J]	survived
MUENZ	Dawid				Abraham	Pearl	M	[P]	died 1929
MUENZ	Mirel				Abraham	Pearl	F	[P]	survived
MUENZ	Jakob	1918	Autoschlosser	panel beater	Abraham	Pearl	M	[J], [Y]	perished
MUENZ	Baruch				Abraham	Pearl	M	[L]	survived
MUENZ	Salomon	1940					M	[J]	
MUENZ	Simon	1941					M	[J]	

Krosno, Poland Yizkor Book

Surname	First name		Year	Occupation	Occupation	Father	Sex	Source	Fate
MUENZ	Syna		1924			Reuven	F	[Y]	perished
MUENZ	Chaim				goods		M	[R]	survived
MULLER	Elisheva						F	[L]	survived
NACHTIGAL	David Dr.						M	[L]	survived
NACHTIGAL	Eliazar						M	[R]	survived
NACHTIGAL	Sara		1858				F	[J]	
NAGEL	Nathan		1932				M	[J]	
NAGEL	Markus		1925	Arbeiter	worker		M	[J]	
NAGEL	Tobias		1884	Fleischer	butcher		M	[J]	
NAGEL	Samuel		1914	Fleischer	butcher	Towim	M	[J], [Y]	Auschwitz
NAGEL	Guetl		1917			Towim	F	[J], [Y]	Auschwitz
NAGEL	Jakob		1920	Arbeiter	worker	Towim	M	[J], [Y]	Auschwitz
NAGEL	Markus		1924	Arbeiter	worker		M	[J]	
NAGEL	Rachela		1900				F	[J]	
NAGEL	Markus		1922	Arbeiter	worker		M	[J]	
NAGEL	Halinke		1932				F	[J]	
NAGEL	Sima						F	[L]	survived
NAGEL	Yehuda		1893			Israel	M	[Y]	Biecz
NAIS	Aron						M	[R]	survived
NAIS	Rachel						F	[R]	survived
NEJMARK	Shalom						M	[L]	survived
NEISS	Zipora		1896				F	[J]	
NEISS-AKSELRAD	Sara		1929				F	[J]	
NEISS-AKSELRAD	Majer		1898	Arbeiter	worker		M	[J], [G]	

Surname	First name	Year	Occupation	Name	Occupation	Sex	Code	Fate
NEUMANN	Sime	1902				F	[J]	
NEUMANN	Schaje	1930				M	[J]	
NEUMANN	Abraham	1932				M	[J]	
NEUMANN	Motel	1920		Moshe		M	[Y]	perished
NEUMANN	Menachem					M	[L]	survived
NEUMANN	S		Student		student	M	[R]	
NEUSS	Hirsch	1888	Korbmacher		basket maker	M	[J], [S]	
NIEWIADOMSKI	Chaje	1925				F	[J]	
NIEWIADOMSKI	Berek	1908	Arbeiter		worker	M	[J], [S]	
NISSENBAUM	Jente	1910				F	[J]	
NISSENBAUM	Rosa	1933				F	[J]	
NISSENBAUM	Sala	1937				F	[J]	
NISSENBAUM	Dov					M	[L]	survived
NOBERT	Idel			Dawid		F	[Y]	perished
NOJS	Salusia			Yehuda		F	[Y]	perished
NOJS	Srulik			yehuda		M	[Y]	perished
NOJS	Izrael					M	[R]	
NORBERT	Hirsch	1875	Schneider		tailor	M	[J], [Y]	
NORD	Rosa	1911				F	[J]	
NORD	Jochweth	1917				F	[J]	
NORD	Zipora	1919				F	[J]	
NORD	Jsaak	1924	Schneider		tailor	M	[J], [L]	survived
NORD	Marie					F	[R]	survived
NORD	Rachel	1860				F	[J]	
NORD	Salomon	1881	Kaufmann	Itzhak	merchant	M	[J], [Y]	perished

Krosno, Poland Yizkor Book

Surname	Given	Year	Occupation	Occupation	Father	Sex	Code	Fate
NORD	Dine	1883			Avraham	F	[G]	Belzec
NORD	Chaya	1917			Hersh	F	[J], [Y]	.
NORD	Ryfke	1874				F	[J]	
NOVEMBER	Samuel	1912	Weißbinder	house painter		M	[J]	
NOVEMBER	Menachem					M	[L]	survived
NOVEMBER	Wolf	1876			Henoch	M	[J], [Y]	perished
NUSSBAUM	Henoch	1909	Kaufmann	merchant		M	[J]	
NUSSBAUM	Ida	1909				F	[J]	
NUSSBAUM	Abisch	1935				M	[J]	
NUSSBAUM	Debora	1914				F	[J]	
NUSSBAUM	A					M	[L]	survived
NUSSBAUM	Yaacov					M	[L]	survived
NUSSBAUM	Karol						[R]	shot
NUSSBAUM	Wolf					M	[P]	shot in 1942
NUSSBAUM	Jacob		Tischler	carpenter		M	[B]	survived
OBRYBSKI	Atara					F	[L]	survived
OFNER	Golde	1884				F	[J], [S]	
OKNOWSKI	Josef	1908	Tapezierer	paperhanger		M	[J]	
OKNOWSKI	Aron	1886	Angestellter	employee	Yossef	M	[J], [Y], [G]	perished
OLING	Awraham							
OLING	Leie	1890				F	[J]	
OLING	Malke	1912	Modistin	milliner	Aron	F	[J], [Y]	perished
OLING	Chane	1915	Modistin	milliner	Aron	F	[J], [Y]	perished

OLING	Khaia			Aron	F		[Y]	perished
OLING	Mindel		Schneiderin	tailoress	F		[J]	
OLING	Jakob		Student	student	M		[J]	
OLING	Genia				F		[G]	
OLING	Chaim		Bäcker	baker	M		[R]	
OLING	K		Student	student	M		[R]	
OMACHEL	Leib				M		[L]	survived
ORENSTEIN	Chaim		Krämer	grocer	M		[R]	
ORGLER	Luba	KANNER			F		[L]	survived
ORGLER	Yedwabne				F		[L]	survived
OSTROWSKA	J				M		[R]	
OZIAS	Leibish				M		[L]	survived
PACHER	Avraham Dr				M		[L]	survived
PALANT	Israel				M		[L]	survived
PALANT	Sabina				F		[L]	survived
PALANT	Shlomo				M		[L]	survived
PALANT	Gittel		1880	Yaacov	F		[Y]	survived
PANZER	Mirel		1913	seamstress	F		[J]	
PARNESS	Scheindel		1909	seamstress	F		[J]	
PARNESS	Yaacov				M		[L]	survived
PARNESS	Taube		1900		F		[J]	
PASTERNAK	Toni		1937		M		[J]	
PASTERNAK	Leie		1896		F		[J]	
PASTERNAK	Gerson		1924	Handelsgehilfe	clerk	M		[J]	
PASTERNAK	Dawid Oz.			household	M		[R]	

Krosno, Poland Yizkor Book

PASTERNAK	Mojzesz		merchant	Kaufmann			M		[R]	
PASTERNAK	Tema	1905					F	Mojzesz	[P]	perished
PASTERNAK	Reisel	1916			Moshe	Tema	F		[Y]	perished
PASTERNAK	Rivka	1908			Moshe	Tema	F		[Y]	perished
PASTERNAK	Simon	1875	food		Moshe	Tema	M		[Y]	perished
PASTERNAK	Simon	1894					M		[JJ, [G]]	
PASTERNAK	Leib	1919	merchant	Kaufmann			M		[JJ]	
PASTERNAK	Anshel	1905			Leib		M		[P]	perished
PASTOR	Regina	1914					F		[JJ]	
PASTOR	Ester						F		[JJ]	
PASTOR	Yossef						M		[L]	survived
PATAWAY	Meir						M		[L]	survived
PECKER	Regina	1908					F		[JJ, [S]]	
PELZMANN	Samuel	1933					M		[JJ]	
PELZMANN	Reisel	1878					F		[JJ, [S]]	
PELZMANN	Feige	1920					F		[JJ]	
PELZMANN	Rachel	1921					F		[JJ]	
PELZMANN	Chaje	1928					F		[JJ]	
PELZMANN	Meilech	1872					M		[JJ]	
PELZMANN	Chaje	1903					F		[JJ]	
PELZMANN	Sara Ryfke	1939					F		[JJ]	
PEREL	Riwka				Yaacov		F		[Y]	Belzec
PEREL	Sara				Chaim		F		[Y]	Belzec
PEREL	Chaim	1879			Avraham		M		[Y]	Belzec
PEREL	Jezajasz	1879			Avraham		M		[Y]	Auschwitz

Krosno, Poland Yizkor Book

PEREL	Samuel	1886		Avraham	M	[Y]	Auschwitz
PEREL	Yaacow	1876		Avraham	M	[Y]	Belzec
PEREL	Ruben				M	[R]	
PERETZ	Reuven		student				
PERETZ	U		Student		M	[R]	
PERKIS	Janina	1926		Henryk	F	[Y]	Belzec
PERLBERG	Malka				F	[L]	survived
PERLBERG	Hanoch				M	[L]	survived
PILHARDT	Zalman				M	[L]	survived
PILHARDT	Jakob	1864	Klempner	plumber	M	[J]	
PINKAS	Adele	1908	Schneiderin	tailoress	F	[J]	
PINKAS	Moses David	1906	Tischler	carpenter	M	[J]	
PINKAS	Chaje	1909			F	[J]	
PINKAS	Feige	1927			F	[J]	
PINKAS	Lemel	1901	Kaufmann	merchant	M	[J]	
PINKAS	Freide	1899			F	[J]	
PINKAS	Samuel	1931			M	[J]	
PINKAS	Abraham	1933			M	[J]	
PINKAS	Neche	1935			F	[J]	
PINKAS	Reisel	1937			F	[J]	
PINKAS	Sabine	1941			F	[J]	
PINKAS	Moshe				M	[L]	survived
PINKAS	Malka				F	[L]	survived
PINKAS	Lemel				M	[G]	
PINKASA	N		Friseur	barber	M	[R]	

Krosno, Poland Yizkor Book

PINKUS	Mendel		1886	Arbeiter	worker		M	[J]
PINSEL	Chaje		1886				F	[J], [G]
PINSEL	Fischel		1913	Arbeiter	worker		M	[J]
PINSEL	Brandel		1918	Schneiderin	tailoress		F	[J]
PINSEL	Leib		1922	Arbeiter	worker		M	[J]
PINSEL	Liepe		1924	Arbeiter	worker		M	[J]
PINSEL	Naftali		1929				M	[J]
PINSEL	Rosia	MARGULES					F	[P] survived
PINSLER	Abraham		1934				M	[J]
PINTER	Frieda		1906		Shmuel		F	[J], [S], [Y] Belzec
PINTER	Jsaak		1936				M	[J]
PINTER	Guetl		1935				F	[J]
PINTER	Sara		1878				F	[J]
PIOTRKOWSKI	David		1913	Arbeiter	worker		M	[J]
PIOTRKOWSKI	Moses		1918	Handtaschenmacher	handbags maker		M	[J]
PIRBISK	Hirsch		1919	Handtaschenmacher	handbags maker		M	[J]
PIRBISK	Rachela		1921	Korsettnäherin	woman who makes corsets		F	[J]
PIRBISK	Moses		1940				M	[J]
PIRBISK	Jakob		1904	Arbeiter	worker		M	[J]
PIRBISK	Leie		1907				F	[J]
PIRBISK	Zelig						M	[L] survived
PIVIRT	Chaje		1892				F	[J]

Surname	Given name	Surname 2	Birth	Occupation	Occupation	Father	Mother	Sex	Spouse	Code	Location
PIWONJA	Nuchim		1918	Arbeiter	worker			M		[J], [S]	
PIWONJA	Leie		1919					F		[J]	
PIWONJA	Chaim Hersh				coal merchant			M		[R]	Rzeszow
PLATNER	Mala							F	Chaim	[P]	Rzeszow
PLATNER	Yaakow					Chaim Hersh	Mala	M		[P]	
PLATNER	Mordechai		1879			Chaim Hersh	Mala	M		[YI]	Krosno
PLATNER	Hannah	LUSTIG	1878					F	Mordechai	[YI]	Krosno
PLATNER	Debora-Doba		1913			Mordechai	Hannah	F		[J], [Y]	Szebnie
PLATNER	Joseph	ROITER	1922			Mordechai	Hannah	M		[Y]	Ustrzyki
PLATNER	Beila					Mordechai	Hannah	F		[P]	Szebnie
PLATNER	Genia					Mordechai	Hannah	F		[P]	Russia
PLATNER	Israel					Mordechai	Hannah	M		[P]	Canada
PLATNER	Abraham		1887	Glaser	glazier	Chaim	Mala	M		[J], [Y], [G]	Belzec
PLATNER	Hencia		1887					F	Abraham	[J]	Belzec
PLATNER	Sara		1919	Strickerin	tricotatrice	Abraham	Helene	F		[J], [Y]	Belzec
PLATNER	Rachel		1922			Abraham	Helene	F		[J], [Y]	Belzec
PLATNER	Aron		1925	Glaserlehrling	glazier apprentice	Abraham	Helene	M		[J], [Y]	Belzec
PLATNER	Joseph	WEISSER	1918			Abraham	Helene	M		[J], [Y]	Ustrzyki
PLATNER	Yossef					Chaim Hersh	Mala	M		[P]	Russia
PLATNER	Dwora	HELLER						F	Yossef	Private, [G]	Russia

Krosno, Poland Yizkor Book

Surname	Given name	Year	Occupation	Father	Mother	Sex		Code	Fate
PLATNER	Rivka			Yossef	Dwora	F		[P]	Russia
PLATNER	Avraham			Yossef	Dwora	M		[P]	Russia
PLATNER	Sarah			Chaim	Mala	F		[P]	
PLATNER	Lea			Chaim	Mala	F		[P]	perished
PLATNER	H		Student			M		[R]	
PLATTER	Benyamin					M		[L]	survived
PLETZEL	Peshe					F		[L]	survived
PLETZEL	Chaskel					M		[G]	
PODNER	Shoshana					F		[L]	survived
POLANSKI	Rosa					F		[G]	
PRRUSH	Ozer								
POSNER	Shimon					M		[P]	
POSTAR	Shimon								
POSTAR	Alte Neche	1889				F		[J], [S]	
POZNANSKI	Golde	1911				F		[J]	
PRESSER	Rachel	1879				F		[J]	
PRESSER	Baruch		Ratsmitglied / councilor			M		[R]	
PRESSER	Menachem					M		[L]	survived
PREUSS	Bronia					F		[L]	survived
PREUSS	Mendel					M		[L]	survived
PREUSS	Benyamin					M		[YI]	Krosno
PRIVIRT						F	Benyamin	[YI]	Krosno
PRIVIRT	Lea	1894		Elieazar		F		[Y]	perished
PRIWER	Anna	1912		Avraham		F		[J], [Y]	perished
PROBKER	Sala	1938				F		[J]	

Surname	Given	Year	Occupation	Occupation	Father	Sex	Source	Notes
PROBKER	Ryfke	1940				F	[J]	
PROBKER	Mendel	1918			Shimon	M	[Y]	perished
PROBKER	Moses	1903	Näherin	seamstress		M	[J]	
PRUEFER	Leie	1903				F	[J]	
PRUEFER	Naftali	1930				M	[J]	
PRUEFER	Chaim	1906	Arbeiter	worker		M	[J]	
PRUEFER	Mala					F	[S]	
PURETZ	Samuel					M	[G]	
PURETZ	Feiwel	1909	Schuhmacher	shoemaker		M	[J]	
RABI	Chaje	1916				F	[J]	
RABI	Tile	1872				F	[J]	
RABI	Berl	1938				M	[J]	
RABI	Siegmund	1938				M	[J]	
RABI	Perl	1905				F	[J]	
RABINOWICZ	Rosa	1934				F	[J]	
RABINOWICZ	Abraham	1938				M	[J]	
RABINOWICZ	Eliezer					M	[P]	
RADNER	Feige	1888				F	[J]	
RAKOSZYNSKI	Mordche	1914	Arbeiter	worker		M	[J]	
RAKOSZYNSKI	Samuel H.	1875	Lehrer	teacher		M	[P]	perished
RAMRAS	Ryfke	1876				F	[J]	
RAMRAS	Seindel	1906			Zwi	F	[Y]	perished
RAMRAS	Eidel	1918			Zwi	F	[J], [Y], [G]	perished
RAMRAS	Moses	1920			Zwi	M	[Y]	perished

Surname	Given name	Maiden	Year	Occupation (German)	Occupation (English)	Name	Sex	Father	Code	Note
RAMRAS	Rachel		1939				F		[J]	
RAMRAS	Lazar						M		[G]	
RAMRAS	Moshe						M		[L]	survived
RAND	Ryfka nee	PLATNER					F	Moshe	[P]	survived
RAND	Rachel		1870				F		[J]	
RATZ	Chaim						M		[G]	
RATZ	Josef Leib			Ratsmitglied	councilor		M		[G]	
RATZ	Avraham Mos			Weinhändler	vintner		M		[R]	
RATZ	Hannah						F	Avraham	[R]	
RATZ	Hella	ENGELHARDT					F		[L]	survived
RAUCH	Regina						F		[S]	
RAWSKI	Regina		1883				F		[J]	
RAWSKI	Moses		1903	Schneider	tailor		M		[J]	
RECK	Rachel		1900				F		[J]	
RECK	Rosa		1928				F		[J]	
RECK	Benjamin		1929				M		[J]	
RECK	Regina		1898			Moshe	F		[Y]	Czortkow
REGENBO	Freide		1898				F		[J]	
REIBENBACH	Samuel		1895	Arbeiter	worker		M		[J], [S]	
REIBSCHEID	Adam		1896	Ingenieur	engineer		M		[J]	
REICH	Malke		1912			Yossef	F		[J], [Y]	
REICH	Schulim		1891	Glaser	glazier		M		[J]	
REICH	Rosa		1901				F		[J]	
REICH	Salomon		1930				M		[J]	
REICH	Regina		1935				F		[J]	

Krosno, Poland Yizkor Book

REICH	Yehezkel			M		[L]	survived
REICH	Ruzie			F		[L]	survived
REICHMAN	Frania			F		[S]	
REICHMAN	Leibish						
REINBACH	Wolf	Krosno		M		[P]	perished
REINMANN	Feige	HEMERLING	Krosno		F	Wolf	[P]	perished
REINEMAN	Majer	1923	tires	M		[JJ], [S]	
REINHOLD	Salomon	1906	Arbeiter	worker	M		[JJ]	
REISS	Niche	1899		F		[JJ]	
REISS	Alter	1940		F		[JJ]	
REISS	Seril	1897		F		[JJ]	
RIEDER	Seril			M		[G]	
RIEDER	Josef			M		[JJ], [Y]	Lemberg
RIEDER	Jsrael	1903	Mützenmacher	capper	M	Josef	[JJ], [Y]	Lemberg
RIEDER	Guetl	1889		F		[JJ], [S], [G]	
RIEDER	Mendel	1925	Arbeiter	worker	M		[JJ]	
RIEDER	Leib	1928	Arbeiter	worker	M		[JJ]	
RIEDER	Beile	1930		F		[JJ]	
RIEDER	Sprinze	1920		F		[JJ]	
RIEDER	Leie	1904		F		[JJ]	
RIEMER	Guetl/Tova	1930		F	Jacob	[JJ], [Y]	
RIEMER	Moses	1935		M	Jacob	[JJ], [Y]	
RIEMER	Jakub			M		[G]	
RIEMER	Gusta	1909		F	Yehshua	[Y]	

Krosno, Poland Yizkor Book

Surname	First name		Year	Occupation	Occupation	Father	Sex	Code	Fate
RIES	Cvia					Shmuel	F	[Y]	Russia
RINGEL	Dworah					Shmuel	F	[Y]	Russia
RINGEL	Bila		1912			Zishe	F	[Y]	Auschwitz
RINGEL	Berta					Zishe	F	[Y]	
RINGEL	Hinda						F	[L]	survived
RINGEL	Shaul						M	[P]	
RINGEL	Amalie		1869				F	[J]	
RINGLER	Simon		1898	Kaufmann	merchant		M	[J]	
RINGLER	Malka		1875			Shimon	F	[Y]	
RINGLER	Hersh		1904			Avraham	M	[Y]	Dynow
RINGLER	Pauline		1907				F	[J]	
RINGLER	Abraham		1931				M	[J]	
RINGLER	Malke		1927				F	[J]	
RINGLER	Pepi		1900			Yossef	F	[J]	
RINGLER	Abraham		1937				M	[J]	
RINGLER	Samuel		1898			Avraham	M	[Y]	Auschwitz
RINGLER	Heika	BREITOWICZ					F	[L]	survived
RITTER	Aron		1890	Weißbinder	house painter		M	[J]	
ROESSLER	Ester		1895				F	[J]	
ROESSLER	Isaak		1922	Weißbinder	house painter		M	[J]	
ROESSLER	Moses		1923	Weißbinder	house painter		M	[J]	
ROESSLER	Beile		1925	Schneiderin	tailoress		F	[J]	
ROESSLER	Feige		1884				F	[J]	
ROGALIK	Marjem		1928				F	[J]	
ROGALIK				Zahnarzt	dentist, activist		M	[R]	

Surname	Given name		Birth	Occupation		Father	Mother	Sex	Relation	Religion	Fate
ROMM	Frieda		1877					F		[P]	survived
ROSENBERG	Rachel	AKSELRAD	b.1911			Yossef Bendet	Chana	F		[P]	
ROSENBERG	Miriam							M		[P]	
ROSENBERG	Josef						Rachel	M		[P]	
ROSENBERG	Abraham		1904	Arzt	doctor		Rachel	F		[P]	perished
ROSENBERG	Serl		1920					M	Abraham	[J]	survived
ROSENBERG	Moses		1879					F		[J], [S]	
ROSENBERG	Chaje		1877					M		[J]	
ROSENBERG	Berl		1917	Arbeiter	worker			F		[J]	
ROSENBERG	Ryfke		1918					F		[J]	
ROSENBERG	Frimet		1909					F		[J], [S]	
ROSENBLATT	Chaskel		1936					M		[J]	
ROSENBLATT	Franziska		1885					F		[J]	
ROSENBLUETH	Chawe		1909					F		[J]	
ROSENBLUM	Dr. Leib		1887	Anwalt	attorney			M		[J]	
ROSENBLUM	Franziska		1891					F		[J]	
ROSENBLUM	Ester							F		[J]	
ROSENBLUM	L			Klempner	plumber			M		[R]	
ROSENFELD	J			Schneider	tailor			M		[R]	
ROSENFELD	Moses		1885	Holzarbeiter	woodworker			M		[J]	
ROSENTHAL	Liebe		1885					F		[J]	
ROSENTHAL	Neche		1911	Buchhalterin	bookkeeper [female]			F		[J]	

Surname	First name		Year	Occupation	Occupation	Name	Sex		Source	Status
ROSENTHAL	Eliyahu						M		[P]	
ROSNER	Rosa		1895				F		[J]	
ROSNER	Blueme		1938				F		[J]	
ROSNER	Leiser		1870	Bauer	farmer		M		[J], [G]	
ROSNER	Feiwel		1895	Schneider	tailor	Elieazar	M		[J], [Y]	
ROSNER	Chane		1896			Avraham	F		[JJ], [Y]	
ROSNER	David		1927	Arbeiter	worker		M		[J]	
ROSNER	Chaskel		1928				M		[J]	
ROSNER	Sara		1903			Shlomo	F		[Y]	
ROSNER	Meir						M		[L]	survived
ROSNER	Reuven						M		[L]	survived
ROSNER	Moshe						M		[L]	survived
ROSNER	Yehshua						M		[L]	survived
ROSNER	Majer			Krämer	grocer		M		[B]	
ROSSHAENDLER	Samuel		1890	Kaufmann	merchant	Meyer	M		[JJ], [Y]	
ROSSHAENDLER	Rosa		1898				F		[J]	
ROSSHAENDLER	Elias		1927		motors	Samuel	M		[JJ], [Y]	
ROSSHAENDLER	Irene		1932				F		[J]	
ROSSHAENDLER	Aron						M		[G]	
ROSSLER	Mechel			Glaser	glazier		M			deceased
ROTH	Shprincza	KALB		Glaser	glazier		F	Mechel		deceased
ROTH	Chaskel		1900	Glaser	glazier	Michal	M		[JJ], [Y]	
ROTH	Dora		1902			Michal	F		[JJ], [Y]	
ROTH	Mendel		1902			Michal	M		[Y]	
ROTH	Jta		1920			Michal	F		[JJ], [Y]	

Surname	Given name		Year			Mechel	Shprincza				
ROTH	Lea		1905						F		deceased
ROTH	Zierl		1898						F	[J]	
ROTH	Moses		1928						M	[J]	
ROTH	Guetl		1936						F	[J]	
ROTH	Jhuda		1896	Schäftemacher	upper shoe maker	Avraham			M	[J], [Y]	
ROTH	Shalom		1905			Avraham			M	[J], [Y]	
ROTH	Yehshua		1908			Avraham			M	[J], [Y]	
ROTH	Salomon		1917	Schneider	tailor	Avraham			M	[J], [Y], [G]	
ROTH	Sprinze		1881						F	[J]	
ROTH	Osias		1898	Weißbinder	house painter				M	[J]	
ROTH	Samuel		1933						M	[J]	
ROTH	Avraham			Rabbi	rabbi				M		deceased
ROTH	Lonka		1910						F	[J]	
ROTH	Malke		1905						F	[J]	
ROTH	Aron		1932						M	[J]	
ROTH	Eisig		1936						M	[J]	
ROTH	Schija			Maler	painter				M		Married 1937. Deceased
ROTH	Doba	KALB						Schija	F		Married 1937. Deceased
ROTH	Eisig		1931			Schija	Doba		M	[J]	
ROTH	Mechel		1940			Schija	Doba		M	[J]	
ROTH	Bluma		1882			Eisig			F	[Y]	

Krosno, Poland Yizkor Book

Surname	Given name		Occupation (DE)		Occupation (EN)	Year	Sex	Code	Status
ROTH	Debka						F	[L]	survived
ROTH	Dita	MARGOLIS					F	[L]	survived
ROTH	Berisz				vinegar		M	[B]	
ROTH	Hersz		Händler		trader		M	[R]	
ROTH	Sara					1911	F	[J]	
ROTHENBERG	Josef					1936	M	[J]	
ROTHENBERG	Guetl					1937	F	[J]	
ROTHENBERG	J		Schuhmacher		shoemaker		M	[R]	
ROTKE	Haim			Itzhak		1890	M	[Y]	
ROTT	Regina					1871	F	[J], [S]	
ROTTER	Georg		Arbeiter		worker	1901	M	[J], [S]	
ROTTER	Leib		Schneider		tailor	1882	M	[J], [S]	
ROTTER	Feige					1884	F	[J]	
ROTTER	Saul		Photograph		photographer	1919	M	[J]	
ROTTER	Isaak		Weißbinder		house painter	1923	M	[J]	
ROTTER	Zile					1894	F	[J], [S]	
ROTTERSMANN	Guetl		Verkäuferin		saleswoman	1916	F	[J]	
ROTTERSMANN	Anna					1922	F	[J]	
ROTTERSMANN	Ester		Verkäuferin		saleswoman	1925	F	[J]	
ROTTERSMANN	Suessl					1935	F	[J]	
ROTTERSMANN	Riwka						F	[R]	survived
ROWHELSER	Mina			Moshe		1895	F	[Y]	Auschwitz
ROZNER	F		Schneider		tailor		M	[R]	
ROZNER	Rivka						F	[L]	survived
RUBHEIZER	Oskar		Kaufmann		merchant	1905	M	[J]	

Krosno, Poland Yizkor Book

Surname	Given name	Year				Sex		
RUBIN	Golde	1941				F	[J]	
RUBIN	Mendel	1904	Kaufmann	merchant		M	[J]	
RUBIN	Frieda	1908				F	[J]	
RUBIN	Mechel	1930				M	[J]	
RUBIN	Naftali	1933				M	[J]	
RUBIN	Suessl	1936				F	[J]	
RUBIN	Chane	1890			Menashe	F	[Y]	
RUBIN	Chane	1939				F	[J]	
RUBIN	Jsaak	1915	Arbeiter	worker		M	[J]	
RUBIN	Elieazar	1895			Aron	M	[Y]	Treblinka
RUBIN	Rivka					F	[L]	
RUBIN	Shmuel					M	[L]	
RUBIN	Hersh					M		
RUBIN	Blueme	1895				F	[J], [S]	
RUBINFELD	Wolf	1929				M	[J]	
RUBINFELD	Abraham	1936				M	[J]	
RUBINFELD	Basche	1880				F	[J]	
RUBINFELD	Chajka					F	[G]	
RUBINFELD	Osias					M	[G]	
RUBINFELD	Avraham					M	[R]	
RUBINSTEIN	Chaje					F	[S]	
RUDNICKI	Osias	1898	Vertreter	sales representative		M	[J]	
RUEBENFELD	Chaje	1909	Schneiderin	tailoress		F	[J]	
RUEBENFELD	Alte	1892				M	[J], [S]	

Krosno, Poland Yizkor Book

Surname	Given name	Year	Occupation	Occupation	Name	Sex	Code	Status
RYBACH	Samuel					M	[R]	
SAFRON	Leie	1880				F	[J], [S], [G]	
SALOMON	M		Student	student		M	[R]	
SALOMON	Selde	1905				F	[J], [S]	
SALZ	Jochweth	1917	Schneiderin	tailoress		F	[J]	
SALZ	Mendel		Schuhmacher	shoemaker		M	[G]	
SALZ	J		Schneider	tailor		M	[R]	
SALZ	Jetti	1886	Schneiderin	tailoress		F	[J]	
SAMUEL	Leie	1910	Korsettnäherin	woman who makes corsets		F	[J]	
SAMUEL	Yenta					F	[P]	
SAMIT	Jeremias	1898	Arbeiter	worker		M	[J], [S]	
SAMIT	Yente							
SAND	Sala	1908				F	[J]	
SAND	Samuel	1931				M	[J]	
SAND	David	1933				M	[J]	
SAND	Chaim	1937				M	[J]	
SAND	Frimet	1920	Maniküristin	manicurist		F	[J]	
SANDOWSKI	Itzhak					M	[L]	survived
SCHACHAR	Yaacov					M	[L]	survived
SCHACHAR	David	1886	Arbeiter	worker		M	[J]	
SCHACHNER	Guetl	1880			Itzhak	F	[J], [Y]	
SCHACHNER	Helene	1918				F	[J]	
SCHACHNER	Moses	1936				M	[J]	

Krosno, Poland Yizkor Book

Surname	Given name	Year						Sex		
SCHACHNER	Salek	1910	Elektromonteur	electrician				M	[J]	
SCHACHNER	L.D							M	[G]	
SCHACHNER	Abraham	1877						M	[J]	
SCHALL	Leie	1885						F	[J]	
SCHALL	Ziwie	1920						F	[J]	
SCHALL	Moses	1904	Elektromonteur	electrician	Avraham			M	[J], [Y]	Mathausen
SCHAMROTH	Moshe									
SCHAMROTH	Chaje	1910					Moses	F	[J]	perished
SCHAMROTH	Jsaak	1934			Moses	Chaje		M	[J]	perished
SCHAMROTH	Rachel	1936			Moses	Chaje		F	[J]	perished
SCHAMROTH	Zelde	1886	Bauer	farmer				F	[J], [G]	
SCHAMROTH	Regine	1914						F	[J]	
SCHAMROTH	Lola	1906						F	[J]	
SCHAMROTH	Reuven	1910	Arbeiter	worker				M	[J], [L]	survived
SCHAMROTH	Wolf							M	[J]	
SCHAMROTH	Suessl							F	[J]	
SCHAMROTH	Marjem							F	[J]	
SCHAMROTH	Leie	1886						F	[J], [S]	
SCHAPIRO	Feiwel							M	[J]	
SCHARF	Rosa	1920						F	[J]	
SCHATTEN	Ester	1922						F	[J]	
SCHATTEN	Michael						Dawid	M	[Y]	Korczyna
SCHECHTER	Moses							M	[S]	
SCHEFFLER	Dora	1892			Raphael			F	[Y]	
SCHEFFLER	Salomon				Pinhas			M	[Y]	Stryj

Krosno, Poland Yizkor Book

SCHEFFLER	Adolph				M		[S]	
SCHEIBE	Mendel	1857			M		[J]	
SCHEINBACH	Osias	1896	Angestellter	employee	M		[J]	
SCHEINBACH	Regina	1897			F		[J]	
SCHEINBACH	Serl	1923	Kassiererin	cashier [female]	F		[J]	
SCHEINBACH	Chaim	1930			M		[J]	
SCHEINBACH	Elias	1898	Arbeiter	worker	M	Mendel	[J], [Y]	
SCHEINBACH	Chane	1901	Modistin	milliner	F		[J]	
SCHEINBACH	Josef	1931			M		[J]	
SCHEINBACH	Serl	1937			F		[J]	
SCHEINBACH	Mechel				M		[G]	
SCHEINBACH	Yaakow				M		[P]	
SCHEINBERG	Abraham	1910	Kutscher	coachman	M		[J], [G]	
SCHEINBERG	Yaacov							
SCHEINER	Rachel	1912			F		[J]	
SCHEINER	Naftali	1858			M		[J]	perished in Krosno
SCHEINER	B		Student	student	M		[R]	
SCHEINER	Ryfke	1875			F		[J], [S]	
SCHENKER	Dawid	1882			M	Yaacov	[Y]	
SCHENKER	Sara	1910			F	Dawid	[Y]	
SCHENKER	Mendel	1922			M	Dawid	[Y]	
SCHENKER	Jsaak	1905	Arbeiter	worker	M		[J], [S]	
SCHENKER	Ester Sara	1905			F		[J]	
SCHENKER	Moses	1937			M		[J]	

Surname	Given name		Year	Occupation		Father	Mother	Sex	Source	
SCHENKER	Rachel		1940					F	[J]	
SCHENKER	Mordechai H							M	[S]	
SCHENKER	Rosa		1854					F	[J]	
SCHENKER	Dawid							M	[G]	
SCHENKER	Wolf							M	[G]	
SCHENKER	Sabine		1912					F	[J]	
SHEINOWITZ	Malka		b.1910			Yossef Bendet	Chana	F	[P]	
SHEINOWITZ		AKSELRAD						M	[P]	
SCHERER	Leib		1870			Asher		M	[J], [Y], [G]	
SCHIFF	Ester		1872			Aron		F	[J], [Y]	
SCHIFF	Moses		1904	Arbeiter	worker			M	[J], [G]	
SCHIFF	Debora		1862					F	[J]	
SCHIFF	Itzhak					Leib		M	[Y]	
SCHIFF	Ita		1900			Itzhak		F	[S], [Y]	
SCHILDKREUT	Selig							M	[S], [G]	
SCHILDKREUT	Itzhak							M	[L]	survived
SCHILLER	Mendel							M	[L]	survived
SCHIRTS	Israel		1885	Arbeiter	worker			M	[J]	
SCHLAF	Anna		1890					F	[J]	
SCHLAF	Rosa		1920					F	[J]	
SCHLAF	Hella		1922					F	[J]	
SCHLAF	Leie		1928					F	[J]	
SCHLAF	Moses		1896	Kürschner	furrier			M	[J], [S]	

Krosno, Poland Yizkor Book

Surname	Given		Year	Occupation	Occupation	Father	Sex	Mother/Spouse	Code	Notes
SCHLANGER	Miriam Z									
SCHLANGER	Ryfke		1906				F		[J]	
SCHLANGER	Feige		1929				F		[J]	
SCHLANGER	Selde		1862				F		[J]	
SCHLANGER	Chaim			Kürschner	furrier		M		[S]	
SCHLANGER	Nathan						M		[L]	survived
SCHLANGER	Leib						M		[G]	
SCHLEIDENFELD	Feige		1908				F		[J]	
SCHLEIEN	Ryfke		1876				F		[J]	
SCHLEIEN	Marjem		1912	Schneiderin	tailoress		F		[J]	
SCHLEIEN	Alter						M		[G]	
SCHLEIEN	Malke						F		[S]	
SCHLEIEN	Wolf		1902	Schäftemacher	upper shoe maker		M		[J]	
SCHMALBERG	Fryda		1881			Shmuel	F		[Y]	Sieniewa
SCHMIDT	Nathan	KINDERMAN					M	Ides	[P]	Russia
SCHMUTZ	Ides						F	Nathan	[P]	Russia
SCHMUTZ	Yaakow					Nathan	M	Ides	[P]	Russia
SCHMUTZ	Itzik					Nathan	M	Ides	[P]	Russia
SCHMUTZ	Moshe						M		[P]	
SCHNEIBAUM	Golda						F	Moshe	[P]	
SCHNEIBAUM	Aisik					Moshe	M	Golda	[P]	
SCHNEIBAUM	Lucia					Moshe	F	Golda	[P]	
SCHNEIBAUM	Dworak					Moshe	F	Golda	[P]	
SCHNEIBAUM	Regina			Metallarbeiter	metalworker		F		[R]	
SCHNEIDER	Mechel		1900	Arbeiter	worker		M		[J]	

SCHOENBACH	Dora	1898			F	[J]	
SCHOENBACH	Leib	1931			M	[J]	
SCHOENBACH	Sime	1937			F	[J]	
SCHOENBACH	Jakob		builder	Baumeister	M	[R]	
SCHOENBERG	Salomon	1894			Pinhas	M	[Y]	Stryj
SCHOENBERG	Yaacow						
SCHONFELD	Sara	1898			Pinhas	F	[Y]	Auschwitz
SCHONFELD	Mose Hersh				M	[G]	
SCHONKER	Safran				M	[L]	
SCHPIGELMAN	Zelig Dr.				M	[L]	survived
SCHPILER	Leon				M	[L]	survived
SCHPRINGER	Zalman	1903			Mendel	M	[Y]	
SCHREIBER	Ite	1893			F	[J], [S]	
SCHREIER	Abraham	1919	worker	Arbeiter	M	[J]	
SCHREIER	Aron				M	[G]	
SCHREIER	Aharon	1920			Jacob	M	[Y]	
SCHRENZE	Dawid	1922			Jacob	M	[Y]	Russia
SCHRENZE	Faiga	1893			Aharon	F	[Y]	
SCHRENZE	Abraham				M	[P]	
SCHTROIBRINEM	Leib	1903	employee	Angestellter	M	[J]	
SCHULDENFREI	Taube	1902			F	[J]	
SCHULDENFREI	Dora	1932			F	[J]	
SCHULDENFREI	Hirsch	1933			M	[J]	
SCHULDENFREI	Ignacy		doctor	Arzt	M	[R]	
SCHWARTZBART	Alter	1887	merchant	Kaufmann	M	[J]	

Krosno, Poland Yizkor Book

Surname	Given name		Birth	Occupation	Occupation	Name	Sex	Ref	Fate
SCHWEBEL	Anna		1889				F	[J]	
SCHWEBEL	Regina (Rivka)		1922			Alter	F	[J], [Y]	Belzec
SCHWEBEL	Mendel		1923	Arbeiter	worker		M	[J]	survived
SCHWEBEL	Brandel		1926				F	[J]	
SCHWEBEL	Chaje		1929				F	[J]	
SCHWEBEL	Markus		1876				M	[J], [S]	
SEEMANN	Guetl		1875				F	[J]	
SEEMANN	Elimelech						M	[R]	
SEGAL	K			Student	student		M	[R]	
SEGAL	S			Friseur	barber		M	[R]	
SEIDEN	Abraham		1882	Arbeiter	worker		M	[J]	
SEIDENFELD	Rachel		1878		textiles		F	[J]	
SEIDENFELD	Akter Dawid						M	[B]	
SEIFMAN	Naphtali		1908			Michael	M	[Y]	
SEKEL				Leiter einer Jeschiwa	head of yeshiva		M	[P]	
SELIGMAN	Yair	BEIM					M	[L]	survived
SHAVIT	Aaron		1898			Alexander	M	[Y]	
SHERTS	M			Student	student		M	[R]	
SHERZ	Sender						M	[P]	
SHOSS	Shia						M	[P]	
SHOSS	Sender						M		
SOBOL	Miriam						F	[P]	
SOBOL	Shia								
SHPINDLER	Chana							[P]	

Surname	Given Name	Birth Year	Occupation		Father	Sex	Code	Notes
SHTIMMER	Sabine	1903			Moshe	F	[J], [Y]	
SHTIMMER	Miriam Z	1933				F	[J]	
SHTRYCK	Leie	1898	Kaufmann	merchant	Leib	M	[J], [Y]	
SHTRYCK	Wolf	1930			Wolf	M		
SHTRYCK	Leo	1935			Wolf	F	[J]	
SHTRYCK	Guetl	1911	Arbeiter	worker		M	[J]	
SHTRYCK	Majer	1910				F	[J]	
SHTRYCK	Jente	1937				F	[J]	
SHTRYCK	Ester	1885	Kaufmann	merchant		M	[J]	
SHTRYCK	Moses	1888				F	[J]	
SHTRYCK	Anna	1911	Arbeiter	worker		M	[J]	
SHTRYCK	Chaim	1912	Arbeiter	worker		M	[J]	
SHTRYCK	Jsrael	1927				F	[J]	Handwritten notation near the name reads "Roza"
SHTRYCK	Basche	1894	Hausmeister	caretaker		M	[P]	
SHTRYCK	Yaakow					M	[J], [S], [G]	
SHUB	Osias							
SHUB	Osias							
SWATCH	Nute							
SHWEIBEL		1897				F	[J]	
SILBERBERG	Ester	1923	Schneiderin	tailoress		F	[J]	
SILBERBERG	Chane	1925	Arbeiterin	worker		F	[J]	
SILBERBERG	Jochweth							

Krosno, Poland Yizkor Book

SILBERBERG	Anna	1927		[female]		F	[J]
SILBERBERG	Chaim Jakob	1928				M	[J]
SILBERBERG	Dora	1930				F	[J]
SILBERBERG	Feige	1932				F	[J]
SILBERBERG	Moses	1934				M	[J]
SILBERBERG	Perl	1937				F	[J]
SILBERBERG	Chane	1888				F	[J], [S]
SILBERBERG	Chaim	1920	Angestellter	employee		M	[J]
SILBERBERG	Chaje	1925				F	[J]
SILBERBERG	Mendel					M	[S]
SILBERBERG	J		Maler	painter		M	[R]
SILBERBERG	Regina	1901				F	[J]
SILBERMAN	Max	1900				M	[P]	died 1938
SILBERMANN	Abraham	1935				M	[J]
SILBERMANN	Berl	1938				M	[J]
SILBERMANN	Devorah				Itzhak	F	[J], [Y]
SILBERMANN	Dnah				Moshe	F	[Y]
SIMON	Khia				Moshe	F	[Y]
SIMON	Rachel				Moshe	F	[Y]
SIMON	Fradel	1880				F	[J]
SINGER	Leon		Butterhändler	butter merchant		M	[B]
SIODMAK	Isaak					M	[S]
SITZER	Leo	1915				M	[P]

Surname	Given		Year	Occupation (Ger.)	Occupation (Eng.)		Sex		Code
SLOTA	Ete		1915				F		[P]
SLOTA	Mira		1938				F		[P]
SLOTA	Jana		1940				F		[P]
SLOTA	Ester		1890				F		[J], [S]
SMORODINA	Chaje		1924				F		[J]
SMORODINA	Abraham		1929				M		[J]
SMORODINA	Osias		1885	Arbeiter	worker		M		[J]
SOBEL	Feige		1887				F		[J]
SOBEL	Ester		1920				F		[J]
SOBEL	Fradel		1927				F		[J]
SOBEL	Haja		1920			Hersh	F		[Y]
SOLOMON	Siegmund		1899	Kürschner	furrier		M		[J]
SONNENSCHEIN	Simche		1885	Arbeiter	worker		M		[J], [S]
SPANNDORF	Suessl		1887				M		[J]
SPANNDORF	M			Student	student		M		[R]
SPAT	Salomon			Wirt	innkeeper		M		[B]
SPATT	Dora		1915				F		[J]
SPERBER	J.H.			Besenmacher	brooms maker		M		[R]
SPERBER	Ida					Salomon	F		[R]
SPETT	Josef		1900	Angestellter	employee		M		[J]
SPIEGEL	Sara		1899				F		[J]
SPIEGEL	Leie		1917				F		[J]
SPIEGELMANN	Dawid			Gießer	founder		M		[G]
SPIEGELMANN	Moses					USA	M		[P]

Krosno, Poland Yizkor Book

Surname	First name	Year	Occupation	Occupation	Father	Sex	Source	Notes
SPINDLER	Samuel	1904			Itzhak	M	[Y]	
SPINDLER	Chana					M	[P]	
SPINDLER	Genia	1896				F	[Y]	
SPIRA	Guetl	1878				F	[J], [G]	
SPITZ	Schaje	1916				M	[J]	
SPITZ	Srulik					M	[L]	survived
SPITZ	Naftali	1897	Arbeiter	worker		M	[J], [G]	
SPRECHER	Chaje	1900				F	[J]	
SPRECHER	Regina	1934				F	[J]	
SPRECHER	Sala	1912	Hausmädchen	housemaid		F	[J]	
SPRECHER	Gerson	1910	Tapezierer	paperhanger		M	[J]	
SPRECHER	Mojzesz		Blechbläser	brass		M	[R]	
SPRINGER	Rudolfine	1897				M	[J]	
SPRINGER	Sarah	1904			Moshe	F	[J], [Y]	
SPRINGER	Azriel	1909			Moshe	M	[J], [Y]	
SPRINGER	Jsaak	1893	Mechaniker	mechanic	Moshe	M	[J], [Y]	
SPRINGER	Majer	1920	Arbeiter	worker	Ignatz	M	[J], [Y]	
SPRINGER	Leib	1880			Mayer	M	[Y], [R]	
SPRINGER	Heinrich	1922	Autoschlosser	panel beater	Ignatz	M	[J], [Y]	
SPRINGER	Eugenie	1924			Ignatz	F	[J], [Y]	
SPRINGER	Nussek	1925			Ignatz	M	[J], [Y]	
SPRINGER	Erwin	1927	Arbeiter	worker		M	[J]	
SPRINGER	Regine	1872			Tzvi	F	[J], [Y]	
SPRINGER	Ester	1914	Verkäuferin	saleswoman		F	[J]	
SPRINGER	Eugenie	1913	Schneiderin	tailoress		F	[J]	

Surname	Given	Town	Year	Occupation	Occupation	Father	Mother	Sex	Code	Fate
SPRINGER	Dawid			Blechbläser	brass			M	[R]	survived
SPRINGER	I			Glaser	glazier			M	[R]	
SPRINGER	Josef							M	[S]	
SPRITZER	Fania		1886			Hersh		F	[Y]	Belzec
SPRUNG	Mindel		1884					F	[J], [G]	
SROKA	Aron		1906	Schneider	tailor			M	[J]	
SROKA	Anna		1912	Schneiderin	tailoress			F	[J]	
SROKA	Jonas		1919	Friseur	barber			M	[J]	
SROKA	Marjem		1923	Schneiderin	tailoress			F	[J]	
SROKA	Beile		1926					F	[J]	
SROKA	Moses		1892	Arbeiter	worker			M	[J]	
SROKA	Chaim	DUKLA	1898	Schneider	tailor	Tzvi		M	[J], [Y]	Belzec
STADTFELD	Chume		1891	Schneider	tailor			M	[J]	
STADTFELD	Taube		1893			Chaim		F	[J], [Y]	Belzec
STADTFELD	Dine		1891					F	[J]	
STANDTFELD	Hirsch		1925	Schneider	tailor			M	[J]	
STANDTFELD	Chaje		1924					F	[J]	
STANDTFELD	Abraham		1930					M	[J]	
STANDTFELD	Berl		1933					M	[J]	
STANDTFELD	Yossef							M	[L]	survived
STAWY	Chaim		1885	Arbeiter	worker			M	[J]	perished
STEIGBUEGEL	Leie		1889			Chaim		F	[J]	perished
STEIGBUEGEL	Eugen		1925	Arbeiter	worker	Chaim	Leie	M	[J]	survived
STEIGBUEGEL	S							M	[P]	
STEIGBUEGEL	Idek							M	[R]	

Krosno, Poland Yizkor Book

STEIGBUEGEL	Dolek			student		M	[R]	
STEIGBUEGEL	Geniek					M	[P]	
STEIGBUEGEL	Dolek					M	[P]	
STEIGBIELD	Chaskel	1899	Kürschner	furrier		M	[J]	
STEIN	Sara	1901				F	[J]	
STEIN	Meilech	1926	Arbeiter	worker		M	[J]	
STEIN	Feige	1929				F	[J]	
STEIN	Beile	1931				F	[J]	
STEIN	Marjem	1934				F	[J]	
STEIN	Simon	1936				M	[J]	
STEIN	F		Student	student		F	[R]	
STEIN	Freide	1894				F	[J]	
STEINBERG	Salek	1923	Arbeiter	worker		M	[J]	
STEINBERG	David	1924	Arbeiter	worker		M	[J]	
STEINBERG	Bendet					M	[S]	
STEINBERG	M		Student	student		M	[R]	
STEINBROCHER	D		Student	student		M	[R]	
STEINBUCHER	A		Schneider	tailor		M	[R]	
STEINER	Cudik	1911	Schlosser	locksmith		M	[J], [G]	survived
STEINER	Cesia	1915			Zudik	F	[J]	survived
STEINER	Pauline	TEITELBAUM			Zudik		[P]	Second husband, survived
STEINER	Elana				Israel	F	[Y]	
STEINER	Pinkas	1904	Arbeiter	worker		M	[J]	
STEINHORN	Ryfke	1912				F	[J]	

Surname	Given		Year			Father	Mother	Sex		Code	Status
STEINHORN	Moses		1936					M		[J]	
STEINHORN	Baruch		1874					M		[J]	
STEINHORN	Ryfke		1917					F		[J]	
STEINHORN	Sara		1923					F		[J]	
STEINHORN	Hirsch		1882	Arbeiter	worker			M		[J]	
STEINMETZ	Minna		1888					F		[J], [G]	
STEINMETZ	Malke		1920	Friseuse	coiffeuse			F		[J]	
STEINMETZ	Markus		1928					M		[J]	
STEINMETZ	S			Uhrmacher	watchmaker			M		[R]	
STEINMETZ	Chaje		1909					F		[J], [S]	
STERN	Simon		1877	Schlosser	locksmith			M		[J], [G]	
STERN	Chaje							F	Simon	[P]	perished
STERN	Majer		1909			Simon	Mrs	M		[J]	died 1925
STERN	Chaje		1906			Simon	Chaje	F	Majer	[P]	survived
STERN	Chaim		1936			Majer	Chaje				perished
STERN	Chane		1912	Schneiderin	tailoress	Simon	Chaje	F	Simon	[J]	survived
STERN	Ziwie	CESSIA	1915			Simon	Chaje	F	Zudik	[P]	survived
STERN	Eva		1881					F		[J]	
STERN	Anselm		1896			Baruch		M		[Y]	Lemberg
STERN	Naphtali		1902			Baruch		M		[Y]	
STERN	Raisel		1875			Alexander		F		[Y]	
STERN	Esther	BOBKER						F		[L]	survived
STERN	Dawid							M		[G]	
STERN	Moses							M		[G]	
STERN	Oskar							M		[S]	

Surname	Given		Year					Sex		Code	Place
STERNLICHT	Gusta		1877					F		[J]	
STIEBER	Joachim		1894	Arbeiter	worker	Moshe		M		[J], [Y], [G]	
STIEFEL	Charlotte		1894					F		[J]	
STIEFEL	Marcin		1923	Schlosserlehrling	locksmith apprentice			M		[J]	
STIEFEL	Moses		1925	Arbeiter	worker			M		[J]	
STIEFEL	Josef		1928					M		[J]	
STIEFEL	Rosa							F		[S]	
STIEFEL	Izak					Yonah		M		[Y], [R]	
STIEFEL	Henryk					Yonah		M		[Y]	
STIEFEL	Shmuel							M		[P], [R]	
STIEFEL	Dorothea	GITTER					Shmuel	F		[P]	
STIEFEL	Helena					Shmuel	Dorothea	F		[P]	
STIEFEL	Alicia					Shmuel	Dorothea	F		[P]	
STIEFEL	Stefan					Shmuel	Dorothea	M		[P]	
STIEFEL	K			Student	student			M		[R]	
STIEFEL	U			Student	student			M		[R]	
STIEFEL	Szymon							M		[R]	
STILMAN	P			Student	student			F		[R]	
STILMAN	Chaim		1895			Tzvi		M		[Y]	Belzec
STORCH	Szymon		1893			Tzvi		M		[Y]	Katyn, Russia
STORCH	Salomon			Fleischer	butcher			M		[R]	
STORCH	Nuchim		1889	Schneider	tailor			M		[J], [S], [G]	
STRASSFELD	Scheindel		1922					F		[J]	

Surname	Given name	Occupation (Ger.)	Occupation (Eng.)	Name	Year	Sex	Code	Notes
STRASSFELD	Regine				1923	F	[J]	
STRASSFELD	Jente				1926	F	[J]	
STRASSFELD	Berisch				1928	M	[J]	
STRASSFELD	Mendel					M	[R]	
STROH	Anna				1876	F	[J], [S]	
STROH	Beile			Alter	1876	F	[J], [Y]	Rzeszow
STROHBING	Abraham	Arbeiter	worker		1906	M	[J]	
STRUMER	Meilech	Arbeiter	worker		1907	F	[J], [S]	
STUHL	Salomon				1941	M	[J]	
STUHL	Ester				1914	F	[J]	
SUESSHOLZ	Rosa				1918	F	[J]	
SUESSHOLZ	Mendel					M	[R]	survived
SZERF	Riwka			Yossef	1920	F	[Y]	
SZPEICHER	Fryda			Mayer	1880	F	[Y]	
SZPRINGER	Jakow			Matityahu	1909	M	[Y]	
SZPRINGER	Jehuda			Leopold	1910	M	[Y]	
SZTAIBEL	Ita			Michael	1913	F	[Y]	
SZTAIBEL	Shaindel			Chaim	1889	F	[Y]	
SZTRINGER	Ch	Klempner	plumber			M	[R]	
SZYJA	J	Bäcker	baker			M	[R]	
SZYJA	Samuel	Fleischer	butcher		1912	M	[J]	
SZYJOWICZ	Scheindel				1913	F	[J]	
SZYJOWICZ	Blueme				1940	F	[J]	
SZYJOWICZ	Isaak	Arbeiter	worker		1889	M	[J]	
TABACZNIK	Ryfke				1888	F	[J]	

454

Krosno, Poland Yizkor Book

Surname	Name	Year	Occupation (German)	Occupation	First name	Sex	Source	Fate
TABACZNIK	Ides	1922	Schneiderin	tailoress		F	[J]	
TABACZNIK	Sara	1923	Schneiderin	tailoress		F	[J]	
TABACZNIK	Hirsh	1876			Shmuel	M	[Y]	
TABISEL	Szeindel	1885			Wolf	F	[Y]	
TABISEL	Avraham					M	[L]	survived
TABISEL	Meir					M	[L]	survived
TABISEL	Dawid		Klempner	plumber		M	[R]	
TABISEL	Salomon	1872				M	[J], [G]	
TANZ	Scheindel	1878				F	[J]	
TANZ	Brandel	1906				F	[J]	
TANZ	Golde	1908				F	[J]	
TANZ	Ester	1914	Schneiderin	tailoress		F	[J]	
TANZ	Debora	1916	Schneiderin	tailoress		F	[J]	
TANZ	Ryfke	1920	Schneiderin	tailoress		F	[J]	
TANZ	Moses	1882	Kaufmann	merchant		M	[J]	
TAUBENFELD	Moshe							
TAUBENFELD	Mania	1921				F	[J]	
TAUBENFELD	Wolf	1908	Arbeiter	worker	Mozes	M	[J], [Y]	Belzec
TAUBENFELD	Josef	1917	Arbeiter	worker	Mozes	M	[J], [Y]	Belzec
TAUBENFELD	David	1919	Arbeiter	worker	Mozes	M	[J], [Y]	
TAUBENFELD	Zisha					M	[G]	
TAUBENFELD	Sala	1904			Tzvi	F	[Y]	Warsaw
TEICHER	Mirjam	1902				F	[J]	
TEICHER	Chaje	1876			Asher	F	[J], [Y]	
TEITELBAUM	Mechel	1904	Hausmeister	caretaker	Chaim	M	[J], [Y]	

TEITELBAUM	Ete	1900			F	[J]
TEITELBAUM	Mirjam	1927			F	[J]
TEITELBAUM	Basche	1930			F	[J]
TEITELBAUM	Chane	1931			F	[J]
TEITELBAUM	Benjamin	1933			M	[J]
TEITELBAUM	Osias	1917	Arbeiter	worker	M	[J]
TEITELBAUM	Debora	1914			F	[J]
TEITELBAUM	Ester	1937			F	[J]
TEITELBAUM	Moses	1901	Angestellter	employee	M	[J], [G]
TEITELBAUM	Liebe	1902			M	[J]
TEITELBAUM	Hirsch	1931			M	[J]
TEITELBAUM	Sara	1933			F	[J]
TEITELBAUM	Samuel	1910	Arbeiter	worker	M	[J]
TEITELBAUM	Abraham	1891	Arbeiter	worker	M	[J]
TEITELBAUM	Berta	1901			F	[J]
TEITELBAUM	Minna	1926			F	[J]
TEITELBAUM	Moses	1932			M	[J]
TEITELBAUM	Josef	1936			M	[J]
TEITELBAUM	Josua	1895	Arbeiter	worker	M	[J]
TEITELBAUM	Feige	1906		Melech	F	[J], [Y]
TEITELBAUM	Freide	1934			F	[J]
TEITELBAUM	Mechel	1938			M	[J]
TEITELBAUM	Simon				M	[S]
TEITELBAUM	Jsaak	1932			M	[J]
TEITELBAUM	Jakob	1882	Angestellter	employee	M	[J], [G]

Krosno, Poland Yizkor Book

TENENBAUM	David					M		[P]	survived
TEPLICKI	Liebe	1883				M		[J]	
TEPLICKI	Anna	1913				F		[J]	
TEPLICKI	Helene	1923				F		[J]	
TEPLICKI	Esther	1911			Jakow	F		[J], [Y]	
TEPLICKI	Avraham					M		[L]	survived
TEPLICKI	Cesia					F		[L]	survived
TEPLICKI	Lewi					M		[R]	survived
TEPLICKI	Mathilde	1900			Leib	F		[JJ], [Y]	
TEPPER	Feige	1924			Aron	F		[JJ], [Y]	
TEPPER	Eidel	1889				F		[J]	
TEPPER	Hinde	1916	Schneiderin	tailoress		F		[J]	
TEPPER	Scheindel	1921				F		[J]	
TEPPER	J		Uhrmacher	watchmaker		M		[R]	
TEPPER	Mshe	1884			Aron	M		[Y]	
TERSKI	Feige	1889				F		[J]	
TESTYLIER	Emma	1920	Schneiderin	tailoress		F		[J]	
TESTYLIER	Mordechai					M		[P]	
THALER	Mordechai								
THALER	Sala	1929				F		[J]	
THALER	Bruche	1905				M		[JJ], [S]	
THALER	Markus	1887	Angestellter	employee	Pinhas	M		[JJ], [Y]	Belzec
THALER	Hene	1880				F	Markus	[J]	perished
THALER	Scheindel	1913			Markus	F	Hene	[JJ], [Y]	Belzec
THALER	Pinkas	1921	Arbeiter	worker	Markus	M	Hene	[JJ], [L]	survived

Krosno, Poland Yizkor Book

THALER	David	1909	Bäcker	baker	Itzhak		M	[J], [Y]
THALER	Golde	1911					F	[J]
THALER	Emanuel	1939					M	[J]
THALER	Hawa					survived	F	[L]
THALER	Jakob	1904	Kutscher	coachman			M	[J]
TISCHLER	Reisel	1905					F	[J]
TISCHLER	Rachel	1932					F	[J]
TISCHLER	Anna	1933					F	[J]
TISCHLER	Sala	1934					F	[J]
TISCHLER	Chiel	1935					M	[J]
TISCHLER	Josef	1872					M	[J]
TISCHLER	Chaje	1875					F	[J]
TISCHLER	Berel	1905	Weber	weaver	Josef		M	[J], [Y]
TISCHLER	Zipora	1910			Dawid		F	[J], [Y]
TISCHLER	David	1936			Bernard		M	[J], [Y]
TISCHLER	Genia					survived	F	[L]
TITOV	D		Bäcker	baker			M	[R]
TRALEZ	Markus	1894	Kaufmann	merchant			M	[J]
TRATTNER	Rosa	1891					F	[J], [G]
TRATTNER	Abraham	1924	Arbeiter	worker			M	[J]
TRATTNER	Moses	1925	Arbeiter	worker			M	[J]
TRATTNER	Ester	1932					F	[J]
TRATTNER	Efraim	1855					M	[J]
TRATTNER	Freide	1905					F	[J], [S], [G]

Krosno, Poland Yizkor Book

TRATTNER	Getzel				M	[P]	
TRAUBER	Mania				M	[P]	
TRAUBER	Samuel	1859	Fleischer	butcher	M	[J], [G], [R]	
TRENCZER	Anna	1872			F	[J], [Y]	Belzec
TRENCZER	Gene	1905		Yossef	F	[J], [Y]	Belzec
TRENCZER	Leiser	1887	Arbeiter	Zelig	M	[J]	
TRENCZER	Helena			worker	F	[P]	survived
TRENCZER	Josef	1917	Angestellter	employee	M	[J]	
TRENCZER	Osias	1913	Angestellter	employee	M	[J]	
TRENCZER	Bianka	1914			F	[J]	
TRENCZER	Chaje	1890			F	[J]	
TRENCZER	Chawe	1883			F	[J]	
TRENCZER	Schifre	1914			F	[J]	
TRENCZER	Getzel	1886	Fleischer	butcher	M	[J], [S], [Y]	Belzec
TRENCZER	Feige	1858		Mannis	F	[J]	
TRENCZER	Mathilde	1887		Leib	F	[J], [Y]	Belzec
TRENCZER	Anna	1911		Getzel	F	[J], [Y]	Belzec
TRENCZER	Moshe	1908		Getzel	M	[Y]	Antwerpen
TRENCZER	Itel	1914	Schneiderin	tailoress	F	[J]	
TRENCZER	Erna	1923	Verkäuferin	saleswoman	F	[J]	
TRENCZER	Ignaz	1926	Arbeiter	worker	M	[J]	
TRENCZER	Chawe	1882	Schneiderin	tailoress	F	[J]	
TRENCZER	Rosa	1916	Schneiderin	tailoress	F	[J]	
TRENCZER	Matel	1909	Arbeiterin	worker	F	[J]	

			[female]				
TRENCZER	Fischel	1901	Arbeiter	worker		M	[J], [G]
TRENCZER	Ete	1911			Getzel	F	[J], [Y]	Belzec
TRENCZER	Salomon	1935				M	[J]
TRENCZER	Jsrael	1906	Fleischer	butcher		M	[J]
TRENCZER	Freide	1912				F	[J]
TRENCZER	Charna					F	[G]
TRENCZER	Dwora					F	[L]	survived
TRENCZER	Markus					M	[L]	survived
TRENCZER	Moshe					M	[L]	survived
TRENCZER	Yeshayahu	1897				M	[L], [R]	survived
TRENCZER	Tonka	1901				M	[P]	survived
TRENCZER	Ester	1880				F	[J], [S]
TUERK	Markus	1923	Arbeiter	worker		M	[J]
TUERK	Leie	1925				F	[J]
TUERK	Beile	1888				F	[J], [S]
TUREK	Zipora	1917	Schneiderin	tailoress		F	[J]
TUREK	Joel	1918	Arbeiter	worker		M	[J]
TUREK	Frimet	1919	Schneiderin	tailoress		F	[J]
TUREK	Suesskind	1921	Schneider	tailor		F	[J]
TUREK	Malke	1923	Schneiderin	tailoress		F	[J]
TUREK	Moses	1925	Arbeiter	worker		M	[J]
TUREK	O.		Schneider	tailor		M	[R]
TUREK	Israel					M	[G]
TURK	Aron		Rabbi	rabbi		M	[P]	deceased

Krosno, Poland Yizkor Book

Surname	Given	Year	Occupation (German)	Occupation	Name 1	Name 2	Sex	Name 3	Code	Fate
TWERSKI	Rosa						F	Aron	[P]	perished
TWERSKI	Moshe	1892	Rabbi	Rabbi	Aron	Rosa	M	Moshe	[P]	perished
TWERSKI	Freida				Simcha		F		[Y]	Belzec
TWERSKI	Tzivia	1894			Moshe	Freida	F		[P]	Auschwitz
TWERSKI	Sima				Aron	Rosa	F		[Y]	survived
TWERSKI	Naphtali						M		[L]	
TZIPORI	Taube	1876					F		[P]	
UBERFUHRER	Neche	1913	Näherin	seamstress			F		[J]	
UNGER	Moses	1939					M		[J]	
UNGER	Chawe	1900					F		[J], [S]	
UNGER	Salomon						M		[S]	
UNGER	Malka						F		[L]	survived
UNGER	Leib						M		[L]	survived
UNGER	Schije	1895	Konditor	confectioner			M		[J]	
UNIKOWSKI	David						M		[L]	survived
URLBAUM	Yehoshua						M		[L]	survived
URLBAUM	Joseph Leib	1915							[R]	shot
URTEM	Josef	1893	Arbeiter	worker			M		[J], [S]	
VERSTAENDIG	Beile	1907					F		[J]	
VERSTAENDIG	Mechel	1932					M		[J]	
VERSTAENDIG	David	1929					M		[J]	
VERSTAENDIG	Malke	1935					F		[J]	
VERSTAENDIG	Frimet	1924	Schneiderin	tailoress			F		[J]	
VOGEL	Feige	1924	Modistin	milliner			F		[J]	
VOGEL	Josef	1927	Schneider	tailor			M		[J], [S]	

Krosno, Poland Yizkor Book

Surname	Given name	Year	Occupation		Name	Sex	Name	Notes	Code
VOGEL	Mechel	1928				M			[J]
VOGEL	Samuel		products			M			[R]
VOGEL	Jsaak	1882	Arbeiter	worker		M			[J], [S]
VOGELFLUEGEL	Regina	1905			Leon	F		Dabrowa	[J], [Y]
VOGELHUT	Adolf	1929				M			[J]
VOGELHUT	Jakow				Israel	M			[Y]
VOGELHUT	Sara	1887				F			[J]
WAGSCHAL	Chane	1914				F			[J]
WAGSCHAL	Samuel	1918	Schäftemacher	upper shoe maker		M			[J]
WAGSCHAL	Ete	1921				F			[J]
WAGSCHAL	Guetl	1925				F			[J]
WAGSCHAL	Israel	1927	Arbeiter	worker		M			[J]
WAGSCHAL	Gene	1923				F			[J]
WAGSCHAL	Debora					F			[G]
WAKS	Yehiel Melech					M			[P]
WALLACE	Hannah					F	Yehiel Melech		[P]
WALLACE	Shyfra	1912			Sender	F		survived	[Y]
WALD	Miriam					F			[L]
WALD	Sali	1925				F			[J]
WALDNER	Therese	1916				F			[J]
WALDNER	Feige	1890				F			[J], [S]
WALDNER	Aron					M		survived	[L]
WALLACH	wife					F	Aron	survived	[P]

Krosno, Poland Yizkor Book

WALLACH	Lucia					Aron	F		[P]	survived
WALLACH	Yehuda					Aron	M		[P]	survived
WALLACH	David						M		[J]	
WALLER	D						M		[L]	survived
WALTER	Tzwi		1880				M		[P]	
WALTER	Moses		1880				M		[J]	
WANDER	Anna		1922				F		[J]	
WANDER				Zahnarzt	dentist		M		[R]	
WANDSTEIN	Zelig						M		[P]	
WARFEL	Mendel						M		[P]	
WARSCHER	Sheindel Sa.	FUSSMAN					F	Mendel	[P]	
WARSCHER	Joseph		1911			Mendel	M		[P]	
WARSCHER	Hersh					Sheindel Sa.	M		[P]	
WASSERSTRUM	Rosa		1920		clothing		F		[J]	
WDOWINSKI	Josef						M		[G]	
WEBER	Jda		1893				F		[J], [S]	
WEHRMANN	Berl		1913	Arbeiter	worker		M		[J]	
WEHRMANN	Richard		1921	Arbeiter	worker		M		[J]	
WEHRMANN	Zile		1921				F		[J]	
WEHRMANN	Moses		1938				M		[J]	
WEHRMANN	Itzik						M		[YI]	Krosno
WEINBERG							F	Itzik	[YI]	Krosno
WEINBERG	Mendel		1904	Arbeiter	worker		M		[YI]	Krosno
WEINBERG	Sime		1921				F		[YI]	Krosno
WEINBERG	Nissan						M		[YI]	Krosno

Surname	Given name		Year	Occupation	Occupation	Father	Mother	Sex	Spouse	Code	Fate
WEINBERG	Chaje							F		[J]	
WEINBERGER	Saul		1885		restaurant			M		[J], [G]	
WEINBERGER	Sara		1882					F	Saul	[J]	
WEINBERGER	Nathan		1917		motors			M		[J]	
WEINBERGER	Schmerl		1908		motors			M		[J]	
WEINBERGER	Taube		1900					F		[J]	
WEINBERGER	Chane		1934					F		[J]	
WEINBERGER	Samuel		1936					M		[J], [S]	
WEINBERGER	Meschulim		1877	Angestellter	employee	Leib		M	Margola	[J], [Y]	Rzeszow
WEINBERGER	Margola	KINDERMAN					Meschulim	F	Meschulim	[P]	perished
WEINBERGER	Isaak					Meschulim	Margola			[P]	perished
WEINBERGER	Naphtali		1914			Meschulim	Margola	M		[Y]	Rzeszow
WEINBERGER	Emanuel					Meschulim	Margola			[P]	perished
WEINBERGER	Ruzia					Meschulim	Margola			[P]	perished
WEINBERGER	Minna		1888					F		[J]	
WEINBERGER	Chaskel		1898	Arbeiter	worker			M		[J]	
WEINBERGER	Chane		1900					F		[J]	
WEINBERGER	Chaje		1934					F		[J]	
WEINBERGER	Jsaak		1879					M		[J]	
WEINBERGER	Sime		1920					F		[J]	
WEINBERGER	Ephraim							M		[L]	survived
WEINBERGER	Shmuel							M		[P]	
WEINFELD	Suessl		1889					F		[J], [S]	
WEINFELD	David		1923	Tapezierer	paperhanger			M		[J]	
WEINFELD	Naftali		1924	Tapezierer	paperhanger			M		[J]	

Krosno, Poland Yizkor Book

WEINFELD	Chane		1926			F	[J]
WEINFELD	Jsaak		1888	Angestellter	employee	M	[J]
WEINFELD	Rachel		1894			F	[J]
WEINFELD	Jsrael		1914	Weber	weaver	M	[J]
WEINFELD	Hadassa		1916	Modistin	milliner	F	[J]
WEINFELD	Salek		1918	Monteur	fitter	M	[J]
WEINFELD	Ascher		1897	Kaufmann	merchant	Shmuel	M	[J], [Y], [G]
WEINFELD	Rachela		1897			F	[J]
WEINFELD	Hirsch		1917	Arbeiter	worker	M	[J]
WEINFELD	Naftali		1930			M	[J]
WEINFELD	Reisel		1931			F	[J]
WEINFELD	Markus					M	[G]
WEINFELD	Mordechai					M	[S]
WEINGOLD	Rachel	KANNER				F	[L] survived
WEINKRANTZ	Hannah	TAUBENFELD				F	[L] survived
WEINMAN	Ziril		1870		Aron	F	[Y]
WEINREB	Hersh			Eisenhändler	ironmonger	M	[B]
WEINREB	Wolf		1896	Geschäftsmann	merchant	M	[J]
WEINSTEIN	Margule		1894			F	[J]
WEINSTEIN	Suessl		1926			F	[J]
WEINSTEIN	Gene		1928			F	[J]
WEINSTEIN	Jonas		1931			M	[J]
WEINSTEIN	Jsrael		1902	Kutscher	coachman	M	[J]
WEINSTEIN	Malke		1908			F	[J], [G]
WEINSTEIN	Scharne		1938			F	[J]

Surname	Given name		Year					Sex		Status
WEINSTEIN	Chane		1940					F	[J]	
WEINSTEIN	Pinkas		1908	Arbeiter	worker			M	[J]	
WEINSTEIN	Leib		1907	Arbeiter	worker			M	[J]	
WEINSTEIN	Hene		1873					F	[J]	
WEINSTEIN	Zile		1907					F	[J]	
WEINSTEIN	Salomon		1906	Arbeiter	worker			M	[J]	
WEINSTEIN	Shymon			Arbeiter	worker			M	[P]	
WEINSTEIN	Reisel	PASTERNAK	1892					F	[J]	
WEINSTEIN	Gershon		1919			Shymon	Reisel	M	[R]	survived
WEINSTEIN	Zvi		1920			Shymon	Reisel	M	[P]	perished
WEINSTEIN	Samuel		1924	Arbeiter	worker	Shymon	Reisel	M	[J]	perished
WEINSTEIN	Josef		1934			Shymon	Reisel	M	[P]	perished
WEINSTEIN	Pinkas		1935			Shymon	Reisel	M	[J]	perished
WEINSTEIN	Hirsch		1924	Arbeiter	worker			M	[J]	
WEINSTEIN	Jsaak		1928					M	[J], [L]	survived
WEINSTEIN	Chemje		1900	Kutscher	coachman			M	[J]	
WEINSTEIN	Beile		1902					F	[J]	
WEINSTEIN	Chaim		1935					M	[J]	
WEINSTEIN	Samuel			Mehlhändler	flour trader			M	[B]	
WEINSTEIN	Jechezkel		1914			Shmuel		M	[Y]	
WEINSTEIN	Mosze		1894			Shmuel		M	[Y]	
WEINSTEIN	Nissan		1898			Shmuel		M	[Y]	
WEINSTEIN	Shalom							M		
WEINSTEIN	Szymon					Shalom		M	[G]	perished
WEINSTEIN	Ozjas			Mehlhändler	flour trader			M	[B]	perished

Krosno, Poland Yizkor Book

Surname	First name		Year			Sex	Code	Notes
WEINSTER	Icchak					M	[R]	survived
WEINSTER	Wolf		1896	Gemeindediener	municipality servant	M	[J], [G]	
WEISER	Brandel		1900			F	[J]	
WEISER	Israel		1930			M	[J]	
WEISER	Chume		1923			M	[J]	
WEISER	Suessl		1924			F	[J]	
WEISER	Mendel		1927	Arbeiter	worker	M	[J]	
WEISER	Sali			Arbeiter	worker	M	[J]	
WEISS	Beile		1891			F	[J]	
WEISS	Leiser		1890	Arbeiter	worker	M	[J]	
WEISS	Feige		1921	Näherin	seamstress	F	[J]	
WEISS	Poje		1924			M	[J]	
WEISS	Jakob		1928			M	[J]	
WEISS	Elias		1907	Angestellter	employee	M	[J]	
WEISS	Jutta		1909			F	[J]	
WEISS	Rudi		1935			M	[J]	
WEISS	Sali					F	[S]	
WEISS	Sarah	GREEN				F	[L]	survived
WEISS	Ilona		1900			M	[J]	This is probably a mistake, as no other women are marked in this column
WEISSBERGER	Eva		1922	Stenotypistin	stenotypist [female]	F	[J]	
WEISSBERGER	Berta		1925	Näherin	seamstress	F	[J]	

Surname	Given name	Year	Occupation (German)	Occupation (English)	Name	Sex	Code	Notes
WEISSBERGER	Avraham					M	[R]	
WEISSMANN	Rosa	1914				F	[J]	
WEISSMANN	Beile	1939				F	[J]	
WEISSMANN	Markus	1886	Spediteur	shipper	Moshe	M	[J], [Y]	
WEISSMANN	Zile	1890				F	[J], [G]	
WEISSMANN	Hirsch	1925	Arbeiter	worker		M	[J]	
WEISSMANN	Itzhak					M	[L]	survived
WEISSMANN	Hava					F	[L]	survived
WEISSMANN	Menachem					M	[L], [G]	survived
WEISSMANN	Yossef		Krämer	grocer		M	[L]	survived
WEISSMANN	Lazar					M	[G]	
WEISSMANN	Dawid			building supplies		M	[B]	
WEISSNER	Itzhak		Tischler	carpenter		M	[B]	
WEISSNER	Rosa	1899			Itzhak	F	[J], [Y]	Auschwitz
WEISSNER	Aron	1900			Itzhak	M	[Y]	
WEISSNER	U		student	student		M	[R]	
WEISTRICH	Berl	1868				M	[J], [S]	
WELKES	Baruch	1924	Arbeiter	worker		M	[J]	
WELKES	Chaim	1911	Arbeiter	worker		M	[J]	
WELKES	Malke	1913				F	[J]	
WELKES	Guetl	1912				F	[J]	
WELKES	Chane	1922				F	[J]	
WELKES	Sala	1921				F	[J]	
WELKES	Beile	1868				F	[J]	

Krosno, Poland Yizkor Book

WELKES	Jsaak	1889	Arbeiter	worker		M	[J]	
WENIG	Rosa	1889				F	[J]	
WENIG	Freide	1914				F	[J]	
WENIG	Guetl	1918				F	[J]	
WENIG	Salomon	1919	Arbeiter	worker		M	[J]	
WENIG	Naftali					M	[G]	
WENIG	Taube	1892			Menashe	F	[Y]	
WERNER	Chaja	1886				F	[Y]	Belzec
WERTHEIMER	Henia	1920			Pinkas	F	[Y]	
WERTHEIMER	Pinkas	1887			Pinkas	M	[Y]	
WERTHEIMER	Hinde	1923	Arbeiterin	worker [female]		F	[J]	
WERTHEIMER	Raphael				Selig	M	[Y]	
WERTHEIMER	Salek	1912			Pinkas	M	[Y]	
WERTHEIMER	Blueme	1864				F	[J]	
WESTREICH	Feivel					M	[P]	
WESTREICH	Rosa	1899			Feivel	F	[J], [S], [Y]	
WESTREICH	Yossef					M	[L]	survived
WESTREICH	Chane	1904	Hausmädchen	housemaid		F	[J]	
WICHNER	K		Uhrmacher	watchmaker		M	[R]	
WIEDOR	Isaac		Klempner	plumber		M	[R]	
WIELOPOLSKI	Itzhak					M	[R]	
WIENER	Chane	1909				F	[J]	
WIENER	Rosa	1935				F	[J]	
WIENER	Jakob					M	[R]	

Surname	Given Name	née	Year	Occupation	Occupation	Father	Mother	Sex		Code	Fate
WIENER	Dory					Jakob	Dory	R	Jakob	[R]	
WIENER	Rachel		1903					R		[R]	Auschwitz
WIENER	L			Student	student			M		[R]	
WIESEFELD	Moses		1883	Angestellter	employee			M		[J], [S]	
WIESENFELD	Rosa		1885					F		[J]	
WIESENFELD	Rachel		1914	Lehrerin	teacher			F		[J]	
WIESENFELD	Adolf		1919	Arbeiter	worker			M		[J]	
WIESENFELD	Jakob		1921	Arbeiter	worker			M		[J]	
WIESENFELD	Chaim		1907	Arbeiter	worker			M		[J], [S]	
WIEZOWSKI	Guetl		1913					F		[J]	
WIEZOWSKI	Mordche		1939					M		[J]	
WIEZOWSKI	Hella							F		[L]	survived
WILK	Yehuda Leib							M		[L]	
WILNER	Chaya Eidel	FREUND						F	Yehuda Leib	[L]	
WILNER	Dov					Yehuda Leib	Chaya Eidel	M		[L]	survived
WILNER	Moses		1929			Yehuda Leib	Chaya Eidel	M		[J]	
WILNER	Shmuel					Yehuda Leib	Chaya Eidel	F		[L]	
WILNER	Chaya					Yehuda Leib	Chaya Eidel	F		[L]	
WILNER	Rysia					Yehuda Leib	Chaya Eidel	F		[L]	
WILNER	Chana					Yehuda Leib	Chaya Eidel	F		[L]	

Surname	Given name	Year	Occupation	Occupation	Father	Mother	Sex	Code	Notes
WILNER	Freide	1931			Yehuda Leib	Chaya Eidel	F	[J]	
WILNER	Nathan	1898	Bäckergehilfe	baker assistant	Yehuda Leib	Chaya Eidel	M	[J]	
WILNER	Sala	1896			Yehuda Leib	Chaya Eidel	F	[J]	
WILNER	Freide	1925	Verkäuferin	saleswoman	Yehuda Leib	Chaya Eidel	F	[J]	
WILNER	Salomon	1920	Arbeiter	worker			M	[J]	
WILNER	Naftali	1931					M	[J]	
WILNER	Leib	1896	Arbeiter	worker			M	[J], [G]	
WILNER	Chaje	1884					F	[J]	
WILNER	Berisch	1922	Gerber	skinner			M	[P]	survived
WILNER	Leie	1924	Schneiderin	tailoress			F	[J]	
WILNER	Jsrael	1935					M	[J]	
WILNER	Helene	1889					F	[J]	
WILNER	Sulamith	1925					F	[J]	
WILNER	Leie	1927					F	[J]	
WILNER	Eidel	1932					F	[J]	
WILNER	Shimon						M	[L]	survived
WILNER	Tzvi						M	[L]	survived
WILNER	Leja	1892			Moshe		F	[Y]	
WILNER	Jakob	1886	Arbeiter	worker	Israel		M	[J], [Y], [G]	
WINTER	Sara	1900					F	[J]	
WINTER	Leie	1870					F	[J]	
WINTER	Israel Ber						M	[G]	

Krosno, Poland Yizkor Book

Surname	Given name		Year		Occupation		Sex		Code	Notes
WINTER	Liebe			Krämer	grocer		M		[B]	
WIRTEIM	Milla		1918	Schneiderin	tailoress		F		[J]	
WISTREICH	Beile		1900	Lehrerin	teacher [female]		F		[J]	
WITTKIND	Moses						M		[G]	
WITTMAN	Jakob						M		[S]	
WOHLRAUCH	Sarah		1882			Eliyahu	F		[Y]	Belzec
WOLF	Avraham						M		[L]	survived
WOLF	M			Schneider	tailor		M		[R]	
WOLF	Kalman				honey and nuggets		M		[P]	
WOLF	Peshe	HERZFELD					F	Kalman	[P]	
WOLF	Leibish						M		[P]	
WOLF	Berl		1941						[J]	Could be WELKER; hard to tell
WOLKER	Chaim		1900	Arbeiter	worker		M		[J]	
WOLKER	Chaje		1910				F		[J]	
WOLKER	Hirsch		1939				M		[J]	
WOLKER	Leie		1917				F		[J]	
WROBEL	Berel-Bernard		1876				M		[J], [S], [G]	
WROBEL	Debora		1886				M		[J]	
WROBEL	Guetl		1920				F		[J]	
WROBEL	Freide		1924	Arbeiterin	worker [female]		F		[J]	
WROBEL	David		1921	Schneider	tailor		M		[J]	

Krosno, Poland Yizkor Book

Surname	Given Name	Maiden Name	Year	Occupation	Father	Mother	Sex	Spouse	Code	Fate
WROBEL	Mosze		1890		Baruch		M		[Y]	
WURMAN	Naphtali						M	Naphtali	[P]	Russia
ZAFERN	Hawa	HERZFELD	1883				F		[P]	Russia
ZAFERN	Shija-Wolf		1906		Naphtali	Hawa	M		[P]	survived
ZAFERN	GITCHA	RUBINFELD					F		[P]	
ZAFERN	Chana Dworah						F		[P]	
ZAFERN	Raisel					Chana Dworah	F		[P]	
ZAFERN	Aaron Meir						M		[P]	perished
ZAFERN	Itche Leib						M		[P]	perished
ZAFERN	Chaja Rachel						F		[P]	perished
ZAFERN	Pinkas		1915		Naphtali	Hawa	M		[P]	perished
ZAFERN	Sima				Naphtali	Hawa	F		[P]	Russia
ZAFERN	Nathan-Nuta				Naphtali	Hawa	M		[P]	Russia
ZAFERN	Shprincze		1927		Naphtali	Hawa	F		[P]	perished
ZAFERN	Guetl		1904		Naphtali	Hawa	F		[P]	
ZAFERN	Feige		1931		Naphtali	Hawa	F		[P]	
ZAFERN	Malke		1932		Naphtali	Hawa	F		[P]	
ZAFERN	Yossef		1935		Naphtali	Hawa	M		[P]	
ZAFERN	Isaak		1937		Naphtali	Hawa	M		[P]	
ZAFERN	Yehoshua						M		[L]	survived
ZAHLER	Ele	ELIAS	1913	Arbeiter / worker			F		[J], [S]	
ZAJDOW	Jochweth		1880				F		[J]	
ZAJDOW	Moshe						M		[L]	survived

Krosno, Poland Yizkor Book

Surname	Given Name	Maiden Name	Year	Occupation	Second Name	Occupation	Sex	Father's Name	Ref	Fate
ZALTZ	Chaja		1908		Yona		F		[Y]	
ZAMD	Rachel				Jakob		F		[Y]	
ZAUER	Henka						F		[L]	
ZEIDMAN	Eliasz						M		[R]	
ZELLER	Eliyahu							Eliasz	[R]	survived
ZELLER	Blima						F		[L]	
ZELLER	Frida						F		[P]	
ZELLER	Sara						F		[R]	
ZELMAN	Zeew						M		[P]	
ZELTZER	S			carpenter		Tischler	M		[R]	survived
ZEMAN							M		[L]	survived
ZIGEL	Meir						M		[L]	
ZILBERMAN	Chaje		1884	seamstress		Näherin	F		[J]	
ZIMET	Hersh						M		[G]	
ZIMET	Leib						M		[G]	
ZIMET	Samuel						M		[G]	
ZIMET	Jekel						M		[P]	
ZISSEL	Sara						F		[P]	perished
ZISSEL	Stucia	STEIN					F		[L]	survived
ZOHAR	Al						M		[L]	survived
ZOHAR	Yvonne	KOENIG					F		[L]	survived
ZOHAR	Natan			barber		Friseur	M		[R]	
ZORNA							M		[L]	survived
ZUCKERBERG	Kalman						M		[P]	
TZUCKERMAN	Miriam	KATZ					F	Kalman	[L]	survived

Krosno, Poland Yizkor Book

Surname	Given name	Year	Occupation	Occupation	Father	Mother	Sex		Code	
TZUCKERMAN	Elisheva				Kalman	Miriam	F		[P]	
TZUCKERMAN	Hadassa				Kalman	Miriam	F		[P]	
TZUCKERMAN	Nuta		Krämer	grocer			M		[B]	
ZUKIER	Jakob	1889	Schneider	tailor			M		[JJ], [S], [G]	perished
ZWASS	Marjem	1886					F	Jakob	[J]	perished
ZWASS	Hillel	1923	Schneider	tailor	Jakob	Marjem	M		[J]	perished
ZWASS	Markus	1926	Schneider	tailor	Jakob	Marjem	M		[J]	perished
ZWASS	Aron	1927	Arbeiter	worker	Jakob	Marjem	M		[J]	perished
ZWASS	Blueme	1870					F		[JJ], [G]	
ZWICK	Awraham						M		[P]	
ZWICK	Gedalia		Mützenmacher	capper			M		[B]	
ZWIEBEL	Jakob	1889	Bäckergehilfe	baker assistant			M		[J]	
ZWIEBEL	Feige	1891					F		[J]	
ZWIEBEL	Chaim			clothing			M		[R]	
ZWIEBEL	Salomon	1902	Friseur	barber			M		[J]	
ZWIRN	Feige	1905					F		[J]	
ZWIRN	Hirsch	1904	Schneider	tailor			M		[J]	
ZYCHHOLZ	Leie	1925					F		[J]	
ZYCHHOLZ	Chaim	1928	Schneider	tailor			M		[J]	
ZYCHHOLZ	Sara	1929					F		[J]	
ZYCHHOLZ	Genendel	1884					F		[S], [J]	
ZYZAK	Ester	1921					F		[J]	
ZYZAK	Yaakow						M		[P]	

Chapter XVIII

The city of Krosno pays hommage to the Jewish residents of the city that were killed in the Shoah

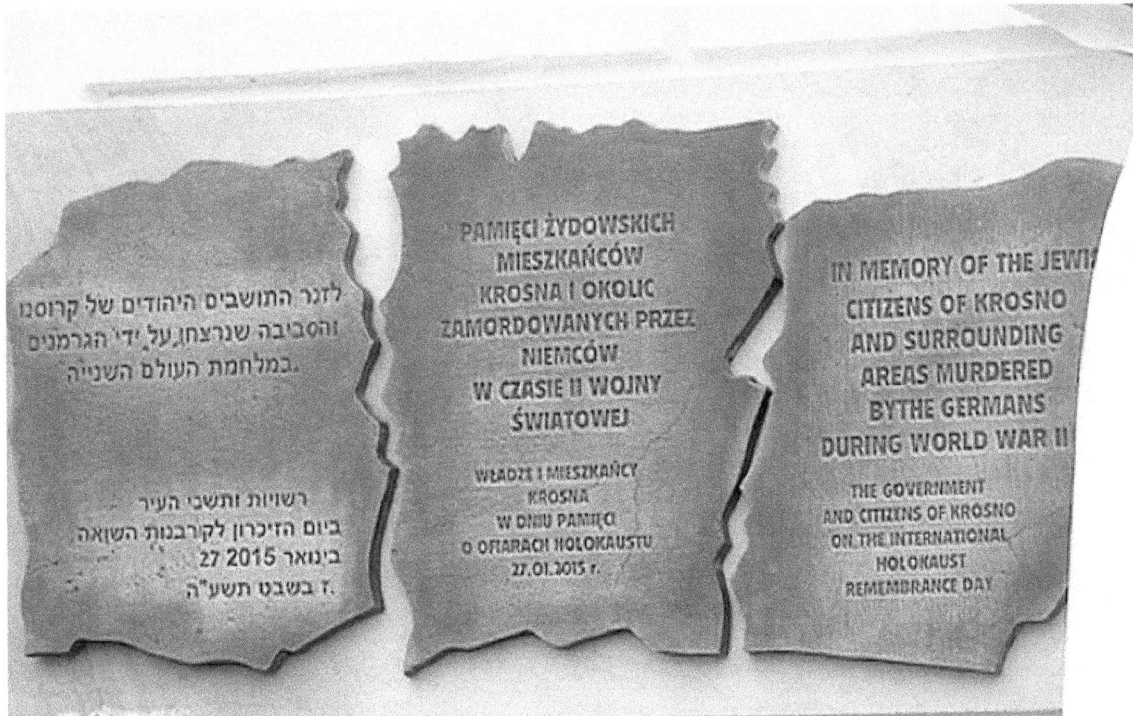

Memorial plaque erected by the Krosno municipality honoring the Krosno Jews that perished during the Shoah. The ceremony took place on January 27, 2015 in Krosno

The plaque was erected along Francziskanski Street # 9 that was the ghetto area in Krosno during World War II

Index

Index does not include the appendix below

Krieger, 102, 103, 275, 400
Krieler, 24
Krieller, 400
Kriger, 174, 316
Krill, 20, 24, 26, 174, 253, 261, 264, 277, 298, 300, 310, 315, 401
Kronkopf, 369
Krosno, 350, 386
Krukierek, 201, 203, 204, 205, 207, 208, 210, 211, 215, 216, 218, 219, 220, 222, 270
Kucziborski, 401
Kudler, 103, 401
Kuenstlinger, 103, 401
Kufic, 315
Kuflick, 45, 160, 174
Kuflik, 103, 401
Kupfermen, 275
Kuppermann, 103, 401
Kuref, 314, 366
Kurschner, 20
Kurz, 20, 401, 402
Kurzer, 103, 402
Kurzmann, 103, 402
Kwill, 257
L
Lacher, 160
Lachner, 103, 402
Lam, 24, 34, 45
Lamberg, 103, 104, 402
Lambig, 402
Lambik, 32, 104, 257, 402
Lamm, 104, 402, 403
Landau, 24, 34, 104, 174, 259, 403, 404
Landgarten, 104, 404
Landsberger, 160
Landstein, 174, 404
Lang, 10, 12, 13, 15, 20, 21, 24, 44, 50, 52, 53, 54, 57, 59, 105, 143, 144, 151, 174, 230, 315, 404
Langbaum, 105, 405
Langblum, 24
Langsam, 152, 154, 157, 297
Laskowski, 405
Lass, 297
Laufer, 174, 277, 315, 405
Lautman, 105
Lautmann, 405
Lehrer, 24, 82, 96, 102, 104, 105, 106, 108, 135, 312, 339, 372, 386, 388, 399, 405, 406, 407, 408, 412, 429

Lehrman, 105
Lehrmann, 405
Leib, 30, 32, 34, 36, 46, 71, 72, 77, 79, 80, 81, 82, 84, 86, 88, 90, 92, 94, 95, 96, 97, 98, 99, 103, 107, 113, 114, 116, 117, 118, 125, 126, 132, 134, 160, 171, 174, 178, 219, 221, 222, 275, 276, 297, 300, 306, 315, 316, 324, 325, 326, 336, 341, 343, 344, 345, 347, 348, 351, 353, 354, 358, 362, 363, 365, 368, 372, 375, 378, 381, 385, 386, 387, 388, 390, 392, 401, 405, 407, 410, 423, 424, 426, 430, 431, 433, 436, 441, 442, 443, 445, 448, 456, 458, 460, 463, 465, 469, 470, 472, 473
Leibel, 105, 405
Leibner, Xix, Xx, Xxi, 40, 52, 53, 54, 57, 197, 207, 211, 212, 224, 230, 231, 253, 282, 320, 406
Leicht, 406
Leichtberg, 105, 406
Leichter, 192, 193
Leidner, 406
Leiner, 52, 105, 406
Leiser, 28, 105, 107, 117, 133, 312, 315, 398, 404, 405, 406, 411, 434, 458, 466
Leitberg, 34
Leiter, 275, 407, 444
Leizer, 174
Leker, 243
Lem, 32
Lemberg, 105, 106, 407
Lempel, 175, 407
Lerman, 160
Lerner, 106, 407
Lessig, 107, 407
Levanini, 175, 407
Lewaj, 407
Lewinski, 172, 367
Libenschow, 250
Liber, 251, 315
Liberman, 312
Lichelet, 106
Lieber, 24, 106, 148, 160, 162, 175, 314, 408
Lieberman, 46
Liebermann, 106, 408
Liebeskind, 408
Lielberg, 250
Lilbera, 248

Perlberg, 176, 425
Pferferbaum, 160
Pflauman, 152
Pieniowski, 304
Pilhard, 176
Pilhardt, 425
Pineles, 138, 182
Pinkas, 14, 32, 36, 74, 78, 85, 88, 95,
107, 111, 113, 114, 119, 122, 128,
132, 133, 148, 160, 176, 194, 229,
241, 275, 312, 314, 323, 333, 344,
362, 367, 385, 412, 416, 418, 425,
450, 456, 465, 468, 472
Pinkus, 25, 76, 176, 275, 337, 426
Pinsel, 34, 114, 426
Pinsler, 426
Pinte, 114
Pinter, 9, 114, 426
Piotrkowski, 114, 426
Pirbiak, 114
Pirbisk, 426
Pittman, 36
Pivirt, 426
Piwirt, 176
Piwonja, 114, 427
Plant, 171
Platner, 4, 15, 23, 25, 28, 30, 59, 114,
115, 176, 177, 259, 267, 310, 335,
362, 376, 427, 428, 430
Platter, 277, 428
Pletzel, 177, 428
Podner, 30
Pogon, 34
Polaner, 157
Polanski, 177, 182, 298, 428
Porush, 25
Posner, 428
Possner, 36
Postach, 25
Postar, 428
Poster, 25
Potocki, 3
Poznanski, 115, 428
Presser, 25, 115, 171, 278, 428
Pressman, 167
Preuss, 177, 428
Privirt, 428
Probker, 115, 428, 429
Proper, 167
Prrush, 428
Pruefer, 115, 429

Pudelko, 190, 192
Puretz, 30, 429
R
Rab, 177
Rabi, 115, 160, 429
Rabinowicz, 115, 429
Rabinowitz, 165
Raczy, 20, 231, 253, 282, 320
Rakoszynski, 115, 429
Ramras, 30, 34, 115, 429, 430
Rand, 177, 430
Ranozy, 20
Rapowicz, 236
Rappe, 269
Raschwitz, 58, 185
Ratz, 34, 36, 115, 255, 256, 275, 278,
430
Rauch, 177, 430
Rawski, 430
Reck, 115, 430
Regenbo, 430
Reibenbach, 430
Reibscheid, 116, 430
Reich, 116, 177, 255, 270, 271, 299,
316, 430, 431
Reichman, 25, 177, 431
Reinbach, 431
Reinhold, 116, 431
Reinmann, 431
Reiss, 116, 431
Reizer, 20
Rettig, 20
Rezmovits, 20
Riedel, 312
Rieder, 25, 34, 116, 431
Rieger, 334
Riemer, 34, 116, 431
Ries, 432
Riess, 160
Ringel, 25, 177, 432
Ringler, 25, 116, 432
Ritter, 177, 432
Rivka, 411
Roessler, 432
Rogalik, 116, 432
Romm, 268
Ronchyn, 233
Rosenbaum, 46
Rosenberg, 46, 117, 198, 219, 220,
301, 326, 433
Rosenblatt, 117, 433

Taub, 361
Taubenfeld, 25, 32, 127, 157, 178, 454, 464
Teicher, 128, 454
Teitelbaum, 23, 25, 34, 127, 450, 454, 455
Tenzer, 160
Teplicki, 128, 178, 268, 269, 315, 456
Teplitzki, 170, 324
Tepper, 128, 276, 456
Terski, 456
Testylier, 128, 456
Thaler, 25, 128, 148, 154, 178, 340, 456, 457
Thon, 271
Tischler, 128, 457
Tiszler, 301
Titov, 178, 457
Tralez, 275, 457
Trancher, 25
Trattner, 32, 129, 457, 458
Trauber, 25, 458
Trencher, 15, 25
Trenczer, 15, 20, 28, 30, 32, 36, 129, 157, 178, 230, 263, 314, 315, 458, 459
Trenczew, 257
Trum, 160
Truncher, 15
Trynopolski, 160
Tuerk, 459
Turek, 130, 275, 459
Turk, 34, 160, 459
Turst, 299
Twerski, 9, 10, 11, 26, 45, 142, 147, 225, 227, 460
Tzeller, 25
Tzipori, 178, 460
Tzuckerman, 163, 168, 473, 474
Tzwibel, 25
Tzwik, 25
U
Uberfuhrer, 460
Unger, 130, 160, 178, 315, 460
Unikowski, 130, 460
Urlbaum, 178, 460
Urtem, 300, 460
V
Verstaendig, 130, 460
Vogel, 15, 130, 460, 461
Vogelfluegel, 130, 461
Vogelhut, 130, 461

W
Wagschal, 130, 461
Wagshal, 275
Waks, 30, 461
Walach, 315
Wald, 178, 316, 461
Waldner, 131, 461
Walker, 25, 131
Wallace, 332, 461
Wallach, 44, 178, 461, 462
Waller, 462
Walter, 25, 178, 462
Wandenstein, 296
Wander, 131, 219, 462
Wandstein, 301
Warfel, 25, 462
Warscher, 462
Wasserstrum, 14, 15, 242
Wdowinski, 131, 462
Weber, 36, 132, 457, 464
Wehrmann, 131, 312, 462
Weinberg, 43, 462, 463
Weinberger, 15, 36, 46, 131, 178, 259, 265, 267, 277, 316, 380, 463
Weiner, 34
Weinfeld, 25, 32, 36, 48, 132, 463, 464
Weinfelds, 157
Weingold, 464
Weinkrantz, 178, 464
Weinman, 25, 178, 464
Weinreb, 464
Weinstein, 15, 28, 32, 36, 132, 133, 178, 464, 465
Weinster, 316, 466
Weintraub, 271
Weisenberg, 301
Weiser, 133, 466
Weisman, 28, 30, 34, 178, 242, 284, 289, 315
Weisner, 25, 134
Weiss, 133, 178, 466
Weissberger, 132, 133, 466, 467
Weisser, 427
Weissman, 20, 48, 173, 176, 179, 370
Weissmann, 133, 134, 467
Weissner, 467
Weistrich, 467
Weivhert, 62
Welkes, 134, 467, 468
Wenig, 30, 134, 468
Werner, 468

APPENDIX – The Jewish Cemetery

Introduction to Appendix

Our grateful thanks to Grzegorz Bozek

We, the former Jewish residents of Krosno, the descendants of Krosno and the residents of the city, owe Grzegorz Bozek and his co-workers a great moral debt for their dedication and perseverance in restoring the Jewish cemetery of Krosno, an integral part of the city's history.

Mr. Bozek also provided us with a large number of pictures that describe the actual restoration project. Many of the pictures are in the Krosno Yizkor book.

Our sages tell us that the "Mitzvah" or good deed of burying or tending to the deceased is the highest ranking mitzvah since the departed will never be able to repay the party. Nobody will be able to repay Mr. Bozek and his assistants for their hard and merciful work.

Permit me to say Thank You.

William Leibner

With the end of the war most of the Jewish population of Krosno had perished, the beautiful synagogue was gone, the entire Jewish physical presence in the city of Krosno had disappeared except for the Krosno Jewish cemetery. The cemetery was consecrated by Rabbi Shmuel Fuhrer soon after his becoming rabbi of the Krosno Jewish community in 1904. At the time, the cemetery was an isolated place, fenced in by a protective wall. This wall apparently protected the cemetery from total obliteration by the Germans as was the case in many towns and hamlets in Poland and conquered Europe.

The Krosno Jewish cemetery after the war

The few Jewish survivors who returned to Krosno were alarmed by the scene at the cemetery and started to restore it. It was soon clear that most of the tombstones had been removed. Adolf Minc, an influential resident of Krosno who survived the war in the Soviet Union, began an active search to discover what had happened to the burial stones. They were soon located outside the city of Krosno. The owner refused to return the stones and was taken to court where he claimed that he had bought them during the war. The court ignored his defense and ordered the stones to be returned to the Jewish cemetery in Krosno.

Jewish tombstones from the Krosno Jewish cemetery saved from destruction in 1946

The stones were returned and some were re-erected in their proper place while others were left on the side of the cemetery since the names were erased or damaged beyond recognition. Still then the cemetery was restored and cleaned. In the following years, the few Jewish Shoah survivors of Krosno left the city and nobody tended to the cemetery. The plants and greens overgrew the cemetery, which became a jungle of plants. Sheep were grazing, the drainage clogged, tombstones fell and broke. For years the place was deteriorating, becoming an ecological disaster area for the city of Krosno, which had expanded so that the cemetery was now surrounded by local inhabitants.

Grzegorz Bozek

In 2002, Grzegorz Bozek, a teacher in Krosno deeply involved in the preservation of the environment, decided to take matters in his hand. He enlisted a group of young Krosnians under his direction. They went to work. With a little help from the municipality and the Jewish communities over the next five years until 2007, these young people sweated removing the rubbish and the overgrowth of bushes, plants, and trees. They renovated the cemetery gate and mounted new and well-secured information boards, removed unimaginable amounts of weeds and hauled out tons of rubbish.

Vegetation covering the Jewish cemetery of Krosno

The Krosno Jewish cemetery surrounded by homes

A young volunteer cutting the dense vegetation that overtook the cemetery

Krosno volunteers clearing the underbrush of the cemetery

Painting of the fence

Restoration of the drainage at the cemetery

The clearing operations continues

Volunteers resting

Young local volunteer workers

Bags of garbage collected in clearing the Krosno Jewish cemetery

Signs being attached to the gates explaining the cemetery to the local residents

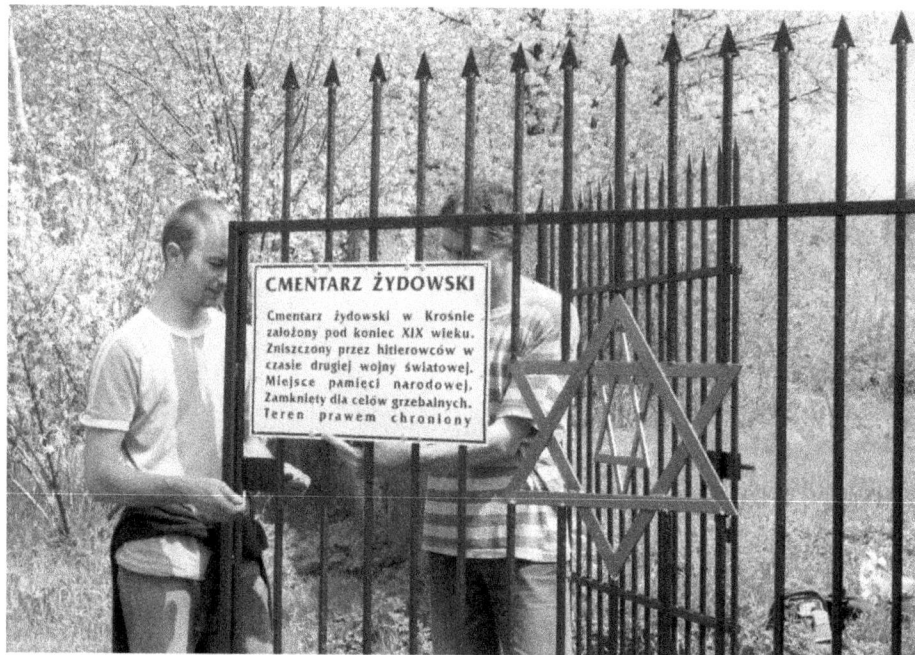

The sign reads: "The Jewish cemetery. The Jewish cemetery of Krosno was consecrated in the last years of the 19th century. It was devastated by the Germans during World War II. This is a Jewish memorial place protected by the law."

Following the hard work of cutting, cleaning and restoring, the cemetery came into view. Now the paths had to be restored along with the fallen tombstones.

A few of the Krosno Jewish cemetery tombstones

Restored tombstones

A section of the restored cemetery

Tombstones damaged beyond recognition.

Individual tombstones

The tombstone of Jozef Bodner, born 1870 and died December 1941.
The words engraved on the tombstone are written only in Polish.

The tombstone of Moses Springer

Tombstone of Bernard Mincwho died in Krosno in 1930

Tombstone of Israel Dov Beir who died on the 11th day of the month of Elul (September 9) in Tartzacha (1935)

Tombstone of Yehiel Proper, murdered by blood thirsty killers.
He was born in Sanok in 1881and murdered August 17, 1945

The restored Krosno Jewish cemetery in the winter

The Krosno Jewish cemetery painted white by Mother Nature

The restoration process took many years. On July 3, 2005, the Embassy of Israel in Warsaw and the Jewish Historical Institute in Poland granted Grzegorz Bozek an honorary diploma for his activities to protect the heritage of Jewish culture in Poland. The diploma "is granted to extraordinary Poles, Polish organizations and cities that restore the Jewish past." In 2007, the project was finally finished. The Krosno Jewish cemetery became and still is one of the best restored Jewish cemeteries in Poland.

Mr. Bozek did not rest on his laurels but continued to tend to the cemetery. He also participated in the erection of a tombstone at a grave containing the remains of about 120 Jews of Krosno who were murdered during the liquidation of the Krosno Jewish ghetto. The tombstone is located within the Jewish cemetery of Krosno.

The tombstone was erected May 20, 2009

The inscription on the tombstone reads:

"Here were buried in a brotherly mass grave the saintly Rabbi Shmuel Fuhrer, Asher Zelig.

Rabbi Fuhrer was also presiding judge of the Jewish religious court in Krosno. Also buried here are

Rabbi Shmuel

Zvi Demarez

Zvi Hertzfeld

Zeev Nussboim

Zvi Margoliot

Asher Boigen

All were killed solely for being Jews, on the first day of the month of Tevet (December 9) in the year Tashag (1942).

Also buried were men, women and children who were killed on the fourth day of Chanukah (December 7, 1942) in the year Tashag (1942).

May they rest eternally in peace."

Dr. Alexander White speaks before an audience in Krosno about the Jews in Krosno before the war.

Dr. White located the grave of his grandmother Mala Platner in the Krosno Jewish cemetery

Grzegorz Bozek lights a memorial candle at the tombstone.

Grzegorz Bozek not only tends to the Jewish cemetery in Krosno but also organizes exhibitions on Jewish life in Krosno. He and his group also organize receptions for visiting Krosno Jews Like Dr. White.

Grzegorz Bozek and his group meet at the Jewish cemetery to memorialize the Jewish past on the day dedicated by the United Nations as the International Holocaust Remembrance Day 27 Jan 2015

Candles are lit at the mass burial tombstone at the Krosno Jewish cemetery

The city of Krosno erected plaques in memory of the Jewish population of Krosno that were murdered during the war.

Grzegorz Bozek and his group of Olszowa deserve the greatest of merit for their devotion to the history of Krosno and to the memory of the Jews who inhabited this city.